Lewis and Clark Among the Nez Perce

Strangers in the Land of the Nimiipuu

LEWIS AND CLARK AMONG THE NEZ PERCE

Strangers in the Land of the Nimiipuu

ALLEN V. PINKHAM *and* STEVEN R. EVANS

Foreword by FREDERICK E. HOXIE

wsupress.wsu.edu I wsupress@wsu.edu I 800-354-7360

The Dakota Institute Press
of the Lewis & Clark Fort Mandan Foundation

Library of Congress Control Number 2013943287
ISBN-13 978-0-9834059-8-6 (Hardcover)
ISBN-13-978-0-9834059-9-3 (Paperback)

Distributed by The University of Oklahoma Press

Created, produced and designed in the United States of America
Printed in Canada

Book layout and design by: Margaret McCullough
Corvus Design Studio www.corvusdesignstudio.com

The paper in this book meets the guidelines for permanence and
durability of the Committee of Production Guidelines for Book Longevity
of the Council on Library Resources.
10 9 8 7 6 5 4 3 2 1

Cover Image: "Watching Over the Promised Land"
by Nez Perce artist John Seven Wilson III

The Dakota Institute Press
of the Lewis & Clark Fort Mandan Foundation
2576 8th Street South West   Post Office Box 607
Washburn, North Dakota 58577
www.FortMandan.com
1.877.462.8535

MIX
Paper from
responsible sources
FSC
www.fsc.org
FSC® C016245

Dedicated to Our Friend and Mentor

Alvin M. Josephy Jr.

May 18, 1915 - October 18, 2005

Alvin Josephy at the Josephy ranch in Wallowa County, Oregon.
Photograph by Steve Evans.

Table of Contents

Map: Ordway Junket

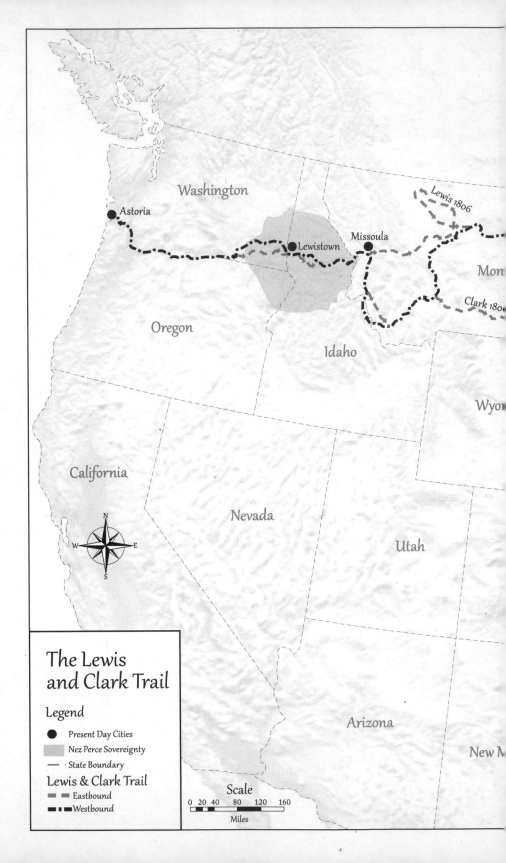

The Lewis
and Clark Trail

Legend

●   Present Day Cities

  Nez Perce Sovereignty

---- · State Boundary

Lewis & Clark Trail

▪ ▬ Eastbound

▪ ▬ Westbound

Scale

0 20 40   80   120   160

Miles

Washington

Astoria

Lewistown

Missoula

Lewis 1806

Clark 180

Mon

Oregon

Idaho

Wyor

California

Nevada

Utah

N
W   E
S

Arizona

New M

A Message From the Nez Perce Tribal Chairman, Silas C. Whitman February 22, 2013

The following are some comments in reference to the book authored by Steve Evans and Allen Pinkham. Reading the manuscript allowed me to reflect back to a time when I heard several elders recount the Lewis & Clark Expedition's emergence into Nez Perce territory. First of all I feel that the book opens a critical view of how the tribe dealt with the "discovery." It shows how history played out, shedding new light on why the Nez Perce allowed themselves to let a more narrow "history" take its course. This new view will generate future questions and more research, more recounts of a culture--much of it forever lost--facing hard changes after showing both compassion toward the initiators of and reluctance toward the inevitability of "manifest destiny pressures."

The tribal views of the "Discovery Party" (for want of better terms) as motley-looking, smelly, and, in the words of one elder, "churlish," were reinforced by several tribal groups outside of the Twisted Hair-Red Bear camps. What I also was told by several aunts is that they were spiritually "disconnected." A female cousin, her brother, and my older sisters indicated that this meant that they were walking "dead people" with their heads upside down: bald men with beards. I hadn't heard that description from other tribal people except from an uncle and aunt who were always saying that they could have "cursed" the digging grounds at Musselshell Creek and Meadows in Idaho and that they should have gotten rid of the "discoverers" then, as some tribal men wanted during that encounter. I feel that this mentioning of a "curse" was more aligned with the future problems that we as Nez Perce would face with the unrelenting change brought on by these new people. My uncle told of the long-ago prophecy of the coming of these strangers from afar, a prophecy (or a people?) with a name that I couldn't remember. It was a reflection of anxiety from that time as elders used to remember.

Another unfathomable action taken by the Discovery Party was the continued desire for dog meat. While generally offensive to the tribal people, there were some that were extremely offended that they would immediately kill the animal that was so depended upon by families for a

number of purposes before the advent of the horse. I feel certainly that
the completion of this book should well lead to at least another book
that completely airs the feelings and viewpoints of the Nez Perce people
while there are still some people left who could contribute remembrances
gathered from their family elders. This is important to pass to the coming
generations as "truthfulness" and qualification to a history often tainted by
non-Nez Perce desires to shape history into commonly accepted myths and
interpretations for their learned institutions and non-Nez Perce groups.

There are other things that could be mentioned but aren't cogent to
the purposes of this particular book. I congratulate the authors for their
fine work which opens the door wider that others might follow their lead.
I would urge a fully-compatible book on Nez Perce counterpoints to the
"Discovery."

Silas C. Whitman iii

Foreword

"What Every American Schoolboy
Should Know"

In 1955, the Supreme Court of the United States rejected an Alaskan Native group's claim to be the original owner of a tract of unceded tribal land by declaring that the Indians' long occupation of the territory counted for nothing. "Every American schoolboy knows," Justice Stanley Reed wrote, "that the savage tribes of this continent were deprived of their ancestral ranges by force and that, even when the Indians ceded millions of acres by treaty in return for blankets, food and trinkets, it was not a sale, but the conqueror's will, that deprived them of their land." (348 U.S. 272)

The images triggered by Reed's declaration are telling:

"Savage tribes of this continent." Translation: all Indians were and are—the same: backward, illiterate, disconnected from "civilization."

"Ancestral ranges." Translation: Indians "range" across the land like animals. They have no history, only a record of occupation.

"Force ... Ceded." Translation: the Indians' dispossession was produced by warfare; Native people and the United States have no common history.

"Blankets, food, and trinkets." Translation: The United States generosity enabled the Indians to survive; nothing provided through treaties was the result of agreements between equals.

"Conqueror's will." Translation: Events of the past were triggered by American initiative; Indian motives and actions counted for nothing.

We might call Reed's images "stereotypes," but his words carry a deeper meaning. They reveal that (at least in 1955) the history "every American schoolboy" knew was the one-way story of American expansion and the relentless tale of "civilization's" triumph over "savagery."

Today "school boys" (and school girls) are exposed to more events and more Indians, but the deep structure of the nation's history remains unchanged. The Founding Fathers continue to get top billing despite their common insistence that Indian people, in George Washington's words, were "wolves." Best-selling biographies of Andrew Jackson ignore or dismiss his central role in the brutal Indian removals of the early nineteenth century.

We revere Abraham Lincoln, forgetting his direct order to execute thirty-eight Santee Sioux men who, in 1861, had rebelled against the cruel treatment they suffered on their Minnesota reservation. We celebrate the separation of church and state without seeing the decades when United States tax dollars subsidized Indian missions and schools. And so on.

"Good" Indians, like Pocahontas and Squanto, make it onto our children's lunch boxes and into their textbooks, but nothing seems to alter the basic American story. Justice Reed might be pilloried today for his crude language, but few would question his declaration that America's size and wealth were produced by "the conqueror's will."

Words of protest have failed to change this structure. Insisting that stereotypes are inaccurate or offensive has little effect when those stereotypes are self-satisfying and popular. Listen to the defenders of teams called "Warriors" and "Braves," and you will hear deep affection and an endlessly repeated loop of national self-congratulation praise: we are great; they were noble; we conquered them; it was inevitable.

Now we honor them. It's all good. This deep affection produces a sense of belonging ("we" honor "them") and even optimism—conquest is progress, backwardness yields to civilization. We are on our way up. Relax. Pop a brew. The Redskins are on!

But the history in this book will certainly change that nationalist tune. *Lewis and Clark Among the Nez Perce: Strangers in the Land of the Nimiipuu* is modest in scope, but its ambition and its meaning resonate far beyond Washington, Idaho and Oregon. The story Pinkham and Evans tell began "a long time ago," when ancient peoples came to occupy and study the Snake, Clearwater and Salmon rivers' drainages and then to make a life there for themselves and their descendants.

The actors in the story are men, women and the other creatures— material and spiritual—who shared this magnificent landscape with them. And the Americans who enter their story arrived late, disrupting settled lives, rather than delivering "civilization" to the book's main actors, the Nez Perce.

Historians often claim they are "context" builders. They describe settings, motives, and alternatives. For good historians, rich contexts mean that outcomes are not "inevitable." In this sense, Pinkham and Evans are wonderful historians. Through them we can see how the Americans who stumbled into their homeland late in 1805 were frightening, yet intriguing.

We learn to imagine Twisted Hair and his relatives reviewing the rumors and prophecies that would explain the newcomers and tell them what to do next. We come to understand the human geography of the area—the locations of villages and neighbors—Walla Wallas, Umatillas, Yakamas, Wanapums and others. We witness the Nez Perce's tentative decision to help the Americans and their gradual transition to friendship.

But the real eradication of words like "savage" and "conqueror" from our national narrative can come only when Americans are exposed to the true "grit" of history: daily events, specific people, tiny interactions, and real life incidents that make us unmask the silliness of broad labels. For example:

- The Nez Perces debating the murder of the entire American party.

- An Indian man disgusted at the Americans' apparent preference for dog meat.

- The Yakamas dancing with the Americans.

- And perhaps the climax of Pinkham and Evans's story: the May 1806 grand council where the Nez Perce and the United States became allies.

They write, that at that moment the Nez Perce and the Americans became "brothers, like the Sahaptin brothers the Palus, Yakamas, Umatillas, Walla Wallas, Klikitats, everyone all the way to the Wyam… and then of course they would share everything." Following this event, the Americans settled into their camp along the Clearwater to wait for the snow to clear from the passes through the Bitterroots. They became neighbors, living alongside the Nez Perce for the next month.

As the Americans finally leave the Nez Perces—more than a dozen chapters after they first arrived—readers of *Lewis and Clark Among the Nez Perce* will understand a relationship that was far more complicated and interesting than Justice Reed's self-serving tale of savagery, trinkets, blankets, and conquest. Lewis and Clark's band and the Nez Perce finally parted ways on July 4, 1806, but readers of this fine book will see that, in the decades to come, the two groups would be a part of each other's history. Their new friendship had been triggered by mutual need, intimate contact and a desire to find common ground. There was no "conqueror's will" at work here and nothing every "American schoolboy" could know about them at that moment except that their friendship was a function of history and their common humanity.

The authors of *Lewis and Clark Among the Nez Perce* make it possible for readers to see the explorers and the Nez Perces through fresh eyes, leading us to understand these people of the past as two distinct communities: two collections of fascinating individuals, each with its own values and each with unformed hopes for the future. Pinkham and Evans teach us that nothing in American history was "inevitable." And that is a lesson every American school boy and school girl should learn.

Frederick E. Hoxie

Preface

Lewis and Clark traveled from St. Charles, Missouri, to the Pacific Ocean and back again, between May 14, 1804, and September 23, 1806. They traveled 7,689 miles altogether. They encountered more than 50 Indian tribes along the way. Most of their encounters were necessarily brief. They were in a hurry. In fact, they were on a mission. They seldom spent more than a couple of days with any given tribe, sometimes to the consternation of tribal leaders, who were eager to learn what they could of the strangers and extend them proper hospitality.

Lewis and Clark lingered with just three tribal communities. They spent a long, at times brutally cold, winter among the Mandan and Hidatsa at the mouth of the Knife River in today's North Dakota (October 26, 1804–April 7, 1805). They built an encampment near several villages of Clatsop Indians near the mouth of the Columbia River in today's Oregon (December 12, 1805, to March 23, 1806). And they spent a significant amount of time with the Nez Perce (Nimíipuu) Indians, both on the outbound journey in the fall of 1805 and on their return to the United States in the late spring of 1806.

Lewis and Clark could not accomplish their mission without passing through sovereign Nez Perce country twice. In both instances they were outside the boundaries of the United States, as determined by the Louisiana Purchase Treaty.

The time Lewis and Clark spent with any one of these tribes—Mandan-Hidatsa, Clatsop, Nez Perce—was greater than they spent with all of the other tribes they encountered combined. The case can be made that their time with the Nez Perce was both the most important and the most satisfying of the transcontinental journey. Until recently, the story of Lewis and Clark among the Nez Perce has not received the historical attention it deserves. But with the publication of David Nicandri's pivotal *River of Promise: Lewis and Clark on the Columbia* (2009) and now Allen Pinkham and Steve Evans's *Lewis and Clark Among the Nez Perce: Strangers in the Land of the Nimíipuu* (2013), for the first time that important chapter of the journey is beginning to receive the attention it merits.

On the outbound journey, William Clark and a small group of explorers made first contact with the Nez Perce on September 20, 1805, at Weippe Prairie, in the western foothills of the Bitterroot Mountains. Meriwether Lewis, traveling at a slower pace with the bulk of the expedition's men, caught up with Clark's advance party on September 22. After a rough beginning, expedition members were able to recover their health, engage in diplomatic activities with the available Nez Perce leadership, construct makeshift dugout canoes near today's Orofino, Idaho, temporarily dispose of its horse herd, and then begin to make its journey down the Clearwater, Snake, and Columbia rivers on October 7, 1805.

Although Lewis and Clark soon passed out of Nez Perce territory, they were accompanied on their downriver journey by two extraordinary Nez Perce leaders, Twisted Hair and Tetoharsky, who accompanied the expedition all the way to Celilo Falls. The tribes Lewis and Clark encountered between October 6 and October 27, 1805, were all Sahaptin speakers, peoples with languages sufficiently similar to Nez Perce to enable Twisted Hair and Tetoharsky to converse with them.

At Celilo Falls, in David Nicandri's words, "the expedition had reached a cultural divide between the Sahaptin-speaking tribes, such as the Nez Perce, and the Chinookan-speaking people downriver, a divide every bit as important to an understanding of the peopled Columbia as the falls were to the physiographic one." Lewis was not keeping a journal at this point. The more reliable Clark noted unceremoniously, on October 27, "The Chiefs deturmined to go home.   we had them put across the river."

Lewis and Clark had spent 37 days with one or more individuals of the Nez Perce tribe.

On the return journey in 1806, Lewis and Clark made contact again with the Nez Perce on April 18. Clark reported, "early this morning I was awoke by a Indian from the nieghbourhood of our horses, he had he arived here yesterday & this morning found a Small bag of powder and ball which had been left when we exposed our goods yesterday and brought it to me." That unnamed individual, soon joined by several Nez Perce families, accompanied Lewis and Clark upriver along the Columbia River and then the Snake River, and helped the expedition make the most of a longer meeting with Walla Walla leader Yelleppit, whom they had neglected the previous fall but promised to visit with greater attention on the return journey. With help and guiding services from the hospitable Nez Perce, Lewis and Clark made part of their return journey overland. They arrived back at the villages of the Nez Perce leader Twisted Hair on May 8, 1806.

Captain Lewis desperately wanted to get back to St. Louis during the 1806 traveling season. He believed that, if he didn't get through the Bitterroot Mountains by early summer, he might have to spend a third (really fourth) winter in the wilderness. Lewis was a naturally impatient commander, and all the members of the expedition were eager to return to their homes and families in the United States. The captains remained at what is known as Camp Chopunnish or Long Camp between May 14 and June 10 waiting for the snow to melt. At that point, they chose to ignore the sensible advice of the Nez Perce leadership, that the journey through the Bitterroot Mountains would have to wait until the end of June at the earliest.

Presuming that they knew better, the captains pushed on ahead to Weippe Prairie, and a little beyond, and discovered that the snows were too deep to permit them to make the transit without jeopardizing their horse herd and the security of the expedition. After five frustrating days among the impassable snow pack, Lewis and Clark turned back—one of the few retrograde motions of the entire expedition—and chomped at the bit for an additional week before attempting the mountain crossing again, this time guided by several young Nez Perce men.

Thanks to the generosity of the Nez Perce, Lewis and Clark arrived safely on the other side of the Bitterroot Mountains on June 30, 1805. They had made the crossing in just six days. This time, Lewis was effusive: "we were entirely surrounded by those mountains from which to one unacquainted with them it would have seemed impossible ever to have escaped; in short without the assistance of our guides I doubt much whether we who had once passed them could find our way to Travelers' rest in their present situation… these fellows are most admireable pilots." It is hard to imagine higher praise from the pen of Meriwether Lewis than this.

At Traveler's Rest (in today's Montana) the expedition split first into two, later into four, smaller strands. Clark made his way to the Yellowstone River. Lewis returned to the Great Falls, this time with the Nez Perce guides in the lead, by a more direct route that took him over what is now known as Lewis and Clark Pass. On July 4, Lewis finally bade farewell to these young Nez Perce who had led them through the Bitterroot Mountains. In doing so, he said farewell to the resourceful Nez Perce forever. It is not known whether any veteran of the expedition ever encountered the Nimíipuu again. Certainly Lewis did not. On that day, Lewis wrote: "These affectionate people our guides betrayed every emotion of unfeigned regret at separating from us." Just what Lewis felt on the occasion of this final farewell is unclear.

When all of these adventures, from April 18 to July 4, 1806, are added together, the total number of days Lewis and Clark spent with the Nez Perce on the return journey comes to 77.

In sum, Lewis and Clark spent 114 days with one or more individuals of the Nez Perce tribe in 1805 and 1806.. This compares with the 167 days that the expedition spent with the Mandan, and 101 days the expedition spent among the Clatsop Indians.

However, these statistics do not tell the whole story.

The case can be made that the Nez Perce did more for Lewis and Clark than any other tribe. They fed the pale strangers at their moment of greatest vulnerability, at a time when some members of the expedition had reached nutritional collapse. They decided not to kill all the members of the expedition when it would have been easy enough to do so and when, *we now know* some members of their tribe thought it a prudent idea. They taught Lewis and Clark the Nez Perce technique of manufacturing canoes, thus hastening the expedition on its way in 1805, and they tried to teach Lewis and Clark their method of castrating stallions, which proved to be superior to the system used by the Anglo-Americans.

The Nez Perce sent along significant leaders to pave the way for Lewis and Clark along the Clearwater, Snake and Columbia rivers to the furthest extent that their linguistic skills held out. They superintended Lewis and Clark's horse herd during the expedition's five-month absence, and they overlooked a number of cultural annoyances and provocations— from dog-eating to unauthorized intrusions into Nez Perce dwelling places. In fact, in no instance did the Nez Perce do anything that could be construed as inhospitable, unless it was the notorious incident involving a puppy dog of May 8, 1806, which Allen Pinkham and Steve Evans explain in a refreshing new way in this book.

Nez Perce individuals showed the eastbound Lewis and Clark a shortcut back to the heart of the Nez Perce country. They gave Lewis and Clark eminently intelligent advice about the snow conditions in the Bitterroot Mountains and then entertained members of the expedition during the frustrating interim that followed. They entered into a formal economic and military alliance with the United States at the "Grand Council" of May 11-12, 1806, and, as the authors of this book proudly remind us, the Nez Perce never broke the sacred agreement.

For a long time in Lewis and Clark historiography and tradition, Sacagawea was regarded as the "Indian guide" of the expedition. This myth was based on Clark's statement on July 13, 1806, that Sacagawea had piloted his half of the expedition over today's Bozeman Pass, and his statement, on October 13, 1805, that "The wife of Shabono our interpetr we find reconsiles all the Indians, as to our friendly intentions   a woman with a party of men is a token of peace." It is true that Sacagawea performed her official and informal duties admirably, and she added something important, but ultimately unmeasurable, to the success of the expedition. But the truth is that her contributions were comparatively modest.

Virtually all of the actual guiding of the expedition was done by Nez Perce individuals:

- the boys who took them on first contact on September 20, 1805, to the main Nez Perce villages

- Twisted Hair and Tetoharsky, who both guided the expedition and served as key emissaries for the strangers among Sahaptin-speaking tribes (October 7-27, 1805)

- the unnamed individuals who showed Lewis and Clark the overland shortcut between the mouth of the Walla Walla River to the present site of Lewiston, Idaho (April 24-May 8, 1806).

- the five young men who led Lewis and Clark over the still-deep snowpack in the Bitterroot Mountains all the way to today's Missoula, Montana (June 24-July 4, 1806). Only "Old Toby" of the Shoshone played a guiding role that bears any comparison with the work of these Nez Perce individuals.

Most of the Indians Lewis and Clark met in their travels were friendly and hospitable during the brief periods that the expedition spent among them, but they did not have the opportunity to teach the Enlightenment travelers much about their cultures and their traditions of hospitality. In histories of the expedition, the Mandan have always received high praise for their friendliness and hospitality, slightly more than their Siouan-speaking neighbors the Hidatsa. The Clatsops have tended to receive mixed reviews. But it was the Nez Perce who aided the expedition in more significant ways than any other tribe and, pursuant to Jefferson's strategic objective, allied themselves with the United States most forcefully, and in the end, tragically. It is hard to imagine Lewis and Clark achieving their full success without the hospitality, guiding services, diplomacy, equestrian management and friendship of the people who call themselves the Nimíipuu.

Clay S. Jenkinson
Editor-in-Chief
The Dakota Institute Press

Introduction

The Nimíipuu, often called the Nez Perce today, have always lived in the same location. But there was a time when no human beings occupied the region at all. Then the *titokan* (human beings)[1] arrived, came forth from the earth and bonded with it (you will find a glossary on pages 293-296 that provides translation of all of the Nimíipuu words used in this book. In most instances, the English equivalent will also be placed in parentheses in the body of the book). As time passed, they adapted as necessary to survive. Climate changed, the plant and animal gifts of Mother Earth changed, but the Real People, the Nimíipuu, adapted.

Other people arrived, and the Nimíipuu fought with them and drove them off. Sometimes they accommodated the new arrivals, making strangers into friends and sharing resources, goods, information, and stories. Then thousands of years passed, and thousands more in this fashion, precursors of change and then change and adaptation.

Long before white men appeared in Nimíipuu territory, change was heralded by strange new sicknesses sweeping through villages. This was probably a generation before any American exploration. The time before the white man was marked by the entry of metal goods, axes, knives, arrowheads, and cooking pots, as well as beads, both metal and glass. Horses appeared also, soon after 1700, along with their equipment and new ideas about trade and war. By this time, certainly some Nimíipuu traveling outside the tribal homeland had seen white men.

The first whites to penetrate Nimíipuu homeland of which there is historical record were the American explorers William Clark and Meriwether Lewis, co-leaders of the fledgling American government's Corps of Discovery. Through carefully thought out decisions based on enlightened self-interest, humanitarian considerations and a tradition of hospitality, the Nimíipuu not only allowed the explorers to pass through their nation unharmed but, through sign-talk and ceremonies, made diplomatic agreements which represented a permanent commercial and military association.

Our story is an exploration of that fleeting moment in time the Nimíipuu shared with the American explorers and the impact of this most notable contact. The tribal largess is readily appreciated when one imagines something like the reverse of the Lewis and Clark expedition. Thirty or so young and well-armed men of the Nimíipuu nation set out through a fledgling United States, with the goal of traveling to the Atlantic and back. What kind of reception, what type of aid might they expect from the people they met and the governmental entities they encountered? Would they have hired a multi-lingual guide, with a pregnant teenaged wife? Would the frontier people of America have fed them, helped them build watercraft appropriate for the Mississippi and Ohio rivers, and provided guides and maps for hundreds of miles, along with a general description of the balance of the journey to the sea? Could our friendly warriors have expected leaders from the first American community met to secure their horse herd and riding and packing equipment for eight months, and would those American village leaders have traveled ahead of our young warriors, diplomatically smoothing the route from settlement to town?

On the return route, would American strangers have traveled along, showing shortcuts and the best places to camp? Would the white leaders have traveled out to meet and guide them, as did Ram's Horn (later known as Looking Glass, Senior), at Pataha Creek and Alpowai Creek? Would Anglo America, on its own turf, have formally allied itself to the travelers, promising peace, friendship, and trade? And would the villagers met by the Rocky Mountain tribesmen have cemented the alliance by sharing their young women? This imaginative re-creation offers insight into the enormity of the Nimíipuu contribution to the Corps of Discovery, as it reflects some major examples of the heartfelt hospitality given by the Nez Perce.

Despite suspicions that the arrival of white people would somehow bring them harm, and prophecies that many terrible happenings might befall the people who treated with the whites, the Nez Perces offered food, shelter, and community. In addition, Nez Perces guided Clark to the Clearwater River, and Twisted Hair took him back to the prairie near present-day Weippe to welcome Meriwether Lewis and the balance of the party. Twisted Hair then led them to a good camping spot at the juncture of the Clearwater and North Fork of the Clearwater rivers. There, at the Canoe Camp, Twisted Hair and likely Red Grizzly Bear (unidentified by name in the 1805 journals) helped construct the large canoes necessary to carry all the personnel, trade goods and equipment of the expedition. In addition, Twisted Hair drew a map on a white elkskin showing the way, and although he and "Tetoharsky" (Te-toh-kan Ahs-kahp, or Looks Like Brothers) did not launch with the flotilla on October 7, they met them downstream the following day. The headmen then helped guide the Americans safely all the way to the Narrows of the Columbia, below Celilo Falls. This took two weeks and three days of their time, not counting the time for their approximately 300-mile horseback ride back to their Clearwater River homes.

The following spring (1806), a Nez Perce was at Celilo when Lewis and Clark arrived on their return upstream to Nimíipuu country.

This unnamed person was joined by another Nimíipuu family, who accompanied and helped other friendly Sahaptins direct Lewis and Clark away from the Snake River route to a time-saving cross country trail that would bring them back to the juncture of the Snake and Clearwater rivers. Thus, near the mouth of the Walla Walla River, the whites abandoned the last of their canoes, and took what was called "the Nez Perce Trail" to the Clearwater country.

It was along this trail that the headman Ram's Horn (We-ah-koomt, Flint Necklace), "the big horn Chief,²" later renowned as Chief Looking Glass, Sr., met the expedition and brought them safely down the Alpowai drainage trail and back to the Snake River.

Lewis and Clark came back into the Nez Perce country in 1806, at a time of hunger and privation for the tribe. Yet, now reduced to a minimum of trade items, the explorers were able to sustain themselves until they reached the Kamiah region, where the tribal headmen, representing the bands of their nation, entered into a formal alliance with the United States, as represented by Lewis and Clark.

From that date forward (May 12, 1806), the men of the Corps found trading for food easier, and their diet was supplemented by unlimited horse steak offered by Chief Tunnachemootoolt (the Broken Arm). Both Chief Tunnachemootoolt and Nusnu-ee-pah-kee-oo-heen (Cut Nose) helped make maps, including one which revealed a short cut to the Great Falls of the Missouri. It was the *qoqáalx 'iskit* (spelled Cokahlarishkit by Lewis) or the Buffalo Trail, up Montana's Blackfoot River.

In the sense that history is understood in Western civilization as founded on written records, the coming of the Lewis and Clark expedition was the beginning of history for the Nimíipuu. Thus the encounter of the Nez Perces with the Lewis and Clark expedition was a watershed in tribal history. From the time of those explorers to the present, there have been ever-increasing written accounts of the tribe. The first accounts were those kept by American, British and Canadian traders, and then by the mountain men, missionaries, adventurers, government agents, and ultimately by the Nimíipuu themselves.

The Nez Perces would find great meaning in the promises of Lewis and Clark because the Nimíipuu *mim'yoóxat* (chiefs/headmen) had smoked tribal pipes with the captains, the representatives of the United States, and Nimíipuu villages flew the 15-star American flag given to them by the captains. Headmen even wore the peace medals awarded by the captains. The pipe, the flag, the medals were the symbols of the American Alliance, the outward manifestation of the heartbond of the two nations. These symbols were the tools for the *mim'yoóxat* to teach the people, and the reminders to the headmen themselves that the agreements of peace, trade, and friendship were real. Through these symbols, Nez Perces believed they understood clearly that they were allied with the Americans.

American men, just as other individuals from other allied nations, were acceptable to the Nez Perce as marriage partners. And it was natural, acceptable, expected, and desired that the marriage alliances would produce children which would make the Nez Perce-American bond perpetual, a living alliance of commercial, political, and military cooperation. Nez Perce tribal history during the last two centuries is unexplainable except through an understanding of the government-to-government relationship initiated by the interaction between Lewis and Clark and the Nimíipuu headmen in 1805 and 1806, and this alliance includes the intermarriages which resulted from and reinforced that relationship.

For the Nez Perces, the coming of Lewis and Clark, quickly followed by the establishment of the Canadian fur trading posts such as Kootanae House (1807), Saleesh House (1809), and Fort Spokane (1811), brought the tribe more directly into trade with whites, with whom they had only been marginally involved in the late eighteenth century. In July of 1806, Lewis and Clark left Nez Perce territory never to return, but tribal involvement in the fur trade had begun and soon began to accelerate. The Nimíipuu and America would never be the same again.

ENDNOTES

1   The reader will generally find the English translation in parentheses. The au-
    thors realize that most readers are more comfortable with standard English
    names for places, things, and individuals, but we also believe that the time has
    come to normalize Nez Perce terms as much as is possible without creating any
    confusion.

2   Gary E. Moulton, ed., *The Journals of the Lewis & Clark Expedition,* 13 vols.
    (Lincoln: University of Nebraska Press, 1983-2001), 9:304.

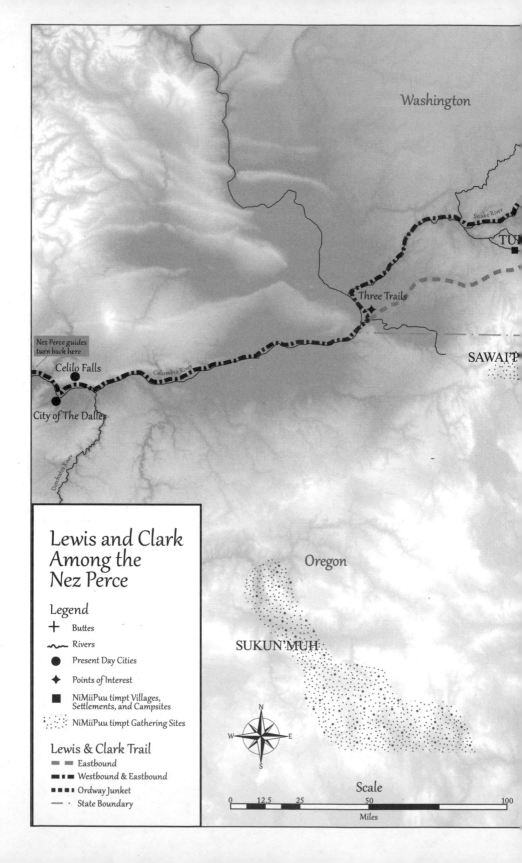

Washington

Snake River

TU

Three Trails

Nez Perce guides
turn back here

Celilo Falls

Columbia River

SAWAI'P

City of The Dalles

Deschutes River

Lewis and Clark
Among the
Nez Perce

Legend

+   Buttes

∿   Rivers

●   Present Day Cities

◆   Points of Interest

■   NiMiiPuu timpt Villages,
      Settlements, and Campsites

⋯   NiMiiPuu timpt Gathering Sites

Lewis & Clark Trail

– –   Eastbound

■-■-■   Westbound & Eastbound

■■■■   Ordway Junket

– ·   State Boundary

Oregon

SUKUN'MUH

N
W   E
S

Scale

0   12.5   25   50   100

Miles

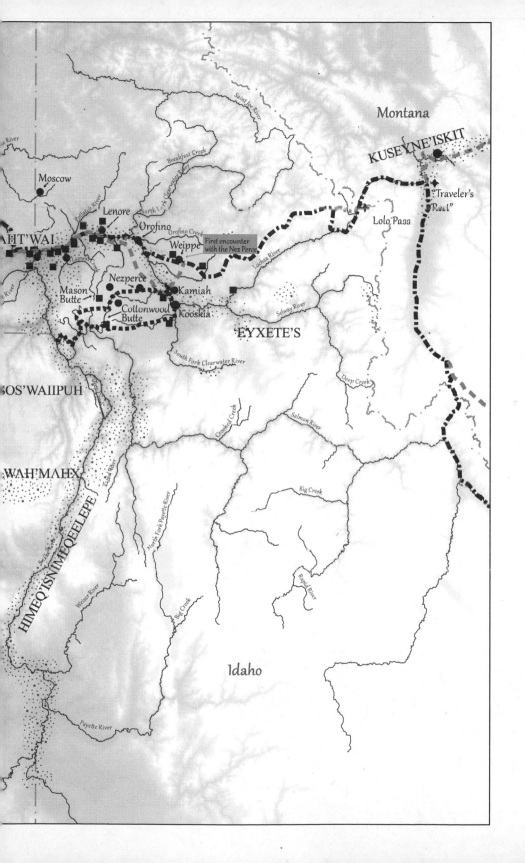

Montana

KUSEYNE'ISKIT

"Traveler's
Rest"

Saint Joe River

Moscow

Breakfast Creek

Lolo Pass

Lenore

North Fork Clearwater River

Orofino

ΛΗΤ'WAI

Orofino Creek

Weippe

First encounter
with the Nez Perce

Lochsa River

Nezperce

Kamiah

Selway River

Mason
Butte

Collonwood
Butte

Kooskia

EYXETE'S

ĠOS'WΛIIPUH

South Fork Clearwater River

Deep Creek

Crooked Creek

Salmon River

WΛH'MΛHX

Big Creek

North Fork Payette River

HIMEQ'ISN'IMEQEELEPE

Weiser River

Rapid River

Big Creek

Idaho

Payette River

Chapter 1

A Long Time Ago

Waqipani´x (a very long time ago)[1] there was a land of mountains so high there was no timber on the tops, only rocks and snow and ice. Water in tiny rivulets ran off of the peaks and ridges in the spring, summer and fall. As it tumbled, it joined with other rivulets to form raucous creeks and loud-roaring rivers that pounded through volcanic soils and rock until merging with the west flowing river, Xuyeełp (Columbia River).

Between the mountain peaks and the big bend of the Columbia, where the Pik'úunen (Snake River) empties into the Columbia, lay a most perfect country. Within the greater land there rose the Bitterroots, the Clearwater Mountains, the Salmon River Mountains, the Blue Mountains, the Wallowas and the Seven Devils Mountains, all with heavy timber: spruce, red and white fir, tamarack, lodgepole, ponderosa, white pine, cedar and hemlock. Some mountains plunged straight to canyon bottoms, while others benched out into massive plateaus where the timber was thin or nonexistent, but there was plenitude of good grass, edible roots and berries in the high meadows and the open ridges.

Through the canyon bottoms ran some of the great rivers of western North America: the Selway, Lochsa, north and south forks of the Clearwater and the Clearwater proper, the Grande Ronde and its branches, the Little Salmon and big Salmon, which finally joined the even more powerful Snake.

In movement, life was found. Above the canyons, above the prairies and mountains, the clouds appeared and disappeared, moved by the invisible force of the wind. In canyon bottoms, the creeks and rivers persisted in their incessant rush to the western ocean. In the sky above and the water below, there was movement within movement. As the air moved, insects and birds moved within it. River currents pushed boldly downstream, and the otters swam in the powerful flow, emerging to play along the banks. Geese flew overhead, flying north during *weweexp* (spring season) and south during *sexnim'* (fall season).[2] Ducks, too, were in the air, swam on the river's surface and dove beneath it.

Of all the moving elements, water was the most vital; the streams and rivers were the threads that held life together. And waters were the most powerful and mysterious moving force, the one which bound the sky to the earth.

This great country, with its water veins reaching to the Pacific, had been made by the Creator as a home to large animals like the woolly mammoth, the giant bear, the giant elk and the giant bison, much larger than *qoq'aalx̣* (modern buffalo). One legend refers to a large woolly animal, resembling the muskox, which lived and was hunted here.[3] Even the condor, called *qu'nes,*[4] once flew in the skies of the Nimíipuu homeland. There was a miniature three-toed horse, and other animals, like the familiar mule deer and whitetail, regular-sized elk and moose, bighorn sheep, mountain goat, cougar, black bear, grizzly and *hi'miin,* the wolf.

In the cold clear streams, migrating sturgeon, chinook salmon, coho salmon, steelhead and eels made their home. The beaver went about his work of winter food storage and dam building, and the otter and muskrat blended their lives with the waters, too. Overhead, the winged ones flourished—everything from grouse to woodpeckers, owls, and eagles. All the fish and birds and all the animals could speak and communicate with each other.

One day, the Creator decided the world must change to make way for another creature, the human being. Creator called all the animal people together for a council and told them about the change that was coming. The animals were asked to choose three judges from among themselves to give names and lifestyles to all the rest to help the human beings when they came. To qualify, the animals were told, "each of you must act out how you want to be and state how you can help the human beings when they come. Not all of you will survive but, if you do, you will be given your traits and a name for the coming generation." The council was to be held on a hill high above the lower Clearwater Valley. As the council time arrived and some of the animals straggled in late, Creator turned them to stone, and their remnants can still be seen.[5]

Each animal, fish, bird, and even insect acted their part. The deer would live in the hills and the high ridges and would make themselves available for buckskins and for meat. The elk would be similar to the deer, but would be more difficult to find; however, the meat would be more than that of the deer, and the bull's antlers would be more useful for making tools.

Scavenger birds—magpies, crows, ravens and vultures—would be the clean-up crews, along with some of the insect people, all helping to keep the land tidied up from the wastage of humankind and the large predators. Eagle wanted to rise higher in the sky than any other being and offered to act as a mediator and brother for the human beings. He would one day contribute his feathers as a reminder and symbol of bravery, spirituality and many other things.

So this is how it went, each acting out the way in which it would live and the manner in which it would aid the humans when they arrived. Then the coyote, *'iceyéeye,* came into the council; he was late, but Creator listened as he announced that he would be large, ferocious, and feared by all creatures. He said he would be as the grizzly bear, but that was not possible, because grizzly was already qualified and established. Then coyote said he would be a large, high-flying predatory bird, but that was eagle, who was already established, so coyote could not be that either.

Finally, Creator was amused by *'içeyéeye* (coyote) and took pity on him, giving him his own special powers as a world traveler and to act as Creator's agent for the coming of the human beings. Coyote would be a teacher to the human beings, silly at times, but clever and a survivor. He could only exist in one dull color; he must always be gray.

This is the world that the Native People came into—the Nimíipuu and other tribes. There are several stories of the beginnings of their creation, but the best known and most universally accepted by the Nez Perces is the story of how Coyote brought them about by killing a giant monster who had made his home in the Kamiah Valley of the Clearwater River.

In all variations of the story, coyote acts as the creating agent by combining the heart-blood of a large monster with the soil of Kamiah valley. The following version is adapted from an account given to the authors by tribal elder Oliver Frank (1906–1992), who heard it many times from his own grand relative Ipnaatkian, a woman who resided near the monster's heart, upon the spot where the monster's liver came to rest in the valley of Kamiah.

Monster and Coyote *('ilcwéew'cix kaa 'iceyéeye)*

as told by Oliver Frank

Sometime before the coming of the Indian, Coyote was making a kind of fish ladder by tearing down the Waterfalls known as Celilo. This work the Coyote was doing so that the Salmon could go upstream for the coming people to catch at their various places of settlement. The fancy-stepping Coyote was very busy engaged at his work until a voice came to him from somewhere. "Why are you working and spending your time, when all the (animal) people are gone? The Monster has consumed them all."

Coyote hesitated for a moment and finally replied to himself, "I'll just continue and work because I was doing this for the people." But he rethinks what he must do and realizes he must confront the Monster— "And now maybe I'll be consumed by the Monster, too."

The coyote then began to trot upstream towards the Salmon River via the Columbia and the Snake rivers. While Coyote was traveling, he accidentally stepped on Meadow Lark's leg and broke it. In a cry of pain and anger, the Meadow Lark shouted at the Coyote: *"Nee saa wai loo* (Coyote), *Yee ya weets a koo saa* (It's a pitiful thing you are doing)—what chance do you have in finding the people?"

Coyote replied, "My friend, please tell me all you know of the disappearance of the people, and I'll make you a leg out of *kaak sun ma* (sturdy brush)." So Meadow Lark told Coyote that, as far as [he could recall], all the people were consumed by the mighty Monster. So Coyote completed the task of making Meadow Lark an artificial limb. Then, in loneliness and despair, Coyote said to his only companion, "I, too, might as well go and be consumed or swallowed by the Monster."

So Coyote continued on his journey, saying to himself, "I must be clean and acceptable for the Monster." Therefore he took a sweatbath. Coyote also decided to make himself strong and immovable, so that if the Monster swallowed him, he would not be able to spit him out. Coyote also gathered for himself some hemp rope with which to tie himself around the waist, so that when the Monster swallowed him, he would have some anchor or protection from entering the Monster too fast.

He decided to anchor himself to three different mountains ranges: the Wal'waamaxs or Wallowa mountains, Siseeqiymexs or the Seven Devils [Mountains], and Epa tok maaux, known as Chimney Peak in the Selway Crags. Coyote continued his journey over many hills, vales, valleys, prairies, and ridges. While traveling, he also prepared himself with garments, including a helmet of bunch grass that would make him difficult to see.

First Glimpse of the Monster

All of a sudden, as Coyote was traveling along the Camas prairie, he got his first glimpse of the Monster's huge head. The Monster was looking for something to make prey of, something to swallow or destroy.

Coyote hid himself behind some waving bunchgrass from where he could see the gigantic body of the Monster. "Oh, Monster! We are going to have an inhaling contest." The big head of the Monster swung from side to side as his bright eyes began to gaze about to see where the voice was coming from. The Monster thought to himself that the voice sounded familiar. It took him quite some time before he discovered the clever Coyote who now was thoroughly prepared for the occasion.

Weapons of Death

On his back, Coyote wore his bundle in which he carried his equipment of death. It contained five good knives made of sharp-edged stone, some *papc'icqiy* (pitch from a fir tree) and, lastly, some flints with which to start a quick fire. After some deliberations, it was agreed that Coyote would try to inhale the Monster first. The challenger tried with all his might, strength and wisdom to inhale his mighty foe, but to no avail. The Monster just barely weaved or shook, so Coyote finally gave up, crying to the Monster, "It's your turn, you might as well inhale me, swallow me in with the rest of your victims, because I'm alone and lonely anyway." The Monster, as he drew in his breath, sounded like roaring wind and, as he inhaled, Coyote flew toward the mouth of the great Monster.

Along the way, Coyote was sprinkling along the way some different kinds of edible roots, berries, and herbs for the coming generation. The first anchor snapped, and the second anchor was getting very tight so Coyote cut himself free. During this time, Coyote was inspecting all of the ways by which to avenge and destroy his foe, not for his own glory, but for the future and the betterment of the coming human race. Finally, the third anchor got so tight that Coyote had a hard time releasing himself to prevent being cut in two.

Inside the Monster

At last Coyote was completely inside the dangerous and unconquered Monster. Walking down the throat of his foe, he could see dry bones scattered all along the way. There and then Coyote understood why there wasn't anybody on the outside anymore. He discovered some small creatures and asked directions to the Monster's heart. On their way to the heart, they were rushed by grizzly bear, but Coyote just snarled, stepped aside and gave the grizzly a kick on the nose as he went by. Grizzly would be a part of the new generation, but his nose would always be upturned.

As Coyote continued to wend his way he heard the rattle of the rattlesnake, but Coyote just gave him one stomp on top of his head and pronounced that, from this point forward, rattlesnake would have a flat, smashed-looking head. While still en route towards the heart, Coyote was charged once again, this time by the common bear. Coyote told him teasingly, "So it is you who is the Monster's last choice for protecting the heart," and then gave him a swift kick in the backside. He exclaimed to bear, "Now your rump is all rounded and you will from this day on have a rounded rear, and the coming generation will recognize you by that."

At Last the Heart

Finally they arrived at the heart. This was the beginning of the end of the great, unconquered Monster. Immediately Coyote commanded everyone to gather all the wood available and pile it just as close to the heart as they could. During this excitement, Coyote's bosom buddy, *tilípe'* (the Fox), came up and was commanded to gather wood the same as the rest of the [animal] people.

As the wood was being prepared, Coyote cried to the people, "You poor ignorant people, why do you die of starvation and thirst?" And immediately he unpacked his bundle, took his first stone knife and began slicing off slabs of fat and meat from the Monster's heart. He fed many of the dying animal people who were in a state of starvation.

Then Coyote started up a fire with his flint and pure fir pitch which he had prepared before entering the Monster. Soon smoke drifted up and out of the eyes, nose, ears, and anus of the once great Monster. The Monster squirmed and quivered all over, wanting to release the Coyote.

Cry of the Monster

The fire blazed away and soon after the Monster cried out, "I was a little afraid of you, Coyote, why not let me cast you out?" But Coyote answered, "What would the people say of me when they would spy me? 'There goes Coyote who almost became our hero, but instead of freeing us out the nose, eyes, ears, and anus of the Monster he thought only of himself?' No, no, I'm staying in."

Thus, Coyote refused to be cast out of any of the Monster's openings. Coyote knew that the people would never refrain from ridiculing him for doing something for the glory of himself instead of setting the example for the coming generations. The Monster tried one last time to eliminate Coyote out his anus but failed.

Beginning of the End of the Monster

The Monster began to groan and moan in pain as the clever Coyote started cutting away on the heart with his stone knife. The first knife did not last too long, and the second knife did not make it long either. Here Coyote commanded the people to gather all the bones and carry them to all of the [Monster's] outlets mentioned before, so that it would be easy to kick out all of the bones when the time would permit.

And during this same time, Coyote also ordered that all the elderly be permitted to position themselves to be first out of the various openings. All the while, Coyote was cutting away at the heart of the Monster with his third knife, but it, too, broke. He started cutting with the fourth knife and cut for a time, but with quite a large chunk remaining to be cut, it too broke. Then with the fifth and only knife left, Coyote kept on cutting, hoping and praying that his plan of operation might succeed for the benefit of posterity. Then the last knife broke.

All of his knives now were broken and useless, yet a small portion was left of the heartstrings. With a last desperate effort, Coyote hurled himself on the piece of heart still hanging and luckily ripped it off. In the Monster's suffering and convulsions, he yielded all of his various outlets and, as ordered before, the bones were first kicked out, followed by the elders and then all the remaining beings.

Freedom at Last

Just as the animal people filed out followed by the heroic Coyote, and as the Monster started to fall into his eternal defeat, all of his body's outlets started to close. By some error a Muskrat still was partly in the Monster and, with the help of the Coyote, he barely squeezed out, catching just his tail in the anus of the Monster and pinching off all of his tail-hair as he escaped. There and then Coyote declared that Muskrat would forever be that way (with no hair on its tail), even after the coming of the new generation.

Dry Bones to Live Bones

At last the people were free, but the pile of bones remained, and once again good old Coyote ordered the people to gather all the bones and arrange them accordingly. As this was done, Coyote finally said, "We are going to carve the Monster." The Coyote then smeared blood on his paws and sprinkled it on the bones and suddenly, all the dry bones and body parts came to life.

As this occurred, Coyote looked up to the Creator of the Universe, then flung the new life in all directions. He forenamed many of the nearby tribes of people, such as the Coeur D'Alene, Cayuse, Flatheads, Crow, Blackfoot, Sioux, Paiute, Bannock, Shoshone, Ute, and many others.[6] And during this time, Coyote had consumed all the good parts of the Monster, as well as the blood, not realizing he had omitted anyone.

Small, but Mighty

After all the parts of the body and blood were exhausted, once again an old buddy, the Fox, reminded Coyote that he had unintentionally omitted [to make provision for] himself, as well as the local people who would dwell in the beautiful valley forever. The Coyote scolded his buddy, the Fox, on why he did not remind him of the oversight sooner. But once again Coyote relied on his people and commanded them to bring him some water.

As the people did so, the Coyote, in his final declaration, dipped his paws, which were still bloody, into the water, [wrung] his hands several times, then sprinkled the blood on the soil of the Kamiah valley. At the same time, he commanded: "You [the Nimíipuu] may be the last to be blessed, but you shall and will be known to the Human race as small but mighty." *Waʼko kalo* (that's all).[7]

Coyote left a portion of the monster's heart in the beautiful Kamiah Valley of the Clearwater River, and it still stands as testimony to the truth of the story of the terrific struggle which took place so long ago. Photograph by John W. Fisher

Oliver Frank, Kamiah Nez Perce, raised by Chief Joseph's sister, Debora Corbett. He served on the tribal council and was a repository of Nimiipuu legend and lore. Photo courtesy Nez Perce National Historic Park: NEPE-HI-2967.

Coyote left a portion of the monster's heart in the beautiful Kamiah Valley of the Clearwater River, and it still stands as testimony to the truth of the story of the terrific struggle which took place so long ago. This was the beginning of the Nimíipuu, and if one asks a Nez Perce where their people originated, no one will answer that they have come from across the Bering Strait. Invariably, Nez Perce will insist, "We have always been here."

Coyote was the creative agent acting on behalf of the Creator. The evidence is in the legend and in the stone mound at Kamiah. For modern science, there is skepticism surrounding the word "always," but it must be remembered that in any discussion within the oral history context, "forever" and "always" delineate time "beyond memory." And since there is nothing in tribal tradition, legend, or myth suggesting migration to this region, "forever" properly describes the permanent residence in the steep river canyons and canyon bottoms, prairies and timbered benches of "home."

Thus, the stories of the Real People reach back into time immemorial. They not only explain the birth of the people from *weetes* (earth), but the generation of the animal traits and the topography of the Nimíipuu world, as well. Hells Canyon was dug by Coyote. Coyote warned Ant and Yellow Jacket to stop their feuding and, when they ignored his warning, he turned them to stone.

Coyote stopped all salmon from advancing up Potlatch Creek, but the salmon escaped by jumping over the ridge separating Potlatch Creek from the Clearwater and, in so doing, they dragged their tail fins to create a notch in the skyline. Everything in nature is explained in stories among Nez Perce and some surrounding native tribes. Native people traveled widely and listened to the stories of their neighbors who likewise shared their own perspectives of places and events far and wide.

There are no migration stories for the Nimíipuu or Real People. If science suggests Nez Perces migrated into their homeland, the theory would have to be about a time before civilization in China or India, or Rome or Greece, or the pyramids of Egypt. The time would be before writing, before history, before time mattered. Within the framework of legend, myth, oral history, and written history—in other words, in every dimension vital to a description of human beings in relation to place—the Nez Perces have always been where they remain today.

And the tribal memory does reach far, far into the past. Large hairy beasts are described which might easily be ancient conceptions of creatures for which scientists have recovered skeletal remains.[8] Nez Perces knew of these animals, such as the wooly mammoth and the miniature three-toed horse, which were slain and eaten by the tribe's ancestors.

Likewise there are stories of exploding volcanoes and darkened skies. Such catastrophic incidents occurred deep in the past. The eruption of Mount Mazama (now Crater Lake, Oregon) is dated by scientists at nearly 7000 years ago. There are even stories from earlier, when great destructive floods swept everything before them, except those few bands who escaped by ascending to high places within the homeland, such as Steptoe Butte, Kamiak Butte and Moscow Mountain.[9]

It was always in the winter season that the stories were told, around a crackling fire in the dark. These stories constituted an important portion of youth education. The topography, birds, fish, animals, and weather were all described by myth and close observation.

The collective memories of thousands of relatives over thousands of years ensured that the stories were all true, not necessarily in the literal sense, but full of life's truths. The memories were often confirmed by their universal authenticity and their continuing applicability to the world in which we live, such as not undertaking a serious venture without first going through the sweat ritual or without securing all proper equipment like sharp stone-knives and good fire-making materials in advance. Plan each move in advance, too, and have a counter-plan, a fall-back move for every move of your adversary. Try to avoid appearing ridiculous, such as starving while surrounded by food. Lead by example and never give up, even while in the belly of the monster.

Like all excellent educational systems, Nimíipuu storytelling ultimately served the society by fostering the traits that would perpetuate the wisdom and well-being of the people. The stories were also immensely entertaining, with wide use of surprise, mystery, and magic, as well as the personal mimicry, gesture and voice of the storyteller that insured an individual style would be stamped on every episode.

One of the important themes of the Nimíipuu myths is an ongoing concern over food. Another theme is adaptation. Both are essential to survival through the time of legends, through the tens of thousands seasons and the earth's rotations around the sun. This was all before history or even the concept of history. Through the time of glacier ice and exploding volcanoes with their liquid glowing-floating stone, the people understood that everything that moved was alive and that they were a part of that life. They adapted ways of protecting and feeding themselves, even in times of great difficulty, ways to live and thrive.

Killing a woolly mammoth required organizational and technical skills and ultimately a good quantity of personal courage. These were the qualities of the Nimíipuu hunters. Even after the disappearance of the mammoth and the extinction of saber-tooth cats, the giant bison, and others, the same hunting skills remained essential. However, hunting big game, by its nature, was not a consistent or dependable source of food.

The rivers—the Snake, Salmon, and Clearwater—were the tribe's primary home for hundreds of centuries, since time before memory. Like the bear, otter, beaver, and muskrat, the people centered their lives on the living rivers, seasonally teeming with varieties of fish. Chinook, or king salmon, known as *naco'ox,*[10] was the most important species, but there were many kinds of fish and fish harvests. This river orientation, in fact river dependence, was especially strong before the eighteenth century, and the entrance of the horse.

Big game hunting was primarily the arena of the men, and both men and women fished. But it was root discovery, root garden-tending, and harvesting by the women that resulted in the most dependable sustenance. Nimíipuu forebears lived in winter villages along the river and creek bottoms from which the women, soon after the first snow melt, sought the first spring roots, *qeqí it,* that occasioned a thankful first roots ceremony.

It was a great honor and an important rite of passage for Nez Perce girls to accompany the older girls and women to dig their first roots. As spring gave way to summer, root gathering proceeded upslope to higher elevations, especially for the rich *qém'es* (camas). During these times, people often lived in large temporary structures that more closely resembled camps than villages. Roots were prepared for immediate consumption and also preserved for winter sustenance and inter-tribal trade.

Likewise, the high country also produced berries, wild onions, turnips, and carrots. Some of these, too, were eaten fresh, while the rest were stored for trade or winter reserves. Nimíipuu women were revered and generally enjoyed a high status. This was, in part, because of the women's expertise in the collection of the Nez Perce nation's most important food resources, but also, like the men, they often sought *wéeyekin* (guardian spirit) power, and they disciplined themselves by sweating and swimming in cold waters.

In olden times their ability to run long distances was hardly less than that of the men.[11] And many Nez Perce women rose to high positions of power and leadership within their villages and bands. Lewis and Clark did not anticipate female leadership among the Indians they met and did not recognize it when they witnessed it.

Water was critical to both the physical and spiritual lives of the Nez Perce. Spring water, and water from the streams and rivers themselves, was the ultimate medicine, the ultimate visible tangible power available. This is why the Nimíipuu often began each day with a drink of water and ritually drank water before each meal.

Water is a mysterious, regenerating power substance. This was revealed through witnessing the growth of plants following the rains, the cleansing of wounds with cold water, and the dependence of the young of all mammal species on the milk of their mothers, a reflection of the dependence of all life on the milk of the mother earth. And the power was revealed not only in observations, but also in dreams that brought further revelations. Some of these were the source of myths that explain the water gifts to the Real People.

The Sweat Bath

The most ancient of all Nimíipuu rituals involving water was the Nez Perce sweat bath. It originated in mythology as a gift to the people, female and male, a multi-purpose and necessary gift with spiritual, social, and physically practical properties. The sweat bath was also part of a complex of rituals that included use of an emetic stick, the hot bath soak, and the hot mud bath, all accompanied by cold-water bathing known as the swim. Much of the complex ritual is no longer or rarely practiced, except for the sweat bath, which today can be found all over Nez Perce country, exhibiting a strikingly similar format to the old-time sweat.

There were several styles of sweat house construction, but with each the goals were the same: recreational and social, religious and curative. It was a cleansing and a renewal; when used in conjunction with the emetic, the supplicants were cleaned from the inside and out. Specially selected rocks were heated in an outside fire and ceremonially placed inside the sweat house in a special pit lined with flat rocks. As each rock was placed, a *koos háama* (waterman) splashed water with *qawsqáaws* root on the rocks—"washing the old man's face," as it was and continues to be called.

Later, when all were inside the sweat house, more water was "thrown on" for each person in the circle inside and prayers were offered as the steam rose. Many believed the steam carried the prayers appropriately. When all had been prayed for, one last splash was offered for *Qi'iwn* (Old Man) the personification of the sweat house.

After the rocks quieted or "stopped speaking," the *piskis háama* or doorman howled like a coyote, and everyone swam in the nearby creek or stream and relaxed. (Today, participants use a bathtub and pour a pitcher of water over their heads.) This described the end of the first round; often there would be at least three rounds. Men and women would sweat separately in their respective sweat houses, and the elders of each sex often used the occasion as an opportunity to tell stories intended to entertain and instruct. For the men, the stories were often on the subjects of hunting, fishing, and war.

The "swim" or cold water bath could be, and often was, used alone for cleansing and conditioning, especially in warm weather, but for some it was a year-round activity. It was much easier to enter the water after a sweat or hot water bath because of the much higher body temperature. However, cold water would toughen the individual, and both little girls and boys were required to bathe in cold water daily for hygiene and conditioning. Children would enter the river in the presence of an elder who would encourage them to remain deep, over their shoulders, by switching them about the shoulders should they be exposed.

One informant remembers being sent running to the river to jump in and returning to the house where the elder, an uncle and veteran of the 1877 war, told them *náaqc* (once), now *náaqc héenek'e* (once more) and down the hill they charged and back into the Clearwater. This was repeated until the uncle deemed that it was enough.[12]

Small children who cried or whined for no apparent reason had cold water flicked in their faces while in the act; the discipline stopped when the crying ended. Babies were taken to the rivers by their mothers and taught to swim, they never had a memory of not being able to swim and no informant could remember any Nimíipuu who could not swim.[13]

Nez Perce were taught to cross rivers whenever it was necessary. Anyone could cross the largest rivers by pushing a drift log into the current at a good spot, a place where the current would carry the individual towards the opposite shore where there was a place to get out. Studying or knowing the currents was the key point because many places existed in rivers, like the Salmon and Snake, where the current might carry the swimmer to the opposite shore, and a sheer bluff or whirlpools might be encountered.

Many of the best swimmers simply entered the river and swam unaided to the opposite shore, a relatively easy feat in low water conditions and where good judgment is exercised, but a dangerous and risky stunt at medium or high water. Yet it was possible to cross streams under those conditions, as well.

Horses and Canoes

A variety of tribal traditions explain how the Nimíipuu acquired their first horses and their first Appaloosa horses, the latter of which are considered nearly synonymous with *si'k'em,* or horse, in Nimíipuu legend. Several stories that seem logical claim that the first horses came from Shoshone neighbors to the south. The Pueblo Revolt of 1680, initially successful, resulted in thousands of horses becoming available to the western tribes.

It staggers the imagination to consider what the first sightings of horses meant to Nimíipuu observers. There was likely no single tribal introduction, but a variety of experiences and a rapid absorption of horse power into tribal culture. The bunchgrass of the northwest was a great natural horse pasture, and once introduced, horses proliferated. The horse revolutionized Nimíipuu trade and travel, which was essential to tribal culture from its genesis. The Lolo trail, already worn by thousands of moccasined feet over millennia, would be cut wider and deeper by the hooves of unshod ponies.

Intertribal conflicts would escalate, and the use of horses would both increase the frequency of wars and lead to the development of a new style of warfare. Securing new horses became a reason for war. Horses altered all aspects of tribal culture, even marriage, as horses became an important consideration in dowries offered for an *'iwéepne* (wife).

The Nimíipuu word for the horse is *si'k'em.* The word for dog is *ciq'áamqal.* These similar terms reflect that horses were similar to dogs in many ways. Both were pack animals, early alert agents for approaching enemies, and fighting companions. But horses, like dogs, could be much more than that. They became important spiritual links between humankind and the rest of the natural world.

Upon the first encounter, a lot of people were probably skeptical of the horse's power or value. Perhaps it was the youth and more venturesome adults who first embraced the possibilities of the new creature. Is it unfair to suggest that some people of the older generations did not like the portent for change that the horse brought and that some people clung to their canoes and their river way of life? No matter, the horse had come to stay and many individuals developed almost immediate bonds with individual horses. For the Nimíipuu, the horse soon became both a practical and aesthetic necessity, but the tribe recognized a deeply spiritual dimension, too.

Seeking spiritual guardianship in equestrian skills was warmly embraced. This is illustrated by the emergence of many horse-related *wéeyekin* powers, of which the following example may suffice.

Charlie Amera, grandfather of informant Cecil Carter on his mother's side and recognized bronc-rider, war-dancer and musician, his skills were augmented by the spirit power of the grouse on a limb in the wind. Photograph courtesy Nez Perce National Historic Park: NEPE-HI-2054.

Charlie Amera's *Wéeyekin* (Guardian Spirit)

as told by Cecil Carter

There were two men named Charlie Amera. One was a Mexican cowboy who married into the tribe. The other Charlie Amera was his step-son who took the name, but was not the blood relative of the Mexican. The younger Amera had a *wéeyekin* (guardian spirit) power. He was taken out in the mountains and left, and he was told 'stay where you are.' He wasn't told when anyone would come and pick him up, but just to stay awake and remain in that one spot. He was supposed to remain there until someone came and got him.

Later he heard a voice, and the voice told Charlie that he would help him in his horseback riding. He could hear the voice, but when he looked at the person he saw a grouse. The person became a grouse. And the grouse was perched on a limb, and the wind blew the branch, but the grouse remained calm, only his legs moving back and forth with the blowing branch.

That grouse had great balance, and that balance was the power that Charlie would have in riding broncs and breaking horses. He could see right through that grouse. He could see the ribs and everything, and that grouse person gave him a song. It was an Indian song, and, after he would sing this song… his power would be especially strong. It was the power of balance, the power of balance and rhythm. It was said he was a great horseman, and later he became a good musician, too. *wáaqo' kalo',* that is all.

───────────

This story is just one of many that could be cited regarding the union of horsemanship and the spirit power of *wéeyekin* (guardian spirit). It also illustrates how everything to the Nimíipuu was interconnected: horsemanship, fishing, even success in love and gambling were not separate from spiritual strength.

As horseback hunting increased, the relatively small numbers of buffalo west of the Rocky Mountains decreased, and the traveling of the Nez Perces to the buffalo country on the east side of the mountains accelerated. While east of the Bitterroot Mountains, they often allied with Salish or Crow and camped in large *tamacilpt* (tipi circles) for protection.

Meeting new people and making new friends was adventuresome and fun. However, conflict with enemy tribes increased, too, with the coming of the horse. The circle of the people had to be defended against raiders looking for horses, women, and children to steal.

Through all of their trading and travel experiences, the Nimíipuu came to be aware of the Spanish. One of the first questions they posed to horse-owning tribes to the south was, "Where did these animals come from?" The answer always led back to those who came from across the water, had settled in the southwest, and lost their horses to the Pueblos.

These Spanish who lost their horses also lost the equipment that went with the horses, including metal objects such as bits for the horse bridles. There is even the legend that a Spaniard was for a time amongst the Nez Perces. He was won in a gambling game called stick game, along with a small group of mares, a stallion, and a female captive.

A favorite gambling game of the Nimiipuu and many other indigenous tribes witnessed by the Lewis and Clark Expedition members in Kamiah Valley in 1806. Photo courtesy University of Idaho Special Collections and Archives, #38-1214. Stephen D. Shawley Collection.

Legend of Stick Game Victory

as told by Gordon Fisher

This all happened near the headwaters of the Salmon River in Shoshone country where Nimiipuu and others were meeting with the Lemhi Shoshone to trade. While camping near each other, they decided to play stick game. In this game, two sides are on their knees facing each other. There is a bundle of 20 sticks that are painted and sharpened on one end, and each team has 10.

The object of the game is to win all of your opponent's sticks. To win a stick, a team leader must guess which hand of the opposing team leader holds a marked piece of bone. There are two bones held, but only one is marked. The team leader exchanges the two bones hidden in his or her hands, while the leader's teammates try to distract the guessing team with songs, joking, and laughter.

In this particular stick game, a team of Nimiipuu men played a team of Shoshone men. The game first went one way, and then, as the day wore on, it went the other, and so the game continued. As the Nez Perce team guessed correctly another stick was stuck in the ground in front of their leader, but before all the sticks could be secured, the Shoshone men would next get lucky and the sticks would begin to shift to their side, yet neither team could win all the sticks—all 10 that it took to win the match. The two teams faced each other most of the day, and each team sang its songs accompanied by rhythm pounded out with sticks on a log placed in front of each team member. An audience backed each team cheering wildly and beating on their hand drums as their team's momentum would threaten to end the game. Anyway it was drawing [towards] night and the Shoshones had sixteen of the twenty sticks stuck on their side, they had won that many. They wanted to bet more and win more from the Nez Perces, and there were many side bets too, because anyone in the crowd could bet on who might win one stick or two sticks or any [side] bet you wanted to make. One Shoshone put up six mares and a stallion, and he had a Spanish slave, a horse trainer that he was tired of, he put him in the bet too, and the Nez Perce leader signed [through Indian sign language], 'and the woman too,' because he saw that the Shoshone had an attractive captive woman. The momentum shifted to the Nez Perces and they began to win back [all] their sticks, then they won the sticks of their Shoshone opponents as well. All these horses and both people then were won by the Nez Perces. They had a big and famous victory. This is how it was that this group of Nez Perces got horses and a horse-trainer at the same time. They were lucky that time when it happened because often the win would go the other way and they would lose many valuable possessions. *Waaqo' kalo'* (that is all).

The Nez Perces are famous for their spotted horses, the Appaloosa, a spotted breed almost synonymous with horse. The Nez Perces are often credited with creating the Appaloosa by selective breeding of other horses, which they learned from the Spanish. There are several existing stories of the coming of the Appaloosa among the Nez Perces. The first refers to the first spotted horses in the Kooskia-Kamiah region and was told by the late Harry Wheeler (1884–1963) of Stites, Idaho, and a graduate of Carlisle Indian School.

Harry Wheeler, son of War of 1877 veteran, Weeahweoktpoo (later known as Presbyterian minister Rev. William Wheeler, d. 1918), and father of authors' informant Wally Wheeler, Harry Wheeler was an oral historian who helped Clearwater County, Idaho historians Ralph Space and Zoa Swayne with their works. Photo courtesy Clearwater County Historical Society, Orofino, ID.

Tsuts Pilkin and the first spotted horses

as told by Harry Wheeler

The first ones were brought to Cottonwood Creek just west of Stites, Idaho, by Tsuts Pilkin. He was a great big man… and an excellent roper and bronco buster. He and some others traveled to Salt Lake to steal horses from the Shoshoni, Bannock and Ute tribes. There he met some Mexicans who were impressed with his ability with the lariat.

They induced him to return with them to Mexico, going by way of St. Louis. Several years later he returned with two spotted mares and a spotted stallion. There was no moral rule broken in stealing horses.[14] It was a game, and one gained fame as a good horse thief.[15]

Another story, a myth, is told of the first spotted horse to appear in the Palouse country which came about as a result of the dream of a Nimíipuu prophet, named Imatsinpu. He dreamt, then foretold that a small Nimíipuu band living in the Palouse [modern eastern Washington] region would bring to being an unusual horse that would benefit the entire people, would serve them, and bring honor.

The Origination of
Maamin [Mormon] or the Appaloosa

as told by Oliver Frank

In the eastern part of the state of Washington where the small community of Palouse stands today a *Maamin* or, as it is known today, an Appaloosa, was given to a small band of Nez Perces for the benefit of the entire tribe. [It was] an unusual horse, an animal strong and sturdy, a war horse that could run all day long, with unusual features on its body, different spots around its nostrils, encircling spots and dots on its eyes which showed much white and resembled the eyes of a human being. It had beautiful dots on its body and rump and hips. The Nez Perces called it *Maamin,* an Appaloosa, a horse with the heart of stone for its strength, sturdiness, and endurance.

Imatsinpun, the Dreamer prophet, had a vision of such a horse, and he asked all tribal leaders to come to upper Palouse River, where lived a small band of Nez Perces. They came and listened to the Dreamer. The meeting was opened with a prayer, thanking the Great Spirit for life and the preservation of life, praising the Creator for the sun, moon, the stars, sky, clouds, and the rainbow. He thanked the Creator also for all insects, beasts, animals, and birds and fish of all types, and for the earth provider, mother of all the human beings, with its day and night and water for all.

Next, the Dreamer made his speech to all *mim'yóoxat* [chiefs/headmen] and others who were gathered at the long house. He told them of his vision about the unusual war horse and how it would come about. A woman carrying a baby in her body would be cared for in a certain way before the coming of the child. But a mare must be selected and instead of the careful way of the human mother, not to become too excited, the mare must be kept in an agitated state, the opposite to that of the human mother.

When the time comes for the selected mare and she is with colt, we must all meet again. We will gather at the place and have a big sweat bath in a large sweat lodge and we will gather and welcome all with singing and dancing and have a big feast. Next morning, after eats, all will dress in their most colorful regalia with the young men's faces painted and with unusual paint spots of all kinds upon their bodies. We will all gather with our horses, bows and arrows, *kopluts* (war clubs), and knives as if going to warpath.

The maidens and women will be in their best farewell

outfits, then we will form a large circle, followed by a moment of silence and a prayer by the group. Thanks will be given, and the pipe smoked for everyone in attendance and for everyone who cannot come.

The time arrived the following spring, and every procedure was followed through the sweating, dancing, prayers, body paints, and smoking. The mare is brought to the center and surrounded by everyone. Imatsinpun rides up on his horse painted with spots, all decorated with fancy and bright colors. He carries a staff and rides forward, and waves the staff towards the mare who is held by young and husky Nez Perce men. The Dreamer speaks loudly for all to hear:

We all know, have seen and heard of human being
mothers having at times born children with various
kinds of marks and spots, so today we try the same with
this mare to gain the horse I saw in my dream.

Then began the singing, the charging of the mare by the young men on their wildly painted horses, the dancing too of the women and everyone singing, shouting and attempting to get the mare as nervous and excited as possible and to let her see all the colors and the young men hollering and brandishing their war weapons. This ceremony lasted until late in the day and then that evening another big feast in the long house and the Dreamer prayed and held more religious ceremony followed by an all-night social ceremony. In the next few days the group disbanded and departed for their respective homes in different areas and just waited for word of the results of their endeavors.

The results of this first gathering was not successful and several other gatherings were held at different locations and again, no specially marked horse arrived. New meetings were called for with excitements, bright colors, war paints, sweat baths and prayers and smoking and nothing happened. It was getting to be disgusting to the Nez Perces wondering about Imatsinpu and his dream.

Finally, back on the upper Palouse, on the location of the original ceremonies, the dream of Imatsinpu came true and the first horse colt was born which matched the vision. This was the beginning of a special horse of the Nez Perces, a horse to match their mountainous homeland, a horse with an eye like a brother. I have spoken.

"Mode of crossing rivers by the Flatheads[Salish] and other Indians."
Nimiipuu and Salish use same techniques crossing rivers. Penrose
Library, (Box 2, Native American Collection) Mullan's Military Road
Report, artist Gustavus Sohon from Mullen expedition.

After the horse became part of the Nez Perce culture, the dependence of the people on the rivers remained strong, but the power and speed of their horses enabled them to range further from their river bases and return in less time with more big game or to raid more effectively against tribal enemies. Horses had to cross rivers, too. Horses, like tribal youth, were encouraged to overcome any fear of water by wading and then swimming. This began when the colts were small and taken to the rivers by the side of their mothers. When they were two years old or older, they were led into the river where they were mounted by young riders from already trained horses. The water discouraged them from bucking, which was too exhausting for the young horses and, if they should pitch and buck and dislodge the rider, the odds of riders being injured were lessened by the river.

By this time, the horses already knew how to cross rivers, since they had likely made crossings on the downstream side of their swimming mothers. Riders would enter a river at a well-chosen spot and, when the water became too deep for the horses to touch, the rider would slide off on the downstream side and hang onto the mane or saddle. If they missed either of these, the rider had the option of holding onto the tail until the far bank was reached.

In small bands or even large herds of horses, the best riders and horse swimmers would plunge in first, while the remaining riders would push the rest of the herd into the water, it being the horses' nature to follow the herd leader. This entire process was so common in the Nimíipuu homeland that it was referred to as *sap-soo-wayikt*.[16]

Whether swimming a river or swimming horses across a river, it was imperative to know the river in question, that is, the currents and manners of a particular stretch to be crossed. Because of the mountainous nature of the Nimíipuu homeland, crossings had to be chosen carefully, and certain of these could be used only at specified river levels, which ordinarily changed radically from season to season, sometimes changing overnight due to an upstream melt or thunderstorm. These crossings were well-recognized and named by the Nez Perces.

Of course, crossing rivers could be accomplished by building rafts from driftwood, called *we-dhuh, we-tuh,* or *Wit-uh.*[17] These rafts were used to transport people and goods downstream, as well as across rivers, and required great handling skills in white water. Panic drowns many victims of water accidents, and plenty could go wrong under the best of circumstances. However, in Nez Perce country, everyone on board— men, women, and all but the tiniest children and the most elderly— were at home in raging cold waters and strong currents. Rafts had the disadvantage of going only across water or downstream; there was little or no upstream raft travel. Upstream water transportation was by canoe.

Nez Perce canoes were dugouts made from a single tree. Pine, red fir, cedar, or even cottonwood—the log available was the one used. Canoes were all sizes, up to 50 feet long and sometimes small enough for just one woman to propel herself across river using no paddle, only her hands.[18] Canoes were used for extensive downstream travel and, perhaps somewhat surprisingly, could be taken upstream, as well as by a special technique, which the Nez Perces and others on Northwest rivers also used. There were two keys to upstream canoe travel: one was knowing the currents and using back eddys to advantage, and the other was the means of propulsion. The most common was a simple pole called *'iyehneno's.*[19]

The Nez Perce also used a special pole/paddle combination called the *eaus,* which was 10 or more feet long, light and strong, usually made from red fir. It was used as a pole by standing boatmen in the bow and stern to maneuver between rocks and to brace against the current. In shallow water, the boatmen could simply hang on and wade upstream, pushing the canoe. In quiet sections of the river, as in the many deep holes between rapids, the canoe was "paddled" with the *eaus.*

Canoes required a great deal of time and hard labor to construct and were consequently valuable. They were especially valuable in the great untimbered country which began about 10 miles above the mouth of the Clearwater River and continued down to below the Celilo Falls on the Columbia, a distance of several hundred miles. Raft making and canoe building were economic activities for the Nez Perce because they could use their rafts and canoes to move trade goods, and then both rafts and canoes became potential merchandise. Rafts were often dismantled and their materials used in long house and slab house construction by downstream tribes.

Before horses, the Nimíipuu would walk home or work their way back upstream in a canoe. After the adoption of horses, canoes and rafts might be exchanged for saddle horses for the trip back to the Clearwater River or Salmon River country. Although the coming of the horse certainly lessened the association with rivers that existed from the beginning, the bonds between the people and rivers obviously remained strong into the eighteenth and nineteenth century, the time of the coming of Lewis and Clark.

The spirit power of the *weeyekin* (guardian spirit) that was embraced on select ridge and mountain summits was sometimes visited in other secret places in the rivers. It is said that some tribal youth were sent into deep holes in the Salmon River, for example, over and over, each time holding their breath as long as possible and looking at the river bottom for something of meaning. They would describe what they observed to a *tiweet* (spiritual and medicinal doctor) who would help them interpret the meaning of their experience.

Another story is that, at certain levels of the Salmon, underwater shelves can be located with air pockets and sitting places. Here a supplicant might wait day and night with no food until visions came. Outside the underwater cave, a prearranged small group would await the individual's emergence.

Similar to a candidate climbing down from a high place like a mountain top or ridge, the individual would swim out from the air pocket and pass out upon reaching support. The visions or hallucinations would not be spoken of except to *tiweet* or *tiwata'aat* (male and female spiritual leaders), who would aid the youths in interpreting the experiences.

Part of the revelation would be a name, and many of the known historic names of Nez Perces show the close association of *weé yekin* (guardian spirit) and the rivers of the Nez Perce home. Any name with reference to the otter was referenced to a strong power. Chief Peo-Peo-Ta-likt (Bird Alighting, 1855–1935) said the otter held "much big power, strong."

River otters were common in the Clearwater, Snake, and Salmon rivers and are currently making a comeback. Beaver and muskrat are two other common mammals associated with the rivers. Grizzly Bear was associated with strong powers as well and, as the grizzly of the Clearwater country utilized the salmon as its primary source of protein, grizzly power was associated with water power, too. The birds whose names were used by Nez Perces, reflecting many *weyekin* (guardian spirit) powers, are ducks, geese, swans, dippers, ospreys, and bald eagles.

What were the special powers that were represented by the names of individual Nez Perces? It is impossible to fully know, appreciate, or understand; that they were water- or river-related there can be no doubt.

One individual with known water power, Charlie Oatman, was told to swim the fishing spots at low water and learn all the hiding places of the salmon—all the rocks, currents, and eddies of the salmon's home. He did this his life long, even swimming portions of the tumultuous waters below Celilo Falls of the Columbia. He was known as a great fisherman and would catch salmon when other fishermen struggled.[20]

Leadership was more than a simple sum of practical skills and good judgment. The mysterious and the unseen also had to be taken into account. Sorcery had to be dealt with, requiring a person who specialized in spiritual matters. This trained individual was the shaman, or *tíwéet*, along with the female equivalent, *tiwata'áat*. These individuals carried their own specialties, that varied widely depending upon their spirit helpers. A shaman might have specific pharmacological knowledge, or even be adept at osteopathy, but they would likely have knowledge of how to counteract evil spells and might be able to remove a curse.

The training for shamanism took many years, and curse removal could be a long, drawn-out affair. It might even require the reinforcement of a second or third shaman. Many, no doubt, were excellent psychologists who possessed intimate knowledge of the patient's personal circumstances and family background.

The knowledge of the individual's tutelary power (the power received during the vision quest) was significant, also, in determining treatment. These powers were ordinarily demonstrated at winter dance ceremonies and were accompanied by appropriate songs, a representative bundle, and specific dances. Shamanistic practices were a necessary antidote to sorcery.

Each village was autonomous, and the bands consisted of the different villages within a watershed. Each village had a *mim'yoox̣at,* a leader chosen by the elders of the village, and the various village *mim'yoox̣at* chose one leader to serve as spokesperson for the band. The *mim'yoox̣at*[21] chosen were from families who were recognized as producers of leaders. Youth with perceived aptitude for leadership were specially trained to understand the exercise of leading and the responsibilities thereof. One way to conceive of a village or band leader is to think of someone whose judgment was universally respected, someone who could end divisive disputes and exercise an acute sense of justice.

Often the leaders of various villages and bands were related because certain families dominated the leadership positions. Band leaders represented the highest form of permanent political structure. There was no permanent political structure at the tribal level but, at different times of emergency or crisis, a temporary leader might be recognized to exercise leadership over matters of concern for the entire tribe, especially in times of warfare.

Within this political framework were all kinds of sophisticated nuances that permitted the recognition of other forms of leadership. For example, the fishing leader, who would make the important decisions regarding the time and taking of the various fish and the methods of the catch, would likely be a man who would also make judgments regarding the distribution of the fish caught. He insured that all received a share and that no one was left out.

The Fish Leader would suggest how much of a catch might be prepared for winter storage and how much would be prepared for inter-village or inter-tribal trade. These were practical matters. Sometimes the Fish Leader exercised diplomatic authority as well, such as determining which family held the most advantageous fishing locations and ensuring that all ceremonial rituals relative to fishing be properly executed within his village jurisdiction.

Of course, everyone did not fish all the time, and the same village members or even band members who submitted to a particular leader for guidance in fishing might look to someone else entirely at times of the hunt. This would be especially true for the buffalo hunt, which demanded the high degree of organizational skills needed to get an entire village moved from, say, the Salmon River country of modern Idaho to Montana's Judith Basin or Musselshell Basin. On the occasion of the buffalo hunt, there was the ever-present possibility of confronting enemies. This would require the emergence of a war leader, a man of proven defensive skills.

ENDNOTES

1   Haruko Aoki, *Nez Perce Dictionary* (Berkeley, CA: University of California Press, 1994), n. 82. Hereafter cited as Aoki, *Nez Perce Dictionary*.

2   Names from Herbert Joseph Spinden, 1908. "The Nez Perce Indians." *Memoirs of the American Anthropological Association* 2(3). Lancaster, Penn. (Reprinted: Kraus Reprint, New York and Millwood, 1964, 1974), pp. 237–8. Hereafter cited as Spinden, "The Nez Perce Indians."

3   Allen P. Slickpoo Sr. and Deward E. Walker Jr., *Noon Nee-Mee-Poo (We, the Nez Perces): Culture and History of the Nez Perces*, Vol. 1 (Lapwai, ID: Nex Perce Tribe of Idaho, 1973), p. 5. Hereafter cited as Slickpoo and Walker, *Noon Nee-Mee-Poo*.

4   Aoki, *Nez Perce Dictionary*, p. 1134.

5   These large basalts are located on the south slopes of the Clearwater River breaks, opposite and slightly downstream of the mouth of Hatwai Creek, located approximately 7 miles from the confluence of the Snake and Clearwater rivers.

6   Coyote, of course, did not use their modern names, but their titles as identified by the Nimíipuu.

7   From manuscript of Oliver Frank (1906–1992), in possession of authors.

8   Tribal Elder Oliver Frank (1906–1992) told of his Kamiah, Idaho, friend Sigurd Grove who dug up mammoth bones in Kamiah Valley in 1957. This story is printed in the *Lewiston Morning Tribune* (Lewiston, ID) September 25, 1994.

9   Lloyd M. Cox, *In the Days When the Rivers Ran Backwards* (Lewiston, ID: Norbon's Copy Cabin, 1994, 1995), for an explanation of how the Clearwater River ran backwards during a series of catastrophic floods. Hereafter cited as Cox, *In the Days When the Rivers Ran Backwards.*

10 Aoki, *Nez Perce Dictionary*, p. 464.

11 Lillian A. Ackerman, "Marital Instability and Juvenile Delinquency Among the Nez Perces," *American Anthropologist* 73:3(June, 1971) pp. 595–603. Hereafter cited as Ackerman, "Marital Instability and Juvenile Delinquency Among the Nez Perces."

12 From Jesse Redheart Spalding Sweathouse.

13 In recent times, some do not learn to swim, and some are poor swimmers. There have been many lives claimed by the Clearwater in the 20th century.

14 In Jefferson's Virginia, horse theft was a capital crime, whereas in Nimíipuu culture, stealing horses was a specialized virtue. Legal theft of land was a virtue to Jeffersonian Americans, but inconceivable to the Nez Perce.

15 D.E. Warren, "Spotted Horse No Recent Arrival," *Lewiston Morning Tribune* (Lewiston, ID), January 6, 1963.

16 Information from Eugene Wilson, Lynus Walker and Alex Pinkham.

17 See Stephen D. Shawley, Appendix I: Nez Perce Names and Notes, *Nez Perce Trails* (Moscow, ID: University of Idaho), p. 103.

18 Info on women's canoe from Mylie Lawyer.

19 Aoki, *Nez Perce Dictionary*, p. 502. See also Lucullus V. McWhorter, *Hear Me, My Chiefs!: Nez Perce History and Legend*, edited by Ruth B. A. Bordin (Caldwell, ID: Caxton, 1952), p. 19 n. 4. Hereafter cited as McWhorter, *Hear Me, My Chiefs!* Also, Bob Chenowith, "Waliimliyas: the Nez Perce National Historical Park Dougout Canoe Collection and Dugout Canoe Use Among the Nez Perce Indians," *Journal of Northwest Anthropology* 42 no. 2 (Fall 2008).

20 Story from Marcus Oatman about his brother.

21 Deward E. Walker, Jr., *Conflict and Schism in the Nez Perce Acculturation: A Study in Religion and Politics* (Pullman, WA: Washington State University Press, 1968), p. 16. Hereafter cited as Walker, *Conflict and Schism in the Nez Perce Acculturation.*

Chapter 2

The Coming of the White Man
(weye 'úuyit sooyáapoo)

The Nimíipuu had many other visionary leaders just like Imatsinpu, both men and women who took in all that they saw and heard, who considered long and well the needs of the people, and who prayed and sought visions for the proper course of action. In the sweat house, when the water with the good *qawsqáaws* medicine was thrown upon the cherry-red stones, the stones would speak. *wistitám'o* (the sweat house), was the gift of the Creator to the people, and when the water strikes the rocks, they speak to you. Rocks are the oldest part of the earth, and thus the wisest, and the wisest leaders listened carefully to what the earth had to say.

They said that there would come another new being. It would be the across-the-water people, the hat wearers, the white people. They would be strange in many ways and would bring many good things and bad things, also. They would have a powerful technology, but their presence would bring more of the new death and sickness that had already been visited upon the Real People and many of their neighbors. There would be a creature with horns like the buffalo (cattle) that would be on the hills around the Clearwater River. The new people would point at the land and say "This is mine, this is mine," and they would draw lines upon the earth and try to divide it up. Shamans made up songs about such things to make the prophecies indelible in the minds of the people.

If these things were to come about, the question naturally arose as to how the tribe should react. What should the leaders do about this coming event? There were more and more reports from traveling Nimíipuu regarding white strangers and increasing reports, too, from neighboring tribes who witnessed white people. In the west, they had been seen on the lower Columbia and on the upper Missouri to the east. In both instances, they came by water, and many, especially their leaders, wore elaborate hats. *Soya* is a Nez Perce term referring to crossing water and *poo* or *puu* refers to people, these were the across-the-water people. Also, some of the white men referred to their headgear, their hats, as "chapeau." It is easy to understand how the word *soyapuu* or *sooyáapoo* and chapeau were blended into a word meaning both across water people and hat wearers.[1]

Over the tens of thousands of years of Nimíipuu existence in the Clearwater, Salmon, and Snake rivers country, they had absorbed many changes. Their memories, as preserved in their mythology, legend, and oral history, all reflect their courage and resiliency. They had seen flooding and the destruction of many of their people; they had witnessed the fire and ash of multiple volcanic eruptions. Sickness was dealt with by herbs, the sweat bath, and spiritual living.

With the Columbian "discovery" of America, new diseases came for which the old cures proved useless, yet the tribe lived on. The horse came and, in a short time, was embraced and absorbed into the deepest recesses of tribal ways of life. Every challenge had been met, and the Nez Perces had survived each, maintaining the courage and strength to defend their beautiful homeland and hunting grounds east of the Rocky Mountains against all comers. Would a new threat conquer and displace the sovereignty of "forever"? Around the campfires in the long houses and tipis of the Nimíipuu, conquest did not seem likely. "Let us wait and see," they said.

The first time a Nez Perce met any of Lewis and Clark's party may have been on the upper Missouri. Peo-Peo-Tah-likt (Bird Alighting), in his narration to his cousin Many Wounds (Sam Lott), told of Twisted Hair and a few followers who accompanied some Shoshones to the Mandan and Hidatsa villages at the mouth of the Knife River in today's North Dakota. This was during the Corps of Discovery's stay at Fort Mandan (October 26, 1804-April 7, 1805). The only written evidence is the oral history written down by Sam Lott in 1935. Is it true?

This is a difficult question, but the story is plausible because one of Sergeant John Shield's hatchets, traded to local Indians at Fort Mandan, found its way into a Nimíipuu's hands. The five Mandan and Hidatsa villages in today's North Dakota were the center of a vast continental trade network that had been in place for many centuries. Goods of every sort, both before and after white contact, made their way from the Knife River to every corner of North America, including the lands west of the continental divide. It is not at all surprising that the hatchet preceded Lewis and Clark to a Nez Perce village in the fall of 1805. Also noted by Lewis and Clark was the fact that a handful of Nez Perces already possessed firearms, ostensibly secured in the upper Missouri trade. Twisted Hair heard the message brought by the explorers, a message of peace and subsequent prosperity. As a result, the Nimíipuu sent out three emissaries of peace to their Shoshone neighbors.

The first bona fide historical encounter between the Corps and tribal members occurred on Sunday, September 10th, 1805. U.S. Army Captain

Meriwether Lewis wrote: "this evening one of our hunters returned accompanyed by three men of the Flathead [Salish] nation whom he had met in his excurtion up *travellers rest* Creek. on first meeting him the Indians were allarmed and prepared for battle with their bows and arrows, but he soon relieved their fears by laying down his gun and advancing towards them. the Indians were mounted on very fine horses of which the Flatheads have a great abundance; that is, each man in the nation possesses from 20 to a hundred head."

U.S. Army Captain William Clark wrote: "Colter, met with 3 <Flatheads> Tushapaw Indians who were in pursuit of 2 Snake Indians that hade taken from <the three from> ther Camps on the <Columbia> head of Kooskooske River 21 horses, Those Indians came with Colter to our Camp & informed by Signs their misfortune & the rout to ther villages and &c. &c. one of them Concluded to return with us. <I> we gave them a ring fish hook & tied a pece of ribin in the hare of each which appeared to please them verry much, Cap Lewis gave them a Steel & a little Powder to make fire, after eating 2 of them proceeded on in pursute of their horses."[2]

These Indians were, in fact, Nez Perces, not Flatheads, which is evident in their descriptions of their home on the Kooskooske River, today's Clearwater River in Idaho. The man who at first agreed to guide the expedition over the Bitterroot Mountains to his relatives, changed his mind the following day and continued after his brethren in pursuit of the Snake horse thieves. It is obvious that the journal keepers could not differentiate between the Salish, who spoke the Salish language, and the Nez Perces, who spoke Sahaptin. The confusion over the identity of the two tribes persisted in the Corps's records despite the Corps's considerable exposure to both.[3]

Twisted Hair's possible meeting with the Lewis and Clark Expedition at Fort Mandan and the brief interchange between the Corps and the three young Nez Perces near Travelers' Rest while in pursuit of their horses, does not furnish the drama of the later meeting at Weippe Meadows. The Weippe encounter came as a result of the difficult passage the expeditioners experienced, as their Shoshone guide, "Old Toby," led them over the Bitterroots.

With their livestock worn beyond lean and the travelers' rations running low, they were in desperate need of relief. Clark, with a half dozen followers, forged ahead of the main party in hopes of finding game and breaking out into easier country. The trail generally followed the dividing ridge between the Lochsa River and the North Fork of the Clearwater and, from a high point, prairie country could be seen in the distance. However, the snow, sleet, and rain, combined with steep sidehills criss-crossed with fallen timber, made travel tedious, brutal, dangerous, and disheartening.

Clark was riding towards an area known today as Weippe Prairie. The Nimíipuu simply called it Weippe (Weippe is the modern spelling for 'Oyáyp),[4] It was one of the principal root-gathering grounds controlled by the tribe. The principal root was *qém'es,* later called "camas" by the whites. People came from many different bands to dig *qém'es,* after which they roasted it in pits. Following this procedure, it could be stored for winter consumption or utilized as a trading commodity.

Not only friends and relatives from other Nimíipuu bands showed up at Weippe to share in the resource, but also friends and relatives from other tribes, such as the Cayuse, Umatilla, Walla Walla, and the Palouse. Other groups might be represented in the *qém'es* trade, too, from as far as the mid-Columbia—tribes such as the Klikitat, Wishram, and Yakama. Representations from non-Sahaptin speakers such as the Coeur d'Alene, Spokane, and Flathead might also be found. While *qém'es* remained the premier attractant resource at Weippe, the social life made possible by such a large gathering was the equivalent of urban living.

A popular game of "follow the leader" was played on horseback. Did the riders dare to "follow the leader," in tearing through the brush and dashing down steep slopes and jumping creeks and logs? This could develop into a dangerous situation where broken limb, if not life, was risked and courage proven. Foot races and horse racing were popular, too, with the young, and those who did not participate directly might gamble on the outcome. The "stick game" was a more direct means of enjoying the raw excitement of pure gambling between guessing teams, each vying to prove their observation skills and spirit guidance in their guessing power.

Hunting skills were developed in the arrow and hoop game. The hoop was rolled across the ground and arrows shot through the hoop. The game was competitive, fun, and sharpened the manual dexterity and eye-hand coordination required in hunting and war. This was most popular with the boys, but the girls had their own pretend games, usually mimicking the activities of their female elders.

One popular sport involved a rawhide ball used to "score" when a team would advance the ball beyond a goal, which might be two upright poles placed in the ground or even pine trees. The teams were made up from anyone in a village, male or female, young or old, and one village was pitted against another.

It was a rough and tumble affair in which a team could kick the ball or run with it or throw it to a teammate. The area of play was a little longer than a modern football field, and the sidelines extended to the natural boundaries. The youth were the most active players, and the game began whenever young people from their respective villages could gather. The game did not end until all players quit, usually at dark.

Players could come on and off the field at will, there was no limit on the size of the teams, and both sides were cheered by village members not playing. The villages themselves are best described as temporary camps made up of various dwellings, tipis, elongated tipis or "long tents," and camp huts of pole frames covered with fir boughs. When the game was played with "sticks," some compared it to shinny and field hockey.

At Weippe, trade goods were exchanged with travelers far and wide, along with trade items and all the latest news, accented, no doubt, by gossip. There was always excitement in the air at Weippe during the root gathering, and the prairie was punctuated by the ripple of laughter in the days of happiness and wailing in the bad times.

In September 1805, wailing sounded on the prairie. Most of the residents of a Nimíipuu village on the north side of the Clearwater River in the Kamiah valley were wiped out in a raid by the Tewelke, their Shoshone enemies. This raid was particularly gruesome in that many of the Nez Perce victims were disemboweled or had their heads cut off or their bodies otherwise desecrated.[5]

The Shoshone generally were a traditional enemy, and the raids and counter-raids had been going on longer than the oldest tribal members could remember. Between raids, truces were negotiated in order to trade and, with gun-bearing Blackfeet threatening both Nez Perces and Shoshones in the buffalo country, the two tribes sometimes allied. Increasingly, the Lemhi band of Shoshones of the upper Salmon River country were considered as potential friends and allies against the even greater Blackfoot threat.

In their most recent visit to the Minitarees (the Hidatsa), Twisted Hair and other Nez Perces heard the message of peace and friendship proposed by the Americans, either directly from the Americans or from other tribal leaders. This message was not lost on the Nez Perces. They wanted peace in order to stop the continuous loss of their numbers to the incessant intertribal wars. Because they recognized that peace would be mutually beneficial, the *mim'yooxat*, the "chiefs," sent three diplomat warriors with a pipe offering of peace to the Shoshone.

In early September the news spread rapidly through Nez Perce country that all three emissaries had been murdered. Mourning for these three was added to the wailing for the slain at Tamataha village. After considerable deliberation, the village and band leaders agreed that only vengeance would salve the pain of loss, and on September 17, 1805, all able-bodied warriors of fighting age left Weippe, adding additional warriors to their total as they rode south to avenge the killings of Nimíipuu.

This was the situation on September 20 1805, when Captain William Clark and six men came down from the timber several days in advance of the main party. In preceding years, perhaps a handful of wide-traveling Nez Perce had seen white men on the lower Columbia, on the Missouri, and in the southwest, but the majority of the tribe had only heard of these strange creatures. They were about to experience the entrance of whites into tribal territory that had been predicted and prophesied. It was known as "the first coming," the *weye 'úuyit*.[6]

The *weye 'úuyit*, the Coming of the White Man

Eight-year-old Aleiya, the son of Chief Twisted Hair and his two companions, Is-coat-time and another, whose childhood name has been forgotten,[7] were hunting small game about a mile from the easternmost village located on the Weippe Prairie. With a little dried meat in their quivers they could remain afield for some time. When they observed riders approaching, they ran and hid in some tall grass. Their three small hearts were pounding as they intently watched the red-haired leader rein in his horse and begin looking for the boys he had observed. He found two of them and gave each a small piece of ribbon and gestured for them to go towards the village.[8]

The boys quickly relayed the news of the white men's entrance into Nimíipuu territory, and at the same time described the intruders as having glassy eyes the color of the sky on a cloudless day, making their eyes appear fish-like. They wondered, too, if they were not related to dogs or bears since they had a bad odor and hair on their faces. Later, it would be said that some of the white men's faces appeared upside down, because some had hair on the bottom of their heads and little on top. Many women and children mounted ponies and headed into the timber to watch developments from a safe distance. Others hid in the tipis.[9]

As Clark approached the first village, it was likely Chief Twisted Hair's brother, Al-We-Yas, who came forward to greet him. Clark wrote in his journal, "a man Came out to meet me with great Caution." Tribal elder Mylie Lawyer stated that it was Al-We-Yas, the village leader or *mim'yooxat* of the easternmost village at Weippe Prairie,[10] who "came forward." Unseen by Clark, some Nez Perce men, according to Chief Peo-Peo-Tah-Likt, placed themselves strategically and awaited developments with bows strung. Others, like Al-We-Yas, cautiously approached the strangers.

This was the first historical meeting, confirmed by government records, between a tribal leader and an official of the United States government: September 20, 1805. The ribbons exhibited by the boys were correctly seen as a sign of an invitation to trade and, with most of the warriors gone, Al-We-Yas improvised the prudent wait-and-see policy until a plan could be formulated.

Clark and the others put their right hands forward and grasped the elders in a handshake. This was a new thing to the tribesmen, and they did not understand it or like it. Some of the old men said *"hin-Olt-Sin,"* "they dawdle as if we were children."[11]

Al-We-Yes escorted Clark and his six hunters to "a lage spacious lodge" and they were treated to "a Small piece of Buffalow meat, Some dried Salmon beries & roots in different States, Some round and much like an onion which they call *(Pas she co)* quamash the Bread or Cake is called Pas-she-co Sweet, of this they make bread and Supe they also gave us the bread made of this root all of which we eate hartily." In fact, they ate, too, "heartily." Later that evening, Clark recorded, "I find myself verry unwell all the evening from eateing the fish & roots too freely."[12]

While Clark and his companions were eating, Al-We-Yas sent riders to all villages on the Weippe Prairie and to all nearby villages on the Clearwater proper in the canyon below, with the message of the *weye 'uuyit,* the coming of the white man. The arrival, which had been so long prophesied and expected, had arrived unexpectedly, and now some decisions had to be formulated that had been continuously debated and long postponed.

The Plot to Kill Lewis and Clark

as told by Irvin Watters

A lot of tribes people wanted to kill Lewis and Clark and all their party. There were several reasons for this. First, they bore a lot of weaponry, rifles and steel knives and tomahawks and, with most of the warriors gone, the whites posed a real threat. A lot of the stories about the whites seemed to indicate that they were treacherous, and any negotiations with them would merely play into their hands and contribute to the tribal demise.

Treachery was especially felt as a possibility when the people saw the Shoshone man and boy and recognized Sacajawea,[13] too, as a member of an enemy tribe, although generally a woman with a child would not travel with a war party. There was concern, too, over York, Clark's black manservant; the meaning of his skin color was not understood, and many thought he was painted for war, perhaps in mourning and seeking vengeance.

Observers noticed that, after Clark's group ate, they became sick and incapacitated. So they talked up a plan to wait for all of the expeditioners to be at one village on the prairie and feed them. When the last person took his last bite of food and all were in a vulnerable state, they would attack, strip them of their weapons and kill them. That would have been the end of them.

———————

Peo-Peo-Tah-Likt, Bird Alighting, a veteran of the 1877 war, told his cousin Sam Lott his story of the coming as he learned it from his father who, as a boy, had witnessed the coming. In 1935, Sam Lott transcribed Peo-Peo-Tah-Likt's description, as follows:

> [L]ots [of] Indians camping up in Clearwater River Valley. Some dig roots, some grind roots to make Indian bread. Some woman getting sticks to make fire. Indian men hunt for meat, fish and do other Indian custom things. When women get wood and do other work, and children play, they hear noise. When they look to see what makes noise in brush they see something and makes them all much scared. All womans run in brush and hide and children too run and hide and peek to see what it is. Some go in teepee and men get bows and arrows quick, and all talk lots. All scared. They see strange whitemans coming down Lolo trail, Indian trail--never Nez Perce see white mans like this before. They afraid bad white spirit come bring evil to Indians. Then they talk and Indian men was going to kill white men.

Were Lewis and Clark aware of a debate concerning the life or death of their party? The journals suggest there were concerns. Clark wrote on September 21 that he "Sent out all the hunters early in different directions to Kill Something and delayed with the Indians to prevent Suspicion..."[14] He must have thought that the Nez Perce villagers were feeling some "suspicion."

When Lewis came onto the prairie on the 22nd with the balance of the party, he wrote, "on our approach to the village which consisted of eighteen lodges most of the women fled to the neighbouring woods on horseback with their children, a circumstance I did not expect as Capt. Clark had previously been with them and informed them of our pacific intentions towards them and also the time at which we should most probably arrive. the men seemed but little concerned, and several of them came to meet us at a short distance from their lodges unarmed."

This statement concerning the women and children does indicate that something was afoot, that they had heard enough of the debate over what was going to happen next to concern them about the well being of themselves and their children.

When the Corps of Discovery was desperate for horses, they were fortunate in meeting the Shoshone and Sacajawea's brother, Chief Cameahwait. As they now made contact with the Nez Perces, they were fortunate once again—they met the people who knew the territory better than anyone on Earth, people who understood the nature of the waters that led 300 miles in the direction the Corps needed to travel through quickly. Winter was coming and Lewis and Clark were running out of time in the traveling season of 1805.

The Americans desperately needed Nimíipuu help to get downstream. Ultimately, the captains won tribal support and established successful relations, but the beginnings were fraught with tensions and considering whether to kill the white men—to thwart the prophecy that bad things would come of the encounter and to obtain the expedition's impressive arsenal of weapons. It may have been that one woman's argument tipped the scales in favor of the explorers. Her name was Watkuweis, and her story is legend among the Nimíipuu.

Her name, Watkuweis, meant "returned from a far country," and was an apt name that matched her saga. Like Sacajawea, she was captured by enemies on the plains as a young girl. She was exchanged often, always eastward, and finally ended up near one of the Great Lakes.

The story is so old that many details are lost. However, she was exhausted and worn down when finally married to a white man. The man and his community welcomed her and embraced this woman and were kind to her. She regained her health and strength, eventually bearing a child—whether a boy or girl, no one remembers. Her husband found it necessary to go across the ocean, but the woman refused to go any farther away from her mountainous homeland.

After a year, her husband had not returned, and she was exceedingly homesick. With her small child, no older than two, she left the Lakes region and began her westward sojourn, the small child sometimes walking, sometimes being carried by its mother, but always they followed the setting sun. They had to hide from enemies many times, and they were often hungry and cold. Once, lost in a snowstorm, she called upon her *weeyekin* (guardian spirit) for pity and help. She spied people ahead, and they signaled her to follow. They turned into wolves, but they left meat for her. A wolf was her Guardian Spirit.

Finally, late in the fall, she was discovered by Salish Indians, friends and relatives of the Nimíipuu. Her child had perished, and the woman had buried her little one in a rockslide in the mountains. The Salish kept her one winter while she healed; the next summer, buffalo-hunting bands of her own tribe took her in. They gave her the name Watkuweis. Watkuweis then grew old among her own people, always telling them of her adventures and of the kindness of the white people in the east, where the men wore big hats and owned many goods that would be good to have.

By September 1805, Watkuweis was near death. She was lying down in her tipi which stood at the edge of Chief Red Grizzly Bear's root-digging camp. Chief Red Bear was her relative. Tribal oral histories agree that, as she heard of the plans to kill Lewis and Clark and their entire party, she rose up and, seeing some of the men, shouted to "Do Them No Harm!"[15] Her words probably sounded as though she was giving an order but, in fact she was admonishing her people.

There were many reasons to not harm the Americans. Practical matters dictated waiting to make such monumental decisions. Twisted Hair liked the message of the newcomers and began immediately to augment his own agenda of cooperation with Americans to accomplish what they wanted. And what the Americans wanted was to go downstream on rivers they did not know, all the way to the Pacific Ocean.

The Nimíipuu knew the rivers, the Clearwater, lower Snake and mid-Columbia. They understood the uniqueness of each,[16] and they, their neighbors, and relations on the Columbian plateau knew the rivers were a part of themselves, emotionally, mythologically, and spiritually. They knew the different characteristics of all the rivers at all locations under different water levels in all the seasons.

Not that each individual knew it all—of course, they did not—but someone in the various bands intimately knew some of each portion so that it can be said with confidence that collectively the tribe knew every rapid and every hole of every major and most minor streams within their tribal realm. They were experts at navigating them as well, whether it was downstream in a raft or canoe or upstream in a canoe. Additionally, they knew the rivers by swimming, either alone, in a group, or on or beside a horse.

Lewis and Clark were on the Clearwater, which they call the Kooskooskee in their journals and, while the men of the Corps struggled with the conditions of their stomachs on the Clearwater, Clark scouted downstream looking for a suitable location to build canoes for the Pacific journey. In the absence of the war chiefs, the counsel of Twisted Hair and the advice of Watkuweis was adhered to.

It was "a verry hot day" September 25, 1805, and most of the party were complaining and several were "verry Sick" when Clark set out, guided by Chief Twisted Hair and "2 young men."[17] Clark had been furnished a horse, and Lewis, too, although he was so sick he was "Scercely able to ride."[18] Clark's goal was to establish a good camp where the Corps could build and launch canoes on west-flowing rivers that would enable them to reach the Pacific. Clark had already secured several maps from Twisted Hair and another chief which showed plainly what lay ahead.

After riding down the north side of the Clearwater, past "rock dam Creek" which bisects the modern hamlet of Orofino, Idaho, they continued about five miles downstream to the forks where the Clearwater was joined by the North Fork, named the "Chopunnish" River by the captains. They crossed the main fork of the Clearwater River to the south bank opposite the North Fork mouth of the Clearwater. Here they established what has been called "canoe camp."[19] The Clearwater led to the Snake and the Snake to the Columbia. The chiefs knew the way.

Clark had already sampled Clearwater canoe travel when he embarked with Chief Twisted Hair and his son the morning of September 22 and crossed to Twisted Hair's camp on a small island. After eating, he canoed back to the north bank and remounted to ride the trail back up into the Weippe country and a rendezvous with Lewis and the main party. Simultaneous to this activity was the Nimíipuu discussion as to whether Lewis and Clark and all their troupe ought to be killed, and Watkuweis had played out her vital role, unsung by the expedition members but notorious in tribal memory.

Also noted was the favorable impression made upon Twisted Hair's son, about nine years of age who, according to family oral history had witnessed Clark's first entry to the prairie. Yes, young Aleiya or Lawyer, the third youth sighted by Clark when he first approached a Nez Perce village, had not been discovered in the tall grass, had preceded Clark to the Clearwater and, of course, had alerted all camps on the path to the Clearwater as to the coming.

Unknown to Lewis and Clark, the favorable impression Clark made upon Twisted Hair and his son would be pivotal in the history of the expedition and the expansion of the United States into the Pacific Northwest. Twisted Hair's son would grow up to become Chief Lawyer, one of the strongest advocates of a political, military, and economic alliance between the Nez Perce and the United States. This alliance was suggested by none other than the leaders of the Corps, although they could not have foreseen the application of the alliance as envisioned by the Nez Perces.

Once tribal leaders decided not to kill Lewis and Clark and their party, the *mim'yoóxat* or band leaders probably were not in agreement as to the extent that the Nez Perces should co-operate with the goals and wishes of the Corps of Discovery. Twisted Hair and several other band leaders either agreed or acquiesced in a decision to actively aid the military reconnaissance party of the United States. The reasons were manifold, beginning with the pressing need for powder and lead for the existing half-dozen flintlock weapons owned by tribal warriors and the need for even more rifles to catch up in the arms race enveloping the northern plains buffalo range.

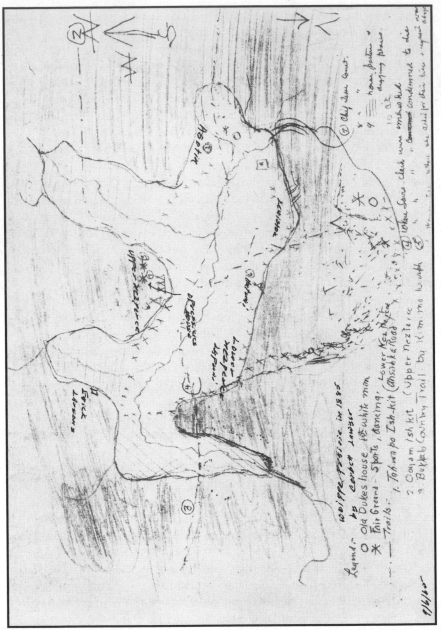

This map was drawn in pencil in 1885, by Corbett Lawyer, grandson of Chief Lawyer. Shown are the various villages that stood on and around Weippe Prairie along with the major trails in and out of the Prairie including those used by Lewis and Clark and where the expedition was to be ambushed. Weippe-Lawyer Map, MA 2000-18, Special Collections & Archives, University of Idaho Library.

If the bands could befriend the Americans and ally with them, the future held promise. That was reality in 1805, and reality dictated that there was no hope of establishing a trade and security relationship with the Americans unless the American envoys could accomplish their goal of reaching the Pacific safely and returning safely to report to their government.

The first step in treating with the Americans was to see that they got their canoes constructed and that they were safely escorted as far as the Nez Perces were able to help them, in both guiding them on the river and smoothing their journey through diplomacy with the many tribes who lived en route.

The idea of peace between people had already been received, if not by Twisted Hair in person, then by an unnamed representative of one of the upper Clearwater bands who had heard it at Fort Mandan or from others who had been there. The murder of three Nimíipuu peace emissaries to the Shoshone led to the retaliatory war party in progress during Lewis and Clark's entrance into Nimíipuu territory. On September 23, while many warriors were gone, "principal Men as well as the Chiefs" heard the peace proposal directly from the captains. This must have had the effect of promoting an alliance and weakening the argument for bludgeoning the expedition and taking all of their weapons and other goods.

Thus, in the journals we find Twisted Hair "with great cherfullness" drawing a map on white elkskin of the river route from his camp on the Clearwater all the way to the falls of the Columbia.[20] This was an important source of information that corroborated information secured from other natives. And it was Twisted Hair who furnished Clark a horse on September 25 and guided him to the forks of the Clearwater where large ponderosa pines were available for canoes.

Lewis and Clark had planted the seed of alliance and suggested its benefits with the gifts passed out on September 23: "2 other Medals to other Chefs of bands, a flag to *the twisted hare,* left a flag & Handkerchief to the grand Chief gave, a Shirt to the *Twisted hare* & a knife & Handkerchief to the grand Chief gave, a Shirt to the Twisted hare a knife Handkerchif with a Small pece of Tobacco to each."[21]

The knives and handkerchiefs handed out were gifts of diplomacy that were, no doubt, appreciated. However, the American flag and the shirt were of great symbolic importance. Weeks earlier, the flag of the Americans had been introduced to the Shoshone chief Cameahwait as the bond of union between the Americans and the tribe. The presentation of the flag to Twisted Hair meant exactly the same thing and was accepted as it was offered, a symbol of peace and union. The Nez Perces felt the power of this symbol deeply and determined to sincerely fulfill their end of the union.

The first step in developing a friendly and productive relationship with the whites was obviously to not kill them. Secondly, they were fed and hospitably furnished with the food which the Nimíipuu women had gathered and prepared: berries of various types, the *qém'es* root bread, and salmon. Thirdly, the captains were given the maps that they requested, not just a drawing in the dirt, but with beargrease and charcoal on a tanned elk skin. A white elkskin indicated that the hide had been prepared by brain curing, a long, tedious, and laborious process. The flag meant union on multiple levels to the Nez Perce, all linked to trade.[22]

Shown here are some major qém'es-root fields, harvested in August and September by the Nez Perces and affiliated tribes. The qém'es has a long "shelf life" and was used as a major nutrient for a source of carbohydrate and protein and was used as a trade item as well.

But one of the highest levels, if not the ultimate, was that of a relative. In fact the Nez Perces recognized non-blood individuals as "relatives" through a ceremony of shirt trading between men and dress trading between women. These ceremonies were augmented by the exchange of smaller gifts, as well. Lewis and Clark may not have understood the full ramifications of their acts, but they struck a chord of real need among the Nimíipuu, and the bands, once committed to a diplomatic course so full of promise, were not going to falter. Yes, they knew the river route for a great distance towards the ill-tasting lake (the ocean), and they would guide them as far as the great falls of the Columbia, far towards the setting sun.

With an eye to the Corps's own voyage from the canoe camp downstream, Clark began notations on Nimíipuu canoes. On September 25, Clark wrote that he witnessed two canoes at the mouth of the North Fork Clearwater that were "loaded with the furnitur & provisions of 2 families, those Canoes are long Stedy and without much rake."[23] Later, after he had crossed with his saddle horse to the south side of the main branch of the Clearwater using a natural ford available only at low water, he began riding the seven or so miles upstream, returning to camp.

About this same time, "one of the Indian Canoes with 2 men with Poles Set out from the forks ... and arrived at our Camp on the Island within 15 minits of the Same time I did, not withstanding 3 rapids which they had to draw the Canoe thro' in the distance.[24] This upstream traveling canoe was no doubt directed by experts using the paddle/pole combination developed for this unique function. But then, the Clearwater was unique, too.

During a series of great Missoula floods, the largest happening approximately 15,000 years ago, the backwash forced massive walls of water to race up the Clearwater canyon and slowly retreat, which formed scoured and rocky bottoms under most of the river and its gravel bars. This rock was erratically thrown about in otherwise unnatural disbursement. Essentially, the Clearwater had run volumes larger backwards in prehistoric times, creating a unique aqua environment that just did not make sense by the standards of normal erosion.[25]

As a result, parts of the river, at low water, would not float a loaded dugout canoe without the passengers disembarking and pulling the craft, yet in a nearby stretch the water might be so deep as to preclude reaching bottom with a long pole, thus the probable evolution of the simple *eaus*.[26] The whites were anxious to get their canoes built and begin their western journey again. The Nimíipuu would help.

ENDNOTES

1   There is a strong case, too, that the Nimíipuu simply borrowed the term for white men from the Salish. Whites were often referred to as the "Long Knives" or "Big Blades," and a Salish sword or long knife is a "sooi-api." From Josephy, p. 35 n. 1, Abridged Edition, quoting Partoll, ed., "Anderson's Narrative of a Ride to the Rocky Mountains in 1834," *Frontier Omnibus*, ed. John W. Harkola, p. 78. See also Salish-Pend d'Oreille Culture Committee and Elders Cultureal Advisory Council, Confederated Salish and Kootenai Tribes. *The Salish People and the Lewis and Clark Expedition* (Lincoln and London: University of Nebraska Press, 2005), p. 12, when Pete Beaverhead spells whiteman as "suyapi." Hereafter cited as Salish-Pend d'Oreille, *The Salish People*.

2   Gary E. Moulton, ed., *The Journals of the Lewis and Clark Expedition*, 13 vols. (Lincoln: University of Nebraska Press, 1983-2001), 5:1978. Hereafter cited as *JLCE*.

3   For a Salish perspective, see Salish-Pend d'Oreille, *The Salish People*.

4   Aoki, *Nez Perce Dictionary*, p. 1262.

5   Oral testimony of Eugene Wilson.

6   Zoa L. Swayne and Carol A.G. Bates, ed., *Do Them No Harm!: An Interpretation of the Lewis and Clark Expedition Among the Nez Perce Indians,* (Caldwell, ID: Caxton Press, 1990), p. 12. Hereafter cited as Swayne, *Do Them No Harm!* See also Haruo Aoki, *Nez Perce Dictionary*, p. 869, "weye," and p. 1105, "?u yit."

7   From Mylie Lawyer, the great granddaughter of Chief Twisted Hair. The third boy was known in adulthood as Barnabus and was a signer of the 1855 Treaty. Mylie could not remember his adult Indian name with which he signed the treaty.

8   *JLCE,* 5:219–22

9   Joseph Whitehouse described as being covered with dressed hides and also many covered with "flags," which were merely lightweight flexible reed mats arranged over a tipi pole frame. The mats were rolled up and easily moved from camp to camp and the tipi poles stood against trees until the following season when they could be reused. *JLCE*, 11:329–31. The mats were made of cat-tail reeds and tule reeds. It is told tribal elder Lynus Walker (1813–2002) that the Nez Perces preferred red fir poles off of north slopes for lodge poles, for their strength, light weight and resistance to rot.

10   Mylie Lawyer, also Swayne, *Do Them No Harm!,* p. 336

11   Robert Lee Sappington and Caroline D. Carley, "Alice Cunninghamn Fletcher's 'Ethnographic Gleanings Among the Nez Perces,'" from *Northwest Anthropological Research Notes* Spring 1995 vol. 9 no. 1 p. 20. Fletcher's spelling, "hin-olt-sih."Hereafter cited as Sappington, "Alice Cunninghamn Fletcher," vol 9. See also Kate C. McBeth, *The Nez Perces Since Lewis and Clark* (New York: F.H. Revell Co.), pp. 25–26. Hereafter cited as McBeth, *The Nez Perces Since Lewis and Clark.* Confirmed by Angel Sobotta with Rachel Zumwalt of Stites, Idaho, and member of the Nez Perce Tribal Elders Council. Authors' spelling from Aoki, *Nez Perce Dictionary*, p. 94.

12   *JLCE*, 5:223.

13   Neither Shoshone nor Hidatsas of the early ninteenth century wrote their names in English. In the course of a lifetime individuals from these tribes and many other western tribes had many names, childhood names, pet names, familial names and later a variety of earned names. Non-Indians developed different spelling traditions for some of these names. The authors are well aware of the different spelling traditions of the name of one of interpreter Charbonneau's wives, the one who accompanied the Lewis and Clark expedition. The authors both learned to spell Sacajawea growing up in the public schools in Idaho, eastern Washington and eastern Oregon. We were taught to spell Sacajawea with the "j".

      This was the tradition applied to the dominant peak in Oregon's Wallowa Mountains, Sacajawea Peak. It is the spelling also in Lewiston, Idaho's,

Sacajawea Junior High School, and the name of a motel in Lewiston, Idaho, Sacajawea Motel and a former museum at Spalding, Idaho, called the Sacajawea Museum. It was called thus because their prize display item was a dress that was allegedly traded to Jane Silcott by Sacajawea at Wind River, Wyoming, in about 1880. Jane was the daughter of Chief Timothy and was named after Sacajawea's nickname, or pet name, "Janie." The name of Sacajawea is acclaimed in many other places with the "j" spelling across the Pacific Northwest.

Sacajawea's relatives at Wind River chose to spell her name with a "j" on the stone at her gravesite on the Wind River Reservation. Spelling Sacajawea's name with a "j" is typical of the spelling of her name in the Lemhi Shoshone country of Idaho, and by citizens and educators all over Idaho, eastern Oregon and eastern Washington and many other places. It is how Nicholas Biddle spelled the name

after conferring with both William Clark and George Shannon (in 1810) of the Lewis and Clark expedition and it is noteworthy that Clark himself in perhaps his last spelling of her name used the "j" after never using it in his journals. Again, we are aware of the different spelling traditions, but feel that Clark's last spelling, the spelling of our own educators and the spelling of her own Shoshone ancestors constitute the best spelling tradition for us to follow.

14   *JLCE*, 5:226.

15   Swayne, *Do Them No Harm!*, p. 54. Zoa Swayne dramatized the phrase by making it her book title.

16   Cox, *In the Days When the Rivers Ran Backwards*.

17   *JLCE*, 5:233.

18   Ibid., 5:232.

19   The name Choppunnish seems likely the name attached by some Nez Perces, as well. Alfred Seton, Donald Mackenzie's clerk at Mackenzie's Post of the Clearwater River, 1812-1813, wrote that the Clearwater called "Shakaptin"[Sahaptin]. see pp 24–32, *Idaho Yesterdays* 18, no.3 (Fall, 1974). Note: Clark's pronounciation of the "Ch" in Choppun should be as if spelled "Sh." For confirmation of this see his spelling of Shoshone August 17, 1805, "This nation Call themselves Cho-shon-ne," *JLCE*, 5:115.

20   *JLCE*, 5:230.

21   Ibid., 5:231. note on same page in his early entry of September 23 that Clark states that one handkerchief and flag were "for the great Chief when he returns from war".

22   See Alan Marshall, "Nez Perce Social Groups: An Ecological Interpretation." Ph.D. dissertation, Washington State University, 1977. See also Slickpoo and Walker, *Noon Nee-Mee-Poo*, p. 24. Marshall, Alan G.

23   *JLCE*, 5:233.

24 Ibid.

25 Cox, *In the Days When the Rivers Ran Backwards.*

26 The name is utilized in the place name for the mouth of the Slate Creek on the Salmon river, called Iuusnima, or place of the [use of] *eaus*, McWhorter *Hear Me My Chiefs!*, p. 19 n. 4, explains "Eausnima is the Nez Perce name of Slate Creek, Idaho. Eaus is an old term almost forgotten by the tribe. Ninety-four-year-old (1936) Phillip Evans says it means the oar or pole used in poling boats, not the flat oar."

Chapter 3

In A Big Hurry

It was obvious to the Nez Perce that the United States Army recon team was in a big hurry, eager to get downstream. In a matter of days, they moved their entire unit from the rugged, wet, and cold Bitterroots to the camas fields of the Oyáyp prairie and beyond to the canyon bottom of the Clearwater. With Nimíipuu permission and assistance, the Americans had simultaneously located appropriate trees for large canoes and established the camp from which the labor would be performed.

They seemed single minded and a little irritable. They handed out small gifts as trade items, including tobacco as would a relative, yet when a young man acted as a relative and helped himself to a small piece of tobacco, they seemed upset. Clark recorded, "I displeased an Indian by refuseing him a pice of Tobacco which he tooke the liberty to take out of our Sack."[1]

For Clark, the taking of a small piece of tobacco seemed like a case of petty theft. But, in tribal culture, it would have been a matter of sharing. It probably seemed a stingy act to the young man who was, after all, helping the Americans build their canoes from pine trees given them by the Nimíipuu. In some ways, it is amazing that there were not a great many more misunderstandings. There were the many cultural differences, but they were undoubtedly aggravated by the difficulty of communication in general.

There was sign language, of course, but only George Drouillard, the half-blood Shawnee, was an expert at that. Then there was the spoken word, but it involved a long and tedious chain of translation. Messages traveled in this fashion: the captains spoke English to Drouillard, who spoke French to Charbonneau, who translated the French to Hidatsa, then Sacajawea spoke the same message in Shoshone to a Shoshone man living with the Nez Perce, and he talked to the Nimíipuu in their own tongue. When the Nimíipuu wanted to convey a message, they could use sign language with Drouillard if he was available, or speak their own language to the Shoshone if he was handy. There were plenty of weak links in the chain of communication, and it is a testimony to the virtue of all that worse problems than the tobacco incident did not come up.

This incident took place even as the Nez Perce men were assisting the whites with their canoe building from trees given them by the Nimíipuu. The biggest canoes were probably near 50 feet in length,[2] and Clark wrote "our axes all too Small."[3] In addition to the inadequacy of their axes, many of the men were simply too sick to work, and the native diet of salmon and roots continued to give them problems.

For a change of diet, hunters were sent out, but the dry conditions did not make for good hunting. Although some game was killed, the white men were finally desperate enough to kill a horse and eat it, which was against tribal practice. However, to be polite, the Nez Perces ate some with their guests. On September 28, Clark wrote that one family arrived from the North Fork on a raft. Patrick Gass wrote about it too, adding that there was a dead mountain goat on board, the first ever seen by the Americans.

The Americans were visited by many tribal people while working at canoe camp, and both Lewis and Clark mention some of these visitors, referring to some as chiefs and, in some cases stating also where the persons came from. But the Corps never introduced any of these people by name. Their main focus was on completing the canoes, and their journal notes mention only the name of Twisted Hair.

Acqywawi (Ahsahka) canoe camp by Nez Perce artist, Nakia Willismson. Image use courtesy of the Nez Perce National Historic Park, Spalding, ID.

That Red Bear saw the white men in 1805, and not merely on the return in 1806, is much more than conjecture. He had led a large contingent of Nez Perce warriors three days south before Clark's arrival at Oyáyp Prairie. Al-We-Yas, Twisted Hair's brother, informed Clark that the war party would be gone about 15 to 18 days.[4] Ten days after Red Bear left Oyáyp would have been September 27, about the same time as the beginning of the canoe camp on the Clearwater (September 26–October 7, 1805).

Sergeant John Ordway described the division of the Corps into five work squads, each to work on a canoe, but mentioned no Indian visitors. Clark mentioned that "Several Indians Come up the river from a Camp Some distance below."[5] However, Patrick Gass noted in his journal on September 27, "In the evening the greater part of the war party came in, and some of the principal men came down to our camp. We could not understand what they had done, as we could only converse by signs."[6]

Clark wrote on September 28 that "Drewyer Sick...." Perhaps the Corps's half-Shawnee Droulliard was too sick to interpret, because the story of a war party could certainly be easily understood by a good sign reader. Neither Clark nor Lewis nor Joseph Whitehouse even mention the war party despite the fact that the absent leader had been described by Twisted Hair's brother, or interpreted by Clark, as the "great Chief." Clearly Gass did state that the war party returned, which matches the Indian account dictated by Chief Peo-Peo-Tah-Likt (Bird Alighting) to Chief Many Wounds, Sam Lott. Twisted Hair himself helped not only with selection of the trees to fell but also the actual construction of the canoes. So did war leader Red Grizzly Bear, who worked on a canoe with Charbonneau.[7]

On September 27, the white men began to build the canoes, despite their poor physical condition and the oppressive heat. It was probably hard to conceive that just a few days earlier, their teeth had been chattering as they struggled across snowy slopes of the Bitteroots. Such was the nature of the Nimíipuu homeland; change the elevation and the climate changes, too.

The Corps was clearly on a mission, and even the captains, sick and anxious to get downstream, suffered a diminished interest in tribal diplomacy or protocol, judging by the fact that they ignored writing about the returning war party and "the great Chief." Patrick Gass was feeling better by September 27, and did notice and saw fit to write about the returning war party in his journal, noting further that "Medals were given by the Commanding Officers to 3 or 4 of them as leading men of their nation; and they remained about our camp."[8] The captains were still not well and focused almost entirely on the immediate task of constructing their canoes.

Chief Red Bear's war party likely had their own reasons for withholding a victory ceremony from the eyes of the Americans. A spectacular ceremonial return would typically mark a victorious returning war party and would include a scalp dance and ritual retelling of specific war acts. On this occasion, the ritual events were likely carried out at another village or villages, perhaps to deliberately mask them from being witnessed by the peace-proposers Clark and Lewis.

There were several reasons for this. First of all, there was the presence of Old Toby, his son, and Sacajawea, all Lemhi Shoshone. They likely knew the people recently engaged by the Nez Perces and may even have been related. It would have been impolite to perform the victory dance in their presence. Secondly, as the Nez Perces were already aware, the captains espoused co-operation and friendship with the Shoshones. Lastly, the sickly condition of the white men and their complete focus on canoe building and acquisition of food supplies perhaps led the Nez Perce leaders to wisely postpone any sharing of a national celebration.

Red Bear, leader of the war party and a relative of Chief Twisted Hair,[9] and other *mim'yooxat* (leaders) had undoubtedly been briefed on the recent developments with the whites. As there was no tribal consensus, future possibilities could have been spoiled if the status quo were upset. The Nez Perces would try to aid the whites in completing their immediate goals. There would be plenty of time later to coordinate white activities with the tribal agenda.

Thus, the Nimíipuu continued to be friendly and helpful to the whites, trading supplies for beads and metal goods, while also aiding them in flattening and turning over logs so that the flattened sections became the boat bottoms.[10] In an overhead view, Nez Perce canoes were not pointed, but square on both ends, the bow and stern both raked to match the shore so that people and cargo could go aboard without getting wet. Although the logs from which the canoes were formed were naturally tapered, which caused the finished hull to be wider at the bow, they were, if necessary, reversible. (As sometimes happens in river running, the back end of the craft ends up downstream ahead of the bow. This can be caused by striking a rock which "holds" the bow as the current swings the aft downstream and "pulls" the bow off the rock.) The sides and gunwales were thin, about an inch thick, compared to the bottom and ends, which were intentionally four to six times thicker.

Although the Clearwater and Snake Rivers have long sections that are deep, both have powerful shallow rapids where dangerous encounters with rocks are likely. The high sides of Nimíipuu canoes helped keep waves from splashing inside the craft unduly. The interior shapes of the canoes were created by allowing a series of small fires of grass and pitch to char all wood that they wished to remove. After these were allowed to cool, the remaining charcoal could be chipped out with a sharp stone or the axes and adzes used by the Corps.

Tribal oral tradition, recorded by Red Grizzly Bear's grandson who was known as Many Wounds but also known as Sam Lott, reveal that Chief Red Grizzly Bear and Charbonneau worked on the same canoe and became fast friends.[11] It was hot and dirty work, but easier and faster than trying to hollow a green log entirely with small tools. The Nez Perces, in short, used their canoe building techniques and helped with all other activities that furthered the goals of the American expedition, assuming that there would be plenty of time later to benefit Nimíipuu goals with reciprocity from the whites.

Expeditioners continued on September 28 to fight the heat and their disorderly bowel problems from their change in climate and diet. Finally, the captains ordered another horse killed for food,[12] something that the Nez Perces frowned upon, but the bad hunting and subsequent lack of red meat made the captains consider it a necessity. The small axes and adzes also posed a problem and, for a few days, the Nez Perces watched to see the results of the white men's efforts. No one writes about it in their journals, but the natives who were coming and going were probably shaking their heads in wonder, perhaps laughing out loud at the frantic efforts.

It is believed that tribal members helped, however, because although Clark mentioned on October 2 "Burning out the hotter[hollow?] of our canoes…"[13] giving no credit to the Nez Perces, the day before (October 1) Gass wrote, "To save them from hard labour, we have adopted the Indian method of burning out the canoes."[14]

Sergeant John Ordway wrote, "we Continued on makeing our canoes as usal. built fires on Some of them to burn them out. found them to burn verry well." Again, not specifically mentioning help from the Indians, but mentioning the Indian method. The Indian method was demonstrated to the men of the expedition after tribal members observed several days of the difficult and slow techniques used by the Corps. Nez Perce oral history says that they helped the Corps from the tree selection to the launching:

> Twisted Hair take white mans and show him which tree to cut to make canoes, so they cut first one big pine tree, and make canoes. Chop some with small strange looking ax which Lewis bring. But Indians they get pitch and dry grass and burn more with pitch and grass. Then chop with Indian ax—takes long time and lots hard work to make Indian canoes. Then Lewis and Clark and Indians make more canoes for to go in Clearwater River.[15]

Ya-mok-mokin who tended horses for Lewis and Clark the Winter of 1805-1806. Later he was the tenth signer of the 1855 Treaty at Walla-Walla. Photo courtesy Penrose Library Archives at Whitman College, No. 2408 (on left).
Looking east up the main fork of the Clearwater River. Canoe Camp was located on the south bank. Photo by E.J. Gay, 1889-1892. Photo courtesy Nez Perce National Historical Park, NEPE-HI-1637 (on right).

In fact Chief Peo-Peo-Tah-Likt got the story from his father, who witnessed the council in which the captains asked for the help of the Nez Perce. After everyone smoked, Lewis said: "you chiefs here now tell me this River goes to big waters, the Ocean. I want ask you—if you let me cut trees for make canoes to go to Ocean and if you let your people help me and my people make Canoes."[16]

As the canoes neared completion, the expedition made arrangements for its large horse herd. Horses would not be useful in the down river canoe journey that was about to commence. Chief Peo-Peo-Tah-Likt mentions Twisted Hair keeping the expedition horses ("left in field for winter at Fo[r]ds creek") without any comment on the branding that took place before they were turned over to the Nimíipuu. Was this the first branding held in what is now Idaho? Most likely.

When the canoes were close to ready for launching, the horses were gathered and their topknots cut off. Then the horses were branded, but not using the famous rectangular brand carried by the expedition. While the captains fail to explain the details of the branding, both John Ordway and Joseph Whitehouse do. The horses were branded on the near shoulder using "Stirrup Iron."[17] No Nez Perce today possesses any recollection of any family witnessing the branding, only that it happened. Did they brand using the tread of the stirrup or its curved side as a running iron? Illustrations of wrought iron stirrups from the era show nine types that might have been used, and any of the treads or sides might have made a distinctive brand.[18]

After branding all their stock and cutting the forelock, the captains "delivered them to the 2 brothers and one Son of one of the Chiefs who intends to accompany us down the river..."[19] However, John Ordway stated that "the old chief who we leave the care of our horses with has engaged to go on with us past his nation and leave the horses in the care of his two sons."[20] The Chief who would guide them was Twisted Hair, and the other guide was Twisted Hair's younger brother. Twisted Hair is, of course, identified often in the journal entries of the fall of 1805.

However, the younger guide, Twisted Hair's brother, is not identified by name in the journals until he was met on the return trip (May 4, 1806). At that time he was called "Te-toh-arsky."[21] This name could not have been an accurate rendition as there is no "r" in the Nez Perce language. The name was probably a reference to "Te-toh-kan Ahs-kahp," which meant "People-Coming-Looks-Like-Brother."[22] Thus, in a matter of about two weeks (September 26–October 7), the Corps completed their downriver craft, branded their horses and cached their saddles. They were indeed in a big hurry, but they could not have accomplished so much in such a short time without the cooperation and hands-on involvement of chiefs Twisted Hair and Red Grizzly Bear, as well as their tribal cohorts.

ENDNOTES

1   *JLCE,* 5:245.

2   Bob Chenoweth, Nez Perce National Historic Park (NPNHP) research specialist "conjectural canoe" he figured at 52 feet in length and the Nez Perces used a concoction utilizing bear fat and pitch to seal the craft's surface.

3   *JLCE,* 5:234.

4   Ibid., 5:222.

5   Ibid., 5:235.

6   Patrick Gass, and Carol L. MacGregor, *The Journals of Patrick Gass: Member of the Lewis and Clark Expedition* (Missoula, MT: Mountain Press Publishing Co., 1997), p. 134. Hereafter cited as Gass, *Journals.*

7   See Peo-Peo-Tah-Likt (Bird Alighting) and Chief Many Wounds (Sam Lott), *Historical Sketches of the Nez Perces* (Manuscripts, Archives and Special Collections, Washington State university, Pullman, WA, 1935), Cage #1218, p. 13. Hereafter cited as Peo-Peo-Tah-Likt, *Historical Sketches of the Nez Perces,* Cage #1218.

8   Gass, *Journals*, p. 134, writing on the September 27.

9   Authors were never able to determine the exact relationship between these two, although there was much agreement "they were related." It should be noted here that

nearly all of Nez Perce leadership, and many leaders of adjacent Sahaptin speaking bands, were related in one way or another, by blood, marriage or adoption.

10 Discussion with Bob Chenoweth (NPNHP) Curator, and author of "Dugout Canoes and Lewis and Clark's Journey to the Pacific" unpublished manuscript, presented to NCAI Conference, Portland, Oregon, Feb. 23, 2002.

11 Peo-Peo-Tah-Likt, *Historical Sketches of the Nez Perces*, Cage #1218, p. 13.

12 *JLCE*, 5:244.

13 *JLCE*, 5:244.

14 Gass, *Journals*, p. 35.

15 Peo-Peo-Tah-Likt, *Historical Sketches of the Nez Perce*s Cage #1218, pp. 11-12.

16 Ibid., p. 11.

17 *JLCE*, 9:234, for Ordway.

18 Illustrations of era stirrups are found in George C. Neumann, Frank J. Kravic, and George C. Woodbridge's *Collector's Illustrated Encyclopedia of the American Revolution* (Harrisburg, PA: Stackpole Books, 1975).

19 *JLCE*, 5:246.

20 Ibid., 9:234.

21 Ibid., 7:205–7.

22 Swayne, *Do Them No Harm!*, pp. 33, 321–22. Tribal elder Harry Wheeler explained to author Zoa Swayne the most likely rendition of the journal references to "Te-toh-arsky."

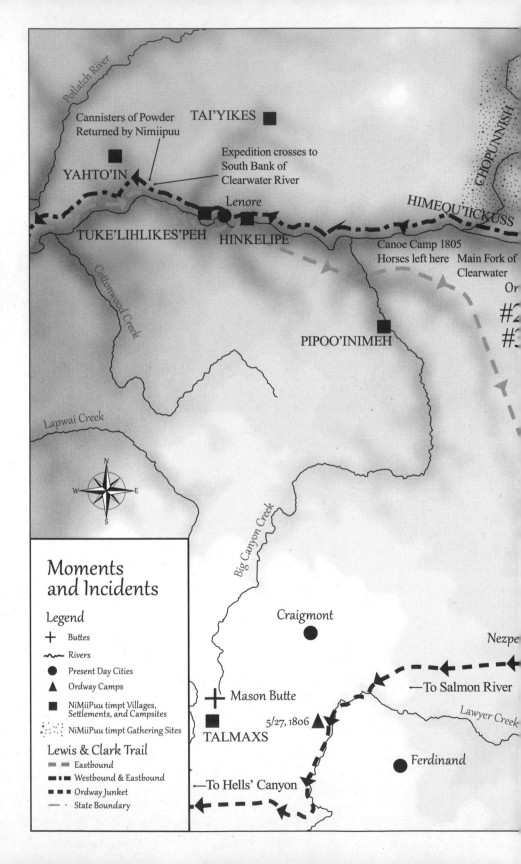

Cannisters of Powder
Returned by Nimiipuu

TAI'YIKES

Expedition crosses to
South Bank of
Clearwater River

YAHTO'IN

CHOPUNNISH

Lenore

HIMEQU'TICKUSS

TUKE'LIHLIKES'PEH   HINKELIPE

Potlatch River

Cottonwood Creek

Canoe Camp 1805
Horses left here   Main Fork of
Clearwater
Or
#2
#3

PIPOO'INIMEH

Lapwai Creek

Big Canyon Creek

Craigmont

Nezpe

←To Salmon River

Lawyer Creek

Mason Butte

5/27, 1806

TALMAXS

Ferdinand

←To Hells' Canyon

Moments
and Incidents

Legend

+ Buttes

～～ Rivers

● Present Day Cities

▲ Ordway Camps

■ NiMiiPuu timpt Villages,
Settlements, and Campsites

⋰⋱ NiMiiPuu timpt Gathering Sites

Lewis & Clark Trail

▬ ▪ ▬ Eastbound

▬ ▪ ▬ Westbound & Eastbound

▬ ▬ ▬ Ordway Junket

— · State Boundary

Moments and Incidents

#1 - Clark comes upon Nimiipuu Village, September 21, 1805.

#2 - The Cut Nose and Twisted Hair argue about horses.

#3 - From May 8th camp Twisted Hair and several young men go to Canoe Camp for expedition horses and equipment left the previous fall. Horses and gear returned 5/10/06.

#4 - Horse castrations take place.

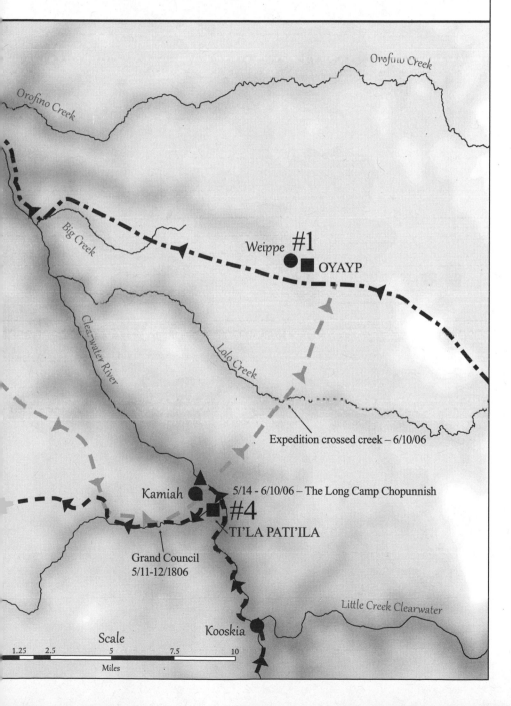

Orofino Creek

Orofino Creek

Big Creek

Clearwater River

Lolo Creek

Weippe #1

OYAYP

Expedition crossed creek – 6/10/06

Kamiah

5/14 - 6/10/06 – The Long Camp Chopunnish

#4

TI'LA PATI'ILA

Grand Council
5/11-12/1806

Little Creek Clearwater

Kooskia

Scale

1.25 2.5   5   7.5   10

Miles

Chapter 4

Down the Koos keihk-keihk
(Clearwater)[1]

There were different families and other small groups who dropped by to see the white men, and some followed along convenient stretches of water after they launched, as recorded by John Ordway as "about 3 o'Clock p.m." on October 7, 1805.[2]

Twisted Hair and Te-toh-kan Ahs-kahp (Looks-Like-A-Brother, spelled "Tetoharsky" by the Americans) apparently had agreed to guide the party downstream as far as the Celilo Falls, called the great falls of the Columbia but, for some reason, they missed the hour of launch. The canoes, using poles and paddles and perhaps some of the Nez Perce combination pole/paddle, began their downstream journey. They did not go far before one of the canoes struck a rock. Clark wrote, "the Canoe in which I was Struck a rock and Sprung a leak."[3]

This was just in the third rapid below their launching point. Striking rock would prove difficult to avoid, as the Clearwater River has little soil on the bottom or banks. All is rock, whether rigid, unmoving, unforgiving rock, or loose rocks thrown up randomly, or in giant bars left by one of the great Missoula floods rushing first up canyon, then flowing downstream and generally westward.

A river guide would have been useful, this first day on the Clearwater, and the leaders must have recognized that fact when Clark wrote that "we missd. both of the Chiefs who promised to accompany us."[4] There is no explanation of how or why the Chiefs were missed, but there is no doubt that their river experience would have been helpful.

It is well known that some of the Frenchmen amongst the Corps were good rivermen, too, but they must have realized what every river guide knows: there is no substitute for the intimate knowledge of locals concerning specific stretches of river, rock locations, water depth, and tricky currents. These were the things the Nez Perces knew about the Clearwater River, their river. Many were born on the banks of the

Clearwater, learned to swim in it, and had in fact swum in much or most of it at some time or another. Many of them, perhaps, had canoed down it and back up it at various water levels in different seasons of the year.

William Sohappy and dugout canoe"(P218:BAG 147) Benjamin A. Gifford Photographs (P 218-SG 1), Oregon State University Special Collections & Archives Research Center, Corvallis, Oregon.

For many of the young men, the Clearwater was a source of recreation and economy both. They gathered driftwood and constructed large rafts, which were then taken from the lower Selway and Lochsa forks and the North Fork timbered regions downstream to the lower Clearwater untimbered region, and to the treeless Snake and Columbia plain beyond, where the timbers were traded.

This was most often done in the spring, after the weather warmed, but when the rivers and their rapids ran high. Where they knew they would be riding exciting waves and there were villagers nearby, they landed upstream, scouted the rapids and announced that they would be coming through. This gave the villagers time to turn out on one or both banks to witness the event and cheer them through.[5]

Early Downstream Problems for Lewis and Clark

As mentioned, Twisted Hair and his brother Al-We-Yas missed the American canoe launch, and the reasons why remain a mystery to this day. Clark wrote on the October 5 that they had left the horses with "2 brothers and one Son of one of the Chiefs who intends to accompany us down the river"[6] but on the 7th, the day the Corps launched, he wrote "we missd. both of the Chiefs who promised to accompany us."[7]

Did the Chiefs, who intended to guide, miscalculate the determination of the whites for an early launch, or was there miscommunication over the time of the beginning of the downriver sojourn? Maybe they did not expect them to launch at 3 in the afternoon, generally a poor time to begin a trip traveling into the afternoon sun through rocky waters. (The authors launched a driftboat at approximately the same time of day almost exactly 199 years after Lewis and Clark [October 4, 2004] and, at times, it was impossible to read the water ahead due to the glare.)

At any rate, the exploration party launched on a cloudy day, so perhaps they were not hampered by an intense glare off of the water. For whatever reasons, the Chiefs were not on hand for the launch. Clark was concerned about the rapids and was apparently counting on the Chiefs to guide them. "The after part of the day Cloudy proceded on passed 10 rapids which wer danjerous the Canoe in which I was Struck a rock and Sprung a leak in the 3rd rapid."

However, they proceeded on and camped for the night near modern Lenore, Idaho, opposite Jack's Creek.[8] They pulled in near dark and fixed the crack in Clark's canoe the best they could, probably using pitch. Although they were gradually leaving the heavily timbered country behind them, there remained a ready supply of scattered pine trees and pitch. They were in a dryer area, but not as yet a treeless region. Clark wrote they had traveled 20 miles, but modern measurement makes the distance close to eleven and one-half miles.[9]

October 8, 1805: Canoe Wreck Day for Patrick Gass

About 9 a.m. on October 8, the Corps started again downriver in their dugouts. The river is relatively deep and slow from their camp, but soon they faced problems similar to the day before. They had 15 rapids to pass through, several of them in diminished channels found on the sides of islands where they were faced with the difficult decision of choosing which channel to attempt.

A wrong choice here could prove disastrous, even with a small canoe showing the way, since the small canoe might easily pass where larger dugouts might strike bottom rocks or even be swept into the cliffs and boulders that marked much of the shoreline. In a few places, the river was so shallow as to prove shoaly or a "rock garden," in the parlance of the modern river runner. Rock gardens are not good places to be in dugout canoes and, in several places, the men were forced into the cold waters of the Clearwater in their moccasins, where they pulled their canoes over rock-strewn shallows and into deeper channels.

Late in the afternoon, at the bottom of one of the islands passed, they beached their canoes at a small camp and were greeted by and smoked the pipe with Twisted Hair and Te-toh-kan Ahs-kahp (Tetoharsky), the chiefs who would be vital to their downstream saga.

These are the two chiefs Clark stated earlier had "promised" to come along. Yet, even with Te-toh-kan Ahs-kahp (Tetoharsky) and Twisted Hair on hand to give navigational advice, towards the end of day, just below the mouth of Potlatch Creek, called Coulter's Creek by the Corps, the canoe "in which Serjt. Gass was Stearing" wrecked.

It is impossible to tell precisely what happened from reading Clark's and Gass's journal entries. Although they were both describing the same event, each writer's focus is quite different. In Clark's story it appears that the canoe got sideways to the current and lodged against some rocks. The canoe nearly turned over, one side split open, and Clark says the vessel "sunk."

It was only their second day out and already the Corps had crashed one of its vessels and lost precious cargo. Clark writes that he had "one of the other Canoes unloaded & with the assistance of our Small Canoe and one Indian Canoe took out every thing & <got> toed the empty Canoe on Shore." Everything was wet and he had it laid out on shore and "Sentinals put over them to keep off the Indians, who are enclined to theave haveing Stole Several Small articles." At the same time, paradoxically, he also noted "those people appeared disposed to give us every assistance in their power dureing our distress—"[10]

Where did this "Indian canoe" come from? Reading Clark, it is easy to get a mental picture of the Corps paddling through the Clearwater country alone in the wilderness. Then another canoe suddenly appears out of the blue. There were a lot more canoes, from many villages along the Clearwater, passed by the explorers on both October 7 and 8. Clark does mention that several encampments were passed and that the Indians were present at the rapids taking salmon. At one such place, he states, "we found our two Chiefs who had promised to accompany us, we took them on board after the Serimony of Smokeing." While the chiefs must have wanted to guide the party safely downstream, it is doubtful if either the Twisted Hair or Tetroharsky considered themselves belonging in any sense to Lewis and Clark.

Gass, the man steering the canoe that wrecked, wrote of the incident as if it was something over which he had little control. Once the wrecking process began, he could probably do little but watch with horror as it developed and hope for the best. He writes, "In the evening, in passing through a rapid, I had my canoe stove, and she sunk. Fortunately, the water was not more than waist deep, so our lives and baggage were saved."[11]

He did not make any more of the incident, and it would be natural for the boatman to play down the negative aspects for which one might be held responsible. He also mentioned that there were lodges of the natives on "both sides of the river;" and that "Two chiefs of the upper village joined us here, and proposed to go on with us, until we should meet with white people; which they say will be at no great distance."[12]

Clark left the impression that the party had been let down initially by the two chiefs who promised to accompany them, but did not show up for the launch. But Gass clearly states that they (the two chiefs) themselves proposed to guide the expedition. It probably occurred to the chiefs that there would be no possible advantage in befriending the whites if they died on the river, thus their proposal to lead the way. After all, in two days' travel, the whites had already wrecked two canoes, and the really heavy water and boiling cauldrons of the Snake rapids lay ahead.

In Clark's account, the reader easily gets the impression he took charge of the situation, and all ended well. In reality, he headed the rescue efforts of his party, got a canoe empty, and sent it out to help. Gass, "headboatman" for one of the canoes, didn't make much of the wreck; after all, the water was "not more than waist deep."[13] It may have only been waist deep, but there was a powerful current.

A quick look at Private Joseph Whitehouse's account probably gives a better picture of the Indian situation and the canoe wreck (although he is still calling the Nimíipuu "Flatheads"). He says the water was rough enough to wash water over the sides of the canoes and that many rocks were struck but that the current was of such force as to push the canoes on downstream. This was all before the second wreck. He also mentions many more natives and villages, horses, and other canoes along the route. There was trading going on, too: beads for roots and salmon, and some of the men were trading for dogs to eat. The Nez Perce had a low opinion of any human that would eat their horse or dog.

Joseph Whitehouse wrote on October 8 at one of the camps, simply, "2 chiefs came with us,"[14] then shortly afterwards, "as we were descending a rockey rapids at the foot of an Island on which was Some Indian Camps, one of the canoes Struck a rock and wheled round then Struck again and cracked the canoe and was near Spliting hir in too, throwed the Stearsman over board, who with difficulty got to the canoe again, but She soon filled with water, and hang on the rocks in a doleful Situation. Some of the men on board could not Swim, and them that could had no chance [of saving themselves] for the waves and rocks. an Indian went in a Small canoe to their assistance."[15]

It is an interesting study, to look at the three views of the canoe wreck. William Clark, one of the expedition's commanders, naturally saw the event from a command point of view. The Steersman of the boat—who in modern river parlance would be the "boatman," the one who was responsible for the safety of the craft and the baggage and persons on board—would naturally play down the difficulty of the situation, otherwise he (or she) would not look good to the other boatman and the commanders.

And finally, we have a more objective physical description from a more distant and "disinterested" party. In this last view, that of Joseph Whitehouse, "It was very fortunate for those Men that an Indian [an unnamed Nimíipuu] who saw their situation from the Island we passed last, came to their assistance with a small Canoe and One of our Canoes went also, and took out some of the loading and landed it safe on the Shore.—"[16]

That the Nimíipuu individual "saw their situation," is a great nutshell account of a riverman's immediate assessment of a development readily decipherable to the experienced eye—what Whitehouse described as a "Sad axident."[17] River running means hitting the correct slot at the head of a rapid. The river guide should know, before entering, whether to enter "river right" (right side as facing downstream), "river left," or "river center," or somewhere in between. With dugouts by their nature being long and heavy, it is especially critical to not only execute a proper entry, but to avoid getting cross-wise against the current and against the rocks.

In Whitehouse's description, the key phrase, left out of all other accounts, is the telling remark, "struck a rock, and wheeled around, where she again Struck another rock." In the annals of river running, there are few stories that end happily that begin with those words. In the case of Gass's craft, the conclusion of the episode is about the best that could be expected: no one killed, few goods lost, and the canoe reparable.

"Every thing wet perticularly the greater part of our Small Stock of Merchindize," wrote Clark. The wet gear, plus the need to repair the canoe, forced the decision to camp near the wreck site, probably no more than one half mile below the mouth of Colter's Creek (now Potlatch River, in Nez Perce County, Idaho). Whitehouse says the "Natives," whom he invariably incorrectly identified as the "Flatt-head Nation," "came to Visit us, and behaved with a great deal of friendship to us all."[18] The men were jubilant, a typical reaction to a harrowing escape from disaster.

Whitehouse writes, "Our party were all rejoiced at the fortunate escape that the Men made that were in the Canoe, and think that nothing but the Interference of Providence was the occasion." Cruzatte played the fiddle and some of the men danced. The tribesmen, Whitehouse wrote, "continued sometime with us & took a friendly leave & departed for their respective camps."[19]

The next day (Wednesday, October 9) was spent drying the wet goods, while two guards were posted because, Whitehouse wrote, "The Natives appear'd round our Camp the most part of this day, and had every appearance of wishing to pilfer or steal from us." Exactly what one looks like while wishing to pilfer remains unexplained, but probably one only had to appear Native American to the corpsmen to appear as "wishing to pilfer."

Clark wrote that the "Indians who are inclined to theave" had already "Stole Several small articles."[20] Some of the white men watched their merchandise dry and others repaired the canoe. With darkness upon them, and their goods not yet dry, the captains made the decision to spend a second night on the Clearwater's north bank, just below the mouth of modern Potlatch Creek.

That evening (October 9), a woman danced and sang in the firelight and began giving her personal possessions away. She was probably beginning the *'isxíipit* ceremony. A complete understanding of its full meaning has been lost to the ravages of time, and it is no longer practiced. It was something that was done for spiritual reasons, perhaps at the compulsion of the women's tutelary spirit, as a way of becoming a medicine woman and developing curing power. According to one testimony, the woman that would become a real medicine person must work herself "into a state of hysteria."[21]

None of the white men understood what they were witnessing. How could they? Clark wrote she "faind madness," and he told how she gave away "in Small potions all She had if they were not received She would Scarrify herself in a horid manner c."[22] Patrick Gass wrote, "At dark one of the squaws, who keep about us, took a crazy fit, and cut her arms from the wrists to the shoulders, with a flint; and the natives had great trouble and difficulty in getting her pacified."[23]

The give-away portion of the woman's ceremony was to enhance her powers. For the exercise to be successful, witnesses had to "receive" goods offered, which the candidate had acquired for a year. To reject a gift, no matter how small or seemingly insignificant, was not considered good manners. The rejection of a gift seems to be the incident which triggered the Nimíipuu woman's blood-letting from self-inflicted cuts by flint stones. Rejection of a gift was a rejection of her proffered relationship with the recipients. This seems most evident when one considers the eye-witness account of Private Joseph Whitehouse. In his account, the evening was going well. There was fiddle music and dancing which, in his view, "delighted" the Natives.[24]

But one of the women, claimed Whitehouse, "was taken with a Crazy fit. This Woman began with singing in the Indian language, [did he expect her to sing in English?] and then gave all that was round her some roots, & all those who she offer'd them to, had to take them.   One of our Men refused taking them from her, at which she grew Angry, and hove them in the fire, and took from her husband who stood near her, a sharp flint stone, and cut her Arms in many places, that the blood gushed out of them, she catched the blood &eat it, She then tore off some beads & pieces of Copper than hung about her neck, & gave all those round her, some of them; she still kept singing, & would at times make a hissing noise. She then ran round the whole of them, & went towards the River.   her Relations followed her, & brought her back; when she fell into a fit, & remain'd Stiff & Speechless for some considerable time.—

The Natives threw Water on her, & brought her too, & then gave her some small Articles at which she seemed much pleased—"[25]

Lewis and Clark came from a society that was male-dominated. They did not recognize female leadership in any form amongst the Nez Perces, nor in most of the other tribes with which they came into contact. Nez Perce women, and Sahaptin females generally, have always been strong and have exercised much more political and spiritual leadership than their contemporary non-Native sisters. They owned their own horses and canoes. The tipis used in ranging out to distant hunting camps and root-gathering locations belonged to them, as did all the cooking equipment, gathering-baskets, pack saddles, riding saddles, beargrass storage bags, and all the winter stores of berries and meats.

Moreover, they could divorce whenever they wanted, leave their men, and take their property with them. Nez Perce women could become respected spiritual leaders, and performance of the *'isxíipit* (woman's power-attaining ceremony) was a prerequisite for advancing towards becoming a medicine woman with healing powers. The candidate was usually assisted by those who supported her.

The woman who danced for the Corps was likely a shamaness or perhaps a person that anthropologist Deward Walker, Jr., has identified as a "near shaman," or possibly a person who possessed a powerful *wéeyekin* (guardian spirit). There were strong similarities in these practices. Like the woman described in the journals, the women who possessed shamanistic power performed "the giveaway," and the subjects chosen to receive goods which had been accumulated by the subject would be wise to be gracious receivers. If not, the true nature of their hearts would be questioned.

At least one of the expedition members refused the gifts, and the temperamental nature of the *'isxíipit* shaman became manifest in the tantrum or "madness" witnessed at the campsite below Potlatch Creek (Colter's Creek). Because the shaman might have the power to injure another through a curse or in some cases a mere wish or look, it was considered wise not to provoke them. The "hissing noise" mentioned by Whitehouse may have been a part of her distinctive *'isxíipit* language that was developed exclusively for use by the shaman.

In Nez Perce society, the shamans often held great curative powers but, because of their power, which might be misdirected, they were also to be feared. Perhaps the woman's behavior was a challenge to the visitors to recognize, or at least acknowledge, female position in Nez Perce society.

Over the decades, this ceremony has been both modified with little or no bloodletting and driven underground. The last public ceremony of this nature was probably performed in the 1940's, and Elmer Paul, a tribal witness then in his twenties saw no blood, only a woman singing, dancing and giving away her possessions. He himself received a sweater and a brain-cured buckskin.[26]

Neither of the expedition's captains was culturally conditioned to recognize female leadership, or perhaps even female importance. It may be telling that, despite the large amount of time spent among the Nez Perce, they register no female's name in their writing. The name Watkuweis, for example, comes from the Nimíipuu tradition, rather than any written account in the expedition's journals. Watkuweis becomes the most "famous" or "best known" Nez Perce woman of this encounter, but ONLY because of the tenacity of the Nez Perce historical tradition.

Goodbye, Old Toby

Another event which occurred at the camp below Potlatch Creek was the exit of the Shoshone guide Old Toby and his unnamed young Shoshone companion. Clark wrote, "at Dark we were informed that our old guide &his Son had left us and had been Seen running up the river Several miles above, we Could not account for the Cause of his leaveing us at this time...." The white water experiences of the first two days of canoe travel on the Clearwater and the prospects of more to come, with the real chance that "his" canoe might be the next to have an unscheduled collision with solid rock, probably proved "enough" for the Snake guides to leave the party for home. The journals do not mention him being harassed by the Nez Perces, but this was a possibility.

Maybe Old Toby was merely thinking of the shorter days and colder nights and deeper snows of the route home; each day could be critical in making it back to the east side of the Bitterroots. The Corps leaders attempted to "Send a horseman after our old guide,"[27] but they were advised that it would be of no use, and that if Old Toby were paid the Nez Perces "would take his things from him before he passed their camps."[28]

Thursday, October 10, 1805

The Corps left at 7 a.m., according to Clark, and continued down the Clearwater from their camp of October 8 and 9, a camp marked by the existence of Indian lodges "on both sides of the river." The Corps was troubled by the river this day, too, but was assisted by the Nez Perces. Clark mentions another canoe striking a rock, forcing a halt for repairs, while Ordway specifically states that "the Indians caught some of the oars &c for us."[29] Ordway also wrote of passing "large. fisherys" and the existence of "pleanty of Small canoes" possessed by the Indians which were used in their fishing.

One of the favored methods of the Nez Perces was to light a torch mounted on the front of these canoes and enter the quiet pools. The light attracted the salmon, and the fisherman could spear the salmon when within range. This canoe fishing method required considerable balance, skill, and knowledge of the river. The fisherman had to stand in the canoe to cast the spear. Consider for a moment, spearing a fighting 40-pound fish while standing in a narrow hollowed log in a deep, cold river, operating only by the light of a torch. The Columbia salmon have great vitality; they continue to thrash and battle for life even out of the water, and must be clubbed hard atop the head with a special club to be subdued.

The Corps purchased their salmon; it was faster and easier. They purchased more dogs, too, and had their mid-day meal while the split canoe was repaired. They were less than three miles from their morning launch when they re-embarked about 2 o'clock.[30]

Tribal oral history places the expedition's October 10 stop at Spalding, Idaho, at the juncture of Lapwai Creek and the Clearwater River. The mouth of Lapwai Creek was the site of several ancient villages. This spot, where the Lewis and Clark party made at least a brief stop, was destined to become one of the more historical locations in the early history of the future state of Idaho. It was here near Lapwai Creek that Peo-Peo-Tah-Likt's (Bird Alighting) father, who saw Lewis and Clark in 1805, would rise to chieftainship.[31] And it was here that Reverend Henry H. Spalding established his mission and a printing press in 1836.

Along the Clearwater River, both below and above the mouth of Lapwai Creek and for a dozen or more miles up the Lapwai Valley, extends rich level land, the kind of terrain at a premium in the rugged canyon-dominated landscape. The creek was named "Cottonwood Creek" by the captains, but it was called Lapwai Creek by the locals and it remains that today.[32]

Just 31-years after Lewis and Clark's visit, the site was selected by Reverand Spalding as the location of a mission to the Nez Perces. Just a few miles upstream, Henry and his wife Eliza would live in a tipi until a cabin was ultimately established just a few steps from the spot where the Lewis and Clark canoes landed. And, at this same location, one of Idaho's first ferries was constructed by Harvard graduate John Silcott in 1862.

Chief Peo-Peo-Tah-Likt's father, who remembered Lewis and Clark, received a partial education at the mission school, as did Chief Peo-Peo-Tah-Likt, a warrior in the War of 1877, waged by the United States against the Nez Perces.[33]

The landscape surrounding the Spalding area is rich in the icons of Nimíipuu mythology. A large stone on the hill was known as Coyote's cradleboard. (This stone was later removed by the Daughters of the American Revolution and made into a monument honoring missionary Spalding.) There is "fresh rock" exposed in a cliff across the river from a lightning strike brought on by the power of a shaman. Downstream, a half-mile below Spalding on the Clearwater's north bank, are the arched backs of the Ant and the Yellowjacket, turned to stone by Coyote for disobedience. This is also the location of the Nez Perce National Historical Park headquarters.

Lewis and Clark were in too big of a hurry to hear any of these explanatory stories, and anyway, winter was the season for storytelling, and it was still only October, but they made a few observations of their own regarding the Nez Perce people. Clark wrote:

> The *Cho-pun-nish* or Pierced nose Indians are Stout likeley men, handsom women, and verry dressey in their way, the dress of the men are a white Buffalow robe or Elk Skin dressed with Beeds which are generally white, Sea Shells—i e the Mother of Pirl hung to ther hair & on a pice of otter Skin about their necks hair Cewed in two parsels hanging forward over their Sholders, feathers, and different Coloured Paints which they find in their Countrey Generally white, Green & light Blue. Some fiew were a Shirt of Dressed Skins and long legins, & Mockersons Painted, which appears to be their winter dress. with a plat of twisted grass about their necks.
>
> The women dress in a Shirt of Ibex, or (Goat) [*X:* Argalea] Skins which reach quite down to their anckles with (out) a girdle, their heads are not ornemented, their Shirts are ornemented with quilled Brass, Small peces of Brass Cut into different forms, Beeds, Shells & curios bones & c. The men expose those parts which are generally kept from few [*X; view*] by other nations but the women are more perticular than any other nation which I have passed in Screting the parts.

The party was indeed on an urgent mission to reach the coast, but still capable, judging by Clark's remarks, of making some remarkable observations.

Clark also thought the people "verry Selfish and Stingey of what they have to eate or ware, and they expect in return Something for everything give us as presents or the Survices which they doe let it be however Small, and fail to make those returns on their part."

His remarks tell us more of the white man's attitude than of the nature of the Nez Perces. That is to say, the whites had an expectation that the natives should serve them. The native peoples generally had heard of the whites in advance of their arrival, and the prophecy of their dual nature had preceded them. The white men possessed great medicine (translated as high technology).

This was as foretold by tribal prophets, but also foretold was that bad things would come with the good. The newcomers, it was said, would oftentimes consider themselves better. They would push old people around in disrespect, and they would draw lines upon the earth. Still, the whites were guests and, by custom and tradition, had to be welcomed. The Nimíipuu must welcome them, but be on alert. Prudence dictated awareness. The Americans were smelly, and they were dog-eaters, after all.

Below the mouth of Lapwai Creek, the party approached a rapid they called the "ragged rapid." Rapid naming is an interesting phenomenon that is still practiced by modern river runners, but "Rugged Rapid" is not the same today as in 1805, thanks to the explosive charges used in the 1860s to destroy the most difficult impediments to steamboat traffic on the Clearwater River. In 1805, the rapid looked formidable enough to discourage the most intrepid of the expedition's voyagers and the captains.

They decided to line the canoes through the rapid, one at a time, yet the ferocity of the river still temporarily claimed one craft, when it "Struck a rock…and broke a hole in hir Side."[34] The Indians, Ordway wrote, "caught some of the oars &c for us."[35] It wasn't the first time, and it would not be the last. The Clearwater was proving to be a considerable challenge to the Corps of Discovery.

Near this area on the Clearwater, Clark observed use of the sweat bath and "hot and cold baethes."[36] The Indian sweat bath is often heard of, but the "hot bath" is different and not so well known. (See Chapter 1 pages 12-14 for more information on the sweat bath.) In both the sweat bath and the hot bath, the cold bath is used alternately. The cold water is easy to enter when the body temperature is raised through the use of the sweat or the hot bath. Just a few miles (no one can tell for sure from Clark's estimates) from the mouth of the Clearwater, Clark saw an Indian practicing the hot bath. He noted that the bath was made hot by "hot Stones thrown into a pon of water."

This was a common practice in the old days, especially after a difficult and exhausting venture. The "pon of water" mentioned by Clark could either be a small natural "pon" or a hole dug in a river or creek bank. A fire was built on the side of the hole or pond, and red hot rocks were rolled with a stick or tossed into the water until the desired temperature was achieved. The bathers could "swim" and rinse off in the cold water or even roll in the winter's snow, then re-enter the hot bath. It was used to toughen and relax as well as cleanse. It might be accompanied by the use of an emetic stick.[37]

At about five in the afternoon[38] all canoes floated into the Snake River, "about 400 yards wide, and of greenish coulour. No timber barron & broken prairies on each Side."[39] There was a new addition to their flotilla, too. A man and his son followed them in a small canoe from where they had stopped for two hours a few miles upstream. There were four Nimíipuu with the party at this stage and people following on both banks on horseback.

Rock bars in the last few miles of the Clearwater required the men to get out of their canoes and drag them fully laden downstream to deeper water. With the confluence gained, they would now have plenty of water. But they would have new problems: the river had so much water, and was dropping at such a rate, as to force them to line their canoes through, or at the very least to stop in the days ahead to allow the non-swimmers to walk around many roaring rapids.

And there was the wind, the omnipresent afternoon upstream wind, blowing especially hard when downstream was west because the dominant wind of the Pacific Northwest is the west wind. The wind blew so hard on the afternoon of October 10 that Lewis and Clark made only a mile on the Snake before they could go no further. They camped on the north shore, their first night in what would become the state of Washington.

Clark wrote they had paddled 20 miles, but it was closer to 16. The contrast in water clarity was remarkable as the expedition canoes left the clear, nearly translucent waters of the Kuus kayxkáyx (clear or translucent water) and entered the green Kimooenim or Snake. This was deep water.[40] The Snake is the larger and longer of the two rivers. It acquires its color while running through a nutrient-rich environment, unlike the Clearwater, originating in the nutrient-weak Idaho batholith.

ENDNOTES

1   Olin D. Wheeler, *The Trail of Lewis and Clark, 1804-1904: A Story of the Great Exploration Across the Continent in 1804-06; with a Description of the Old Trail, Based Upon Actual Travel Over It, and of the Changes Found a Century Later* (New York: G.P. Putman's Sons, 1904), vol. 2, p. 119 (hereafter cited as Wheeler, *The Trail of Lewis and Clark),* correctly addresses the difficulty in any two non-Nez Perce hearing a Nez Perce word the same or learning the Nez Perce name for a river. First, many names used were close but different in meaning. For example, Lewis and Clark tend to use kooskooskee as synonymous with the Clearwater River, but the Rev. Samuel Parker *(Journal of an Exploring Tour Beyond the Rocky Mountains in 1835–37,* published 1940) wrote that the name should have been "Coos-coots-ke," or "the Little River." Secondly, the Nez Perce did not name rivers as the white men did—the same from top to bottom. "Indians," wrote Wheeler, "do not name streams as such" (Ibid.). This statement is consistent with the authors' informants who described sections of river areas named or described but not the entire stream. Wheeler provides a good example: below the north fork (of the Clearwater), the river was described as keihk-keihk or clear, while above the north fork it was called Sélwah (Ibid., 121).

2   *JLCE*, 9:234.

3   Ibid., 5:249.

4   Ibid.

5   This description provided by the late Reverend David Miles, Sr. Nez Perce
    tribal member and instructor to a Nez Perce language class at Lewis-Clark State
    College, Lewiston, Idaho.

6   *JLCE*, 5:246.

7   Ibid., 5:248.

8   Clark wrote they went 20 miles, Gass wrote that there were 4 large canoes and
    1 small one "to look ahead" (Gass, *Journals*, p. 135). Clark was lucky that the
    afternoon of launch proved to be a cloudy one. Proceeding primarily west, the
    late afternoon sun glaring on the Clearwater has caused many a modern boater
    concern for the rapids and rocks.

9   Olin D. Wheeler gave the railroad survey from canoe camp to the confluence as
    39 miles; the journals estimated 57 (*JLCE*, 5:255).

10 *JLCE*, 5:251.

11 Gass, *Journals*, p. 136.

12 Ibid.

13 Ibid.

14 *JLCE*, 11:341.

15 Moulton suggests, *JLCE*, 11:343, that the Stearsman was Clark (in a ft. nt.);
    however, Clark states clearly, and is quoted by Moulton, that the Stearsman was
    "Serjt. Gass" (*JLCE*, 5:251).

16 *JLCE*, 11:343.

17 Ibid., 11:342.

18 Ibid., 11:343.

19 Ibid.

20 Ibid., 5:251.

21 See Walker, *Conflict and Schism in the Nez Perce Acculturation*, pp. 25-26.

    See also Aoki, *Dictionary*, pp. 1083–4. See Carolyn Gilman, *Lewis and Clark:
    Across the Divide* (Washington, D.C.: Smithsonian Books, 2003), p. 70, de-
    scribes a similar practice by mid-Columbia people. She sites Robert Boyd,
    People of the Dalles: The Indians of the Wascopam Mission (Lincoln: University
    of Nebraska Press, 1996). Hereafter cited as Gilman, *Lewis and Clark: Across
    the Divide*.

22 Clark writing on Oct. 9, quoted in *JLCE*, 5:253.

23 Gass, *Journals*, p. 137.

24 *JLCE*, 11:345.

25 Ibid.

26 Elmer Paul to co-author (Evans), 1996.

27 *JLCE*, 5:252.

28 Ibid., 5:253.

29 *JLCE*, 9:236.

30 Highway 12 runs parallel to the Clearwater River and on the odometer the distance between Potlatch Creek (Coulter's River) and Lapwai Creek (Cottonwood Creek of the Journals) is only 3.1 miles. Since they camped on October 9 below Coulter's River the actual distance would be likely even less than 3 miles. Clark's estimate of the total miles from canoe camp to the Snake River was 60 miles; the actual miles of river as measured by the Corps of Engineers is 41.

31 Peo-Peo-Tah-Likt, *Historical Sketches of the Nez Perces,* Cage #1218, p. 10.

32 Cottonwood Creek name is used in modern times for the creek emptying into the Clearwater seven miles upstream from Lapwai Creek. It is about four miles from modern Cottonwood Creek to the mouth of Potlatch Creek (Colter's Creek) and about three miles downstream from Potlatch Creek to Lapwai Creek. The primary trail running south from Clearwater River to Salmon River paralleled Lapwai Creek and today's Highway 95, Idaho's only north-south highway also parallels Lapwai Creek.

33 Peo-Peo-Tah-Likt, *Historical Sketches of the Nez Perces,* Cage #1218, p. 1. This version has two pages labeled "1"; our citation refers to the first page "1."

34 *JLCE*, 9:236.

35 Ibid.

36 *JLCE*, 5:259.

37 See Deward E. Walker, Jr., "The Nez Perce Sweat Bath Complex: An Acculturational Analysis" *Southwester Journal of Anthropology* Vol. 22 (1966), pp. 133-71.

38 *JLCE*, 11

39 *JLCE*, 11:346.

40 Snake River travels a long distance and is nutrient-rich; the Clearwater comes from the Idaho Batholith and is not as rich in nutrients.

Chapter 5

Down the Snake

Overnight the wind shifted and began to blow downstream. This allowed the Corps to launch and paddle with the wind at their backs (the morning of October 11). While the journals of the expedition only mention two Nez Perces traveling with Lewis and Clark at this point, Chief Peo-Peo-Tah-Likt (Bird Alighting) claimed that there were six Nez Perce. Four turned back partway down the Snake, and two led on to the Celio Falls area on the Columbia.[1] Acting as guides and leading the way in a small canoe were Te-toh-kan Ahs-kahp (Looks-Like-A-Brother, spelled "Tetoharsky" by the Americans) and Twisted Hair.[2] Twisted Hair had the expedition land a few miles below their camp of the night before.

This stop was at the Alpowai village, near the mouth of Alpowai Creek, which entered the Snake River from the south side. Here lived Chief Ta-Moots-Tsoo, who had been at Oyáyp (Weippe) when the explorers were there, with his young son, later known as Chief Timothy. But Ta-Moots-Tsoo had gone downstream to prepare for the Americans, who they knew must pass their home village at Alpowai. Their village location was vital in the untold annals of this area of the Snake, as ancient overland travelers and war parties used the route along Alpowai Creek to connect with the Snake River or cross at a rare low-water ford just below the mouth of the creek.[3]

Chief Tamootcin was at 'Oyáyp with his young son also known as Tamootcin when Lewis and Clark were there. They rushed downstream to the mouth of Alpowai Creek on the Snake River to greet the explorers when they arrived. The younger Tamootcin, later known as Chief Timothy, was missionary Henry H. Spalding's first convert. Chief Timothy, a Smithsonian photograph by Antonio Zeno Shindler, 1868. Photo courtesy Nez Perce National Historic Park, NEPE-HI-1796.

Like the Lewis and Clark party, the Northwesterners of Montreal and Hudson Bay folk would soon be visiting this village as they used the route. So did missionary Reverend Henry H. Spalding and his wife on their way to establish their station in 1836. Ta-Moots-Tsoo's son, also sometimes known by the name Ta-Moots-Tsoo, became Chief Timothy and was Spalding's first convert to Christianity.[4] And Colonel Edward J. Steptoe crossed to the south side of the Snake River and to safety at this location on May 18, 1858, following his defeat by the Coeur d'Alene and Spokane warriors the day before near modern Rosalia, Washington.

Ta-Moots-Tsoo the elder, the Alpowai band leader, was likely disappointed that the captains remained in the vicinity of this village only about an hour.[5] The Alpowaima, the people of the village, were already well provided with "pleanty of beeds and coppertrinkets, copper kittles &C which must have come from white people," according to John Ordway.[6] But they traded fish and dogs to the whites anyway, so that the party might feed itself on its downstream journey. Joseph Whitehouse mentions trading, too, for "Some dryed haws &c",[7] a reference, no doubt, to the bland-flavored and fibrous berry of the prolific Columbian Hawthorne.[8]

They continued downstream, passing over more rapids "where the waves roled high"[9] and finally camped with "a fishing party of Indians."[10] Gass recorded that, at this camp, on the south bank of the Snake River near (today's) Riparia, Washington, they met an Indian of a different nation who told them they might reach "the falls" in four days. No one knows the tribe to which this individual belonged.

On the morning of October 12, the explorers launched early. The two "chiefs," meaning Twisted Hair and Te-toh-kan Ahs-kahp, "remained on board with us," Gass wrote. (He still called the Nez Perces 'Flatheads.') Two others, the chief's men, were in a small canoe and had the stranger from another tribe with them, leading the way. Guides with first-hand local knowledge led the way. This was and remains the way of intelligent travel in rugged and unknown waters.

Most of the Snake at this point was tranquil and smooth, at least on the surface. The bed of the Snake River consists of hard rock formations that cause strange and dangerous currents, sometimes boiling to the surface. Of course, periodically the canoeists also faced outright rapids, where both massive waves and jagged rocks threatened not just to make a hole or crack in a canoe, but to bash a dugout to kindling. In such rapids, it was only good sense to send an experienced crew in a smaller craft to act as guides and pilots, and this was the role played by the Nez Perces and "the stranger."

Those who followed only had to watch the guides, then choreograph their own route to pass safely. That evening (October 12) the expedition arrived at a particularly difficult stretch of water, which the guides passed safely through. However, the water was particularly difficult "to read" while looking west into the sun. It was not a place to venture blindly, and the captains chose instead to wait and run the rapid the next morning, when there would be no vicious headwind or sunlight in their face. If one is going to possibly wreck in a rocky rapid on a large powerful river, it is best to do so with daylight visibility and daytime temperatures. There would be enough danger without clinging to a rock through a cold night in wet buckskins.

They were still in Nimíipuu country, but were fast approaching that of the Palouse tribe. These people were, in nearly every respect, similar to the Nez Perces and in fact intermarried with them on a regular basis. Their language family was Sahaptin, the same as that of the Nez Perces, and the two tribes often camped together along this section of the Snake. Distinct tribal differentiation existed but was not emphasized within the Sahaptin language group until the American government demanded it in treaty negotiations and people were "divided up." Further downstream, Nimíipuu neighbors such as the Walla Wallas and Yakamas also spoke Sahaptin. There were dialectical differences between the languages spoken by these related tribes; those in closest proximity were the most linguistically similar. The village on the south bank was likely a Nez Perce village or a combined village of Nez Perce-Palouse. The Palouse, like their Nez Perce relatives, were equally at home in their dugouts in strong currents or on rough slopes and open prairies on horseback.[11]

The morning of the 13th was rainy and the party did not set out until late in the morning. By noon, all canoes were safely past the rapid that had caused sufficient anxiety the previous evening to halt the expedition. The captains took the precaution of having the non-swimmers walk around the rapids carrying cargo. This insured the safety of those at risk of drowning and, at the same time, lightened the load of the canoeists responsible for their craft.

They passed two important drainages emptying into the Snake; the first, on river left, was called the Tucannon.[12] The second river, the Palouse River, begins in the timbered mountains of modern Idaho, far to the north and east of where it empties into the Snake River. Most of its course runs through the undulating Palouse Hills, a timberless country. The river runs generally west, paralleling the Snake, then turns radically South and plunges over several spectacular falls and through a deep narrow gorge a half dozen miles before feeding into the Snake.

The Palouse Falls are upstream from where the Palouse River empties into the Snake. The Palouse Indians had a large fishing village on the Snake at this juncture which was passed by Lewis and Clark on October 13, 1805. They called the Palouse River "drewyers River." Photo taken by Richard Storch.

Origin of the Falls of the Palouse and Lower Gorge

The story is told that these falls and the gorge itself were created a long, long time ago by a Giant Beaver. This Giant Beaver had once terrorized the people, but was challenged and ultimately killed by Three Warrior Brothers. Each time they thrust a lance into Giant Beaver, he would become enraged and chew the basalt riverbed, finally in his anger and agony creating Palouse Falls and the narrow gorge downstream that reaches all the way to the Snake River.[13]

At the mouth of the lower gorge, at Palouse village, a mere seven years and eight months after Lewis and Clark's brief visit, the first "recorded killing of an Indian by a white man in the inland Northwest" took place. An Astorian, John Clarke, executed an Indian for the theft of his silver goblet.[14] The village site at the lower end of the sacred Palouse Canyon is, at present, beneath the resevoir waters behind Lower Monumental Dam.

The expedition had struggled to acquire firewood on the lower Clearwater and, once on the timberless lower Snake, the lack of warming and cooking fires became increasingly acute. Lewis and Clark could hardly help but notice that the Indians had large quantities of timber, which they used in the construction of their homes, stored on islands and on shore. But the whites knew this timber had been obtained, with great difficulty, from far upstream or in trade with those young men who would raft the timber to them. This timber, along with the many caches of fish along the river, the explorers generally left alone because they respected the property of the tribes despite their own need.

Two Indians, Clark says "from the upper foks over took us and continued on down on horse back, two others were at this mouth of the

Creek."[15] What did Clark mean by "upper foks"? Likely he meant the North Fork of the Clearwater and the lower "foks" would have been the confluence of the Snake and Clearwater. If so, then these riders were Nez Perces and the other two Palouse.

Now there was a cavalcade of Sahaptins traveling with the expedition: Twisted Hair and Te-toh-kan Ahs-kahp (Tetoharsky) in the Gass canoe, two other Nez Perces, and the unidentified Indian in another small canoe leading the way. No modern Nez Perce knows exactly who these Indians were. One of the few oral histories, written down in earlier years through the recollections of Chief Peo-Peo-Tah-Likt, even pronounced that the Nez Perces, six in number by his count, turned back near Riparia, after the night of October 12. Clearly he must have been mistaken, for the journals state unequivocally that the Nez Perces continued on. Even the short riders, by both descriptions of Clark and Whitehouse, continued with the party, racing their horses against the speed of the canoes in a two-mile-long chute of rock-bordered foam. At one point, they even swam with their horses from the south to the north side of the river and continued their ride downstream. That afternoon (October 13), another hard west wind greeted the travelers, and today, almost every afternoon, it still blows.

The next day, the Indians on horseback continued to follow the downriver party. When the canoes came to another rapid, they got to witness two of the canoes slamming into rocks and barely escaping. Later, in another rapid, Gass struck a rock with his canoe, and it swung sideways in the current and began to fill with water. Some of the goods washed out, and the remainder became soaked. The men were standing on rocks a "half leg deep in the rapid water untill a canoe came to our assistance."[16]

By the time that happened, two Nez Perces already "Swam in & Saved Some property," according to Clark. We know that one of the rescuers was Twisted Hair, who was about 65 years old at the time.[17] With men from a rescue canoe removing cargo, the lodged canoe "got lightened" and "She went of[f] of a sudden & and left myself [Ordway] and three more Standing on the rock."[18] Another canoe came to their rescue. The small canoe with three other Indians, two Nez Perces and the unidentified rider, were below the wreck and out of sight. However, they saw oars in the river, grabbed them, turned around, and brought them back upstream.[19] This rapid, like all others of the lower Snake, no longer exist, as all are beneath the stilled waters created by the dams. There are four dams on the lower Snake today. From downstream and working upstream, they are Ice Harbor, Lower Monumental, Little Goose, and Lower Granite. It might be an amusing consolation to Ordway and the others that the scenario of wrecking boats in rapids is repeated dozens of times throughout the modern west by recreational river runners, even Native American river runners, who make some of the same errors and suffer similar consequences.

There is no cold like soaking wet cold, and the Corps needed fire to dry their men and their gear and to cook the ducks they shot for supper on October 14. The Indians' wood scaffolds, so carefully stacked and stored and covered with rocks as a precaution against high water, were too tempting and too essential now. Lewis and Clark "took" the precious wood of the Palouses who were gone onto the prairies in their hunts for antelope, but Ordway says they only took "Some." We can safely assume it was not squandered, and they were respectful of the Palouse winter stores of dried salmon, also carefully cached. If the whites who followed Lewis and Clark were one half as considerate, much trouble and bloodshed might have been avoided.

The expedition delayed starting on October 15 while they continued to dry equipment soaked in the boat wreck of the 14th, but finally they were on their way at 3 p.m. They made good time, the river being fast and, Gass believed, "handsome, except at the rapids, where it is risking both life and property to pass; and even these rapids, when the bare view or prospect is considered distinct from the advantages of navigation, may add to its beauty, by interposing variety and scenes of romantick grandeur where there is so much uniformity in the appearance of the country."[20] This quotation indicates that, despite the mission to rush to the Pacific, there was at least some appreciation of the beauty of the river and landscape through which they were passing, a river and landscape both beautiful and sacred to the Native inhabitants.

All together, they passed seven rapids on October 15, some of them bad. Towards evening, the hills became much less pronounced, with still no timber and one of the worst rapids yet. Clark described the boiling cauldron: "for 3 miles… the Clifts of rocks jutted to the river on each Side compressing the water of the river through a narrow chanel; below which it widens into a kind of bason nearly round without any proceptiable current, at the lower part of this bason is a bad and dificuelt and dangerous rapid to pass."[21]

Twisted Hair, Te-toh-kan Ahs-kahp (Tetoharsky) and the other three Indians were all waiting for the Corps at the head of the rapids. They had gone ahead earlier in the day and stopped at this dangerous place in order to warn Lewis and Clark and to thoroughly scout and plan passage. Clark found the rapids even "more dificuelt to pass than we expected from the Indians information. a Suckcession of Sholes, appears to reach from bank to bank for 3 miles which was also intersepted with large rocks Sticking up in every direction,. and the chanel through which we must pass crooked and narrow."

This would have been altogether a difficult and dangerous run even with modern equipment, such as rubber boats and life jackets. But they did not have modern equipment or life jackets. They did, however, have thoroughly adept Indian guides, and the corpsmen were determined and increasingly experienced students of the river.

As they wisely chose on a previous occasion, they encamped, leaving the dangerous water for the morrow. They were making progress, heading generally west, getting closer to the Pacific with each mile traveled. In fact, the whites were measuring the trip in miles. Ordway wrote they traveled 27 miles on October 15, Whitehouse jotted 17 miles, Gass figured 18 miles, and William Clark calculated 20 miles. For the Nez Perces and the other "Indian" present, it was no doubt "one day's travel."

First, the three Indians in the smallest canoe ran safely through, and then the small canoe of the Corps was followed by the four large canoes. All went well until the last canoe, Sergeant Pryor's, was "run on a rock near the lower part of the rapid and Stuck fast."[22] They had the drill down by this time. Rescue canoes were emptied and sent out to lighten the weight of the stuck canoe, and again, with urging, she broke loose and they were all on their way again, "without any further injory than, the wetting [of] the greater part of her loading."[23] This might have signaled a crisis earlier in the trip, but by now it was seemingly routine.

In the afternoon the guides signaled to "pull in." The last difficult rapid on the Snake lay just ahead. It was a long risky rapid, but passage looked possible. A heavy boat generally is a less maneuverable craft and a lighter canoe naturally rides "higher and dryer." To increase their odds of a successful run and not risk lives unnecessarily, the captains again decided to portage some of the baggage nearly a mile. The canoes, lightened in this way, were then sent two at a time and ultimately all came through safely. Next, the canoes were repacked below the rapid, and the expedition continued on. Several more rapids were run that afternoon, but none as dangerous as those already passed. Since the morning of October 11, the white men believed they were on the Columbia River but, in the evening of October 16, they came to another large river which Clark measured across as 860 yards. Now, at last, they were on the true Columbia.

ENDNOTES

1   Peo-Peo-Tah-Likt (Bird Alighting) and Chief Many Wounds (Sam Lott), *Historical Sketches of the Nez Perces* Manuscripts, Archives and Special Collections, Washington State University, Pullman, Washington, 1935), Cage #4681. Hereafter cited as Peo-Peo-Tah-Likt, *Historical Sketches of the Nez*

Perces, Unpublished manuscript, Cage #4681. Hereafter cited as Peo-Peo-Tah-Likt, *Historical Sketches of the Nez Perces,* Cage #4681.

2   Swayne, *Do Them No Harm!,* pp. 321–2. Harry Wheeler explained the probable meaning of "Tetoharsky" by pointing out the Americans were probably trying to say Te-toh-kan Ahs-kahp which, combined, expressed the thought "People are coming. They look like brothers." A literal translation might be *Tetoken,* "Indian," and *Askap* (asqap), "younger brother," therefore "younger Indian brother."

3   Van Arsdale, "History of the Alpowai," unpublished manuscript in possession of the authors. This crossing appears at low water (before dam construction) and is caused by a stone ledge extending across the Snake. Some called this Red Wolf Crossing due to its proximity to Red Wolf village. Others called the crossing Coyote's Penis.

4   Rowena L. Alcorn and Gordon D. Alcorn, *Timothy, A Nez Perce Chief, 1800–1891* (Fairfield, WA: Ye Galleon Press, 1985). Alcorn has calculated young Ta-Moots-Tsoo's age at five years in 1805; Chief Peo-Peo-Tah-Likt suggests he may have been as old as ten years. At either age, Chief Timoty was old when he died in 1891. Hereafter cited Alcorn, *Timothy, A Nez Perce Chief.*

5   Gass, *Journals,* p. 137. Gass says they were only at the village about an hour.

6   *JLCE,* 9:237.

7   *JLCE,* 11:348.

8   The Hawthorne exists at river level and up to four thousand or more feet in elevation. In Nez Perce country there is both the Red Hawthorne,"Red Haw," and the Black Hawthorne, "Black Haw."

9   *JLCE,* 9:237.

10   Ibid.

11   Clifford E. Trafzer and Richard D. Scheurman, *Renegade Tribe: The Palouse Indians and the Invasion of the Inland Pacific Northwest* (Pullman, WA: WSU Press, 1986). Hereafter cited as Trafzer, *Renegade Tribe.*

12   See *JLCE,* 5:268 n. 2. Now Tucannon River, Columbia County, Washington. *Atlas* map 73. "Ki-moo-e-nimm" (and similar spellings) may come from the Nez Perce term *qemuynem.* The etymology of the word is not clear but may have to do with the Wallowa valley region of the Nez Perce homeland in northeastern Oregon and apparently is unrelated to the Tucannon River, or at least only in a very distant geographical sense. Haruo Aoki, personal communication." Maybe because the river, followed to its source leads to the crest of the Blue Mountains (in today's states of Oregon and Washington) and is an avenue into the home of the Wallowa Nez Perces. The other river was called "drewyers River" after George Drewyer or Droulliard. The Nez Perces called the river Ipeluut and the people who lived there Peluucpu. This was the site, too, of those people's largest village, Paluso, Trafzer, *Renegade Tribe,* p. xiv.

13 Adapted from Clifford E. Trafzer, *Grandfather, and Old Wolf: Tamánwit Ku Súkat and Traditional Native American Narratives from the Columbia Plateau.* (Michigan State University Press, East Lansing, 1998).

14 Trafzer, *Renegade Tribe*, p. 156.

15 *JLCE*, 5:268

16 *JLCE*, 9:238.

17 *JLCE*, 5:271–2 (Clark).

18 *JLCE*, 9:238.

19 *JLCE*, 5:271–2.

20 Gass, *Journals*, p. 139.

21 *JLCE*, 5:275 (Clark).

22 *JLCE*, 5:276–7 (Clark).

23 *JLCE*, 5:276 (Clark).

Chapter 6

Down the Columbia

On the upstream side of the mouth of the Snake, a peninsula extended between that stream and the Columbia. This is where the Corps set up their camp, near an Indian village, probably the Palouse village called Qosispah.[1] The Indians appeared friendly; most likely they were in a hospitable mood because the Nez Perce "chiefs" had gone ahead two days previously in order to inform their neighbors (and relatives) that the white men were coming and that they professed "friendly intentions towards all nations &c."[2] This diplomacy, performed by Nez Perces and quite likely several Palouse leaders, in addition to the presence of Sacajawea and her child, undoubtedly did a great deal to smooth the way for the United States Army reconnaissance who were now far from the United States and their homes.[3]

The Natives approached the Corps's camp about 200 men strong, "Singing and beeting on their drums Stick and keeping time to the music."[4] This was a welcoming song and was a ritual performed for all friendly visiting nations. The rawhide drums of the mid-Columbia people are single-sided and usually held in the left hand while the right is used to thump on the rawhide stretched over a wood frame perhaps 16 to 20 inches in diameter.

A large number of drums in unison, accompanied by the singing of a chant and chorus, is bold and impressive, a great booming of the heartbeat of their nation. The drums of all the tribes of the interior northwest were an integral part of their religous ritual practice. One religious leader of the mid-nineteenth century, Smohala, explained the significance of the drum among his worshipping group: "The drum is life. It is the sound of life within you. It is the sound of life in the world."[5]

After the drumming and singing welcome presented to the Americans and their guides came the smoking, another ritual as significant to the interior Northwest peoples as it was to any on the continent. The captains handed out a large medal to the "principal chief" and a couple of small ones to a "2nd Chief" and to "the Chief who came down from the upper villages,"[6] likely a reference to a village up the Columbia. The "principal chief" was named "Cuts-Sah nim,"[7] which sounds much like the Nimíipuu word *qacano* or a variant *qacnot* which is a descriptive word referring to "versatile, competent, capable, fearless."[8]

Perhaps he was the Palouse leader called Ke-Pow-Han, whose son Watai-Wattai How-Lis was quoted (in an 1854 report by government agent James Doty) as saying that his father had been given the medal. This may be the same medal discovered in a canoe grave at the mouth of the Palouse River in 1964.[9] When the rituals were over, local tribesmen returned to their camp, and Twisted Hair and Te-toh-kan Ahs-kahp (Tetoharsky) negotiated with them for firewood. With a cooking fire by the river bank, the expedition party could enjoy roasted fish and dog.

On October17, Clark took a side trip with two of his men and ascended the Columbia for a distance to see what he could of the terrain, the rivers, and the natives. The people on the river generally had sore eyes. This was brought on by ultraviolet ray damage and the subsequent development of cataracts, as well as continued exposure to campfire smoke.[10] Clark wrote a couple of paragraphs on the dress of the women. The water of the Columbia, he noted, "is Clear, and a Salmon may be Seen at the deabth of 15 or 20 feet."[11]

Everyone in camp either worked on equipment for the trip down the Columbia or was engaged in hunting locally for sage grouse, "a large fowl...the Size of a Small turkey."[12]

On the 18th, the captains held a council, Clark wrote, "in which we informed of our friendly intentions towards them and all other of our red children; of our wish to make a piece between all of our red Children in this quarter &c. &c. this was conveyed by Signs thro: our 2 Chiefs who accompanied us, and was understood, we made a 2d Chief and gave Strings of wompom to them all in remembrance of what we Said."

It was a presumptuous and patronizing message, in that the boundary of the United States officially ended at the headwaters of the Missouri and, in 1805, even that was merely a claim. The occupying Nations had not been consulted in the Louisiana Purchase, and the west slope of the Rockies in both Northwest and Southwest were beyond the territory of the United States.

The captains assumed sovereign authority and, in fact, were making a claim by their presence and the presence of their men and their arms. None of this was understood in that sense by the Palouse or the Nez Perces, or any of the Nations of the Columbia, who had their own realms of which they were a part. The Nimíipuu and the other tribes of the interior Pacific Northwest knew the limits of their own tribal regions. However, they held no concept of private ownership in the manner of land title. If understood, the Euro-American idea would have been considered nonsensical, as tribal regions were only "owned" collectively. Further, there was no word for "empire" in the Sahaptin vocabulary.

The captains were making use of one of the most powerful tools in communications within a non-literate society: the capacity of objects to represent or symbolize ideas. Objects stood for something; they could be ideas or concepts, even stories. This *wompom* distributed on October 18 stood for the message delivered that day. The extent to which the message was understood was due in part to the Nez Perces Twisted Hair and Te-toh-kan Ahs-kahp (Tetoharsky), and both would continue for a time with the *sooyáapoo* (white men) on the Columbia, acting as guides, diplomats, and informants.

There was no denying that white men had arrived with a message. They had some strange ideas, and they looked funny, smelled bad, and ate dogs, just like the Nimíipuu's uncivilized and bad-mannered enemies to the south. However, they seemed to have a high opinion of themselves, and their technology was impressive and possibly useful. Also, they were personally likeable. Therefore, prudence and wisdom both dictated a watchful waiting. Three natives turned back upstream from the camp at the mouth of the Snake River. One was the unidentified river guide of the lower Snake, and the other two were his young Nez Perce companions.[13]

The zenith of the salmon fishing season was over, and the spawned out salmon were lying dead along the shore of the Columbia. The white explorers did not understand the salmon cycle,[14] but the fall Chinook run was in full migration. Some tribal fishermen persisted in their attempts to secure more salmon for their winter stores and for trading, while others hunted the prairies for antelope and still others, the mountains for deer and elk.

One of the conditions which made diversified food gathering possible was the low rainfall and dry humidity of the interior Columbia basin. The conditions allowed for the drying of salmon outside on racks constructed by the Indians out of timber rafted down the various feeder streams. They used large timbers rafted down, as well, for the construction of their large A-framed dwellings that were covered with reed mats. These lodges, sometimes with floors dug down a foot or two, allowed fires down the center, and a long slit in the top allowed the light to filter in and the smoke to escape.

Another feature of this style of dwelling was the portable reed mats, which were made of cattail or tule. They were constructed in manageable sizes and layered upon the timber frames, beginning on the bottom, then overlapped like shingles all the way to the top smoke opening. They could be removed if necessary or desirable and hauled (or floated) to a new location and installed on a different frame. Sometimes tipi-style frames were covered with the mats and, at other times, they could be used in conjunction with cured elk and bison hides, and, later, even beef hides and commercial canvas and tin. Normally, there was no rain, and the reed mats would breathe; rain would swell and tighten the reeds and a cold wind would freeze them, forming an ice shield against the winter. The stored frames even served as emergency firewood.

These are the styles of housing that predominated on the mid-Columbia and constitute the type that Lewis and Clark observed in their travels with Twisted Hair and Te-toh-kan Ahs-kahp's sojourn from the mouth of the Snake to the Celilo Falls of the mighty Columbia. These dwellings, sometimes called *kuhét'iniit* (long house), or *tok'ó'niit* (tule house) by the Nez Perces, allowed reasonably secure and versatile living in an environment that ranged from above 100 degrees in the summer and well below zero in the winter.[15]

These dwellings, sometimes called kuhét'iniit (long house), or tok'ó'niit (tule house) by the Nez Perces, allowed reasonably secure and versatile living in an environment that ranged from above 100 degrees in the summer and well below zero in the winter. Nez Perce National Historic Park: NEPE-HI-0440.

When the Corps camped on October 18 after paddling only a few hours in the afternoon (they did not launch until 4 p.m.), they formed a camp on the south bank, a short distance below the mouth of the Walla Walla River. Clark wrote that they went 21 miles that day,[16] so they did well for the few hours traveled. The canoes had slipped right past another village, which Twisted Hair and Tetokan Askap (Tetoharsky) informed the captains was the home of "1st Chief of all the tribes in this quarter."[17] The Nez Perces informed Clark, too, that the chief had called for them to land and that he had plenty of wood, etc.[18]

The captains did not understand what was happening until they had already passed the village. At that point, they sent Twisted Hair and Te-toh-kan Ahs-kahp (Tetoharsky) up the bank to invite the chief down for a smoke and a talk. The chief returned with twenty of his men too late for a powwow, and put up a camp nearby. The next morning (October 19) all had their smoke and talk.

The chief's name was "Yel-lep-pit."[19] Chief Yel-lep-pit and his people were Walla Walla Indians, although some scholars believe him to be Cayuse. At any rate, he understood the language of the Nez Perce, even though there was some discrepancy in their vocabularies. Yel-lep-pit was described by Clark as "a bold handsom Indian, with a dignified countenance about 35 years of age, about 5 feet 8 inches high and well perpotiond."[20]

The chief wanted the whites to remain at their camp until noon so his villagers could come and look at them, but the Americans were eager to move on and promised to remain a day or two on their return trip. Many Indians canoed to their camp to look at them anyway before the explorers launched about 9 a.m.[21]

This day on the Columbia (October 19) brought many new adventures for the exploring party and, as usual, the Nez Perces were important participants. The reaction of the numerous Natives was marked more by fear than curiosity, which Clark noted but could initially do nothing about since the people located themselves at positions where it was difficult, if not impossible, for the large, heavy-laden canoes to land.

At a very bad rapid[22] the party pulled to shore in order to do the necessary scouting for the best route. Clark took both Nez Perces, plus Charbonneau, Sacajawea, and presumably their son with him in a walk around the rapid. Clark looked at the river from a height and determined the best route (always easier to see from above than at water level).

Only one channel seemed suited for the large canoes—on the opposite side (north side) of the river. He then sent Charbonneau and family, accompanied by the Nez Perces, to the flotilla with directions to seek the channel on the north side of the rapid. The smaller canoe with three men aboard was sent down the south (left) bank as Clark requested, to wait at the bottom of the rapid.

He then climbed several hundred feet above river level for more observations. Clark could see a mountain to the west which he thought might be St. Helens, the snow-capped peak mentioned by British Captain George Vancouver as seen from the mouth of the Columbia a dozen years earlier. Clark was wrong, he was really seeing Mt. Adams to the east of St. Helens.

He could see that, across the river, Lewis and the others were struggling to get through the difficulties of the rock-strewn channels. Clark could see, too, that Lewis and the men were being observed by Natives who went towards their lodges downstream as fast as they could travel. Clark's fear was that "those people might not be informed of us."[23] This must have been a group that missed the usual briefing by Te-toh-kan Ahs-kahp (Tetoharsky) and Chief Twisted Hair.

Clark then determined to put them at ease and, with the small canoe and the three men in it, he crossed the river, approached a lodge, and found it shut fast. With his pipe in hand, Clark entered the lodge and there found "32 persons men, women and a few children Setting permiscuesly in the Lodg, in the greatest agutation, Some crying and ringing there hands, others hanging their heads."[24] Clark gave them small articles of trade merchandise and offered his hand to them. He sent in Droulliard and the Field brothers to try and convince them that the visit was a friendly one.

Only when the other canoes arrived, and Twisted Hair and Te-toh-kan Ahs-kahp (Tetoharsky) came forward, and one of them spoke did the villagers begin to relax. The sight of Sacajawea and her baby boy did more than anything else, Clark wrote, to ensure "those people of our friendly intentions, as no woman ever accompanies a war party of Indians in this quarter."[25] The men came forward at last and had a smoke. It came out in council that they had witnessed Clark shooting a crane and some ducks and, seeing the results of his "thunder," became alarmed; they had not seen many whites or firearms. All they knew is that they had heard a crack of thunder and suddenly a crane had dropped out of the sky. The Nez Perces told these folk, possibly a band of fellow Sahaptin-speaking Umatilla, of where the whites came from, where they were going, and gave them generally "a friendly account of us," Clark wrote.[26]

After smoking, council, and finally trading for fish and berries, the exploration party moved on, paddling a few miles downstream and landing on the south shore.[27] Many natives came to their camp in canoes and some brought firewood, although the party had selected a spot with a few willows with which they could at least heat their food.

The next morning the expeditionaries began by breakfasting on dog and sharing a smoke with the Natives who shared their fires with them. The morning was still cool as they launched their canoes, leaving about 200 Indians on the bank. The river ran powerful and smooth, with only a few rapids passed that day (October 20). Many lodges were passed, mostly on the north shore and on the islands, for there was a general fear of attacks by enemies from the south. The Indians, the journals noted, possessed an increasing number of European-manufactured goods. Clark saw one tribal man with what must have been considered a stylish sailor's jacket. A few days later, he would spy another.

The curiosity of the American party brought them to stop at some islands with wooden structures, which proved to be a type of burial chamber.[28] There was no mention of the "old chiefs" on this day, but perhaps they informed the Corps of the purpose of these structures. After a few hours of paddling, camp was established on the north shore (near Roosevelt, Klickitat County, Washington), at the base of high, open, and rocky hills. The south shore was open desert, a rocky sandy plain with not a tree in sight on either side.

While Clark described the morning of October 20 as "cool," he called the next morning "a verry Cold morning" and, to add to their discomfort, there was not enough firewood even for breakfast, so they launched early and headed downstream to look for food and fuel.

Columbia River Drive-in

Fending for yourself gets tiresome and monotonous when you're traveling on a budget and undersupplied. Once in a while, it's good to splurge and just pull over and get a bite to eat and fuel up. This was the decision of the captains on October 21. After maybe a couple of hours of paddling, they came to a village known hereafter as the "Columbia River Drive-In," where they "bought some wood and breakfast" from some villagers who "recived us with great kindness, and examined us with much attention."[29]

They spoke the same language as those upstream, so Twisted Hair and his companion could speak directly with them. The men of the expedition saw several more cloth blankets and another sailor's coat in this village.[30] Downstream from breakfast a couple more miles, all canoes stopped again, this time to look at some more rapids before attempting to "run" them. This pattern continued throughout the day; pull in to scout the water, then run. It was slow tedious going, and dangerous, but not as risky as "running" without scouting. At an exceptionally terrible looking stretch of white water, the worst one, they "put out all who could not Swim to walk around,..." because the run looked "verry dangerous...."[31] As they passed different villages, the people were all drying fish; this river and salmon were their lives.

While all stroked the current with their paddles, Twisted Hair pointed out where "a great battle" had taken place not too many years previously, between the Sahaptins and the Snake Indians.[32] The captains selected a campsite on the north side of the Columbia a little below the mouth of "a Small river on the Larboard Side"[33] and a little above the mouth of the Deschutes River.

Were Twisted Hair and Te-toh-kan Ahs-kahp the first Nez Perces to taste beer?

That evening, John Collins presented to "us," wrote Clark, "Some verry good *beer* made of the *Pa-shi-co-quar-mash* bread, which bread is the remains of what was laid in as [X; *a part of* our] Stores of Provisions, at the first flat heads or Cho-pun-nish Nation at the head of the *Kosskoske* river which by being frequently wet molded & Sowered &c," had fermented into a passable wilderness beer. How much beer did Collins make? He used the *qém'es,* the mainstay of Niimiipuu vegetable food supply, to make that beer. Inquiring minds of beer makers worldwide want to know how he did it, and was there enough to go around? Was there even a taste for Twisted Hair and Te-toh-kan Ahs-kahp (Tetoharsky)? If so, it would be a historic first, worthy of note.

Alas, there is no hint in the Clark account of who received the beer. Perhaps the captains got all that was offered by Collins. Neither Sergeants Gass or Ordway, nor Private Whitehouse mention any beer whatsoever. Surely if the journal-writing army sergeants had beer, it would have merited at least a mention. None of the journal keepers except Clark mentioned the beer. Twisted Hair and Te-toh-kan Ahs-kahp (Tetoharsky) probably got no beer either, and the historic moment of the first Nimíipuu drinking a beer was probably several decades away.[34]

The morning of October 22 was "A fine morning calm and fare."[35] There was no mention of a hangover. The Columbia River ran smooth for a few miles and then "a verry bad rapid at the head of an Island close under the Stard. Side."[36] Successfully passing this rocky, risk-strewn route, the captains traveled river left to investigate the mouth of a river entering the Columbia from the Southeast. Both hiked up this river, now called Deschutes, Clark checking out a "verry Considerable rapid," where he "beheld an emence body of water Compressd in a narrow Chanel of about 200 yds in width, fomeing over rocks maney of which presented their tops above the water."[37] Lewis joined him at the rapid after examining some roots the Indians had been harvesting in "great quantities in the bottoms of this River."[38]

From the mouth of the Deschutes, it was a short canoe ride downstream on the Columbia and around a left turn in the river to more lodges on an island. On the north bank there was another village, with all of the usual fish-drying racks. The villagers at this location still spoke the Sahaptin tongue and, despite vocabulary differences, the Nez Perces could converse with them. The explorers were now immediately above the Great Falls of the Columbia, called Celilo. This region was a natural climatic dividing line between a semi-desert and a wet and woodsy clime. The climate transition was also a linguistic one; the tribes downstream spoke the Chinookan tongue.

Celilo

There never was, nor will there ever be again, a place on this planet such as the Great Falls of the Columbia, or the Celilo Falls. Massive basalt blocks from ancient volcanoes constitute the bottom of the river, yet portions of this rock protrude above the level of the river's surface and form several large islands in the center of the river. The mass of water that originates high in the Rocky Mountains (in modern Canada), and the waters of the Snake and Salmon, beginning in modern Wyoming and

Idaho, all join and attempt to force themselves down the north side, the right side of the river as you face downstream.

At extreme high water in the springtime, the current succeeds in running down the right side but, as the spring flows recede, the stony bottom seems to push up and through the water surface and relatively more and more of the river backs up and drops over a 20 foot perpendicular drop that runs diagonally out to first one, and then two, of the largest stone islands. These islands and peninsulas themselves become increasingly large with the dropping of the flow volume in the summer and early fall season.

Salmon that run in the spring flows swim against a nearly impossible current. The fall fish must jump an 18-foot waterfall, then a short run through frothing cauldrons, followed by another 20-foot jump. They are on their way to the place of their births, traveling desperately to their own breeding beds, making their last valiant gesture before they die. But they leave new life in their wake, for their own salmon people and for the Chinook tribes below and the Sahaptin and Salish above.

In the early twentieth century cable cars proliferated to enhance fishing opportunities at Celilo. Photo by Joy Simpson, mother of co-author Evans, Athena, Oregon, 1949.

This was the kind of fishing that made Celilo one of the greatest fisheries of the world, but after thousands of years of fishing and a government promise that it would always remain, the United States destroyed the site in 1957 when water backed up behind the Dalles Dam. Photo by Joy Simpson, Athena, Oregon, 1949.

Otters swim in the rapids below the falls, taking their meals at their leisure. The seagulls fresh from the saltwater, and the ravens and crows from the mountain realms, make their own language and their own wars and truces over the gut piles and bodies of the salmon brothers lining the abandoned pools amidst the rocky islands and rocky shores of the water-shorn and worn basalt so smooth that the Frenchmen who first saw it called the rock "dallage," because it reminded them of flagstones. In time, the name morphed into "The Dalles."

This washed lithic condition existed intermittently for a half dozen miles. It existed from Celilo on downstream through both the short narrows and long narrows, where the Columbia was choked by black monolithic faults into snarling, roaring chutes that were a mere stone's throw across. The bottom of the river was so uneven as to never allow the surface a rest; waves, foam, whirlpools, upheavals, and sprays both constant and unpredictable all happened in unison.

Everything above Celilo, the Great Falls, was the dry desert and desert-like open sage-, grass-, and rock-strewn terrain of the interior basin. Rugged interior mountains bordered the basin: the Ochocco, Blue Mountains, Bitterroots on the southeast and east, and the Okanogan and Selkirks to the north and northwest. These mountains and their foothills were the homes of many tribes, such as the Nimíipuu, and many more who relied on the waters and migratory fish but also rode their horses to the buffalo country or traded with those who did.

Below Celilo, both Narrows, and The Dalles, the climate changed, with the abrupt beginnings of the brush-covered, then timber-clad, benches and ridges leading to the mighty Cascade Range. In a thousand miles of north-to-south-reaching glaciated and volcanic heights, there is but one water route connecting the basin to the Pacific: the Columbia River and the gap known as the Columbia River Gorge.

The Columbia Gorge, from the Celilo Falls to and including the Pacific coast about the mouth, was home to Chinook people, who were people of the salmon and the cedar. The low river valleys, their navigable waters, were plied by them in their exquisitely designed, sharp-prowed, cedar canoes. Their life-ways were integrated with deep woods, fog-shrouded waterways, estuaries, and perpetual rains.

These Chinook who lived on the coast and on the lower Columbia had been trading with upstream Natives for 10,000 years and with white men since Spaniards and Russians first dropped anchor in their waters more than a century earlier. The British and the Americans, "the Bostons" dropped by, too, trading primarily for sea otter to trade for great profit in China.

That was the region Lewis and Clark were then approaching, and they were excited. They were about to enter a new bioregion, an area that would bring them closer to their goal. They better understood the currents of the Columbia than the cultural and political forces of Wyam[39] (the Celilo falls area), the Narrows, and The Dalles. This was the ancient trade mart, where buffalo robes were traded for sea shell earrings, where the name Pierced Nose was more than just a name; it was descriptive of both Sahaptin-and Chinook-speaking villages.[40]

When the first salmon were caught each spring, a religious ceremony was held, and multi-village gambling took place, off and on, all summer long. Women had their own trades and trading partners, people they met with annually to check the year's news and gossip and to exchange goods, baskets, beads, tanned elk hides, you name it. Old flames of trade rivalries, even wars, were kindled alongside old friendships and new romances. Whites from downstream had left the area just days ahead of Lewis and Clark's arrival from upstream. What was the experience of the tribes with these whites? Lewis and Clark did not know, but some of the tribes were not to give the downstream party a friendly reception.

The Expedition had to get their canoes, men, and equipment below the Wyam, the Celilo Falls. The Nez Perces helped negotiate with local tribesmen on the north shore, above the Falls, and pack horses were engaged to move the supplies and equipment of the party 1200 yards across the rocky shore (streambed at high water) and down a sand dune to a large eddy below the falls.[41] This spot was selected as camp the nights of October 22 and 23. The following morning, Clark, "with the greater part of the men Crossed in the Canoes to opposit Side above the falls and hauled them across the portage of 457 yards."

In the portage, they avoided an initial 20-foot drop, but shortly came to an additional drop nearly as high, and through this they decided to allow the canoes to float empty with ropes attached, a technique called "lining." All went well, except one of the canoes "got loose by the Cords breaking." The Indians caught the canoe downstream and sold it back to the captains.

It was three in the afternoon on October 23rd before all the canoes and men were safely back in camp below the falls. They traded in one of their canoes and got a new model from the Chinooks, designed to handle the big wind-driven waves of the lower river and the ocean. The "nativs," Clark said, "not being fond of Selling their good fish, compells us to make use of Dog meat for food, the flesh of which the most of the party have become fond of from the habits of useing it for Some time past." There were only eight dogs, and they were small, but they were "fat."[42] Clark, Twisted Hair, and Te-toh-kan Ahs-kahp (Tetoharsky) did not eat dog, so that left more for the others.

Twisted Hair informed the captains that the "nation below" were planning to kill them, and Clark wrote that "our two old Chiefs appeared verry uneasy this evening."[43] But all the men were "at all times & places" on their guard, and no attack came. Maybe the warning and the obvious defensive arrangements helped preclude an attack, or maybe the anti-Nez Perce rivalry of the Chinook speakers deliberately allowed the two elders to overhear a threat that was merely a warning. Next morning the "chiefs" again informed the captains they were ready to return home, as "they Could be of no further Service to us, as their nation extended no further down the river than those falls."[44]

The captains, however, wanted two more days from the Nez Perces, and they agreed. The motives of the captains seemed to be that there were more falls "at no great distance below." There was also the President's order: make peace between the tribes—and, as the Nez Perces had informed them, there was war between themselves and the nation below. All succeeded in passing through the rapid called Short Narrows, with the canoes crashing against "whorls and Swills," into what Clark called a "gut Swelling, boiling & whorling in every direction."[45]

That afternoon a camp was formed near another village and above "the long narrows." An opportunity came to effect a peace between a "Great Chief" of this village and the two Nez Perces. Everyone smoked and "Peter Crusat played the *violin*."[46] Clark now believed that peace "and good understanding" were accomplished between Twisted Hair, Tetokan Askap (Tetoharsky) and the "Great Chief," and that "those two bands or nations are and will be on the most friendly terms with each other."[47]

Friday, October 25, 1805, was the last day Twisted Hair and Tetokan Askap (Tetoharsky) saw the members of the expedition until the following spring. All in all, it had been a rather amazing association. Twisted Hair had invested more than five weeks with the American expedition, smoking, talking, helping with the selection of the trees with which to construct the canoes, and had been instrumental in showing the technique of burning and scraping to create the canoes Indian-style. Twisted Hair had drawn or helped draw a map on elkskin that informed the captains of a great deal of landscape of the Nez Perce country, and had advised on the techniques of running specific rapids in the Clearwater, Snake, and Columbia Rivers that were life-threatening.

In addition, Twisted Hair and Te-toh-kan Ahs-kahp (Tetoharsky) were both acting in the role of diplomats with the strategically located Palouse and other downstream Sahaptin speakers, such as the Walla Walla, Umatilla, Yakama, Wanapums, and others. There was to be more between the Nez Perces and the Corps of Discovery on the Corps's return trip in the spring of 1806, following a long wet winter at Ft. Clatsop. But on October 25, the brothers purchased two horses with two buffalo robes and, following a farewell smoke, began their return journey to their home on the Clearwater.

Today, there is no more Celilo Falls, no more Short Narrows, and no more Long Narrows. Everything that existed, the greatest Indian fishing spot in North America, one of the greatest fisheries in the world, has been drowned out by the rising waters behind The Dalles Dam. The completion of this dam in 1957 was a gross error, even a colossal sin, to the Yakima, Confederated Umatilla, Warm Springs, Nez Perce, and all the tribes who were promised in sacred treaties (1855) that they would always have this portion of the river to fish and to maintain their way of life. Chief Tommy Thompson of Celilo Village refused to negotiate with the agents of the United States government. The American government allowed the construction anyway. Allen V. Pinkham, Sr., co-author of this book, well remembers traveling home on leave from the United States Marine Corps just after the dam was built:

> The bus proceeded up the Columbia River, then crossed to the Washington side, probably at Hood River. As the bus approached and passed The Dalles, I expected to see Celilo Falls and the village where, as a boy, I had fished [with my father] and walked about the islands. The water was high and smooth—no village or falls. My heart sank.[48]

ENDNOTES

1   The men of the expedition referred to these people as Flatheads, a name they seemed to apply to several groups on the west slope of the Rockies, including the Flatheads, Nez Perces, Palouses and others. This village site has positively been identified as Palouse, see Trafzer, *Renegade Tribe,* p. 4.

2   *JLCE*, 5:278.

3   There are several references to the effect of the woman and child in the journals, for example, *JLCE*, 5:268; 5:306.

4   *JLCE*, 5:278.

5   Chick Relander, *Drummers & Dreamers: The Story of Smowhala the Prophet and His Nephew Puck Hyah Toot, the Last Prophet of the Nearly Extinct River People, the Last Wanapums* (Caldwell, ID: Caxton Printers, 1986), p. 84.

6   *JLCE*, 5:278.

7   *JLCE*, 5:294.

8   Aoki, *Nez Perce Dictionary*, p. 569.

9   Cheryll Halsey and Robert R. Beale, *Lewis and Clark and the Shahaptian Speaking Americans* (Fairfield, Washington: Ye Galleon Press, 1983), p. 25.

10   From personal interview with John W. Fisher, author of *Medical Appendices of the Lewis and Clark Expedition* (Juliaetta, ID: privately printed, 2006).

11   *JLCE*, 5:288.

12   Ibid., 5:287.

13   Ibid., 5:298.

14   Ibid., 5:286.

15   Harvey S. Rice, "Native American Dwellings and Attendant Structures of the Southern Plateau," *Eastern Washington University Reports in Archaeology and History*, 1985.

16   *JLCE*, 11:360, says 17 miles.

17   *JLCE*, 5:298.

18   Ibid., 5:298.

19   Info on him in *JLCE*, 5:307 n. 1.

20   *JLCE*, 5:303.

21   *JLCE*, 11:360. Whitehouse wrote 7 a.m.

22   Mussel Shell rapid located near present day McNary dam, see *JLCE*, 5:307.

23   *JLCE*, 5.

24   Ibid., 5:305.

25   Ibid., 5:306.

26   Ibid., 5:306.

27   Moulton has this camp between Irrigon and Boardman, Morrow County, Oregon, *JLCE*, 5:307.

28 *JLCE,* 5:311 for Clark's description of burial vaults seen and investigated.

29 Ibid., 5:317

30 Not sure who these folks were, maybe Methows, see *JLCE,* 5:219.

31 *JLCE,* 5:317.

32 *JLCE,* 5:319-20.

33 Later known as John Day River, called Le Page's River by the expedition in 1806.

34 Individual Nez Perce travelers to California may have tasted beer and maybe several travelers to the mid-west in the 1830s–'40s. The first beer in Nez Perce country probably was not regularly available until gold rush days of the 1860s.

35 *JLCE,* 5:321.

36 Ibid. This is described by Clark but also drawn carefully and beautifully in his Elkskin-bound Journal, reproduced by *JLCE,* 5:316.

37 Ibid.

38 Ibid. Probably a form of the root wapato, Moulton lists two types, *JLCE,* 5:326 n. 9

39 Sahaptin for "echo of falling water" or "sound of water upon the rocks." *Wana Chinook Tymoo*, Winter 2008, p.4.

40 *JLCE,* 5:315.

41 Excellent maps by Clark show the portage of goods on the no.1 shore, the portage of canoes on the south shore, the eddy and the camp location of 22 and 23 October.

42 *JLCE,* 5:327–8.

43 Ibid., 5:328.

44 Ibid., 5:329.

45 Ibid., 5:332–3.

46 Ibid., 5:335–6.

47 Ibid., 5:335.

48 Allen V. Pinkham, Sr., "Childhood Memories of Fishing at Celilo Falls," *Oregon Historical Quarterly,* 108:5, Winter 2007, pp. 586–595. This entire quarterly was a special issue, "Remembering Celilo Falls," and featured twenty-nine contributions.

Chapter 7

Twisted Hair's Return Trip

No one alive knows the route taken by Twisted Hair and Te-toh-kan Ahs-kahp (Tetoharsky) on their way back into the Nimíipuu homeland. That they realized they had been participants in an important experience relative to the tribal future cannot be doubted, when judged in the light of later events. This probability means that they likely did a lot of talking with relatives along their way. This was the Indian way of traveling: work towards home relative by relative.

Journeying in this manner, they did not have to worry about firewood, food, or horse care. Relatives in each village would provide all the help required by a traveler. This was the "moccasin telegraph," and Twisted Hair and his younger brother brought stories and news to each village that extended them hospitality. Everyone would hear the stories and join a thorough discussion of the meaning of the passage of Lewis and Clark and their troop. All talk would be in Sahaptin, without signs, with no holding back as propriety might require of discussions held in the Corps's presence.

Up the south bank of the Columbia they rode. Probably a week passed before they had to make the decision where to turn right, where to leave the Big River and to take a more direct cross-country route home. This cut-off was probably somewhere in modern Morrow County, or perhaps near the modern hamlet of Umatilla (Umatilla County, Oregon). They worked their way towards the foothills of the Blue Mountains, closer to good firewood, the villages of more friends and relatives, and more food: berries, deer, elk, and salmon. A young nephew in one of the villages would watch their horses graze in the bunchgrass and have them ready to go in the morning. The young brother of a good friend would consider it an honor to do the same in the next village.

Each night, the pipe would come out and the elder men's conversations would go long into the night. The younger folk listened, and the opinions of the older and wiser women were offered freely and considered, too. The conclusion was surely reached that change was in the air, fulfillment of prophecy possibly imminent, and the paths of the people should be chosen carefully.

It was said that the Americans were dog-eaters, like the Nimíipuu's enemies, and that the hand-shaking business showed a lack of good manners and a trifling with adults as if they were children. The *soyapoos* (white men) sometimes rudely entered one's lodge with no announcement, they seemed in a big hurry, etc. However, the elders realized that, beyond all these things, the *soyapoos* were bold and courageous and had proven so in threatening situations. While their white-water skills were lacking initially and some of their people could not swim, unheard of among Columbia-Snake basin Indians, they forged downstream despite these handicaps and prevailed in reaching their goals.

In short, they showed dogged determination and seemed to have purpose. Whether they were entirely truthful or not remained to be seen, but their ideas of peace and prosperity made sense. This would be an improvement in the security and peace of mind of all people if, indeed, peace could be achieved.

The black man, York, and the presence of the Shoshone woman and child were surely mentioned, if not discussed thoroughly. Assuredly, Twisted Hair and Te-toh-kan Ahs-kahp talked about the technology of the whites, and the advantages it could bring, at every stop. Keeping the Blue Mountains on their right side, they would cross the Umatilla River, ascend Wildhorse Creek until almost into the Blues, then cross Pine Creek and Dry Creek and enter the Walla Walla Valley. This is probably what they would have done unless they kept on the Columbia until they reached the Walla Walla River then ascended it, then the Touchet. This eastern Washington stream is believed by many to have derived its name from the French trappers, but a Confederated Umatilla man of Cayuse descent, Joe Williams, told the authors the name predated the whites and was a Cayuse name.

Over one more drainage brought them to the Tucannon, which they crossed, climbed a steep ridge and dropped into the Pataha Creek Valley. They ascended this creek until a few miles above modern Pomeroy in Garfield County, Washington. They crossed one more ridge and descended Alpowai Creek. This was the general route followed by Lewis and Clark in the spring when, again, they would be assisted in their path-finding by a Nez Perce guide. This route-finding 200 years after the fact is speculation, as there were many cut-offs and sub-routes; however, most trails that followed the foothills of the Blue Mountains northeast came out, one way or another, at or near the mouth of the Alpowai in present day Asotin County, Washington.

Once reaching Alpowai Valley, Twisted Hair would not have missed the opportunity to smoke-talk with his good friend Chief Ta-Moots-Tsoo.

This meeting was one of many such meetings beginning in the Fall and overlapping into the winter story time. Ta-Moots-Tsoo[1] was at Oyáyp (Weippe) with his son, by the same name, in September of 1805 when the explorers had emerged from the forest. He had rushed to his home village to prepare for their coming after learning of their plans to travel downstream.

The party did not delay long at the mouth of the Alpowai, just a few miles below their camp of October 11, on the Snake. Tribal informants, now deceased, told author Rowena Alcorn that the explorers stopped at Ta-Moot-Tsoo's village and held a brief devotion from a book,[2] and that young Ta-Moot-Tsoo, the son of Chief Ta-Moot-Tsoo, witnessed the brief ceremony and was greatly impressed by it.[3]

Tribal Winter, 1805–1806

For the average person, the presence of the American explorers for a few weeks in the Fall probably had little or no impact upon their daily activities. Many had seen the explorers, but probably most had not witnessed them and could only listen with interest to the stories others told. That these individuals were the topic of campfire conversation cannot be doubted, most especially the black one, the red-headed one, and those who played the fiddle. Some of the young women were curious about the young men of the expedition and considered them to be "beautiful."[4]

Xáxaac 'ilpilp (Chief Red Grizzly Bear) from the Salmon River was well known as a war leader and a wise person. He was one of the first Niimíipuu leaders that Clark heard about when Twisted Hair's brother let Clark know Red Grizzly Bear was the owner of the lodge to which Clark was conducted. The lodge's owner had left three days previously to make war against enemies to the southwest and would return in 15 or 18 days.[5]

Although Clark makes no mention of it, Patrick Gass plainly states in his entry of September 27 that "the greater part of the war party came in, and some of the principal men came down to our camp."[6] One of these "leaders" was certainly Red Grizzly Bear—Peo-Peo-Ta-Likt (Bird Alighting) said he helped Charbonneau with one of the canoes.[7]

There are several reasons Red Grizzly Bear did not make a grand entrance and seek a high profile introduction. The most likely reason is that he was not the dominant leader of that (Clearwater) region, but a band leader of the Salmon River Nez Perces. The victorious Nez Perces probably had a victory celebration on the Salmon River, after which the warriors returned to their respective villages. Lewis and Clark had already left Red Grizzly Bear gifts, including an American flag, so his status had already been recognized. He might have perceived a grand entrance and a war-like demonstration as adverse to the larger interests of the collective tribe.

No doubt he had been told of the purpose of the explorers' visit, including the admonitions about inter-tribal peace, and had been told of the presence of Toby, his son, Sacajawea and her son, all Shoshones. He could not have failed to be cognizant of the fact that the whites were in a preoccupied hurry and were heavily armed. He hung around and watched closely, helped with the burning out of the canoes, and in the process took a personal liking to Charbonneau.[8]

Red Grizzly Bear counciled, like Twisted Hair, that an alliance should be made with these white men. Wetkuweis, Red Grizzly Bear's sister's daughter, had reported on the goodness of the white people to him. She had stressed the *tá'c* (many good things) they possessed, and there was no denying the effectiveness of their technology. Red Grizzly Bear himself had witnessed the men's target practice, watching them shoot across the Clearwater at a large rock and hearing the roar of the explosive powder and the consistent slap of the lead bullets finding their mark on the stone.[9]

The *mim'yóoxat* talked all winter, traveling from village to village, and they urged that, if everything went well upon the return of the whites, they should work towards an alliance with them. There were many arguments against dealing with the Americans, including the risks alluded to in general prophesies about whites and their untrustworthiness. This did not seem to fit these Americans, but they should be watched closely and perhaps a permanent trade relationship should be established.

Then, instead of being dependant upon upriver (Columbia) trade for metal goods and beads or long dangerous trips to the Missouri River traders (in today's North Dakota) by themselves, the Nimíipuu could become the bead merchants of the vast region from the buffalo country to Celilo Falls and below. They would travel safely, backed by the fine rifles they would acquire from the Americans. Their rifles would then shoot better than the guns their plains enemies got from King George's men.

The white men also merited investigation for other reasons not unrelated to those above. The winter was a time of the *wéeyekweecet* (winter spirit dances). This was a ceremonial time in which people had the opportunity to dance in regalia dictated by a guardian spirit, singing spirit-directed songs to the rhythm of drums or rattles, sticks on logs, whistles, or any combination, as the spirit directed. These spirits, that had relationships with individuals only allowed themselves to be revealed at these special times. Only those who had "gone on the mountain," or other sacred place, and had received strong spirit guardianship would ever amount to much in Nimíipuu life. This principle applied to both males and females. Within this framework of the *wéeyekin* power, the people were curious about the spirit power of the Americans and their messages to the tribe regarding peace with their neighbors, trade with the Americans, and a subsequent better life. Their words appealed to the wise elders who had quizzed Lewis and Clark briefly about religion in the Fall; they would ask more of them in the Spring.[10]

While Winter was slowly releasing its icy grip on the Nez Perce homeland, the people were down to their last stores. *Qáaws* and *qeqi'it* (wild potato) were the first roots to reveal themselves in the Spring on low south-facing rocky slopes, and *wew'i imn*, a celery-like plant, grew there, also, and in abundance along the rocky streambeds throughout the canyon system of home. These foods were eagerly anticipated even as the deep snows lingered in the high country that surrounded and protected them.

The Corps of Discovery abandoned Fort Clatsop on March 23, 1806, and with a "new" canoe, stolen from their neighbors, were paddling against the Columbia's rising currents. Now they were not dodging rocks as in their downstream saga, but were combating the beginnings of a massive release of spring run-off that made the Columbia into a river many times more voluminous than that of any October.

The American trading vessel that might have meant an oceanic ride back to the United States, or at least a restoration of food supplies and trade goods, had never arrived. Now the Americans were essentially "broke," and even the powerful surge of the Columbia conspired to slow them. Being broke and impatient is not conducive to the best neighborly or commercial relations. This is how it was as they emerged from the west side of the Cascade Mountains to the dry side at the Dalles, where they arrived on April 15, intent upon trading their canoes for horses to proceed into Choppunish or Nez Perce country and cross the Bitterroots in their homeward quest.

Their winter relations with the natives and some of the exchanges on the 1806 upriver trip were far from ideal, yet the Corps were desperate to trade for horses. On April 15 and 16, they were unsuccessful, and on the 17th Lewis sent Clark a note. The note said to double the price offered for horses and buy fewer horses until they could get farther east, where horses were more abundant and priced lower.[11]

In the early morning of the 18th, Clark was surprised by a Nez Perce man who was from "the nieghbourhood" of the juncture of the North Fork Clearwater (Choppunnish River) and the Main Fork Clearwater (Kooskooske or Kooskheikheik), where the expedition's horses had been left on October 7 of the previous year. The man gave to Clark "a Small bag of powder and ball" that had been left at the trading site of the 17th. This was the first encounter between the Corps and the Nez Perce in 1806. There would be many more than either anticipated.

Meanwhile the party struggled to achieve their trading goals and even to get along with the locals. Lewis on April 20, wrote "they are poor, dirty, proud, haughtty, inhospitable, parsimonious and faithless in every rispect, nothing but our numbers I beleive prevents their attempting to murder us at this moment."[12] There is no doubt that these folk, labeled "E-nee-sher Nation," but probably Wanapams,[13] were sharp traders, but the Americans were neither in a position nor in the mood to appreciate their method. And although Lewis (and Clark, too) used the label "poor" in describing them, Lewis did comment that "These people have yet a large quantity of dryed fish on hand yet they will not let us have any but for an exorbitant price." So really they were not so poor; rather, the Wanapams knew the value of their goods and did not want to give them away.

Clark said he used "every artifice decent & even false statements to enduce those pore devils to Sell me horses."[14] He does not say what the "false statements" were, but the natives must have suspected as much, because they would not part with their horses. Clark next offered the natives twice as much for a horse as the Corps had paid to the Salish, but still they would not budge. They had already been exposed to white traders, and Clark's meager, rusty, trail-worn goods did not much tempt them.

Lewis, meanwhile, was struggling to get upstream to join Clark and struggling, too, to hang on to the horses he had already received. He finally joined up with Clark on April 21 and, amidst many negative statements about the natives and their behavior, he referred to the Chopunnish (i.e. Nimíipuu) man, who had retrieved the shot and lead balls for Clark, as "our guide" and that "he appears to be an honest fellow. he tells us that the indians a little above will treat us with much more hospitality then those we are now with."[15]

That was the idea—to get upstream and away from this (Celilo) place. Another horse, a poor one, was acquired that evening, making travel upstream a little more viable. The price of the horse was "a triffle,"[16] and the Nez Perce "guide" loaned one of his horses for the party to pack, too.[17] The Indians seemed more interested in gambling than trading. The explorers witnessed one village challenging another in several variations of what is called "stick game," an exciting guessing game which led to one side losing all their beads and other goods to the winning village (see Chapter 1 page 17).

On April 22, finally breaking away from the camp at Celilo (on the north shore), the party was delayed by the horse of "Charbono" that tore back towards the last camp. In the mad dash, he threw his saddle and blanket, and an Indian took the blanket, hid it, and nearly provoked a major incident. Lewis sent Charbonneau, the Nez Perce guide, and "Labuish" (i.e., Francois Labiche) after the horse and gear. In the end, they got all, but the robe.

Lewis then sent Sacajawea (typically, he doesn't call her by name, but simply refers to her as "the Indian woman") ahead to tell Clark to send help. He was determined to get the robe back "or birn their houses."[18] Luckily, before the incident could develop further, "Labuish" came to

Lewis with the story of having found the blanket in an Indian lodge "his[d] behind their baggage."[19]

They proceeded on to another village and traded for one more horse. They now had 10 studs and 3 others. Their Nez Perce guide advised spending the night where they were, as it was a long way to the next village and there was no wood or food available. They took his advice, purchasing wood, dogs, and some roots and berries for sustenance. This camp was on the north shore of the Columbia, opposite and upstream a little of the mouth of the John Day River (on the Oregon shore).[20]

Next day (Wednesday, April 23), Clark overtook the same "Choponish man" that had returned the powder and shot to him at the Long Narrows on the 18th. From his entry that day it is clear that the man had a spouse with him, as did the Nez Perce man already serving as guide. This new man, the one Clark caught up with, also had "family" with him, and about 13 head of horses. The Nez Perce women both gave Clark something called "Cake of Chapellell," a small cake made from qém'es.[21] The Nez Perces camped "nearby" the Corps and that night they observed, if not participated in, the dancing of the men to the fiddle or in the Native dances held afterward.

The following day (April 24) the explorers traded off their last two canoes, small ones, for "a few strands of beads." They also "purchased three horses of the Wah-howpums," and "hired three others of the Chopunnish man,"[22] which were added to their pack string. All horses were packed, and they were out of camp by two in the afternoon. There would be no more canoe travel against an upstream current. They were well on their way now to the Nez Perce country and the Bitterroots mountain crossing.

ENDNOTES

1   See notes on spelling of Ta-Moots-Tsoo, Alcorn, *Timothy, A Nez Perce Chief*, p. 63.

2   Alcorn, *Timothy, A Nez Perce Chief*, p. 17. Alcorn writes, "It may have been an Episcopal prayer book, but not a Bible."

3   Rowena Alcorn says young Ta-Moot-Tsoo was 5, Alcorn, *Timothy, A Nez Perce Chief*, p. 17; another tribal tradition has him age 11, in October of 1805, see Peo-Peo-Tah-Likt, *Historical Sketches of the Nez Perces*, Cage #1218, p. 11.

4   *With the Nez Perces; Alice Fletcher in the Field, 1889-92*, by E.J. Gay, edited, with an introduction, by Frederick E. Hoxie and Joan T. Mark (Lincoln, NE: University of Nebraska Press, 1981), p. 148. Hereafter cited as Gay, *With the Nez Perces*.

5   *JLCE*, 5:231.

6   Gass, *Journals*, p. 134.

7   Peo-Peo-Tah-Likt, *Historical Sketches of the Nez Perces,* Cage #1218, p. 13.

8   Mostly surmised, however Peo mentions Red Grizzly Bear liking Charbonneau.

9   Caleb Carter showed a rock to his son Cecil Carter, who lived at Lewiston, Idaho. The rock was upstream from canoe camp and across the Clearwater River, and had been used for target practice by members of the Corps. The target was destroyed during the construction of the Dworshak National Fish Hatchery in 1978. The distance across the Clearwater there is approximately 150 yards.

10   Missonary Kate McBeth's informants told her that the Nez Perces held discussions about religion, McBeth, *The Nez Perces Since Lewis and Clark*, p. 27.

11   *JLCE,* vol. 7.

12   Ibid., 7:146.

13   Ibid., 7:326.

14   Ibid., 7:147.

15   Ibid., 7:153.

16   Ibid.

17   Ibid.

18   Ibid., 7:156.

19   Ibid.

20   Ibid., 7:146.

21   *Qáaws* cake, called *'ápa,* see Aoki, *Nez Perce Dictionary*, p. 973.

22   *JLCE,* 7:163.

Chapter 8

With the Walla Walla Nation

By abandoning the last of their canoes, the Lewis and Clark party were freed from the Columbia's current to push upstream on the north bank on foot and on horseback. The two Nez Perce families riding with them continued along on April 25 (the first day free of the canoes) and camped near them that night. The Nez Perce presence helped in several ways. First, the Nez Perces knew the trails, camping sites, and village locations. Secondly, they could advise the Americans regarding the Walla Walla natives. One of the Nez Perce men "pointed out" the Walla Walla chiefs at a village they entered that evening.[1]

Clark struggled with the Walla Walla name, calling them the "War-war-wa" tribe. The Walla Walla language was different from the Nez Perce, but they were both of the Sahaptin language family, with a similar structure and a great deal of shared vocabulary. The tribes frequently allied both at home and on the buffalo country and were connected by many intermarriages.[2]

The Nez Perce presence with the Americans lent credence to the notion that the white men were friends, and they were given a friendly reception. The Walla Wallas owned many horses, and both the women and the men rode "extreamely well." Despite the Indian horses' "Soar backs," they were in remarkable shape for the season. And the captains needed horses to continue upstream with their men and equipment.[3]

The next day (April 26), the Nez Perces rode along with the Lewis and Clark party all day until all encamped opposite the mouth of the Umatilla River, which entered the Columbia from the Blue Mountains to the south. The following day, one of the Nez Perces suggested that they leave the Columbia, climb a high hill, then parallel the river and descend back to the riverbank at the next Walla Walla village.

Leaving the river on the suggested trail was more direct than following the Columbia, as the river curved sharply at that point and was rimmed by high basalt bluffs. The Americans hoped to trade for more food supplies, as their own stores were running low. The route followed was difficult travel over rocky terrain, and when they got back to the river, they found the Walla Walla village empty. There was a little firewood available, however, so they decided to boil their jerky and make out the best they could. This camp was opposite the Walla Walla river that, like the Umatilla, came in from the Blue Mountains to the south.

While the Lewis and Clark party boiled their jerky, "Chief *Yel-lept*" and "six men of his nation" rode into the village. Chief Yel-lep-pit invited everyone to come upstream to where his people were encamped. Lewis and Clark accepted his invitation and, after eating, everyone continued upstream along the Columbia for about six miles. Chief Yel-lep-pit and the Walla Wallas treated their guests well. Lewis said that Chief Yel-lep-pit was "a man of much influence not only in his own nation, but also among the neighbouring tribes and nations."[4] This observation was certainly one of the leaders' most astute evaluations of Walla Walla, and most Sahaptin leadership, including that of the Nez Perce. The true leadership qualities caused influence to be felt by neighboring bands and tribes.

There were several reasons for this. One was an inherited position. Often the son of a respected leader was raised to exercise responsibility for his immediate band and the welfare of those related. This meant that a wide responsibility was accepted because everyone was related directly by blood or indirectly through marriage or adoption, which was considered just as strong as the blood relationship.

For the leadership to be effective, of course, abilities had to correspond to inherited position, or a leader's "influence" soon waned. Lewis wrote: "Yellept haranged his village in our favour intreated them to furnish us with fuel and provision and then he set an example himself by bringing us an armfull of wood and a plater of 3 roasted mullets."[5]

Here, in a nutshell, was the universal illustration of leadership, "by example." Among the Sahaptins, "chief" is a kind of poor descriptive title because tribal leaders did not order anyone around as an army captain might, but only "influenced" behavior insofar as their person and opinions were respected. Women exercised leadership, too, but this was not in the cultural experience of the whites to recognize—they were not looking for that and, as a consequence, did not see it.

Sahaptin women exercised a lot more freedom than their counterparts in white pioneer America, too, especially in spiritual and ceremonial life, but also in their property rights and the right to divorce. Roots and their products were the staff of life, more important than the salmon, and the "fields" were claimed or "owned" by the females of particular families whose *túuk'es,* or digging sticks, probed the ground, worked it free of plant competition, and allocated its harvest.[6] In pioneer America, it was unusual indeed if a widow with property did not look to remarrying in short order to protect her property. This was not the case amongst Indian women of the interior Pacific Northwest. There are many historical examples that could be cited of unmarried women of property whose rights were respected.

Nez Perce women were rarely involved in raiding and war adventures, but men might achieve status and leadership through success in war. His leadership would be recognized in wartime, but would give way to a "peace chief"—a *miyóoxat*, a strong diplomat, someone who could facilitate or settle disputes, and there was also a *wistamalwiyáat* or travel chief who made decisions at a time of village, band, or tribal travel. Sometimes several types of leadership qualities were found blended into the same individual and this may have been the case with Chief Yel-lep-pit, who undoubtedly had many relatives found amongst his neighbors, such as the Yakama, Cayuse, Umatilla, Palouse, and Nez Perce. A person of substance was always listened to by the people, especially so if the individual was an important relative.

Despite the Americans' eagerness to be on their way, they were convinced by the Walla Walla leader to remain an extra night (April 28). Chief Yel-lep-pit had invited his Yakama neighbors to come visit, to see the white men (and no doubt the black man), to hear the fiddle, and watch them dance. He was particularly convincing because he artfully brought up their promise of the previous fall to spend more time on their way back.

Since the Lewis and Clark canoes were all either burnt for firewood or traded off by this time, they could not cross to the south side of the river without help from Chief Yel-lep-pit and the Walla Wallas. Therefore, Chief Yel-lep-pit gave Clark "a very eligant white horse," and he indicated that he wanted a kettle in return. The Corps had none to spare, so instead he received Clark's "Swoard, 100 balls & powder and Some Small articles of which he appeared perfectly satisfied."[7]

Unfortunately Clark did not say if Chief Yel-lep-pit had a weapon for using the powder and balls. Maybe he had a weapon or anticipated getting one, or perhaps he merely thought to use these items in trade. Clark practiced a little medicine too. That was a harbinger of events to come as the Corps's stock of trade goods dwindled.

The morning of April 29, the wind was quiet and the waves down. Chief Yel-lep-pit did accede to helping the whites take their horses across the mighty Columbia in preparation for taking a more direct cross-country route to the Nez Perce country.

Had the white captains realized how deep the snow in the mountains was at that moment, they might have delayed for a week with no great consequence, and the Indians essentially told them so. Given their usual impatience, the captains consented to spend one extra night (the night of the 28th), and everyone seemed to enjoy the occasion. The fiddle music, the first ever heard by the natives, pleased everyone. The Yakamas, about one hundred strong, along with the Walla Wallas, combined to sing and dance for the Americans. Drums and song continued by firelight until about ten at night, and according to Lewis the Indian people "were much gratifyed with seeing some of our party join them in their dance."[8]

By the time all men and equipment were on the south bank of the Columbia and the horses gathered, the Nez Perce guide informed Lewis and Clark that it "was too late in the evening to reach an eligible place to encamp; that we could not reach any water before night"[9] Thus, they spent the night of the 29th only about a mile up the Walla Walla, a stream described by Clark as "a handsom Stream about 4½ feet deep and 50 yards wide; it's bead is composed of gravel principally with Some Sand and Mud; the banks are abrupt but not high, tho' it does not appear to overflow; the water is Clear."[10]

The Indians informed the Americans that the river came from the mountains visible to the southeast and east. This range of mountains, today named the Blue Mountains, run from northeast to southwest, and for the next few days their Nez Perce guide would lead them on an ancient route northeasterly along the flanks of the northernmost portion of the Blues, terminating near the juncture of the Snake and Clearwater rivers where they had camped on October 10 of the previous year.[11]

The night of April 29, Walla Walla Indians from a village on the south bank of the Columbia wanted to see the whites dance, but bad weather prevailed, and the dance was called off. Clark wrote that several small medals were given to "two inferior Chiefs," and each gave a "fine horse" in return. The captains answered by giving their hosts one of Lewis's pistols and several hundred rounds of ammunition.[12]

Clark mentions that the Nez Perce man had a daughter who was "in a certain Situation." She was in her moon (menstrual cycle) and had to ride a little back from the rest of the family. She could not eat nor touch "any article of a culinary nature or manly occupation." This was one of the customs of the people. Everyone has certain ways of doing things that, for whatever reasons, prove a good mode of behavior. The poor girl could not even camp at night with the family, but had to sleep a short distance away. A young girl's menstrual cycles, especially her first, were accompanied by hormonal changes and often anxieties. Native society met these changes and subsequent needs with what they considered appropriate rituals and taboos.[13]

The white horse given to Clark by Chief Yel-lep-pit was gone in the morning, and when he could not be located, the chief himself, mounted on Lewis's horse, went out to find it. Within half an hour, one of the Nez Perce men brought the horse in, and the party got underway about 11 a.m. They had to leave Reubin Field to collect Lewis's horse upon Chief Yel-lep-pit's return to the camp.

A few days with the Walla Wallas improved Lewis and Clark's impressions of those people and of the Yakamas who had visited them on the north shore village. They did not fail to notice that the women were dressed better than the previous fall; "I prosume the Suckcess of their Winters hunt has produced this change in their attere,"[14] Clark wrote. Lewis sounded a bit whimsical and touched as he wrote, "we took leave of these friendly honest people the Wollahwollahs."[15] Taking leave along with the Americans was their Nez Perce "guide" and another Nimíipuu man and his family.[16] That evening (April 30), everyone enjoyed the crackle and heat of a good wood fire, something they had missed since their camp at The Dalles.

On May 1, the party was on the trail by 7 a.m. They traveled some miles, Clark says nine, up the Touchet River, and the Nez Perce man with the family told Clark of a cut-off trail leading to the left, that he thought best to pursue. Clark could plainly see that they were on a good Indian road, relatively level with water and firewood and hesitated until he could communicate with "the guide," that is, the other Nez Perce man. He held a low opinion of the left fork and seemed "much displeased."[17] He reassured Clark that the road they were on was the best and that if they took the other they would have to remain in that spot all night so as to travel all the next day to reach water and that "there was-no wood; the other [the Nimíipuu man with his family] agreed that this was the case. we therefore did not hesitate to pursue the rout recommended by the guide."[18]

One can only wonder what route they might have followed with no Nez Perces and no discussion of optional routes. So the Nez Perce who suggested the left fork remained behind with his family, determined to travel his cut-off on the morrow. The Corps continued on with the "guide" and his family, slowly ascending the Touchet through "a pleasent looking country" until evening when they again had a comfortable camp.

Another Compliment for the Walla Wallas

That evening three young Walla Walla men came into camp from the village on the Columbia with a trap that one of the men had left behind. Lewis wrote, "this is an act of integrity rarely witnessed among indians. during our stay with them they several times found the knives of the men which had been carelessly lossed by them and returned them. I think we can justly affirm to the honor of these people that they are the most hospitable, honest, and sincere people that we have met with in our voyage."[19]

The Walla Wallas who returned the trap continued with the party until the morning of May 3, when they, along with the young Chopunnish guide, left "reather abruptly." There was no explanation, and the guide's reason for leaving abruptly with the young Walla Wallas will remain a question that can only be speculated upon. Patrick Gass reported that, on the morning of the 3rd, "our guide and the three other Indians went on ahead."[20] Sergeant John Ordway wrote that "our Indians went on this morning intending to git to the forks to day."[21]

The guide knew that the party had but to follow the Indian road to reach the first village on the Alpowai and, in the meantime, there was but little to eat with the Americans. In all likelihood, they knew they could lessen the burden on the food supply of the Corps. In the meantime, they were able to travel much faster on horseback and reach friends and family to alert the people ahead that the Americans were returning. Thus, the Nez Perce "guide," who had begun his duties at the long narrows of the Columbia, was enticed to a new adventure by his Walla Walla friends. At any rate, he had done good duty on behalf of his people. The Nez Perce wanted to meet again with the Americans, and he had guided the Americans over 200 miles back into the Nez Perce homeland.[22]

The Meeting with We-ah-koomt (Flint Necklace), the Bighorn Chief

It is likely that the young Nez Perce guide and his Walla Walla associates met this leader of the Asotin Creek band on the trail because they were headed for the Tseminicum area, where the Snake and Clearwater rivers met at the northern end of the Nez Perce Trail. We-ah-koomt, best known by his ancestral name of 'apaswahayqt, or Flint Necklace,[23] had 10 of his men with him and was headed towards the Lewis and Clark party, so it is likely that he met the departing "guide", and young Nez Perce was able to brief We-ah-koomt (Flint Necklace) on his experiences with the Corps and their approximate location. Subsequently the two groups met at or near what is now the small town of Pomeroy, Washington,[24] in a small grove of cottonwood trees.

A famous chief with many names, this man is known to history primarily as Chief Looking Glass from a small trade mirror given him by Meriwether Lewis, probably in 1806. Looking Glass by Gustavus Sohon, WSHS# 1918.114.9.51.

We-ah-koomt (Flint Necklace) was labeled "the bighorn Cheif" by the captains because he wore a shell of a bighorn ram's horn suspended by a cord from his left arm.[25] (From this point on throughout the book, he will be named as We-ah-koomt [Flint Necklace] unless otherwise noted in a quotation from the journals of the expedition members.) He was instrumental in the Corps receiving a cordial reception the year before by the various Sahaptin villagers. He had ridden his horse to the confluence of the Snake and Columbia ahead of the canoes and "was very instrumental in procuring us a hospitable and friendly reception among the natives."[26]

We-ah-koomt (Flint Necklace), the Bighorn chief and his men rode along with the captains a few miles and camped in a grove of cottonwood trees on Pataha Creek.[27] The weather was spring-spitting wet, a combination of rain, hail, and snow. Luckily there was plenty of willow, cottonwood, and thornbrush in the creek bottom, but unfortunately, they did not have much food.

Lewis wrote, "we devided the last of our dried meat at dinner when it was Consumed as well as the ballance of our Dogs nearly." We-ah-koomt (Flint Necklace), the Bighorn Chief, let them know they were now within a day of the Alpowai Creek and the Snake River. The first Nez Perce lodges encountered would be there.

With a cold wind at their backs, everyone left along Pataha Creek bottom and began the long climb through open, rocky, grass-covered slopes[28] to a high rich plain. The captains noted the richness of the soil and the proximity of timber on the mountains immediately to the south. Crossing into the headwaters of the Alpowai Creek, they began their descent and found themselves back once again on the southern bank of the Snake River.

Up the southern shore several miles they at last arrived at some Nimíipuu lodges, where they hoped to acquire food. They had been traveling over a dozen miles in rough country with nothing to eat. However, the salmon had not yet arrived, and most of the Alpowai Nez Perce were away from the village digging spring roots to tide them until the salmon arrived in earnest. With difficulty, two lean dogs were purchased along with some roots.

Upstream on the Snake from this village, the village of Ta-Moot-Tsoo, the father of young Ta-Moots-Tsoo (the future Chief Timothy), were a couple more lodges where the party stopped. To continue up the Snake on the southern shore would have brought them to an abrupt stone wall descending to the water's edge. There were alternatives: cut around the bluffs on the hilltops and on to the confluence of the Snake and Clearwater where We-ah-koomt's (Flint Necklace) people were gathered on the south shore, or cross the Snake to the north bank.

We-ah-koomt (Flint Necklace), the Bighorn Chief, wanted them to visit with his Asotin creek band which he had led as far as the confluence less than a half dozen miles upstream. This would have made it convenient for his people to see the travelers and would not have forced them far out of their way. But the captains ruled that out as it took them upstream by a more difficult route than the north bank. They could have taken the time to visit We-ah-koomt (Flint Necklace), who was merely attempting to demonstrate his village's hospitality, become better acquainted with the Americans, and hear more of their purposes. Clark said that he gave the chief a small piece of tobacco, and "he went off Satisfied"[29] but, if so, it was temporary.

Clark's gift of tobacco was recorded in his journal entry, but Lewis's gesture was not. Yet it was his gift of a small round mirror with a metal edge and eyelet for hanging that had the more significant impact. Not recorded by the captains, but repeated by some tribesmen to pioneer judge and amateur historian Elgin V. Kykendall, is the story of how Lewis presented the mirror to Ram's Horn [the Bighorn Chief] (We-ah-koomt, Flint Necklace). Lewis, as he handed the small round mirror to the chief, repeated three times the words "looking glass."

In the Nimíipuu tradition, thrice repeating a word was done only in their name-giving ceremony. The Ram's Horn [the Bighorn Chief] (We-ah-koomt, Flint Necklace) and all witnesses believed that Lewis had ordained him with a new title. To his people, he would henceforth be known as Chief Looking Glass.[30]

Chief Looking Glass (We-ah-koomt, Flint Necklace) played an important role in the negotiation of the Treaty of 1855, or Steven's Treaty with the Nez Perces. There at Walla Walla his portrait was drawn by artist Gustavus Sohon. The chief's son, sometimes known as Chief Looking Glass Jr., was famous for his participation (and death) in the War of 1877.

The captains were acting under the advice of Twisted Hair and Tetokan Askap (Tetoharsky) who were at the village. Lewis wrote that *"Te-toh, ar sky"* was "the youngest of the two chiefs" but Clark called him "Te-toh-ar-sky the oldest of the two Chiefs."[31] The two Nez Perces had helped pilot the explorers all the way to Celilo Falls and the Narrows of the Columbia the previous fall.[32] It was from Tetokan Askap (Tetoharsky) that the Corps learned that two of their best horses from the proceeding fall were gone. Toby, the Shoshone guide, and his son, who did not announce their departure or await their pay, had taken the horses on their way home.

Using three small canoes (Gass writes four canoes) from the south bank village, all the men and cargo were moved to the north shore that afternoon. The horses swam across and camp was established by nightfall (May 4). With a small amount of firewood purchased and short rations, the travelers tried to settle in. It wasn't easy. The night was "Cold and disagreeable," and the Indians crowded around the fire to the point, according to both Clark and Lewis, "we Could Scercely Cook or keep ourselves worm."[33] Gass wrote on the same date that they "appear a friendly and well disposed people."[34]

Both captains described a structure which sat apart from the main dwellings of the village. They said it appeared to be a special place exclusively for the women, and they were correct. This was a custom of the Nez Perces that females in their menses had their own lodge, and men were not allowed to approach within close proximity, "and if they have any thing to Convey to the Occupents of this little hospital they Stand at the distance of 50 or 60 paces and throw it towards them as far as they Can and retire."[35] This custom was the same that had demanded the Nez Perce girl to ride and camp apart from everyone else. (See page 114.)

And all in all, the trip from the Columbia to the Snake via the old Nez Perce Trail (now often referred to as "The Forgotten Trail") had been a pleasant learning experience. The Nimíipuu "guides" had shown them the way, along with an alternative route, following the Blue Mountain Foothills with plenty of firewood, horsefeed, and water. They had become much better acquainted with Nez Perce relatives, the Yakamas and especially Chief Yel-lep-pit of the Walla Walla Nation. On a practical level they had secured a few more good horses while also learning they had lost two to their former Shoshone guides Old Toby and his son. Significant to Nimíipuu history they accidently helped create a memorable and historic name for Flint Necklace, known henceforth, as Chief Looking Glass. They had to prepare to cross the Bitterroot Mountains. Again they would look to their Nez Perce friends for support.

ENDNOTES

1   *JLCE*, 7:165.

2   Angelo Anastasio, *The Southern Plateau: an Ecological Analysis of Intergroup Relations* (Moscow, ID: University of Idaho Laboratory of Anthropology, 1975), pp. 135, 141, 146–7. Hereafter cited as Anastasio, *The Southern Plateau*.

3   *JLCE*, 7:165.

4   Ibid., 7:174.

5   Ibid. A mullet is a sucker.

6   See Alan G. Marshall, "Unusual Gardens: The Nez Perce and Wild Horticulture on the Eastern Columbia Plateau," Chapter 9, in Dale D. Goble and Paul W. Hirt ed., *Northwest Lands, Northwest People: Readings in Environmental History* (Seattle and London: University of Washington Press, 1999).

7   *JLCE*, 7:179.

8   Ibid. Authors must mention that some of these songs may have carried religious significance. See Chad S. Hamill, *Songs of Power and Prayer in the Columbia Plateau* (Corvallis, OR: Oregon State University Press, 2012).

9   *JLCE*, 7:181.

10   Ibid., 7:184.

11   Their camp was in what is now Walla Walla County, Washington, and they would cross in succession that county, plus Columbia County, Garfield County, and Asotin County in southest Washington State. Wallula, where the Walla Walla dumps into the Columbia was also the site of Old Fort Nez Perce where the Nez Perce met missionary Henry H. Spalding (1836) to guide him into Nez Perce country over the same general route as the Nez Perce guide routed Lewis and Clark, see McBeth, *The Nez Perces Since Lewis and Clark*.

12   *JLCE*, 7:185.

13   Authors indebted to retired WSU anthropology professor Lillian Ackermann (telephone interview, October 25, 2012).

14   *JLCE*, 7:185.

15   Ibid., 7:187.

16   Ibid. Lewis refers to them as "Chopunnish."

17   Ibid., 7:195.

18   Ibid., 7:196.

19   Ibid., 7:196–7.

20   Gass, *Journals,* p. 182.

21   *JLCE*, 9:304.

22   He left upstream on the Touchet River just a few miles above where Dayton, Washington, is now located in Columbia County.

23   We-ah-koomt is known by many names. His ancestral name, 'apaswahayqt, translated means "Flint Necklace." He is also known by the names of: Chief Ram's Horn, Bighorn Chief, and Chief Looking Glass, a name "given" to him by Captain Lewis inadvertently through the naming ceremony.

24   Pomeroy is the county seat of Garfield County, Washington.

25   *JLCE*, 7:202.

26   Ibid.

27   Just a few miles from Pomeroy, WA, County seat of Garfield County, Highway 12 runs along Pataha Creek.

28 This location, known as the junction of the Three Forks Trail, is commemorated by a turnout and highway history marker on Route 12, Garfield County, Washington.

29 *JLCE*, 7:205.

30 Indian file, Asotin County Historical Society.

31 *JLCE*, 7:206–7.

32 Tetoharsky first given this name in the journals on May 4. He is mentioned, of course, many times in the journals prior to May 4, but never by name. This name was mentioned to a tribal elder, Harry Wheeler, by local historian Zoa L. Swayne, and he explained the name thusly, "Tetokan" = People and "Ahskahp" = Brothers, expressing the thought, "People are coming, They look like brothers." Swayne, *Do Them No Harm!:* pp. 321-2. The spelling would be slightly different in Aoki, *Nez Perce Dictionary*, p. 763, *tito qan,* and p. 976, *?asqap.*

33 *JLCE*, 7:206, 208.

34 Gass, *Journals,* p. 183.

35 *JLCE,* 7:208.

Chapter 9

On the Clearwater's
North Bank Trail

At 7 a.m. on May 5, 1806, the party "set out." Their path was a stony one, with the Snake River on their right and 2000-foot high, open-sloped and basalt-studded hills on their left. They had only traveled about four miles when they arrived at their camp of October 10, 1805, and a mile beyond that, the mouth of the "Kooskooske," the Clearwater River. They could look south, up the Snake River, and they could look up the Clearwater, east toward the sunrise, towards the United States and home. The route they were following was selected because it would get them to Twisted Hair and their horses by the fastest and most direct trail. Still, travel was slow, as many of the men were still walking.

The trail took them by many lodges of Nez Perce, too, and the party rested and visited while Clark practiced his medical skills, but it was all necessary. Some of the Nez Perces had been treated by Clark in the fall of '05 and believed their health restored. Clark was not a doctor, but he had some medicinal skills and a kit. With expedition trade goods depleted, Clark's treatments became a means of exchange, as well as courtesy.

"Eyewater" was a success with many patients, and Clark, observing the esteem with which he was held, tried to make the most of it. "[I]n our present Situation I think it pardonable to continue this deception for they will not give us any provision without Compensation in merchendize and our Stock is now reduced to a mear handfull.   we take Care to give them no article which Can possibly injure them."[1]

One patient gave Clark "a very eligant Gray mare" for a treatment of eyewater. This was at a mat lodge along the north shore trail, one of several they passed that day. The captains had entered the lodge and attempted to trade for some food, but the villagers had none to trade. After they smoked and were about to leave, a man they supposed to be a headman brought forth the mare and proposed the trade. Another good horse, all the better to get home.

And then more good luck. The Nez Perce "guide," the very same young man who had helped the expedition to and through the Walla Walla country, was at the lodge with his family, along with Clark's horse from the previous fall. Clark's horse had somehow become detached from the main herd upstream and had been "in this neighborhood for some weeks."[2]

That was two fresh horses in one day. Continuing on, they came to a place the Nez Perces call Ciwíʹikite, a nice flat along the Clearwater. There was a mat lodge and here the expedition called a halt, traded for "2 dogs and a Small quantity of bread and dryed roots."[3] This was about 1 o'clock, and they decided to eat.

The Puppy-Throwing Incident

Meriwether Lewis on May 5, in the afternoon: "while at dinner an indian fellow verry impertinently threw a poor half starved puppy nearly into my plait by way of derision for our eating dogs and laughed very heartily at his own impertinence; I was so provoked at his insolence that I caught the puppy and threw it with great violence at him and struk him in the breast and face, siezed my tommahawk and shewed him by signs if he repeated his insolence I would tommahawk him, the fellow withdrew, apparently much mortifyed and I continued my repast on dog without further molestation."

It is amazing how the same event is seen differently by different people expressing a different point of view. In 1903, an old Nimíipuu man "Pakaowna" told Alex Pinkham,[4] then a young boy, of the puppy episode at Ciwíʹikite, the flat along the Clearwater River, just downstream from Coyote gulch.[5]

> The *sooyáapoo mim'yóoχat* (white man leader) called Lewis was a dog eater, unlike the other one called Clark. They were coming up the river in the time called *'apa'áal*, the time when *qáaws* bread or *'ápa* is made, now named the month of May. They were all the time looking for *hipt* or food and they traded for our dogs and horses to have something to eat. Sometimes we ate horse with them to be polite and good to them. *Ayeaa!* We never ate dogs with them! We never ate dogs because they helped us while tracking and hunting. Like the horse, you always watch the ears and which way they look when traveling because it might mean danger is close or game is near.
> Peo-Peo-Ta-Likht's (Bird Alighting) grandmother[6] who lived at Ciwíʹikite[7] was talked into trading a dog to Lewis, but she gave

it up reluctantly. She received ribbon and other small items in trade, but later Chief Red Grizzly Bear, her relative, found them to be cheap. If Lewis would have left with the puppy, perhaps what happened next would have been avoided, but he did not leave, he killed the puppy and put it over the coals in a pot. The grandmother's daughter, a little girl, got upset because she saw her playmate being devoured. Another relative, a young man disgusted with the dog eating, took up the little girl's cause and threw another *yú'c ciq'áamqal* (pitiable dog) directly at Lewis. This is not play with Lewis, he picks up the puppy, then throws it, hitting the young man in the chest. Then Lewis picks up the tomahawk and motions to the young man he just might kill him. The young man retreats quickly after trying to take up the cause of the young girl. Can't make fun with these *sooyáapoo!* Their minds don't work right sometimes.[8]

After the meal, this village was abandoned by the eastbound travelers, and the tribal folk were probably glad to see them leave. The Americans did not have much in the way of trade goods. They were heavily armed and out of food, and the puppy lunch episode had to have left a "bad taste." One wonders what Lewis was thinking. Perhaps he was incensed that he was being treated as if he were an uncivilized dog-eater by someone he regarded as a mere "savage." Was he ready to begin a war with the Nez Perces over this perceived insult? Was he seriously going to strike the young man with a steel tomahawk and perhaps begin a general melee? All Nez Perces were not of the same mind that these white men should be tolerated and they and their message embraced.

Four more miles along the north bank trail took them past the Gass canoe wreck site of October 8, and a half-mile upstream from that brought them to another village. This one was at the mouth of Potlatch Creek, which the Americans named Colter's Creek. Here the captains described the village as consisting of two long houses: one had eight families in it and "the other was much the largest we have yet seen. it is 156 feet long and about 15 feet wide built of mats and straw, in the form of the roof of a house haveing a number of Small dores on each Side, is closed at the ends and without divisions in the intermediate Space. [In] This lodge at least 30 families."[9]

A long house. Nez Perce National Historical Park, NEPE-HI-1677.

The headman of the village was "Neesh-ne-park-ke-ook" in Clark's writing. There is no "r" in *Nimipuutímt,* the Nez Perce language, so the inclusion of the "r" is amiss. The translation of "Cut Nose" was correct. His nose was scarred from war, and it was an earned name.

How Cut Nose Received His Name

by Alex Pinkham, father of Allen V. Pinkham

Cut Nose and a few other fighting men went south, to the Country of the *Tiwélqe* [enemy to be fought] also known as Shoshone-Bannock people, seeking retribution for killing of Nez Perce people which occurred earlier. We cannot remember why the killing started because the first killing happened so long ago. The fighting group met the *Tiwélqe* on the trail and challenged each other to have a war. As they engaged in warfare, Cut Nose and a *Tiwélqe* fought with lances around a large chest-high stone. Cut Nose suffered a lance cut across his nose, but he soon felled his foe and the Nimíipuu came away victorious.

When the fight group returned to Yaxtoin [village at the mouth of Potlatch Creek], a messenger was sent ahead to tell the people to gather so the story could be told and if mourning had to be done for those lost. My father [the teller of this story was grandson of Chief Cut Nose] rode his horse around the village with the others of the expedition, sang a victory song, and each told of the great adventure and. what they did in the fighting.

From that day forward my grandfather would be known as Neshne Qine (Nusnu-ee-pah-kee-oo-keen) [in later years, Cut Nose the older]. A name well earned and known to all Nimipuu! *Wáaqo' kaloʼ!* (That's all)[10]

There was a Shoshone-speaking man living in this village and, through him speaking to Sacajawea, Lewis and Clark learned how Cut Nose received his name. But the Americans were not impressed: "he may be a great Chief but his Countinance has but little inteligence and his influence among his people appears very inconsiderable."[11] Despite their belief in Cut Nose's "little intelligence" and his "inconsiderable" influence, Lewis and Clark still gave him "a Medal of the Small Size with a likeness of the President."

Their rationale remains a mystery. Perhaps they were just expressing their sarcasm but, upon second counsel, showed their respect by presenting the medal. Something surefire to cheer a fella up. Cut Nose's apparent lack of influence, from the captain's point of view, may be explained by his role primarily as a war leader; this not being a time of war, he may have been "out of office" until circumstances required his leadership.

It also was a time of gathering. The *qáaws* root was the most important food source during May. The elderly women, who were the best and most experienced at gathering and preparing this important staple, were probably the most influential village leaders at this time, a reality unlikely recognized by these captains from a society dominated by male leadership.[12] Females were not eligible for their prestigious medals.

It was upsetting the way this large band of mostly men imposed themselves upon villages, especially at this time of year. Large parties of travelers did come through the country, but it was at the height of summer, long after the first roots were already harvested, after the first Chinook salmon had appeared in the river, and after much successful hunting. It was maybe even after the return of tribal composite groups from the Buffalo country with scores, if not hundreds, of pack ponies heavy laden with dried buffalo. Then a village could show real hospitality.

Even if a small group, a half dozen or a dozen showed up, that would have been easier to cope with. The people of Yaxtoin, the village at the mouth of Potlatch Creek, were still reeling from an extremely difficult winter. Many people were ill, and even the dogs were pronounced by the captains as "unfit to eat." Upstream folks had cut down pine trees to secure the small, but rich, nuts from the cones and stripped the bark to get at the sweet inner bark on both pine and cottonwood. Also, people had resorted to eating the black moss off the north side of the Yellow Pine, which is baked much like *qém'es* and then reconstituted with water into a kind of mush called *hóopop*. It could be consumed at any time and was best known as a survival food. The sheer size of the Lewis and Clark expedition outnumbered many of the small groups they encountered along the river and surely stressed the available resources at this time of year.

One old man in the village told the others that the men of the expedition were bad men "and had Come most probably in order to kill them."[13] Who this man was and what motivated him is unknown. Perhaps he was one of those elders who had heard stories of bad white people from the east or maybe he was the uncle of the young man Lewis threatened with the tomahawk.

Lewis and Clark responded to the old man's words with important words of their own, which they were able to deliver, albeit through a chain of translation, in the language of the Nez Perce as spoken by a Snake (Shoshone) Indian. This man was a prisoner of war held by the village and who spoke Nez Perce. Sacajawea, of course, could converse in the Shoshone language with him. So Lewis and Clark were able to use that skill, in conjunction with Charbonneau and a French speaker, to make translations from English through the chain to Nez Perce and back again. This was a wonderful opportunity to counteract the voice of the old man.[14]

The captains did not record their message but they delivered it through The Big Horn Chief, who rejoined them at this camp. Sergeant John Ordway wrote that they stated "what our business was and that our tradors would come about the head of the Missourie and trade with them for furs &C.—"[15] Clark wrote that "they appeared well satisfied with what we said to them."[16] He was probably over-optimistic and merely saw native politeness as acquiescence.

A man came to Clark with a proposal: fix the abscess on his wife's back and, next day, he would bring him a horse. This was one of several "applications" they had to help the sick. The travelers were both tired and hungry, and Clark decided to take the man at his word. It was time for the "Dr. Clark Traveling Medicine Show" to spring into action. First, he explained that the case was hopeless. But the applicant wanted to hope, trusted the medicine of the white stranger, and persisted in seeking Clark's help. Clark lanced the abscess on the woman's back and dressed the wound.[17] Now others lined up for treatment, but all were put off until the next day.

On May 6, "the husband of the sick woman was as good as his word, he produced us a young horse in tolerable order which we immediately killed and butchered."[18] Everyone was more "accomodating" this A.M.;

the men received another horse for Dr. Clark's medical help and also were able to purchase some root bread. Lewis traded horses with "We-ark'-koomt," the Big Horn Chief, who gave Lewis a sorrel, "an eligant strong active and well broke horse." In return, the Big Horn received Lewis's horse and "a small flag."

Three "Skeets-so-mish," Coeur d'Alenes, visited with the captains and gave them geographical information. Clark was busy "administering eye-water to a croud of applicants,"[19] for which they received more food, "much to the comfort of all the party."[20]

Twisted Hair's brother, named Al-We-Yas, was now in camp[21] and, along with the Big Horn, was ready to travel upstream after all the horses were collected and packed, which did not occur until about 3 p.m. Al-We-Yas, a village leader in his own right, may have been at the Yaxtoin camp representing his own and his brother's interests. There was a problem with the *sooyáapoo* horse herd that had been entrusted to Twisted Hair and Al-We-Yas in the fall of 1805. Cut Nose was jealous of the honor that had been conferred on the brothers and the material rewards they were to receive for their service. If Al-We-Yas were present with the whites at the same time as Cut Nose, he might be able to thwart all efforts to discredit their custodianship of the *sooyáapoo* horses.

Leaving Yaxtoin on the north side of the Clearwater, the expedition climbed a ridge where they could see up Colter's Creek (Potlatch Creek) on their left and the Kooskooske (Clearwater) on their right. Then they turned to their right and paralleled the Clearwater for several miles. Four miles further upstream, they descended back to the river's edge at a "Lodge of 3 families." Here they could get no supplies, so they continued upstream another five miles to their camping location near another mat lodge, this one large enough for six families.[22]

Chief Weah-Koo-Nut,[23] accompanied by 10 of his people, spent the night at the Pine Creek camp (called Yatoin teméeyenwees or "Coyote's hot bath location"), and left the next morning, May 7. Al-We-Yas, the brother of Twisted Hair, then took over guide duties. The party advanced upstream four miles, where they came to another lodge of Nez Perces, this one with six families. One of the men brought two canisters of powder forward. He said his dog had dug them up and he was returning them. These were the two that had been buried the previous fall near present-day Lenore, and the captains were naturally happy to see their powder returned once again. For the man's honesty, they gave him "a fire steel by way of compensation."[24]

Al-We-Yas told the captains that the trail upstream was easier on the south side of the river and that there was more game, as well. Consequently, they ordered the horses unpacked in preparation for swimming them to the south bank of the Clearwater.

They used one canoe only and got all baggage and horses across in four hours. They ate and then continued upstream, now on the south bank. After a couple of miles, they began climbing the mountain on their right until they were on top, where they found it "perfectly level and partially Covered with the long leafed pine. The Soil is a dark rich loam, thickly Covered with grass and herbatious plants which afford a delightfull pasture for horses."[25]

Chief Cut Nose caught up with them, accompanied by the Shoshone who had translated at the Yaxtoin village at the mouth of Colter's Creek (modern Potlatch Creek), and both rode with Al-We-Yas and the Corps members for several miles. Cut Nose and the Shoshone then turned off to the right, to visit some of the chief's people nearby who were gathering roots.[26] The Nez Perce women were digging *qáaws* root to make their *'ápa* (bread). There were many roots and many root gathering areas, each reserved for use by different villages and according to particular family domination and custom.[27]

Al-We-Yas led the whites across the top of the ridge from whence they could plainly see the Bitterroot Mountains to the east, covered in snow. It was here that the Americans were informed that "the Snow is yet So deep on the Mountains" that they would be unable to cross for another full moon. They descended a long steep trail into Big Canyon, where they found an abandoned village. Chief Cut Nose and the unnamed Shoshone joined them again, and the Corps camped for the night. The captains called this creek "Musquetoe Creek in consequence of being infested with Sworms of those insects."[28] They did observe many deer tracks in the area and ordered hunters to turn out early for deer. Everyone was eager for "the fat plains of the Missouri, and thence to our native homes," as Clark stated in his entry for May 7.

The deep snow was going to hold them back, there was no doubt about that. In the meantime, they made their obligatory observations regarding the people with whom they were relying on for guidance, the people whose home they were currently occupying, the Nimíipuu. Of course, their concept of who was in what tribe, or what on the west side of the Rockies constituted tribalship, was somewhat fuzzy. There was some justification for the captains' lumping together everyone from the Kooskooske River down to Celilo Falls as Chopunnish because, with few exceptions, everyone they had met spoke some version of the Sahaptin language. One exception was the Coeur d'Alenes who had visited the Yaxtoin village.

Lewis and Clark wrote of the several ways in which the dead were buried and noted the nearly universal practice of sacrificing the personal possessions of the deceased, even their horses, the bones of which were scattered about the gravesites. Sometimes the dead were wrapped in robes, bound up and placed on boards in rock slides; several bodies might be interred one on top the other, with rock stacked on top and perhaps a canoe over the top or wooden stakes protruding between the rocks to discourage wild animals from desecrating the remains. These observations were all in response to a list of questions they received in advance of the journey.[29]

Clark wrote, too, of the hunting techniques used by some of the Nez Perces which included the use of "Stocking heads" by which he meant "stalking." These were the heads of deer, skinned out and utilized with small sticks inside to mimic the feeding and looking about of the deer. In this way, hunters could attract deer or approach deer by deceiving them with the stalking heads until the hunters could make their shot. Their favorite hunting method, however, was to hunt while mounted when they could find game in the country through which they could ride. Included in his entry for May 7, Clark wrote, "The orniments worn by the Chopunnish are, in their nose a Single Shell of, Wampom, the pirl & beeds are Suspended from the ears. beads are worn arround their wrists, neck and over their Sholders crosswise in the form of a double Sash-."

This business of nose piercing was not something the Nez Perces typically did. The captains were catching up in their journals, going over much of their recent past "downstream." For example, Lewis wrote his entry on May 6 while he encamped on the Clearwater River, but discussed the renaming of "Clark's river" as the "To-wannahiooks river."[30] There are other examples that could be cited. The Sahaptin speakers who, as a people, pierced their noses were down on the Columbia, near Celilo. Clark wrote on October 22, 1805, that all pierce their noses, "and the men when Dressed ware a long taper'd piece of Shell or beed put through the nose."[31] Neither Ordway nor Gass make any mention of the Chopunnish of the Clearwater or Snake haveing pierced noses. This is because it was not the custom of the Nimíipuu to pierce the nose, although it was doubtless the habit of a few to follow the fashion of the downstream people.[32]

Again, the name was a reference used by the Indians of the upper Missouri to designate the Natives generally west of the Rocky Mountains. They used the same gestures in their sign language to refer to all people west of the Continental Divide. Perhaps the captains had a preconception that the Nimíipuu pierced their noses and, therefore, they "discovered" that the custom existed among the Nimíipuu, even though it would have been a rare individual who observed the practice.

Collars of bear claws were common for the men, but the most important article of dress, the one "on which they appear to bestow most pains and orniments is a kind of collar or brestplate; this is most Commonly a Strip of otter skins of about Six inches Wide taken out of the Center of the Skin it's whole length including the head. this is dressed with the hair on, this is tied around the neck & hangs in front of the body the tail frequently reaching below their knees; on this Skin in front is attatched pieces of pirl, beeds, wampom, pices of red cloth and in Short whatever they conceive most valuable or ornamental—."[33] Every item mentioned as attached to the otter skin came from a long distance off. They were imports and showed connection to distant lands and peoples.

The morning of May 8, the hunters were out early, and those who remained in camp waited for their return. The camp was in a narrow bottom, and it was a long, rocky, open, and steep hillside that the exploring party faced. They did not get anxious this morning because they had seen the pure white of the high country, and there was obviously no need to rush. The hunters returned with deer. Another deer was wounded near camp, and Lewis's dog, Seaman, caught it and killed it. The whites gave Chief Cut Nose and some of his people with him "some venison, horsebeef, the entrels of the four deer, and four fawns taken from two of the does that were killed."

Lewis noted that the "fawns were boiled and consumed hair hide and entrals." They ate the entrails of the adult deer, too; this is called *qo'ópas* or *pilpil'úus*.[34] On this occasion, they even ate some of the horsebeef given them, Lewis observed. But he added, "tho' they will in most instances suffer extreem hunger before they will kill their horses for that purpose, this seems reather to proceede from an attatchment to this animal, than a dislike to it's flesh for I observe many of them eat very heartily of the horsebeef which we give them."[35]

Al-We-Yas and Cut Nose then gave the captains a sketch "of the principall watercourses West of the Rocky Mountains," a map subsequently known as the Cut Nose map, probably because Lewis knew Al-We-Yas only as Twisted Hair's brother.[36]

Lewis wrote "the relation of the twisted hair left us," and then everyone else, including Cut Nose "and sundry other indians," began, at half after 3 p.m., the long arduous climb out of the canyon. It is approximately 1700 feet difference in elevation between the campsite at the bottom and the top of the ridge in less than 2 miles horizontal. Ordway called it a "high hill," and Gass pronounced it "a very high hill." Welcome again to Nez Perce country.

The young Shoshone with Cut Nose was upset that he did not get all the deer meat he wanted and refused to translate through Sacajawea or to talk at all. This made it tough on the captains to understand the problem with Twisted Hair, for when they met him and six of his men, on top of the ridge, he received the whites "very cooly an occurrence as unexpected as it was unaccountable to us."[37]

Twisted Hair and Cut Nose Squabble

Chief Twisted Hair "began to speak with a loud voice and in an angry manner." Then it was the turn of Chief Cut Nose, who answered in kind. This continued for 20 minutes while the members of the Lewis and Clark expedition were standing around, hanging onto their pack horses, wondering what was going to happen next. The entire situation called for some resolution, and the captains did a wise thing in this situation.

They informed the chiefs that they were going to move on to the next campground. Lewis explained that they made this move to help put an end to the dispute, "as well as to releive our horses from the embarasment of their loads."[38] There are reasons to do things in particular ways. When running rapids, you should stop and scout. When packing horses or mules, you don't leave them standing around with their loads on for no good reason.

The party moved forward on the trail about two miles, where they came to a small creek dumping into the canyon on their right. They set up camp and the two factions, that of Chief Twisted Hair and that of Chief Cut Nose, also set up camp, each separated a little from the other. With a series of conferences, held first with one chief and then the other, the facts emerged.

Cut Nose had been away at war when Lewis and Clark traveled through in 1805 and, when he returned, he heard all about Lewis and Clark and Twisted Hair's involvement with them, including the custodianship of the horse herd. Cut Nose did not like the way the horses were being taken care of. That was his primary complaint. The saddles that had been cached near canoe camp had been exposed by high water and, although they were moved to higher ground, the young men of the Twisted Hair band had used some of the equipment and had ridden the Lewis and Clark horses excessively. Verbally attacked again and again by the Cut Nose faction, Twisted Hair had more or less relinquished close supervision of the herd and, although the Indians from the different villages knew the location of the horses, they were widely scattered.

Lewis and Clark had been directed to try to effect peace between the tribes; now they were struggling to produce peace within a single tribe. And they needed to facilitate a settlement in order to get their horses and saddles back and prepare for the hazards and hardships of the Bitterroot Mountain crossing. They needed the help of the young Shoshone, but he was angry for other reasons and refused to help. He said it was the between the Chiefs, and "he had no business with it." Everyone was in "ill humour," according to Lewis's journal.[39]

Fortunately, after about an hour, "Drewyer" Drouillard, the half-blood Shawnee hunter, arrived in camp, and the captains had him go to Twisted Hair with a pipe to smoke with him and seek an explanation through sign language. They directed Drouillard to invite Twisted Hair to come to their camp for a smoke. This got things moving in the right direction. Twisted Hair told his side of the story, how he had been harassed by both Cut Nose and Chief Tun-na-che-moo-toolt (the Broken Arm), who lived in Kamiah Valley up the road they were presently on. He said, too, that he had re-cached the saddles and would send young men to collect and deliver the horses the next day.

This satisfied the captains, who assured Twisted Hair that, when the horses and equipment were delivered they would honor their promise of two rifles and ammunition. Next, having soothed the anger and discontentment of Twisted Hair, Drouillard delivered a pipe and invitation to Chief Cut Nose to come and smoke with the captains and Twisted Hair. Twisted Hair did come to the meeting. There Cut Nose denounced Twisted Hair as wearing "two faces." He reiterated to the captains that both he and the great Chief Tun-na-che-moo-toolt (the Broken Arm) had forbidden Twisted Hair's people the use of the horses because they were being injured.

The Twisted Hair sat and listened to all this. He had already told the captains about the same thing. Maybe the captains were right when they confided to their journals that it was probably over "jelousy."[40]

Twisted Hair wanted the captains to visit him in his lodge, which was a little distance further along the trail on which they were camped. If they would agree to delay there, he would produce what horses he could. The Americans decided to visit Twisted Hair's lodge as he requested and delay there one day on their journey to Chief Tun-na-che-moo-toolt's (the Broken Arm) village, about half a day's ride beyond Twisted Hair's camp. Cut Nose then informed Lewis and Clark that Chief Tun-na-che-moo-toolt (the Broken Arm) had heard of their condition and had sent his son and others with food. Unfortunately, his son had gone by a different trail and missed them. More smoking and general conversation commenced until 10 p.m. when all retired.

At the camp of Twisted Hair

The Americans had their horses packed by about nine in the morning of May 9, and were ready to proceed. Hunters had been sent out with the instructions to meet at Twisted Hair's camp. Twenty-seven-year-old Alexander Hamilton Willard accompanied elderly Chief Twisted Hair off the ridge's steep, timbered, north slope to the canoe camp of October last to retrieve the saddles. Several young Nez Perces were sent off to different locales to round up the horses. Everyone else traveled leisurely, some by foot, others on horseback, about six miles across a table-top ridge covered with a rich topsoil. They soon arrived at Twisted Hair's lodge erected beside a small, lovely rivulet that fell off into a branch of Mosquito Creek.[41]

Clark described the lodges—there were only two—as the "usial form of mats and Straw. The largest and principal Lodge is Calculated for 2 fires only." However, en route he observed the beauty of the country and wrote of it in his journal. Lewis, too, was looking critically at everything and liked what he saw: "a good soil not remarkably stony," for one thing, and there was timber scattered about so firewood and building material would be no problem. Lewis wrote:

> This country would form an extensive settlement; the climate appears quite as mild as that of similar latitude on the Atlantic coast if not more so and it cannot be otherwise than healthy; it possesses a fine dry pure air. the grass and many plants are now upwards of knee high. I have no doubt but this tract of country if cultivated would produce in great abundance every article essentially necessary to the comfort and subsistence of civilized man. to it's present inhabitants nature seems to have dealt with a liberal hand, for she has distributed a great variety of esculent plants over the face of the country furnish them a plentifull store of provision; these are acquired with but little toil, and when prepared after the method of the natives afford not only a nutricious but an agreeable food.[42]

"Hey guys, you know all those statues and signs of Lewis and Clark pointing? You know what they're saying don't you? They're saying, 'I'll take that land, and that land, etc.'" I tell him, "Good joke Cecil." He replies, "That's no joke!" Photo by Steven Evans.

No one had invented the term "Manifest Destiny" in 1806, but Lewis's statement gives no small hint at the prominent ideas later crystallized into an ideology. Probably no one could imagine how little time would pass before the roots gathered by the red people had to give way to the settlers' wheat and pigs. The children of the people helping Lewis and Clark would see it. If the Americans were not an immediate threat, Lewis and Clark's presence represented a threat to the future of the lifeways of the Nimíipuu, as the old man at Yaxtoin village had warned.

While this was a real crisis of the future and as yet largely unseen in 1806, there was a well known and immediate crisis that demanded action. Ancient enemies in the upper Missouri possessed firearms, and to defend themselves the Nimíipuu required new weapons and allies. Good relations with these Americans seemed to be the key component to acquiring both.

Several new tribesmen joined the camp at Twisted Hair's village that evening. They were from the "commearp" creek (Lawyer's Creek) canyon village of Chief Tun-na-che-moo-toolt, (the Broken Arm).[43] That night the wind came up from the southwest blowing cold. Rain began, followed by hail, and then snow. Cut Nose moved in with Twisted Hair, and Lewis wrote that "several indians slept about us."[44]

It snowed all that night until, by 6:30 the next morning, eight inches lay on the ground. There were only roots for a hasty breakfast, and then all proceeded south and east through rolling prairie. They came to a deep chasm and began their descent. As they descended the snow became less and less, but they were on steep slopes and moving among both rocks and mud.

Willard, two boys, and Chief Twisted Hair had returned with 21 of the expedition's horses, mostly in good shape, but a few with sore backs and some few in very low order from being ridden too hard (as Twisted Hair's detractors had claimed). The horses struggled to keep their footing as they walked, then leaned back on their haunches and slid down the slopes of "Commearp Creek" canyon.[45] Lewis estimated the height of the canyon wall at 600 feet, but Clark was closer in his estimate of 800 feet, but the real depth of the canyon at this location is approximately 1,300 feet.

ENDNOTES

1   *JLCE*, 7:209–10.

2   Ibid., 7:210.

3   Ibid., 7:211.

4   Alex Pinkham, 1895–1975, father of one of the co-authors, Allen V. Pinkham.

5   This is the opposite bank and a little downstream of Spalding, Idaho, the site of the Nez Perce National Historical Park Headquarters.

6   Born about 1851, he was a warrior of the 1877 war and died in 1935. There is another version of this story that claims the puppy was purchased in 1805, as the explorers traveled down the Clearwater. This story, too, included a relative of

Chief Peo-Peo-Tah-Likt (Bird Alighting) whose version of the story was written down as he told it in 1935, the year he died. See Swayne, *Do Them No Harm!*, pp. 89–90.

7   Ciwi kite, Coyote Gulch, near Lewiston, Idaho. Aoki, *Nez Perce Dictionary*, p. 41.

8   Story told by Pakaowna to Alex Pinkham.

9   *JLCE*, 7:217.

10 This derived from manuscript prepared by Allen V. Pinkham from his father Alex Pinkham, and published as Chapter 2 in Part 2 of Alvin M. Josephy, Jr., and Marc Jaffe, *Lewis and Clark Through Indian Eyes* (Alfred A. Knopf, 2006), pp. 138–61.

11 *JLCE*, 7:213.

12 This is not to say that women or some woman exercised political leadership of the village. However, the gathering and preparation of the roots and the first roots ceremony, one of the most important of tribal ceremonies, was the realm of the women and the political leadership of the village, whomever that might be, had to confer with, plan with, and show due deference to these women, the matrons who led in all activities related to roots. See Lillian Ackerman, *A Necessary Balance: Gender and Power Among the Indians of the Columbia River* (University of Oklahoma Press, 2003), p. 72, for a thorough discussion of the importance of the First Roots Ceremony.

13 *JLCE*, 7:214.

14 The languages were Nez Perce, Shoshone, Hidatsa, French, and English. see *JLCE*, 9:306.

15 *JLCE*, 9:305.

16 Ibid., 7:214.

17 Ibid., 7:213.

18 Ibid., 7:215.

19 Ibid.

20 Ibid.

21 The Journals do not name him, but his name is offered by Ms. Mylie Lawyer of Lapwai, Idaho, she is the great-great grandaughter of Twisted Hair, the name is written, too, in Swayne's *Do Them No Harm!*, p. 336.

22 This camping location is not agreed upon by scholars. Ralph Space, local historian, *The Lolo Trail: A History of Events Connected with the Lolo Trail Since Lewis and Clark* (Lewiston, Idaho: Printcraft Printing, 1970), p. 25, favors the mouth of Pine Creek. Hereafter cited as Space, *The Lolo Trail*. Martin Plamondon II, in his *Lewis and Clark Trail Maps: A Cartographic Reconstruction,* Volume II, p. 184, also favors the Pine Creek location. So do the authors of this work.

23 Spelling following suggestion of Space, *The Lolo Trail,* p. 25, and his recognition of no "r" in the Nez Perce language and the captains propensity to use "r" for the "ah" sound.

24 *JLCE,* 7:220.

25 Ibid., 7:222–3. They were on Angel Ridge, which separates Jack Creek from Big Canyon Creek.

26 Ibid., 7:223.

27 Ackermann, "Marital Instability and Juvenile Delinquency," pp. 73:3, 595, 598. Alan G. Marshall, "9/Unusual Gardens, the Nez Perce and Wild Horticulture on the Eastern Columbia Plateau," p. 181, in Dale D. Goble and Paul W. Hirt, *Northwest Lands, Northwest Peoples: Readings in Environmental History* (Seattle and London: University of Washington Press, 1999).

28 *JLCE,* 7:223. They were camped either at or very near the small hamlet of Peck, Idaho, in Nez Perce County.

29 See Donald Jackson, ed., *Letters of the Lewis and Clark Expedition, with Related Documents, 1783-1854,* 2 vols. 2nd Ed., (Urbana and Chicago, 1978), p. 158. Hereafter cited as Jackson, *Letters.*

30 *JLCE,* 7:216.

31 Ibid., 5:318.

32 Cecil Carter, quoting his father Caleb Carter and his *piláqa'* (mother's father), Charlie Amera.

33 *JLCE,* 7:224.

34 Aoki, *Nez Perce Dictionary,* pp. 539, 596.

35 *JLCE,* 7:227.

36 This map is reproduced in Gilman, *Lewis and Clark: Across the Divide,* p. 144.

37 *JLCE,* 7:228.

38 Ibid.

39 Ibid.

40 Ibid., 7:232.

41 This is today's Little Canyon Creek, which empties into Big Canyon Creek, called Mosquito Creek by Lewis and Clark. Their camp of May 9, 1806, is in Clearwater County, Idaho, near the boundary with Lewis County on Central Ridge.

42 *JLCE,* 7:234.

43 This man, son of Chief Red Grizzly Bear, was also known by the name of Black or Speaking Eagle, Kate McBeth, quoting elder Billy Williams in McBeth, *The Nez Perces Since Lewis and Clark,* p. 30.

44 *JLCE,* 7:235.

45 Commearp is a corruption of Kamiah. The creek today is called Lawyer's Creek, and the valley near the mouth of the Creek, Kamiah Valley, setting of the small hamlet of Kamiah, Idaho, in both Lewis and Idaho Counties.

Chapter 10

The Grand Council

The son of Chief Tun-na-che-moo-toolt (the Broken Arm) and some of his companions, who had spent the night at the Twisted Hair camp, led the way down the steep side hill, and they arrived at the canyon bottom in the village of Chief Tun-na-che-moo-toolt, at about four in the afternoon. Everyone lived in one lodge, a mat lodge, or *tok'ó'niit* [1] This one was about 150 feet long and had 24 fires down the center. The captains, ever mindful of their military positions, estimated that Chief Tun-na-che-moo-toolt's band "could raise 100 fighting men." [2]

The captains and their men must have felt heartened to see an American flag flying from a pole placed in the ground in front of the *tok'ó'niit* (mat lodge). It was the one they had left for Chief Tun-na-che-moo-toolt the previous fall. The chief met Clark, who was in the lead, at the base of the flagpole and conducted him to a spot a short distance away near the creek where he directed Clark to stop. When Lewis came up, the Americans sat down with Chief Tun-na-che-moo-toolt and other leading men, and all smoked while the captains communicated their need for provisions. The chief had "about 2 bushels of quawmash 4 Cakes of bread made of roots and a dried fish." [3]

Lewis and Clark explained to the chief that their men were not used to the roots, and they desired to trade a good, but worn, horse for a young one for fresh meat, but Lewis reported that "the hospitality of the cheif revolted at the aydea of an exchange, he told us that his young men had a great abundance of young horses and if we wished to eat them we should be furnished with as many as we wanted." The Nimíipuu brought a couple of colts forward, and one was killed immediately and prepared for consumption.

The women were pounding roots into flour between stones; the sound reminded the Americans of a nail factory. [4] Some of the women erected a buffalo hide tipi, and the chief invited the captains to use it for their residence as long as they remained in the area. The Nez Perce tipi was known by several names: *coqóycoqoy* was one, another was *walíim'niit*. [5]

The tipi was roomy and easily packed on horseback. The Nimíipuu used it often for visiting in their own region and exclusively on their plains buffalo hunts. With a small fire, it could be kept warm in cold weather and cool in summer with the sides lifted to create shade and a draft. On the chilly afternoon of May 10th, the fire inside the shelter provided for the visitors felt just right, and a supply of fuel was provided. The Nez Perces seemed ready to take excellent care of their guests.

Chief Red Grizzly Bear rode into camp with 50 warriors, all mounted on "eligant horses. he had come on a visit to us from his village which is situated about six miles distant near the [Clearwater] river," wrote Lewis. Lewis did not know, was not told, or did not understand that Chief Red Grizzly Bear, really Xaxaac 'ilpilp (Red Grizzly Bear), was the father of Chief Tun-na-che-moo-toolt. He dismounted and joined the smoking circle inside the lodge while "his retinue continued on horseback at a little distance."[6]

Everyone was warm, their stomachs full, the conversation good, and the captains handed out a few medals between rounds of the pipe. Maybe the captains forgot they had left a medal for Chief Tun-na-che-moo-toolt in the fall; no matter—they gave him another, this one of the small size with the likeness of President Jefferson, and Red Grizzly Bear received one of the sowing medals struck in the presidency of Washington.[7]

Clark concluded his journal of the 10th with high praise for the locals. He wrote, "Those people has Shewn much greater acts of hospitallity than we have witnessed from any nation or tribe Since we have passed the rocky Mountains. in Short be it Spoken to their immortal honor it is the only act which diserves the appelation of hospitallity which we have witnessed in this quarter."[8]

The smoking and conversation continued until late. Cruzatte played the fiddle, and some of the white men danced, while a number of Indians from other villages came to satisfy their curiosity.

May 11, the men, excluding the hunters, lay about. Drouillard came in; he had been gone all night, but brought in a deer with him. He went out again and was back in the afternoon, this time with two more deer. While the men were hunting and resting, the captains held council. A new chief came into camp about 8 a.m. They called him the One-Eyed Chief because his left eye was missing, and they wrote his name as "Yoom-park'-kar-tim," probably a Virginia-Kentucky rendition of Hiyuumpaaxatimine, which might be rendered as *hiyúum* (mythical grizzly or big one or hibernating animal, like a badger, for example), *páaxat* (five), and *tim'íne* (heart).[9] Lewis described him as "a stout fellow of good countenance about 40 years of age."[10]

Now the Americans had four of the leaders they considered most important all together in the tipi and repeated what they had said the night before. They told the Nimíipuu that the American government intended to establish trade and would bring trade goods, that it was the intention of the Great White Father that all the tribes should be at peace and harmony and, of course, they emphasized the power and wealth of the United States.[11] All of this talk was tedious because everything had to go through the English, French, Hidatsa, Shoshone and Nimipuutímt, the Nez Perce language. The Frenchman, his wife Sacajawea, and the young Shoshone boy were active in these talks. Apparently the young Shoshone man was no longer miffed at the captains.

Nez Perces were reported as telling the captains that three of them had been at the Hidatsa village on the Missouri the previous spring. According to one Nez Perce tradition, it may have been this visit, but altered to have taken place while the expedition was still on the Missouri at Fort Mandan and, in their story, Chief Twisted Hair and several others were in the company of Shoshone friends. This is why Twisted Hair was so friendly and hospitable to the captains during the previous fall; he believed they remembered him. In the tradition, he even dressed as he had on the Missouri, in order that they would recognize him.[12]

After counciling for several hours, Lewis ranked the principal chiefs in what he believed to be the order of their importance. He ranked Chief Tun-na-che-moo-toolt (the Broken Arm) at the top, as did Clark, but Lewis had the Cut Nose in the number two position, while Clark had Red Grizzly Bear. Third slot in the hierarchy of Lewis went to Yoomparkkartim (One-Eyed Chief or Five Big Hearts), where Clark put the Cut Nose. Last place in the top four in Lewis's scheme went to Red Grizzly Bear, and Clark had Yoomparkkartim (Hiyúum páaxat tim'íne) (One-Eyed Chief or Five Big Hearts) there.[13]

Lewis's criteria are unclear, but what he could not know is that the different leaders were not ranked linearly by importance. The Chopunnish did not have rankings that corresponded to the American military or political systems. Each leader's powers depended upon many things, and the power of the local *miyóoxat,* or band leader had to be respected even though other leaders in their own territory might rank higher.

The captains must have felt it was mandatory to show the "power of magnetism, the spye glass, compass, watch, air gun," and there were a lot of people gathered around the only show in town. Everyone was not attracted or able to take the time to travel and see the show. Estimates of the population of the Nez Perces at this time run from about 4000 to 6000 and, from the descriptions in the journals, it does not seem that any more than a few hundred at most gathered at the Chief Tun-na-che-moo-toolt's village.

In fact, at least three of the four "principa[l] cheifs," as rated by Lewis and Clark, were not from the area where their "villages" now stood. Yoomparkkartim (Hiyúum páaxat tim'íne, or One-Eyed Chief, or Five Big Hearts), as they noted, came from south of Lewis's (Snake) River, a large area, maybe now southeastern Washington near the Big Horn chief or maybe further south from the Wallowa Valley in modern-day northeastern Oregon.

The old friend to the captains, Twisted Hair, continued true to his word and brought in another half a dozen of the expeditions' horses. Their horse herd was up over 60 now. Another two horses, a mare and colt, were brought in by a young man and offered to the captains as a symbolic gift. His father had been killed on the plains by the Hidatsas, and the words of the Americans regarding peace and trade "made his heart glad." The mare and colt were a token of his determination to take the advice of the Americans.[14]

Lewis, the bird watcher par excellence, had not failed to note that the menstrual lodge for the "tawny damsels" was present at the Chief Tun-na-che-moo-toolt's (the Broken Arm) camp as at every other village,[15] and both captains mention that the "Chopunnish... are much more clenly in their persons and habitations than any nation we have Seen Sence we left the Illinois."[16]

They and their men could maybe take the time now to do a little cleaning up themselves. When Twisted Hair suggested the people did not appreciate men barging into their dwellings scrounging for food unannounced, the captains took his hint and gave orders to stop the practice. One cannot help wondering the effect of a score or more of heavily armed Indian warriors crashing the food stores of some white frontier settlement with the simultaneous signs that "we are peaceful and will give you trinkets for what we take."

It is likely that at least some of the Americans participated in the sweat bath. One Nimíipuu source maintained that York, Clark's black slave, was led to the creek by some women, signed to remove his clothes, then splashed with water, rubbed, and even had handfuls of sand and gravel rubbed into his skin. Since first sighted in the fall, he had been a source of curiosity because some thought he was painted black in mourning.

Others wondered if he was prepared for war. Some even believed he might be related to *yáaka'*, the black bear. But no, he appeared to be a man, a black man whose color would not come off. Some men took him to the sweat house. Maybe heat and sweat and then rubbing the medicine root, *qawsqáaws*, would take the color away. No, he remained black. They scratched his back and rinsed him off several times, but he remained black.[17] It was considered rude to refuse an invitation to sweat, and there was great symbolism attached to the act itself. Although the Corps wrote little about sweating, it is difficult to imagine them not participating.

The Nez Perces had a variety of styles of sweat houses, but the format of the ceremony had some basic elements, and it was the primary procedure that both sexes used to maintain the cleanliness so admired by the American captains. The men had their own sweat houses, the women had theirs, and both areas were "off limits" to members of the opposite sex. There was a great deal of socializing and laughter at sweat houses, and news exchanged, maybe even some gossip. Stories were told, too, and the younger people were supposed to be quiet, pay attention, and learn from the experiences of the older participants.

The sweat house itself was likely made of a frame of limbs—willow, alder, maybe even red fir—in the shape of a dome. The limbs were stuck into the ground in a circle, bent over about waist high, and tied together to create the shape. Sometimes it was built as a hollow in a dirt bank and only the roof needed covering; sometimes it was only a hole in the ground with rawhides supported by driftwood over the top. Maybe it was the entire dome frame that needed reed mats and a covering of dried mud. The idea was to create an environment that would hold heat.

The heat came from apple-sized rocks made cherry-red by fire then transported into a stone-lined pit inside the sweat house. Forked limbs from a bush would be used to move the rocks from fire to the inside pit. Usually one person did the carrying, "the pitcher," and "the catcher" inside with special sticks caught and arranged them. Everyone sweated nude. You backed into the sweat house and sat on dead grass or inner cedar bark if available. The person nearest the pit had a container of water and had the temporary title of *quus hamma,* the water man or water woman as the case may be. The person nearest the door was titled *piskwaus hamma,* the doorman or doorwoman. The water man regulated how much water was poured onto the rocks, which regulated how much steam and heat was produced. If too much water was poured, you could "burn out," which was considered bad judgement and improper behavior.[18]

In the water was the *qawsqáaws,* a root that came exclusively from the high mountain meadow country. This gave a pungent odor to the steam, and it permeated the skin and stuck with you. Then you would crawl out of the sweat house headfirst, swim in the cold river or splash cold creek water on yourself, and go back into the sweat house three or four times. Your pores would open and the poisons would leave your body. The meditation and prayers that were sent up with the steam would clear your head and purge your soul, and you could walk through a herd of elk, and they would not smell your presence because your scent was the same as a high country bog-meadow, musky.

There was a tea you could drink, too, made from spring water and boiled leaves of a special plant, *mexsem'e pisqu.* It would help a supplicant avoid dehydration. And, of course, there was plain cold spring water. Everyone had their favorite. Cleansing from the emetic stick made one feel light and free. After such cleansing, it was said that some men could run a deer down, not in a sprint but in a day long chase, and wear them down.

Once inside the sweat house, your companions were your "relation"; you had been in the "womb" at the same time. The sweat house was a part of the earth, the mother of everyone. Even when Christianity was introduced, the sweat house was retained. For the "sweaters" of the Lewis and Clark group, a higher level of acceptance would be obvious.

May 12, the Day of the Grand Council

Despite the implications of some of the prophecies and negative opinions of some of the people, the American captains and their retinue were making a good impression. There were some cultural things that were bothersome: their body odor, the dog-eating of some, and other things. But these were circumstances that could be ignored or overcome in time and should not stand in the way of wise decision-making. The Americans were making a clear effort to try to do everything correctly, as evidenced by their patient smoking and counseling.

They had obvious technical superiority in their arms, demonstrated at target shooting and hunting success. And they had a plan, a plan that embraced more security for the Nimíipuu from enemies, trade goods like steel awls and kettles to make the work of the women easier, and the blue beads to make life more beautiful. In fact, the proposals of the Americans, if true, would bring a better life for the people through peace.

The American proposals were discussed in council, and the chiefs wanted to embrace the plan, as there was too much good in it to pass it by and too full of possibilities. The Americans had knowledge the Nimíipuu did not yet have but, with an alliance with the Americans, they could learn, acquire the same types of power, all that the white men knew. The Nimíipuu would make them brothers, like their Sahaptin brothers the Palus, Yakamas, Umatillas, Walla Wallas, Klikitats, everyone all the way to Wyam, the Great Falls of the Columbia, and then they would share everything.

This was all decided in council inside the *kuhét'iniit,* the long house, while Captain Clark demonstrated his skill and dedication through eye wash and other medical procedures and while Captain Lewis answered questions of the people through the interpreters.

One Heart and One Tongue

After the grand council, two young Nez Perces each gave a horse, one to Lewis and one to Clark. The captains, in turn, gave powder and ball to these young men. They must have been two of the six men in Chief Tun-na-che-moo-toolt's (the Broken Arm) camp who already owned firearms secured on the upper Missouri through the British trade. The captains had the chiefs all sit down and presented each with a pint of powder, 50 balls, and a United States flag. Thirty-six years later (1842), when he was at least 90 years of age, Chief Red Grizzly Bear recalled the event to Dr. Elijah White, Indian agent:

> I speak today, perhaps tomorrow I die. I am the oldest chief of the tribe; was the chief when your great brothers, Lewis and Clark, visited this country. They visited me, and honored me with their friendship and counsel. I showed them my numerous wounds received in bloody battle with the Snakes; they told me it was not good, it was better to be at peace; gave me a flag of truce; I held it up high; we met and talked. We never fought again.[19]

Chief Red Grizzly Bear was also known as Chief Many Wounds, for he had 80 distinct scars that he had received in battle. He never used the rifle or bow, always a club of Syringa.[20]

An oration was given by an elder, and it is reported by Lewis that "he observed that they had listened with attention to our advise and that the whole nation were resolved to follow it, that they had only one heart and one tongue on this subject. he said they were fully sensible of the advantages of peace and that the ardent desire which they had to cultivate peace with their neighbours."[21] The old man then summarized the recent past relations with the Shoshone, telling about sending a pipe to them with three warriors, all of whom were killed. A retaliatory raid was conducted, and 42 of the Shoshone were killed, with only 3 losses. The Nimíipuu were now ready for peace.

Lewis reported they "valued the lives of their young men too much to wish them to be engaged in war." The old man expressed his doubts about the willingness of the Blackfeet and the Gros Ventres to establish friendly relations. But he said the Nimíipuu would come to the upper Missouri to trade if the whites put up trading houses. As to the Nez Perces' friendliness to the whites, they "might be assured of their warmest attachment and that they would alwas give them every assistance in their power; that they were poor but their hearts were good."

In his famous instructions of June 18, 1803, President Thomas Jefferson instructed Lewis and Clark to encourage and invite young Indian people to be educated in the United States. The captains explained this opportunity to the Nez Perces, but the leaders told the captains that they would think about it and answer later. The Nez Perce were of a mind that it would be foolish to leave for the mountains too early, or they "would certainly perish."[22] Lewis identified "the orrator on this occasion" as the father of Red Grizzly Bear, but he was mistaken. The father of Red Grizzly Bear was a chief named Pahwainan, who was killed by the Bannocks while Red Grizzly Bear was yet a child.[23]

Perhaps the orator at the grand council was an uncle, the brother of the father, or an adopted father, but he was not the true father of Red Grizzly Bear. The man, whoever he was, held the position *tew'yelenew'éet,* the repeater, sometimes called "Camp Crier"—a trusted elder man of strong voice who recited the decisions of the council so that everyone in the village would know. The report of Lewis on this matter must have resulted from an error in translation or some type of misunderstanding, for Red Grizzly Bear's father had been dead for almost 40 years.

When the women learned of the chief's decision to enter into a formal alliance with the white men, Lewis reported, "the women cryed wrung their hands, toar their hair and appeared to be in the utmost distress."[24] But the men had already consented when they accepted Chief Tun-na-che-moo-toolt's (the Broken Arm) invitation to eat of a feast if they favored alliance with the Americans and to refrain if they did not. Lewis wrote they "swallowed their objections if any they had, very cheerfully with their mush."[25]

Chief Cut Nose gave Drouillard a good horse, and the captains gave Twisted Hair "one gun and a hundred balls and 2 lbs. of powder in part for his attention to our horses and promised the other gun and a similar quantity of powder and lead when we received the ballance of our horses."[26]

Trading Clothes

One of the young men, who at the behest of the tribe gave Lewis a horse, now gave him "a hansome pare of legings," and Chief Tun-na-che-moo-toolt (the Broken Arm) "gave Capt. C. his shirt, in return for which we gave him a linin shirt."[27] This was an important gesture of familial acceptance and was a tradition that accompanied an alliance. There were times when bands from different tribes met and exchanged clothing.[28]

Lewis gave another demonstration of the power of the American rifles after the formalities of the council and accompanying ceremonies. He hit a mark at 220 yards with two balls. We don't know which rifle he shot, how many times he shot it, or the size of the mark, but no matter; it was impressive to the bow and arrow audience, even to those familiar with the trade guns of the British. This is a point usually left out of any analysis of the Nez Perce relations with these first white Americans to tumble onto their turf: the American arms were demonstrably superior in accuracy over the British trade guns of the upper Missouri.

For one thing, the American firearms, such as the type built in Lancaster, Pennsylvania, had rifling, and these cut grooves spun the ball from the barrel, creating flatter shooting and more accurate accounting than the Thomas Barnett-designed trade musket of the British Northwest Company, with its 24-gauge or .58 caliber smoothbore. The "Barnett" was a great night fighting weapon of its day, but only accurate to 50 yards, while the American Lancaster style was good to 100 yards and far beyond in the hands of an expert, as exhibited by the shooting of Captain Meriwether Lewis. People on the plains would soon become cognizant of the skills of the Nez Perces in handling this weapon and its difference from the British trade gun.[29]

The tension of the council and the after-council formalities called for some relief, and the shooting exhibition gave great excitement to the young warriors of the possibilities that would be forthcoming for successful hunting and defense. The recent trading with the Americans also stimulated the commencement of gambling for "beads and other ornaments." The "stick game" as described in Chapter 1, was the favorite game of the gamblers, and it was (and remains) a raucous affair. These were occasions of high excitement, and each team was backed by their "fan base," rooting their people on, jeering the other side, and distracting the opposition team as much as possible.

The stick game songs might include accompanying hand drum playing and humorous lyrics. Side bets were common and general socializing, too. Of course, there were social dances, as well. Sergeant Ordway mentioned fiddle playing and dancing in his journal entries for the 11th (the night before the council) and the 12th (the night of the council), and never mentioned the council at all. The captains emphasized the council and related activities and totally ignored the dancing. They were concerned with moving camp to a new location that would be suitable as a base to launch an assault on the summit of the Bitterroots.

Camp Chopunnish (May 14–June 9)

There were Fort Mandan on the Missouri and Fort Clatsop near the Pacific, then there was this camp, nestled in the Kamiah Valley, recommended by the Nez Perces. This ad hoc camp, established in the Nez Perce midst, was the longest encampment of the expedition outside of a winter fort. The expeditioners did not give it a name, but the scholar Elliot Coues did: he called it Camp Chopunnish. It is also known as Long Camp. Lewis and Clark were in a hurry to get home, just as they had been in a hurry to get to the coast the year before.

Now, even with the certain knowledge that the snow was too deep for a mountain crossing, they seemed anxious to move to the other side of the Clearwater River so that they could prepare for the difficult transit. The Nez Perces were attempting to stall them to protect them from making a rash decision. The captains were told on several occasions, even prior to the "grand council," that it would be a month or a month and a half until it would be possible to attempt a crossing.

The morning of May 13, all the horses were collected, and the Lewis and Clark party, accompanied by a number of Indians also on horseback, started down the Creek headed for the Clearwater River. (In their journals, they are calling it both the Kooskooske and the Flathead River.) They did not leave camp until 1 p.m., but they did not have far to go, only about three miles (Clark says three, Lewis three and one half).

They were only out of camp one mile when they passed "a stout branch," which "flowed in on the wright." This is the modern Seven Mile Creek, named 'Asáha by the Nez Perce.[30] Just below this, the canyon of Commearp Creek (Lawyer Creek) opens into a wide valley surrounded by high hills. A couple of more miles brought the Americans and the Indian cavalcade to the bank of the Clearwater, where they were supposed to meet a man with a canoe in order to ferry men and equipage to the far side. The man with the boat did not arrive until late, so there was not much anyone could do but wait until the following day. The horses were turned out to graze and the river crossing was postponed until the morning of the 14th.

Lewis and Clark were invited to stay in a leather tipi at this location in Lawyer's Creek canyon for the Grand Council with the Nez Perce, May 11 and 12, 1806. Photograph by Al Hilton, 1919. Courtesy Alvin Pinkham.

This delay gave the captains time to catch up a bit in their journals, allowing an interesting glimpse into the society of the Kamiah valley and environs of 200 years ago. It gave the men of the expedition a little time also to try the speed of some of their horses, which the captains found "active strong and well formed." The Nez Perces have "immence numbers of them 50, 60 or a hundred hed is not unusual for an individual to possess." The Nimíipuu men exercised themselves by shooting their bows and riding their horses, "racing &c. they are expert marksmen and good riders."[31]

While waiting on the river bank, Lewis and Clark wrote more of the people with whom they were living and destined to live with for some weeks more: "The Chopunnish are in general stout well formed active men. they have high noses and many of them on the acqueline order with cheerfull and agreeable countenances; their complexions are not remarkable."[32] The Nez Perces liked to gamble and they were eager to trade, but:

An example of a young Nez Perce woman, Pe yah lah wenunmy (Antonia Mathews), photographed in Genesse, Idaho around 1900. She is the maternal grandmother of co-author Allen V. Pinkham. Photo by C.W. Hanson. Courtesy Allen V. Pinkham.

[T]hey do not appear to be so much devoted to baubles as most of the nations we have met with, but seem anxious always to obtain articles of utility, such as knives, axes, tommahawks, kettles blankets and mockerson alls. blue beads however may form an exception to this remark; this article among all the nations of this country may be justly compared to goald or silver among civilized nations. They are generally well cloathed in their stile. their dress consists of a long shirt which reaches to the middle of thye, long legings which reach as high as the waist, mockersons, and robes. these are formed of various skins and are in all rispects like those particularly discribed of the Shoshones. their women also dress like the Shoshones. their ornaments consist of beads shells and peices of brass variously attatched to their dress, to their ears arrond their necks wrists arms &c. a bando of some kind usually surrounds the head, this is most frequently the skin of some fir animal as the fox otter &c. tho' they have them also of dressed skin without the hair. the ornament of the nose is a single shell of the wampum. the pirl and beads are suspended from the ears. beads are woarn arround their wrists necks and over their sholders crosswise in the form of a double sash.[33]

The statement regarding the nose *wampum* has provoked much discussion over the years since it is the contention of all modern Nez Perces that they did not, as a tribe, pierce their noses. Of course, in his statement of May 13th, Lewis is playing catch-up somewhat in his journal, and he is describing "The Chopunnish," which is a designation he used for nearly everyone from Kamiah to Wyam (Celilo Falls) on the Columbia, and so it was not likely intended to be indicative of every Nez Perce in his purview within the Kamiah region. It is perhaps significant that Clark, whose entry for this date is nearly verbatim with that of Lewis, left out the phrase regarding nose *wampum*. Nor is any mention of the practice noted by either Patrick Gass or Sergeant John Ordway.

Both commanding officers mention interesting observations of the body hair of the men and the women. Lewis refers to "savage nations of America," while Clark writes about "Indian Nations of America," but otherwise the comment by both is identical: "in common with other Indian Nations of America they extract their beard, but the men do not uniformly extract the hair below, this is more particularly confined to the females." The captains could readily discern, from simple observation, the conditions of the men's beards and how they plucked their facial hair and, washing in the river or sweating with the men, it seems that some Nimíipuu did "not uniformly extract the hair below."

To what purpose did women "extract the hair below," and how did the captains receive knowledge of the practice? Love medicine is what the hair plucking was about. It is a reference to a variety of practices, beliefs, behaviors, powders, and potions. There was no uniform system. It was highly secretive and mystical. It involved spells conjured up by *tiwata'áat,* women doctors, for success in romance, mate selection, and child bearing for women. Medicine men performed ceremonies and special potions for male romantic success and even as an aid in mare reception in the selective breeding of horses.

While not used by all families, the practice of removing the hair "down below" was part of a love package or practice that might have included down feathers from certain birds in a small bundle with other love ingredients. The use of beaver musk, named *qúuynu,* was another well-known practice in creating love potions. Different families had their different ways of making love potions. A little of the right stuff, strategically placed, could help induce the desired results.[34]

There can be no doubt that the young American men, single (except for York and John Shields) and far from home, which included everybody, were genuinely curious about the young women of the tribes visited. The journals reveal on many occasions that they were extremely observant of everything about the young women that they could observe. Even the captains proclaimed that the Nez Perce women were "more perticular than any other nation in Screting the parts," while the men "expose those parts which are generally kept from few."[35]

Captain Lewis undoubtedly practiced his usual close observation prior to describing the Nez Perce women as "tawny damsels."[36] The members of the expedition had been instructed and encouraged to write of their experiences, but they knew, too, that the army and the public who sponsored the expedition would ultimately be privy to the contents. It would not be prudent to write about "feats of love"; their attention in writing was to be "directed to more useful information."[37]

The soldiers of the expedition probably regarded "feats of love" with Nez Perce women, as mere entertainment while in a strange land and far from home. For the Nez Perce women there were many reasons for liasons with the young American men.

Some Nez Perce women, upon first seeing the white men, thought they were beautiful.[38] And the Nez Perce women were lovely to look at and lovelier still to be with.[39] Lewis the ornithologist, did not write detailed descriptions of any individual Nez Perce woman, like he did his ducks and woodpeckers. However, another ornithologist, John K. Townsend of Philadelphia, traveling through the Oregon country with Nathaniel Wyeth in 1836, immortalized a young woman with his words:

> I observed one young and very pretty looking woman, dressed in a great superabundance of finery, glittering with rings and beads, and flaunting in broad bands of scarlet cloth. She was mounted astride Indian fashion—upon a fine bay horse, whose head and tail were decorated with scarlet and blue ribbons, and the saddle, upon which the fair one sat, was ornamented allover with beads and little hawk's bells. This damsel did not do us the honor to dismount, but seemed to keep warily aloof, as though she feared that some of us might be inordinately fascinated by her fine person and splendid equipments, and whole deportment proved to us, pretty satisfactorily, that she was no common beauty, but the favored companion of one high in office, who was jealous of her slightest movement.[40]

In the practices of the plateau tribes, including the Nez Perces, premarital sex was not frowned upon, and experimentation and exploration were expected. There were methods of birth control and ways of aborting a fetus in the case of unwanted pregnancies.[41] However, children were desirable, and early children, babies born of young parents, were normally reared by the grandparents of one of the parents.

Marriages and sexual liaisons were a way of cementing relations between families, between bands, and between tribes. That is, a marriage could be a basis of political, military, and commercial (trade) alliance. This was the pattern with other Sahaptin tribes like the Palouse, who were often considered merely the westernmost of the Nez Perce, but were really made of independent bands (like the Nez Perce), and others too, like the Umatilla, Walla Walla, and Cayuse.

In fact, it was the same pattern even with non-Sahaptin speakers with whom the Nez Perces needed to ally for mutual protection. This would include the Salish or Flathead of Montana in particular, sometimes the Pend Oreille, Spokane, Coeur d'Alene, even Lemhi Shoshone and Crow. There was even a band of the dreaded Blackfeet with whom the Nez Perces did not fight, the Little Robe band, and that peace was due to a marriage.

Any coming together of sexual partners that was not secretive was considered "marriage"; some lasted a lifetime, others only for the duration of the time allotted by fate. Men in particular had different "wives" in different tribes and bands that they visited on a regular route. A route might include a salmon fishing expedition in the spring to Celilo and buffalo hunting in Montana in the fall, and the relatives of the wives ensured the husband had access to the necessary resources to help his respective families.

This, then, was probably the expectation of the Nez Perces for an alliance with the Americans. They would welcome them, help them do as they wanted, and encourage them to make children with Nez Perce women who were available and interested. Children from these unions would be the living symbol of the alliance and the guarantee that there would never be war between themselves and the Americans. Only a savage would make war upon his own.

Of course, there was a deep commitment to trade with relatives; people were often adopted who were not blood related before trade would begin. The chieftainly families were especially expected to participate in intertribal marriage, and massive trade exchanges were a part of these marriages. The children from "mixed marriages" often spent time in the. country of many relatives and were often trained in the languages and dialects that prevailed among different nations. This was part of their training as diplomats and peacemakers.

This, then, is the context of the meaning of the alliance of the Nez Perces to the Americans. The medals showed the meaning from the American side: the pictures of the national leaders, Washington and Jefferson, plainly implying a kind of fealty to the new government. Perhaps more obvious and better understood by the Indians is the obverse face of the medals: the placement of the pipestem over the handle of the war tomahawk. It is an American republican version of the swords-into-plowshares idea.

Another bond of union between the red and the white man and a symbol of peace was the American flag. As they were traveling through in 1805, Lewis and Clark left a flag to be given to Chief Tun-na-che-moo-toolt (the Broken Arm) when he returned from war. This is the flag they were gratified to see outside his lodge when they came to his Lawyer's Creek (Commearp Creek) on their return on May 10, 1806. In a non-literate society, these symbols served as powerful and sacred "documents" that were, nationally speaking, inviolate. They got the good messages from President Jefferson, messages of trade, peace, and prosperity, but there was another side to Jeffersonian and ultimately American Indian policy that was omitted by the army captains, a dark side that the Nez Perces would learn all too well in the future.[42]

ENDNOTES

1   Aoki, *Nez Perce Dictionary*, pp. 601, 781. *Toko'* may refer to mats of tule, bulrush, or cattail.

2   *JLCE*, 7:239.

3   Ibid.

4   Ibid.

5   Aoki, *Nez Perce Dictionary*, pp. 50, 1052.

6   *JLCE*, 7:238.

7   Ibid. Clark said nothing of the medals at this camp. A good summary of the Nez Perce medals is in James R. and mike Venso's *Across the Snowy Ranges. the Lewis and Clark Expedition in Idaho and Western Montana* (Moscow, ID: Woodland Press, 2001).

8   *JLCE*, 7:240.

9   Aoki, *Nez Perce Dictionary*, p. 747.

10   *JLCE*, 7:242.

11   Ibid.

12   Peo-Peo-Tah-Likt, *Historical Sketches of the Nez Perce,* Cage #1218, p. 11. While some may find the story improbable, it must be remembered that trade goods preceded Lewis and Clark to the Clearwater and that the Nez Perces were not always at war with the Shoshones and, in fact, have a long record of peaceful association with the Lemhi band of Sacajawea's people.

13 *JLCE*, 7:242, 244.

14 Ibid., 7:243.

15 Menstrual lodge for girl's *'elwite s*. Aoki, *Nez Perce Dictionary*, p. 1191.

16 *JLCE*, 7:245.

17 Info from Peo-Peo-Tah-Likt, *Historical Sketches of the Nez Perces*, Cage #4681, p. 5, and from informant Mylie Lawyer. See also McBeth, *The Nez Perces Since Lewis and Clark*, p. 21.

18 For more detailed information of Nez Perce Sweat house, see Walker, "The Nez Perce Sweat Bath Complex."

19 Miss A.J. Allen, *Ten Years in Oregon* (Ithaca, NY: Andrus, Gauntlett, & Co., 1850), p. 185, quoted in Alvin M. Josephy, *Nez Perce Indians and the Opening of the Northwest* (Yale University Press, 1965), p. 228. Hereafter cited as Josephy, *Nez Perce Indians and the Opening of the Northwest*.

20 McWhorter, *Hear Me, My Chiefs!*, pp. 20-21. Incidentally, the syringa bush is used to make both bows and arrows by the Nez Perces, and the syringa is the state flower of Idaho.

21 *JLCE*, 7:247.

22 Ibid., 7:248.

23 From Allen P. descendant of Red Grizzly Bear and account found in McWhorter, *Hear Me, My Chiefs!*, p. 22. This directly from the grandson of Red Grizzly Bear, Wottolen, aged 106, in 1926, he heard the story many times from his grandfather, Red Grizzly Bear himself. Wottolen was a great warrior in his own right, having fought in many inter-tribal wars and having an outstanding war record against the United States Army in 1877. When Chief Joseph gave his famous speech pronouncing, "From where the sun now stands, I will fight no more forever," Wottolen's reply was an equally memorable statement never previously published, that from where the sun now stands "I will never surrender." He never did. Escaped to Canada in 1877, he lived with Sitting Bull's people and returned peacefully years later to die on the Nez Perce Reservation in Idaho.

24 *JLCE*, 7:247.

25 Ibid.

26 Ibid., 7:248.

27 Ibid., 7:249.

28 One example of this behavior in historical times took place between some Nez Perces and Lakotas, see Scott M. Thompson, *I Will tell of my War Story: A Pictorial Account of the Nez Perce War* (Seattle and London: University of Washington Press, Seattle and London in association with the Idaho State Historical Society, Boise, 2000).

29 For example, see Eugene Y. Arima, *Blackfeet and Palefaces: The Pikani and Rocky Mountain House* (Ottawa: The Golden Dog Press, 1995), p. 109. Hereafter cited as Arima, *Blackfeet and Palefaces*. Other information from Authors' black powder buddies Ed Steerman of Lewiston, Idaho and Chuck Knowles of Moscow, Idaho.

30 Aoki, *Nez Perce Dictionary*, p. 975.

31 *JLCE*, 7:252–3.

32 Ibid., 7:253.

33 Ibid.

34 The delicate nature of this subject naturally led to requests by informants to not use their names; however, they nearly all agreed that the sources of their stories were women's sweat houses.

35 *JLCE*, 5:259.

36 Ibid., 7:233.

37 This is suggested in a famous April 5, 1805, entry of Gass, *Journal*, p. 85, However there is controversy over the passage's true author, some believe it might have been added by an editor and the original is not extant.

38 Gay, *With the Nez Perces*, p. 148.

39 Co-authors have both co-habitated with beautiful Nez Perce women.

40 John K. Townsend, "Narrative of a Journey across the Rocky Mountains," reprinted in Reuben Thwaites, *Early Western Travels* (Cleveland, 1905), p. 121.

41 There was a drink made by boiling a certain moss with water for a tea that would bring abortion. Some reports list bear's lard inserted as a vaginal block would prevent pregnancy.

42 James P. Ronda, in his *Lewis and Clark Among the Indians* (Lincoln, NE: University of Nebraska Press, 1984), reveals the duality of the Jeffersonian Indian policy, including the concept of indebting the Indians through trade and taking lands as payment. Hereafter cited as Ronda, *Lewis and Clark Among the Indians*. For a broad treatment of Jeffersonian Indian policy, see Anthony F.C. Wallace, *Jefferson and the Indians; The Tragic Fate of the First Americans* (Cambridge, MA: The Belknap Press of Harvard University Press, 1999). Hereafter cited as Wallace, *Jefferson and the Indians*.

Chapter 11

The Long Camp

According to Nez Perce legend, some young men of the tribe introduced a new gambling game to the troops waiting on the Clearwater's banks for their transportation to arrive.

The Old Badger Gamble

Two badgers were presented, each with a thong attached to a back leg. One of the young men of the expedition was given one thong, while the other was held by a tribal man. At a signal, each was to allow their badger the slack necessary for the badger to begin "digging in," starting a hole to crawl into. Once both badgers had a hole, a signal was given, and each man was to lie on the ground and reach in the hole and grab the badger. The first man to remove the badger from the hole was the winner and the bets, made in advance, were then surrendered by the loser.

This was the game played the afternoon of May 13th while the horses grazed and the men waited for the canoe to arrive. Maybe there was a deal prearranged between the canoeist and the badger-boys. The Indians got the badger from the hole every time before the whites and, thus, won every game.

The Americans never did figure out why the Indians were so fast. The answer was a trick. A badger is a tough animal to get from a hole; it has stiff hair on its back, and it can puff-up, flare its hair, flex its muscles, and take the shape of a wedge. The badger is built to easily go forward but, with determination, it can make itself almost impossible to dislodge. The exception, of course, is when it is squeezed by the testicles, making Mr. Badger lose his determination. In fact, it makes him relax and give up, at which point he was easily hauled out. The soldiers never caught on.[1]

The morning of May 14th was fair. The Indian canoe, with its pilot, had arrived the evening before and, finally, all was in readiness to make the move to the north side of the Kooskooske River (Clearwater River).

With the river running high and cold, this operation consumed the entire morning. The earliest to cross were Collins, Labiche, and Shannon, sent over by their officers to take game for the party, while the balance were employed handling the baggage and crossing the river with the horses.

Crossing the River with Horses

The Kooskooske River or, as it is known today, the Clearwater, is "clear", as its name implies. In fact, one name for the river was the *koos keihk-keihk,* which is to say "translucent."[2] When Clark looked down into the Columbia, he wrote that he could see salmon beneath the surface to 20 feet, and the Clearwater is more clear than the Columbia. Besides being clear, it was running deceptively fast and extremely cold, it was melting snow water, and it was about 150 yards wide.

To cross with horses under such conditions was no small undertaking. The journals of Clark, Lewis, Gass, and Ordway were consulted on this matter, and it will be remembered that, although the journal keepers of the expedition pronounced the day "fair," Patrick Gass wrote that the morning was one of "white frost"; pretty cool for swimming horses.

Ordway simply states, "Swam our horses across." Gass does not make any reference other than "About noon we got all the horses and baggage over safe." Lewis says the horses were driven, and Clark simply wrote "we Crossed our horss without much trouble and hobbled them in the bottom."[3] It was routine to them, none had much to say about the details of the crossing.

It is obvious, from the journals, that many of the Nimíipuu participated in the crossing. Journal entries for the next day say Chief Tun-na-che-moo-toolt (the Broken Arm) and "12 of his young men" left and later Red Grizzly Bear and three old men left camp about 5 in the evening. Perhaps their river-crossing technique was blended with that typically used by the whites, or maybe it is one of those practical affairs whose principles are cross-cultural or universal. This is probably how they did it.

The Nez Perces had a phrase: *sap-soo-wayikt.* It referred to taking lead horses across and the others, pushed from behind, would follow.[4] Choosing the crossing site was an important decision. Care was taken to find a good entry location with an equally satisfactory place to get out on the far bank. At the ideal crossing, the current would help carry the horses to the designated takeout. The best crossings were known by the experienced natives by "reading the water."

Horses, like people, have leaders and swimmers, and the leaders who were the best swimmers were ridden into the water by young riders who themselves possessed the nerve, courage and skills to enter the river on the "leader horses." When the water became too deep for the horses to touch bottom, the horse was guided by the rider towards the far bank. Meanwhile other riders crowded the "follower horses" into the stream and, while there may have been a lot of neighing, splashing, and apparent chaos, it could go alright.

The worst thing was to have the horse's nostrils get into the water. The horse instinctively knew this and held his head high, but sometimes, especially a colt with little river-crossing experience, could get a snootful and panic. It was the obligation of the riders to watch for this and, whenever possible, reach under the chin and lift up on the horse's mouth.[5] If a rider's horse went under, the rider would slide off on the downstream side, hold with one hand on the mane above the withers, and lift under the chin. When the horses touched shore with their feet, or just before, riders would remount and ride up the bank to avoid getting run over by their own or following horses.

The Lewis and Clark crossing involved 60 head of horses, so they mostly swam loose. The position of the horses should be with heads upstream, at an angle to the current. The horse's body would be pulled by its swimming action and pushed by the river's power toward the far shore. The "follower horses" were encouraged by seeing the "leader horses" achieving the far bank.

Another factor incidental to the Kamiah crossing is that the horses were experienced. All had been initially pastured on the north side near Ahsahka, between the main branch and the north fork of the Clearwater River, and all had been delivered either on the plateau between the Clearwater and Lawyer's Creek (Commearp Creek) or in Kamiah Valley, both on the south side of the Clearwater.

The Nez Perce horses also were taught to swim across rivers, just as tribal youth were taught to swim at the earliest possible age, and they were started the same way, by their mother's side under ideal conditions. The May 1806 river conditions were far from perfect, but the training the Nimíipuu horses had already received may help explain how Americans were able, with few problems, to make a difficult crossing appear relatively easy and routine. The U.S. Army could not do this in the Spring 1877 runoff during the war against the Nez Perce.

After crossing to the north side of the Clearwater, the party went downstream a short distance to the extreme low end of the Kamiah Valley. The chiefs picked the spot where the remnants of an old Nez Perce semi-subterranean winter lodge once stood. All that remained was a circular pit about 30 feet across and 4 feet deep, with a berm of 3 1/2 feet around the outside of the circle. Around this, the men erected their camps, facing the outside and placing all their baggage in the center. The site had good grass, good hunting nearby, and was close to the river. In short, since they had to wait for the snows to melt anyway, they were "perfectly satisfyed" with their position.[6]

Nez Perce Chiefs. National Anthropological Archives, Smithsonian Institution, Cited as: photo lot 90-1, #1240. The Long Camp was just to the left in the background of the photo. Lewis and Clark's men hunted these hills and crossed them to Weippe Prairie to begin on the Lolo Trail. Photo location was the village site of the T'ilappalo village near modern day Second Presbyterian Church (Indian), Kamiah, ID.

Soon after the Lewis and Clark party was on the far shore, the two chiefs, Red Grizzly Bear and Tun-na-che-moo-toolt (the Broken Arm), along with a dozen young men, rode upon the opposite bank of the river. They sang for the whites "in token of friendship as is their custom."[7] This was a welcoming song probably accompanied by a few men on hand drums. There were many such songs, some of them routinely performed while riding horseback. This was an old-time custom rarely seen in modern times, where riders en masse guided their horses with their body movements, beat on their one-sided drums and sang in unison.[8] After the men sang, the captains sent over the canoe in several trips to bring the chiefs and some of their followers to their side of the river.

To keep their horses handy, yet allow them some grazing freedom, Nez Perces tied one end of a rope around one front foot of the "horse leaders" and the other end around a sapling. The sapling might flex, but not break. Still, it would restrain the horse. This method was much less likely to result in injury to the horse than a rope around the neck or attached to a halter. The "follower horses," had ropes tied around their necks or one foot, but the other end of the rope was not attached to anything—they would not stray far from the leader horses. This method is called "front-footing" and was remembered by many old time horsemen; it was mentioned by Jane Gay when she was with the Nez Perces during the allotment of 1889–1891.[9]

Horsefeed was not a problem at Camp Chopunnish, for Lewis and Clark were surrounded by top quality grass. However, the Americans did have problems with some of the uncut males. The stallions were noisy, they ran around fighting with other horses, harassed the mares, and were generally troublesome. The men, therefore, attempted to trade them off, even offering two for one, but they could find no takers amongst the local tribesmen. So the captains decided to administer what Gass (or his original editor) called "the quieting operation" (castrating them).

A Nimíipuu man "offered his services" and cut three of the studs.[10] The technique of the Indian was closely observed by the captains: "he cut them without tying the string of the stone as is usual, and assures us that they will do much better in that way; he takes care to scrape the string very clean and to seperate it from all the adhereing veigns before he cuts it."[11]

Drouillard gelded two in the usual way so they had a good opportunity to judge the better method. The Nez Perce method was the same as the Spanish method, and they no doubt learned it from them or from someone else who learned it from the Spanish.[12] As it turned out, the Indian method bled more initially, but allowed the horse to heal faster than the method used in the east. In the end, Lewis acknowledged the Indian method was superior to the American method. The Americans simply shot several of their other stud horses and ate them.

Nimíipuu Grizzly Cook-Out

Two men sent out with John Collins to retrieve the meat from two grizzly bears, a "fat male" and a "meagre female," returned in the evening. The Americans roasted and boiled some of their meat over the open fire, but they gave half of the female bear and the head, shoulders, and neck of the male to the 15 Nez Perces in camp with them. The grizzly was held in great esteem by the Nez Perces, and they esteemed the killing of them equal to that of an enemy.[13] The captains gave the claws to "Hohastillpelp" (Xáxaac 'ilp'ílp' or Chief Red Grizzly Bear, later known as Many Wounds).

The Indians prepared the bear meat in their own way, Ordway wrote: "they cooked it in the Same manner as they Swet their commass roots."[14] They heated rocks in a firepit, then spread the rocks level and placed a layer of pine boughs over the rocks. Next, "they laid on the flesh of the bear in flitches, placing boughs between each course of meat."[15] Finally, the men put about four inches of earth over the entire pile "so that the heap or mass had something of the appearance of a small coalpit on fire." This was, according to Patrick Gass, who said that they left it for an hour and a half.[16] Both Lewis and Clark wrote that the bear was left in the oven for about three hours. Clark did not sample the taste nor the consistency, but Lewis proclaimed it "much more tender than that which we had roasted or boiled," but added "the strong flavor of the pine distroyed it for my pallate."[17]

Ordway said the captains gave the Nimíipuu the bear meat "as [because] they gave us So much & are So kind to us."[18] At about 6 p.m. Francois Labiche returned to camp with the announcement he had killed a female bear and two large cubs. There would be plenty of bear meat for a few meals anyway and, if someone did not like the bear or the horse, there were a few grouse and squirrels brought in to vary the menu.[19]

In the next two weeks, the Corps settled into a routine of camp life and preparation for the hard journey across the Bitterroots. The tribal peoples, too, continued with their regular cycles of food gathering. Lewis and Clark and their party were not a part of daily life in any way for most Nimíipuu once the excitement of the Grand Council was over and the whites were established at Camp Chopunnish on the north side of the Clearwater.

There was near daily continuous contact, however, for a few. Some Nez Perces who had heard of the whites but had not had the opportunity to see them came to visit or to simply gawk at them across the river. Others, who had heard of the healing skills of Clark, came for treatment. Leaders of bands as far away as Salmon River, such as Red Grizzly Bear, remained for a time with the captains and, of course, there were the fairly regular meetings between tribal and Corps hunting parties and even a few local hunts of opportunity.

Initially, movement to distant locations from the long camp was limited by the high water of Collins Creek (Lolo Creek, Idaho), the spring-flowing Clearwater, and the Corps's lack of a canoe. Scarcity of game necessitated that both these situations be overcome. Nothing could be done about the spring run-off, except to endure the wait. Eventually, the Corps began construction of a new canoe to increase accessibility to resources. The lack of provision was ameliorated by trade with the Nez Perce, and a canoe would allow the Americans to initiate interactions. A complete record of all trade would provide the most interesting information, were it only available. After 200 years, the only sources we have are direct statements found in the journals of Lewis, Clark, Gass, and Ordway. As far as we know, Joseph Whitehouse had stopped keeping his journal before the expedition re-entered Nez Perce territory, and the journals apparently kept by other members of the expedition have never been found. Other small tidbits of information have survived in just a few renditions of tribal oral history, and the rest in conjecture and inference based on how business and society were conducted in tribal territories historically.

"Tawny Damsels" Seal the Deal

Lewis, the bird watcher, created the term "tawny damsels,"[20] and the overnight "trading ventures" likely involved liaisons with these young Nez Perce women. As has been indicated, trading and "marriage" of whatever duration often went hand in hand. This was desirable and necessary for the construction of kinship networks that were an expected part of every alliance between plateau peoples, those from the crest of the Rockies to the summit of the Cascade Range. The "wives" of these marriages did not expect that they would remain with their sexual partners. It would have been well understood that only a wife "at home" would remain attached to the man.

These encounters were purposeful in that the female relations of chiefs having children by important personages from other groups, maybe leading men or chiefs, would bring prestige to the family[21] and band and, most importantly, the connection of mutual children would help manipulate future behavior of both groups. The intention here was to seal a permanent peace. "Intertribal peace was made and sustained by intermarriage between the families of the chiefs."[22]

In some instances, tribal elders sat outside the tipi while the young people enjoyed sex. The older adults looked intently at the man involved with their family member to be sure of the child's identity. The offspring would constitute a living symbol of intergroup unity.

The success of an individual in Nez Perce life was always related to his or her power. The power that was most important was for war, as there would be no survival without it. Also, at the top of the hierarchy were the power to heal and salmon power. No one in the Corps seemed to exhibit much salmon power, in fact, they were noticeably lacking in that. But the power of war and hunting they had in abundance, and one man seemed amazing in his power of healing. William Clark must have been considered the single individual with the most power and a good choice for a mate of a chief's female relative.

In the Nimíipuu world, family, band, and intertribal alliances are important enough to be part of the Nez Perce history. So are marriage and trade an integral part of plateau culture in which the Nez Perces played such an important role. When it comes to the specifics of Captain Clark spending quality time with a tribal maid, the discussion is conjectural and unprovable. Where and when did the union, if there was a union, take place? Are there any hints in the journals that lead the curious to "read between the lines"?

Legend and oral history connect a female relative of Chief Red Grizzly Bear to William Clark. Because he was obviously a man with war power and leadership, he may have been targeted as a potential spouse, and so was Lewis for that matter, but in the Nez Perce value system, Clark had the additional attraction of "healing power" (a doctor). Some may say, even in the modern American system, that good-looking women go for the doctors. One story is that the woman who was attracted to Clark or responded to his overtures was the sister or younger half-sister of Chief Red Grizzly Bear. Another version involves a love episode between Clark and Red Grizzly Bear's daughter. If this account is true, she then may have also been Chief Tun-na-che-moo-toolt's (the Broken Arm) sister or half-sister because he was the son of Chief Red Grizzly Bear.[23]

Another oral history describes Clark's involvement with a Nez Perce woman near Deer Lodge, Montana. In this version, from Peo-Peo-Tah-Likt (Bird Alighting), the location is incorrect since Clark was never in the Deer Lodge region. However, Clark may have had relations with another Nez Perce woman from a Nez Perce buffalo hunting task force somewhere else in Western Montana.[24] Peo-Peo-Tah-Likt claims outright that "one beautiful Nez Perce girl she love Clark and she cry when Clark go away."[25] The different renditions of an affair between Clark and a Nez Perce woman affair all share one thing in common: She has a light-eyed baby with reddish hair and names him "Clark."

York received much attention from the beginning of relations between the Americans and the Nimíipuu, and many tribal folks must have contemplated his medicine power. He had a wife back in the United States but she, like him, was a slave. Did anyone explain to the Nez Perces that York was a slave?

The tribal people of the inland Northwest had a concept of slavery themselves, but it was far different from that of the Americans. It was not racially based, nor were the children of slaves considered as slaves, among other differences. York was armed and sent out to hunt and trade, often while among the Nez Perces.

Nothing in the expedition's journals indicates that he had a woman while living on the Clearwater, but this and much more might understandably be ignored in the official journals of a government-sponsored mission. Peo-Peo-Tah-Likt claims "Negro York he do lots dance with feet and looks funny."[26] It was likely the time just after the agreements of the Grand Council that Peo-Peo-Tak-Likt was referring to when he described York's dancing. It was a time when Cruzatte played the fiddle—"all have good time together," and "one girl she love Mr. [Patrick] Gass and then Indian girls love more white mans...."[27]

Tribal traditions favor that York had two "girl friends" while here and had children, perhaps by both. One story says he had a daughter who died. Another legend has it that he fathered a son and that the son fathered several children whose descendants remain on the reservation today.

Several informants point to historical photographs and ask if the features of this man and his brother do not appear to be African American.

Such was the nature of the old timers, too, who closely scrutinized all children for the features of their parents or in some cases the suspected father of a child. In preparing this book, we interviewed some people who were thought to be those descendants. Some tribal members denied any relationship to York, and others said "so what?" None wanted to be quoted. It is all legend now and hearsay.

There is one detail from the oral history tradition which was written and survives. Pco-Pco-Tah-Likt told his literate cousin Many Wounds (Sam Lott) that York "sing loud when he ride in canoe with Indians girl wife."[28] His relative freedom must have made his return to the United States bittersweet, and one biographer has uncovered some evidence suggesting he may have returned west and died among the Crow Indians.[29]

Nearly every day, people were coming and going from the Americans' camp, both Indian and white. Red Grizzly Bear and his son the Chief Tun-na-che-moo-toolt (the Broken Arm) were both in camp on May 15th along with some of their followers, including three old men, who remained all night. On the 16th, an Indian returned Drouillard's horse that had run off. Then Chief Red Grizzly Bear and his retinue were given the head and neck of a bear, killed by Labiche on May 14th, which they took with them about noon. Read Bear and his men were riding upstream to attempt to locate another canoe.[30]

Also, on May 16th, the captains both wrote in their journals that Sacajawea was gathering the fennel root to use as food for the Bitterroot Mountain crossing. Lewis wrote her name as "Sahcargarmeah" while Clark referred to her as simply "Shabonos Squar." They wrote that the men who were not out hunting were rendering the fat from a bear into a five-gallon keg for emergency rations on the trail. Red Grizzly Bear or one of his companions must have been the source for the captains' description of the Nez Perce method of hunting the Grizzly. The Nimíipuu had great fear and respect for the grizzly, and they considered the killing of a Grizzly Bear to be "as great a feet as two of their enimy."

Their favored method of killing the bear was to catch it on level and open lands, pursue it on horseback, and kill it with their arrows. The bears were not easy to bring down; that very day, Drouillard shot three with his rifle and merely wounded all of them.[31] So there was a lot happening on May 16th, according to Lewis and Clark's writing. Gass wrote that an Indian performed the quieting operation on two more studs on the 16th, but neither of the captains mentioned it in their journals Those studs were the lucky ones, as Ordway reported the group ate two more that were "unruly."[32]

May 17th was a little unusual in that no Indians visited the camp, probably because it rained most of the day in the valley and the low hills. On the plain above and, in the mountains beyond the plain, it snowed all day. The elevation differences made for strange weather or variety. Clark noted, "[a]t the distance of 18 Miles from the river and on the Eastern border of the high plain the Rocky Mountain Commences and presents us with *Winter* here we have Summer, Spring and Winter in the Short Space of twenty or thirty miles—."[33]

Next day (May 17th) Sacajawea continued gathering the fennel root, called "Year-pah" by the captains from the Shoshone "Yampa." She continued to dry them for the trip over the mountains. Clark declared them "very paliatiable either fresh rosted boiled or dried and are generally between the Size of a quill and that of a mans fingar and about the length of the latter."[34] Three Indians came from the direction of the Oyáyp (Weippe) Prairie where they had been hunting and found nothing. They stopped for a smoke, and Lewis and Clark gave them a small piece of meat. They took it, indicating they would take it to their children "who was very hungry." Probably the addition of 30-plus extra people, many of whom were hunting with rifles in the same neighborhood in which the Indians were hunting with bows and arrows, stressed the available wildlife resources and made hunting much more difficult.

The Nez Perces in the upper Clearwater were anxiously awaiting the mass migrations of the chinook salmon, which would relieve all their needs for protein. On the afternoon of the 17th, the Americans saw the Indians erect a lodge and a fishing platform on the opposite side of the river in anticipation of the giants from the sea. Baptiste Lepage took the remains of a salmon from an eagle just below camp, which everyone took as a good sign that the salmon run was imminent. Dr. Clark had an elderly couple show up for treatment in the afternoon, also. The man got some eye water, and she received "creme of tarter and flour of Sulphur" for her "gripeing and rhumatic effections."[35]

The people of the canyons and prairies, the Nimíipuu, were remarkably healthy overall. The journals suggest folks with skin problems, rheumatic pain, one fellow with perfectly preserved muscles and yet near complete paralysis. But this is from a population of five or six thousand souls, no one knows for sure. The journals of the expedition pay more attention to Nimíipuu health issues than would have been the case had Clark's medical services not been vitally important to feeding the party.

While Lewis and Clark passed through Nimíipuu territory from east to west, there was 50 miles north and maybe a 150 south they never saw, and there were Nimíipuu living there, also. Part of that vast, rugged, and remote corner of the American west would be penetrated by Ordway, Frazier, and Weiser in a semi-successful fishing trip into what would be known in the future as lower Hells Canyon. (See Chapter 12, page 183.)

The Nez Perces had their own names for dozens of villages in the area and dozens more in places that still remain remote 200 years later. People lived there when Lewis and Clark came through. Maybe they heard something at the time, certainly they heard things later. Anyway, nothing changed immediately for most; they kept fishing in the same ways, hunting in the same ways, and gathering roots as their ancestors had done far beyond the oldest memory, all the way back to times of legend.

A lot of people were not present at the Grand Council, probably not all the important head men of the nation, but those who were there became more important as a result of that interaction and the first-hand knowledge of the whites and a close association with them. These strangers weren't monsters or magicians, and they had some new gadgets and weapons, that they promised to share. They were human enough; the women confirmed it. Yet there were Nimíipuu who avoided the whites and did not want anything to do with them.

Despite all their fire-starting sticks, guns, knives, and metal pots, when it got right down to feeding themselves regularly, the Americans seemed to fall short. Many Indian dogs became a repast, and many a Nez Perce horse was shot, butchered, and eaten. The strangers did acquire some deer and managed to kill *xáxaac* (grizzly bear), but they let many escape to die in secret places, and the meat was wasted to them. The wolves and magpies cleaned it up, that's what they did best.

The white men kept sending out traders to buy roots from the villages, but they did not have much with which to make the purchases. This was the record of the May 19 and many other times. The villagers got a few awls, knitting pins, and armbands in exchange for roots. The Americans were short on items to trade, and the Indians were struggling to feed enough roots to their own people and to provide for the hungry Americans. Everyone knew the protein-rich salmon were coming, but they couldn't get there fast enough for the hungry.

The village they traded with, across the river and upstream a couple of miles, sent down 4 men, 8 women, and a child with medical problems for Clark to doctor. He did what he could for them. He sent all back to their village "well satisfyed" in the minds of the captains, but Lewis called them "poor wretches" and seemed to imply that the doctoring was inadequate, though the villagers "thought themselves much benefited." Lewis was more aware of Clark's medical shortcomings than the patients, but their faith in the doctor was helpful to a cure. Their faith in Clark's eyewash was justified: it was state-of-the-art medical practice at that time and contained anti-bacterial properties.[36]

Food was a big issue. There just was not enough at this time of year. On May 20th another deer and another bear were wounded, but Frazier traded for a "pasel of Roots and bread" and the French-Omaha hunter Francois "Labiech Came in with a large Buck of the Mule Deer Speces which he had killed on Collins's Creek yesterday."[37] This was good for the whites, but hardly enough to feed their entire party. Collins Creek to the north was still too high to cross, and the Americans were dependant on the occasional availability of Indian canoes for access to the opposite bank of the Clearwater.

Now resigned to a long delay before they could pass through the Bitterroot Mountains, the captains realized they needed a canoe of their own. To that end, on the 21st, they began to build a large dugout canoe. It would allow "at will" hunting and trading on the far side of the valley and in the labyrinth of canyons and prairies beyond. Game was becoming scarce, and the captains were entertaining the idea of moving camp downstream towards the mouth of Collins Creek. The new canoe could then be used to move baggage and men below Collins Creek where they could ascend the ridge downstream leading to the Oyáyp (Weippe) Prairie.

This would only be necessary if Collins Creek remained too high to cross. The Kamiah Valley camp had the advantage of being closer to the Lolo Trail, but they knew they had to cross Collins Creek to reach Oyáyp. The fordability of Collins Creek was a big "if" in the spring of 1806. And there still remained the question of whether or not there was a good camp location in the area they were thinking of relocating. They sent out Sargent Nathaniel Pryor on the 22nd to investigate the possibility.[38]

In the meanwhile, the captains had divided up the meager stores of trade goods, and three traders were sent out for more roots. Some "Indians," there is no indication who, gave them another horse to butcher, but the captains chose to save it for emergency rations on the trip over the mountains.

The arrival of the migrating salmon would have relieved the whites and the Indians in the Kamiah Valley, but they were on their own schedule, and they were not yet arrived in force. On the afternoon of the 22nd, the corpsmen who remained in camp were treated to a great exhibition across the river. Mounted Nez Perces were chasing a deer down a wet, steep slope. Lewis wrote, "it is astonishing to see these people ride down those steep hills which they do at full speed."[39] Gass wrote, "These Indians are the most active horsemen I ever saw: They will gallop their horses over precipices, that I should not think of riding over at all."[40]

This style of riding was developed early in Nez Perce youth through the game of follow the leader. A young horseman would ride in the lead and all who dared would follow—good entertainment and good training for the hunt and war.[41] The deer had already been wounded when pursued into the river[42] but, as it swam to the north bank, it was met by Captain Lewis, Captain Clark, and three other men with rifles, who all shot the deer. That must go down as one of the unluckiest deer in the history of deer hunting in the west. It crossed the river at the only place within a thousand miles where five men stood together with rifles.[43] The Indians and the Corps each took half of the deer.

As usual, several Nez Perces visited the Lewis and Clark camp. They informed the Americans that the salmon-trout [steelhead], which stayed in the river all winter, were not in good shape to eat, but that the salmon (migrating Chinook) were now in Tiwelka koos, Lewis's (Snake) River. And they also said it would be "some[time]yet before they would ascend this river as high as this place."[44] Clark described these two young men as "highly decurated in their way."[45]

Another group of Nez Perces rode to the south bank and informed the Nez Perce in the Corps's camp that two nights previous, Shoshones had surrounded a Nez Perce lodge on the south side of the Snake. The occupants discovered them and were able to escape without injury. Where the attack occurred is impossible to tell. "South side of Lewis's river" covers a lot of country; it could have been about anywhere in modern Wallowa County, Oregon, or Asotin County, Garfield County, or Columbia County, Washington.

Goodrich and Sergeant Ordway spent the night of May 21st at a nearby village and returned to camp about 11 a.m. on the 22nd. They must have been "trading," although the record does not indicate they returned with any goods. Ordway did make the observation in his journal, however, that "the most of the women went out eairly with their horses to dig roots. the women do the most of the Slavery as those on the Missourie."

Ordway went on to say the men went sweating while the women worked. What he did not say, or perhaps was not aware of, was that the men might well have been exercising their responsibilities of canoe building, bow making, arrow shaft selection, fish net construction, horse training, saddle making, or any of dozens of other "must do" activities while the women all sweat or, in summer, went swimming. Those women who rode out did so on their own horses, on their own schedule, with a lot more position and status than their white pioneer equivalent. The Nez Perce women did not suffer the intense loneliness of typical Anglo frontier women because the Indian women rarely worked alone, but were surrounded by the women, girls, and children of their immediate family and friends.[46]

Lewis was particularly prone to stereotyping Indian women as slaves or drudges. As a child of the American Enlightenment, perhaps it was too much for him to admit the "savages" might be more enlightened than him and his fellow Americans.

For want of meat, the men of the Corps killed a fat colt. Late in the afternoon, hunters came in with five deer and two of the salmon trout they had purchased from the Indians. The two Nimíipuu who visited on this day (May 22nd) remained the night and aided in getting another deer first thing the next morning. When Sergeant Pryor wounded a deer near camp and Lewis's dog, Seaman, chased it to the river, the two young Nez Perces swam with their horses after it and chased it back into the river where Pryor finished it off. This feat was accomplished while the Clearwater ran "cold and rapid" and about 200 yards wide, according to Gass.[47] Lewis wrote that "we directed half this deer to be given to the indians." They immediately cooked it and, with the help of four others joining them "from the village," ate their half in less than two hours.[48]

Four Indians came to visit (this was still on Friday, May 23rd) from Lewis's (Snake) River, which the Nez Perces informed the Americans was two days' ride away, just to see the whites and to get a little eye water. They were treated and then crossed back over the Clearwater.[49] Hunters returned in the afternoon with little to show for their efforts. The outlook for fresh meat was dim. The next day, more hunters were sent out.

That same day, more sick came to receive treatment, and none were turned away. Sacajawea's baby, Pomp,[50] William Bratton, and an Indian chief who arrived in a canoe also got treated. Bratton had been suffering from a life-threatening back injury for a long period of time—modern scholars believe it was a lower disk inflammation. But after being treated to violent sweats on the 23rd, he was much better and walking around.

The "chief" was a strange case. He had lost the power of his limbs and had been that way for three years. Lewis thought his condition was the result of the root diet,[51] but had never seen anything like his condition before. They had seen him earlier at the village of Chief Tun-na-che-moo-toolt (the Broken Arm), on Commearp (Lawyer's Creek) creek, and had recommended then for him to eat fish and other meat and to take a cold bath each morning. In addition, the captains had left "a few dozes of Creem of tarter and flour of sulpher" to be taken every three days. Now he was back saying he felt a little better, but Lewis could see "no visible alteration."[52] They treated him this day with "a few drops of Laudanum and a little portable soup."

On this day, also, the same young men who made the ceremonial gift to the captains of a horse each during the Grand Council on May 12th, and who are never named in the journals, reappeared at the American camp. The village where they were last seen was the source of the best food the Corps secured on this day, a large quantity of roots that the women gave in exchange for awls the men manufactured out of links from trap chains.[53] The day had been pleasant and warm, but it rained the greater part of the night.

The rain stopped about 6 a.m. May 24th, and the pursuit of food continued with hunters being sent out in various directions and some sent out to trade. Little Pomp was none the better and was first given a "doze of creem of tartar which did not operate," and because of this he was later given an enema. The captains tried to treat the Indian chief with a sweat similar to the one administered to Bratton, but he did not have the strength to support himself upright, so the captains recommended that the Indians take him to their own sweat house and give him horsemint tea.[54]

Lewis reported that, in the evening, Goodrich returned from a trading mission to a village upstream about 8 miles on the opposite bank.[55] He was bearing a small amount of roots but more importantly some information: those Indians had fat fish that had come from Lewis's River (Snake River).[56] Silas Goodrich, arguably the most knowledgable fisherman of the Corps, took special note of the fat and fine fish at the South Fork Clearwater village. That night four Nez Perces remained at the Lewis and Clark camp.[57]

May 26th came and, despite the rain of the night before, turned into a clear, warm, and fair day. Sacajawea's son was better this morning, but the poultices of boiled onion were applied once again on his swollen neck. Lewis wrote that, when the Field brothers returned from their attempted hunt of the day before, "Hohastillpilp" (Xáxaac 'ilpilp or Red Grizzly Bear) and "several other inferior Chiefs and some young men" came with them.

No one could get to the hunting grounds they desired because the creeks were too high. From the descriptions left in the journal entries, it is impossible to understand exactly where they were attempting to go or what villages were visited. It is only sure that they were on the south side of the Clearwater River, and that some substantial creeks kept them from going where they were attempting to reach.

They did visit a village not previously visited by anyone in the American's party, and roots were found at moderate prices. The party was out of meat again, and the captains sent Sergeant Pryor and four men to cross the Clearwater in the just finished canoe and go to this new village to trade. "Charbono York and LePage" were sent out also to the same place for roots, and Reubin Field was sent out to "hunt the horse... which the Indians have given us to kill."[58]

Hope sprang strong on May 27th. Not only did Reubin Field get back in the morning with a large horse which was butchered, but Chief "Hohastillpilp" (Xáxaac 'ilpilp or Red Grizzly Bear) "told us that most of the horses we saw runing at large in this neighbourhood belonged to himself and his people, and whenever we were in want of meat he requested that we would kill any of them we wished; this is a peice of liberallity which would do honour to such as bost of civilization; indeed I doubt whether there are not a great number of our countrymen who would see us fast many days before their compassion would excite them to a similar act of liberallity."[59]

This was the message of both Lewis and Clark: an assurance that they and their men would not want for meat. Red Grizzly Bear was trying and succeeding in making a good impression, only thinking ahead. Other men were out to the different villages looking for roots to trade and hunters, too, were out. If they did not score, there was the horse steak to fall back on. Riding down the hills on the north, Drouillard, Cruzatte, and Labiche brought back five deer, the most killed in a single day since arriving at this camp.

The outlook was good, too, for salmon. One of the men had seen a salmon in the river the day before and Sergeant Ordway, Frazier and Weiser were sent to Lewis's River for salmon, which inexplicably both Lewis and Clark explain as being only a half-day's ride away. Yet on the 23rd they stated plainly that it was two days' distance on horseback.[60]

On the medical front, little Pomp was better. The chief with the immobile limbs, at the request of his father, "a very good looking old man," was given a sweat under the supervision of Doctor Clark. The hole had to be enlarged, which the old man cheerfully accomplished. Then both the son and father could be in the sweat, and the father was able to hold his son in an upright position.

Clark writes that the Nimiipuu, "treat their women with more respect than the nativs on the Missouri." This is one of the earliest photographs known of a Nez Perce woman. It is a tintype circa 1863. Photograph courtesy Richard Storch, Port Angeles, WA.

This occasion prompted both captains to remark in favor of the high respect the people had for one another and that there were the "[s]trongest marks of parental affection. they all appear extreemly attentive to this Sick man," in spite of his having been sick for perhaps as long as five years.[61] Clark added that the Nimíipuu "treat their women with more respect than the nativs on the Missouri."[62] Time and a somewhat more relaxed atmosphere allowed a closer and more accurate opinion to develop. Here Clark corrects the earlier view of Nimíipuu women as drudges, at least. Whether he compared their lives to the status of white women in his own mind is unknown. He certainly did not make a comparison of that nature in his journals.

Of those sent out to trade, "Shabono Lapage & Yourk" remained out all night on their venture. Sergeant Pryor, Gibson, and Shields all returned with "a good Stock of roots and bread."[63] But Ordway, Frazier, and Weiser would be gone for a week, the longest time away from Camp Chopunnish anyone would spend during the long camp, and they would travel farther from the Kamiah Valley than any other members of the expedition. In addition, they would be the last of the party to view the Snake River (Lewis's River), and the only ones to see anything of what would be later called Hells Canyon, the deepest canyon in the United States.

ENDNOTES

1   This story from Harry Wheeler in Swayne, *Do Them No Harm!*, pp. 171 3.

2   This from A.G. Marshall via Sam Watters. See also footnote, ch. 4.

3   *JLCE*, 7:258.

4   Eugene B. Wilson.

5   From Lynus Walker, father-in-law of co-author Evans. Walker was raised by his paternal grandfather, Huisus Mux Mux, a.k.a. John Walker, a warrior of the 1877 War.

6   *JLCE*, 7:256–8. Wheeler, *The Trail of Lewis and Clark*.

7   *JLCE*, 7:256. Likelihood of the welcoming song and style confirmed by retired Nez Perce musicologist Dr. Loren Olsen.

8   This type of an event was witnessed in 1855, at the arrival of the Nez Perces for the opening of negotiation & for the 1855 treaty, now this style is rare only to be seen by a few riders in parades and ceremonies associated with the Pendleton Round-Up each September in Pendleton, Oregon, by Umatilla, Cayuse and Walla Walla relatives.

9   Gay, *With the Nez Perces*. Incidentally, it was also the preferred method of grazing horse control by the French cavalry.

10   *JLCE*, 7:257.

11   Ibid.

12   The specifics of their castration technique and the diffusion of the method is thoroughly discussed in a 1955 work of Douglas Osborne, entitled, "Nez

Perce Horse Castration—a Problem in Diffusion," reprinted in *Northwest Anthropological Research Notes,* 2: (1/2): pp. 113–122.

13   *JLCE,* 7:259.

14   Ibid., 9:310.

15   Ibid., 7:259.

16   Gass, *Journals,* p. 187.

17   *JLCE,* 7:257–8.

18   *JLCE,* Ibid., 9:310.

19   Labich had several grouse with him and young Shannon had several grouse and two "squirrells." *JLCE,* 7:257.

20   Ibid., 7:233.

21   Spier and Sapir 1930:211, quoted in Anastasio, *The Southern Plateau,* p. 181.

22   From Teit, 1930:170, quoted by Anastasio, *The Southern Plateau,* pp. 175–81.

23   Billy Williams on this relationship.

24   See Peo-Peo-Tah-Likt, *Historical Sketches of the Nez Perces,* Cage #1218, p. 13.

25   Peo-Peo-Tah-Likt (Bird Alighting) and Chief Many Wounds (Sam Lott), *Historical Sketches of the Nez Perces* Manuscripts, Archives and Special Collections, Washington State University, Pullman, Washington, 1935), Cage #4681, p. 5. Hereafter cited as Peo-Peo-Tah-Likt, *Historical Sketches of the Nez Perces,* Unpublished manuscript, Account 2.1. Cage #4681.

26   Ibid., p. 2

27   Ibid.

28   Ibid., 8-9.

29   See Robert B. Betts, *In Search of York: The Slave Who Went to the Pacific with Lewis and Clark* (Boulder, CO: The University Press of Colorado and The Lewis and Clark Trail Heritage Foundation, 2000)

30   *JLCE,* 7:265.

31   Ibid., 7:265.

32   Ibid., 9:311.

33   Ibid., 7:268.

34   Ibid., 7:270.

35   Ibid., 7:271.

36   John W. Fisher, *Medical Appendices of the Lewis and Clark Expedition.* 8th edition. (Self-published, 2006).

37   *JLCE,* 7:274.

38 Ibid., 7:277.

39 Ibid., 7:278.

40 Gass, *Journal*, p. 189.

41 Information from tribal elders Irvin Watters, Cecil Carter, and Horace Axtell, who all "played the game" in their youth.

42 *JLCE*, 9:314.

43 The nearest guns were probably on the Missouri, New Mexico, California and Alaska, the deer was retrieved by the Indians on a raft *JLCE*, 7:279

44 *JLCE*, 7:278.

45 Ibid., 7:280–1.

46 See Caroline James, Lillian Ackerman, etc.

47 Gass, *Journal*, p. 190.

48 *JLCE*, 7:280.

49 Ibid., 7:281.

50 Pomp was probably suffering from a staph infection, courtesy John Fisher.

51 *JLCE*, 7:284.

52 Ibid.

53 Ibid., 7:285.

54 Moulton suggests this was probably nettle-leaved giant-hyssop, horse-nettle, see *JLCE*, 7:285 n. 4.

55 Near the hamlet of modern Kooskia, Idaho, at the mouth of the South Fork of the Clearwater River and the main Clearwater.

56 Salmon traveled on their own schedule and appeared sooner in their annual migrations in the Snake than in the Kamiah region of the Clearwater River Kamiah Valley area of the Clearwater River.

57 *JLCE*, 7:286.

58 Ibid., 7:289.

59 Ibid., 7:290.

60 Ibid., 7:281.

61 Ibid., 7:294.

62 Ibid.

63 Ibid.

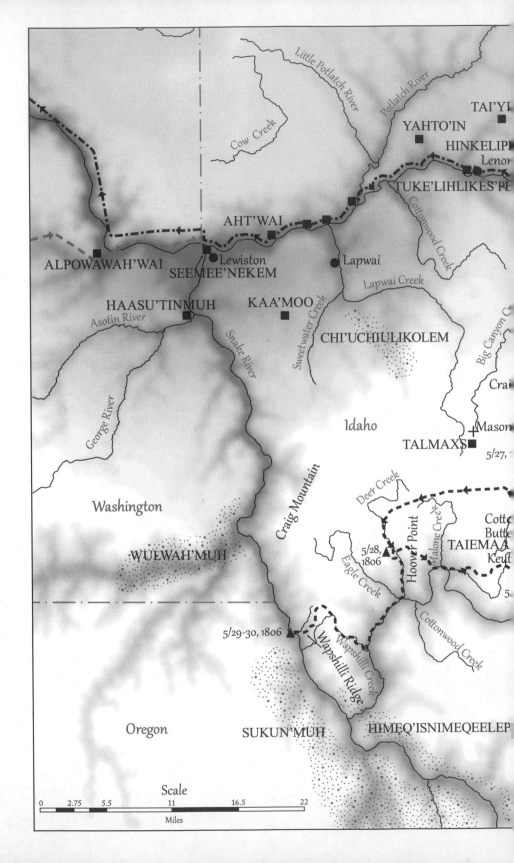

Little Potlatch River
Pollatch River
Cow Creek
TAI'YI
YAHTO'IN
HINKELIP
Lenor
TUKE'LIHLIKES'PE
AHT'WAI
Cottonwood Creek
ALPOWAWAH'WAI
Lewiston
Lapwai
SEEMEE'NEKEM
Lapwai Creek
HAASU'TINMUH
KAA'MOO
Asotin River
Sweetwater Creek
CHI'UCHIULIKOLEM
Big Canyon C
Snake River
Cra
Idaho
George River
Mason
TALMAXS
5/27,
Deer Creek
Craig Mountain
Hoover Point
Malone Creek
Cott
Butt
Washington
TAIEMAA
5/28,
1806
Eagle Creek
Keu
WULWAH'MUH
5
Cottonwood Creek
5/29-30, 1806
Wapshilli Creek
Wapshilli Ridge
Oregon
SUKUN'MUH
HIMEQ'ISNIMEQEELEP

Scale

| 0 | 2.75 | 5.5 | 11 | 16.5 | 22 |

Miles

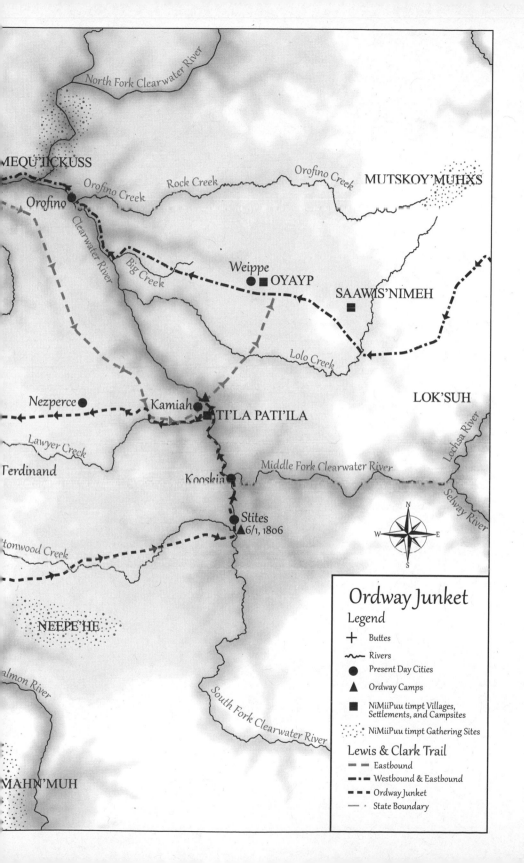

MEQU'IICKUSS

Orofino

MUTSKOY'MUHXS

North Fork Clearwater River

Orofino Creek

Rock Creek

Orofino Creek

Clearwater River

Big Creek

Weippe

OYAYP

SAAWIS'NIMEH

Lolo Creek

LOK'SUH

Nezperce

Kamiah

TI'LA PATI'ILA

Lawyer Creek

Lochsa River

Ferdinand

Middle Fork Clearwater River

Kooskia

Selway River

Stites
▲6/1, 1806

N
W E
S

ttonwood Creek

NEEPE'HE

almon River

South Fork Clearwater River

Ordway Junket
Legend
+ Buttes
〜 Rivers
● Present Day Cities
▲ Ordway Camps
■ NiMiiPuu timpt Villages,
  Settlements, and Campsites
⁛ NiMiiPuu timpt Gathering Sites

Lewis & Clark Trail
⬛ Eastbound
⬛ Westbound & Eastbound
⬛ Ordway Junket
— State Boundary

MAHN'MUH

Chapter 12

The Ordway Junket

One of the most ignored episodes of the activity stirred by Lewis and Clark while waiting in Kamiah Valley for the Bitterroot snows to melt is the trip to the middle Snake River region, a gorge, 7,900 feet deep, that would eventually be named "Hells Canyon." Thirty-year-old Sergeant John Ordway of New Hampshire led the junket and kept a spare record of it in his journal. Robert Frazier was with Ordway and probably wrote of it also but, unfortunately, his journal has not been found. Luckily, Patrick Gass and both Lewis and Clark wrote in their journals some of what was described to them by the participants. It was a rich adventure and perhaps an impossible mission without help from different tribal members nearly every step of the way.

On Sunday, May 25, 1806, Private Silas Goodrich left Camp Chopunnish and traveled about half a dozen miles upstream to a village on the opposite side of the Clearwater River. After doing some trading, Goodrich returned and reported seeing salmon, "fat and fine," which the Nez Perces informed him came from a place on Pik'u-nen (Lewis's [Snake] River). Goodrich's report was probably the inspiration for the captains to send a special three-man task force to "that place" where salmon might be "procurred in abundance."

Sergeant John Ordway and Privates Robert Frazier and Peter Weiser were chosen to go, to trade for salmon, and return the next day if possible. At eight in the morning, on a cool and cloudy Tuesday, May 27, they began with the serious undertaking of swimming their saddle horses and pack stock across the swollen Clearwater River. With their saddles and equipment stacked in the center of their canoe, they poled and paddled for the far bank. Someone held the lead ropes of the horses. In August, this location was an easy ford, but the end of May was a time of icy cold water and deep treacherous currents. There was ample opportunity for catastrophe, but they made their way across safely.

Once on the south bank (modern Kamiah, Idaho), at the camp of Chief Red Grizzly Bear, they were joined by three young Nimíipuu men and, together, they rode back up the trail that initially had brought the Corps of Discovery to the Kamiah Valley. Based on Ordway's journal, it is difficult to trace their route precisely, but they rode about five miles up Commeap Creek (Lawyer's Creek), "left this creek ascended a high hill on a plain and proced. on." So undoubtedly their route took them past or through Chief Tun-na-che-moo-toolt's (the Broken Arm) village and their own camp of May 10–12, along Lawyer's Creek. There were several routes out of the canyon, all of them steep for horse travel, but many that were possible. An old trail led up a ridge parallel to Suzie Creek and may have been the one used. This was the trail descended by the expedition just before the Grand Council.

Once on top, horse travel was easy, and they continued along their old route for a short while. Then they left their old trail and headed generally west, following the open divide between Lawyer's Creek to the south and Long Hollow Creek to the north. They probably passed a little to the south of the modern hamlet of Nez Perce, the county seat of Lewis County, Idaho.

Because Lawyer's Creek flows in a long curve or bow, the Ordway troupe's relatively straight line of travel finally began to bring them back, like a bow string to a bow, into the proximity of Lawyer's Creek and Canyon. Because they were now far upstream, the trail to the canyon floor which took them down had a vertical drop of only about 400 feet. Where they had made their morning ascent, it was about 1,300 feet.

Ordway wrote that they passed a lodge where they struck the creek again, and followed said creek about eight miles farther upstream, and came to one of Chief Twisted Hair's villages. He was the chief who had taken care of their horses during the winter of 1805-06. Ordway never names Twisted Hair in his account, but his description as the one "which took care of the horses," or the "old chief," clearly identifies him. In an earlier journal entry where we know he was referring to Twisted Hair, he also called him the "old chief."

Later, Lewis confirms that indeed Ordway, Weiser and Fraizer were with Twisted Hair when he wrote June 6: "This morning Frazier returned having been in quest of some roots and bread which had left at the lodg of the Twisted hair on his way to the fishery on Lewis's river." While Ordway and crew were listening to the thunder and trying to stay dry huddled by Twisted Hair's fires, both Lewis and Clark were concerned over the whereabouts of Chief Twisted Hair, upon whom they were depending to guide or provide guides for the return over the Bitterroots. What did they expect him to do—hang around Camp Chopunnish and wait for the snow to melt?

They need not have worried. Twisted Hair, a *miyóoxat,* was responsible to many people scattered over a wide region. Besides, he was an an experienced mountain traveler, and knew that it would be weeks before the white men would be able to traverse the Bitterroot Mountains. In the meantime, Twisted Hair relieved the three young men of Kamiah of their guide duties, and they turned back towards the Clearwater River. Twisted Hair would personally conduct the Ordway party to the fishing place.

Obviously there had been some miscommunication over the distance between Kamiah Valley and the Lewis (Snake) River fishery, for they had already ridden, not a half-day's ride, but all day and perhaps 26 miles to Twisted Hair's village, located where Willow Creek flows into Lawyer's Creek. Next morning, Wednesday the 28th, they set out early with Twisted Hair and another Indian leading. Ordway wrote that they rode "on a plain" indicating they were up and out of the creek bottom.

They passed between Mason Butte (Talmaks Butte) and Cottonwood Butte, both heavily timbered, which rise out of the plain. These buttes, both sacred sites as *wéeyekin* locations to the Nez Perces, are obvious landmarks gracing the western skyline from almost anywhere on the prairie; it is too bad neither was mentioned by Ordway, for they would provide obvious reference points.

Ordway, Twisted Hair and the others soon found themselves in the timber and heading west. After a couple of hours, they turned southwest. Still in a forest of ponderosa, lodgepole, and fir, they had entered a large bench country, where the ground sloped upward and finally into a long, rough, table-top ridge known to the Nimíipuu as Wayatinwaus, a place to receive the guardian spirit, later named Craig Mountain by the settlers. This high tableland was incised by a number of creeks dropping off to both the Salmon River on the south and the Snake River on the west.

Two hours' horseback probably brought the small group near the headwaters of Deer Creek, which falls 3,000 feet and enters into the Salmon River about 14 miles up from where the Salmon melds with the Snake. They pushed on through a rugged area that remains remote to this day. The horses struggled against scattered snow patches and downed timber, then "towards evening," Ordway wrote, "we descended a bad hill down on a creek," and "followed it down Some distance and arived at a village where we Camped." From the saddle that day, Ordway counted 14 deer and several mountain sheep.

The village was located partway down the west side of Deer Creek on a bench, about where the timber begins to give way to open basalt-studded breaks. Located far from the river, the "village" was likely a seasonal root-gathering and hunting camp.

The travelers spent another rainy night (May 28), and the next morning it rained more. Ordway wrote that Robert Frazier "got 2 Spanish mill dollars from a squaw for an old razer." And Ordway went on to speculate: "we expect they got them from the Snake Indians who live near the Spanish country to the south." Neither Lewis nor Clark made any mention of the Spanish dollars in their journals, but Patrick Gass, who received the story secondhand, reported that "there are several dollars amoung these people which they get in some way." And he specifically identifies the two dollars that Frazier traded for as having come from around the neck of a Snake Indian whom the Nez Perces had killed some time earlier. Frazier's trade for the dollars reveals the wide-ranging commercial network that linked the Nez Perces to many people in faraway places.[1]

After a light breakfast, Ordway's party, still led by Twisted Hair and his companion, descended along a narrow trail. "Shortly" all arrived at the Salmon River, called by Ordway "a fork of the kimoo-enim or Lewises river," known to the Nez Perces as Tamáanma. The five riders were now in the bottom of the lower Salmon Gorge and, from where they first came to the water's edge, the river runs generally west.

Twisted Hair's guiding brought the party to the Salmon at or near the mouth of Deer Creek, just a half mile above the mouth of Eagle Creek, another of those incising streams coming from the north. The river bank was easily traversed here on foot or horseback, one of the few areas of the lower Salmon where this was possible since the slopes running from basalt bluffs to the water's edge were relatively gentle here. They followed the bank, Ordway wrote, for "Some distance" and then "bore to the right up a creek."

Although he does not say so in his journal, Ordway could not have ridden along the Salmon much farther. It was only about eight more miles down the Salmon to Lewis's or Snake River, and one might wonder why they did not simply follow the Salmon River to its juncture with Lewis's River? One might wonder, reading his journals or looking at a flat map. But Twisted Hair knew what he was doing.

Just three miles beyond the mouth of Wapshilla Creek, the creek they "bore up," would have brought the travelers to "Blue Canyon," where the Salmon runs between high, stone bluffs, dangerous and impractical for any travel. Lewis, who must have quizzed the men on this topic, declared in his own journal that the river was "as one continued rapid about 150 Yds. wide it's banks are in most places solid and perpendicular rocks, which rise to a great hight; its hills are mountains high." Certainly Twisted Hair knew that continuing down the Salmon would be folly on horseback or afoot. He guided them away from danger and towards a more practical route.

Ordway simply recorded: "passd one lodge crossed a steep bad hill and descended down a long hill an a run pass a large lodge and descended the worst hills we ever saw a road made down."[2] The steep bad hill describes Wapshilla Ridge, which separates the Salmon River drainage from the Snake. Following the Wapshilla Creek trail allows the traveler to top out on Wapshilla Ridge at a lower elevation than following China Creek. Still, it is a steep, rugged climb.

To ascend from the Salmon to a saddle leading to the head of Cottonwood Creek, which drains west into the Snake, is to rise more than 3,500 feet in approximately 4 miles. Once on top, you can straddle the Wapshilla divide. The party could look to the east, northeast, about 20 miles and see Cottonwood Butte, passed the day before. Nine miles south, the Salmon River merged with the Snake, but they could not see the waters actually join, as the knarled end of Wapshilla Ridge blocked that sight. But they could see plainly where the canyons joined and, beyond that (another 20 miles), they looked into the heart of what would come to be called Hells Canyon, 7,913 feet deep, with the Seven Devils Mountains on the east, nearly 10,000 feet in elevation, and the equally high Wallowa Mountains to the west.

No one on the Lewis and Clark expedition had ever faced a canyon like this before. Where they began their descent, the Snake Canyon was not as deep as many places upstream, yet it was still formidable at more than 4,000 feet down sharp volcanic rock alternating with steep slopes slick with mud. They crossed through a saddle and into a branch of Cottonwood Creek.

In their descent, they probably worked their way in a northwesterly direction, passing an easy divide between Cottonwood Creek and Big Cougar Creek, then followed down the ridge between the north and south forks of Big Cougar Creek. It was towards evening when they arrived "at the Kimoocnim or Lewises river at a fishery at a bad rapid," wrote Ordway. With moccasined feet and unshod ponies, they had been three days making their "half-day's ride."

There is disagreement over the location at which the Ordway-Twisted Hair party crossed Wapshilla Ridge and, consequently controversy, too, over which route they descended to the Snake. According to Idaho historian John Peebles, the Ordway group ascended China Creek, not Wapshilla Creek and crossed Wapshilla Ridge further to the north and descended to the Snake at Wild Goose rapids.[3] Merle Wells, long-time director of the Idaho Historical Society, has them ascending China Creek and crossing Wapshilla Ridge and descending to the Snake between China Garden Creek and Cave Gulch to McDuff Rapids, a route which parallels the Peebles route, but further south.[4]

We, the authors, are convinced they crossed the saddle at the head of Wapshilla Creek (paralleling the Merle Wells route, but even further south). Although there is no way of knowing exactly where they went, the evidence we saw visiting the locale more than a half dozen times suggests they traveled through the top of Cottonwood Creek, which is like a hand with the fingers spread wide at the top, like a fan, with the fan handle representing the mouth of Cottonwood Creek. They followed a plain trail through a saddle, then descending by crossing several finger ridges and traversed through another saddle into the Cougar Creek drainage and down to Cougar Bar and Big Cougar rapids, the Cochrane rapids and Cochrane Islands.[5]

That the Wapshilla Creek-Cottonwood Creek-Big Cougar Creek trail connecting the Salmon country to the Snake drainage was the best saddle horse route confirmed by Dick Jain (1933–2008) of Lapwai, Idaho, who worked as a cowboy wintering cattle on Cougar Bar. Descending Cottonwood Creek all the way to the Snake was unlikely because that drainage terminates in a series of high, impassable bluffs and waterfalls. Another fact of the terrain that suggests passage into the Cougar Creek drainage is that traveling west in the bowl formed by the headwaters of Cottonwood Creek naturally brings the sojourner to a saddle in the ridge separating Cottonwood Creek from Cougar Creek, which runs southwest.

Ordway noted that they were near a fishery on a "bad rapid," and there was one large lodge which Ordway estimated as "about 100 feet long and 20 wide." Just outside this lodge, Twisted Hair told the men to sit down and not go into the lodge until they were invited. Too many times already the white men had poked their heads into, and then entered dwellings, that did not belong to them, and Twisted Hair had already told Lewis that the people did not like that. Twisted Hair's presence with Ordway helped ensure a friendly acceptance and, at the same time, he successfully got the three white men to recognize appropriate tribal protocol. Thus they waited outside and, at length, were invited in. Robes were spread for them to sit on, and they were fed roasted salmon and some "white bread which they call uppah." Ordway wrote that they ate "hearty of this fat fish but did not eat 1/4 of it."

Because scholars are unsure of the location of this village, the authors planned to take our camping outfit in a dory from the boat launch at Pittsburgh Landing on the Snake, float downstream and investigate the possible village sites. Initially, we planned for a summer excursion, but scheduling conflicts forced the authors to hold off launching into the Snake current until the last week of October, 2002. It turned out to be the coldest week in October on record. Convinced that Cougar Bar was the correct location, we camped three nights in the canyon, closely examining Cougar Bar and several other possible village locations.

We read volume seven of Gary Moulton's authoritative edition of the *Journals of the Lewis and Clark Expedition* as we rowed downstream and found more clues that fit Cougar Bar than any of the other sites. For example, we located a deep rectangular depression where a long house might have been placed. It was 26 paces long and 7 paces wide, close to Ordway's description.

Cougar Bar also fits the general description offered by elder Kew-Kew-Kew'-lu-yah h (Jonathan "Billy" Williams) to anthropologist Alice Fletcher in her 1891 interview. One village was named, See-wy-yah which is descriptive of "a sudden turn or bend of the river around a promontory." This, again, fits the Big Cougar Bar location. See-wy-yah was likely where Ordway and his men found their fishery and began their trade. Other recent investigators have come to the same conclusion.[6]

The next day, May 30, a few small groups of people left the fishery with nearly all the salmon caught, and the Ordway party waited in anticipation of getting some fish, too. In the meantime, they were offered more roasted salmon to sustain themselves. Ordway wrote that they observed "only three dip nets at 3 places a fishing," and most of the fish were being caught on the far side of the river in the "whorls and eddys." Ordway made no comment on any other fishing practices and techniques.[7] If the fish were running upstream in abundance, it is likely the Nez Perces would have been spearing them and using fish traps, also.

The description of this fishing village upon a "bad rapid" does little by itself to identify its location, because there are many bad rapids on the Snake. Yet there are additional clues which point to the village location being near Big Cougar (Creek) Bar and Cochrane Rapids on the Snake River.

See-wy-waa village represented not only a fishery, but also a crossroads between the lower Salmon and Clearwater country (modern day Idaho) and the Wallowa Valley region (of modern day eastern Oregon). It was a meeting place and a trading center, and folks were coming and going, as alluded to in Ordway's remark on the 30th that "a number of [Indians?] left this cairly with nearly all the Salmon which was caught so we had to wait here to day expecting to git some Salmon."

People were coming to the site to trade for early salmon, and obviously there were not yet enough caught to satisfy the demand—thus the wait. And the observation that only three dip nets were in action surely points to the fact that the salmon were not yet running in force. Twisted Hair and his companion did not leave with Ordway on the morning of Saturday, the 31st, "as they had got no fish yet."[8]

Another bit of evidence, suggesting the location of the fishery and the range of activities, is not in Ordway's written account, but in what he must have reported to Lewis, who wrote in his journal on Monday, June 2nd, that "at the fishery on Lewis's (Snake) river below the forks (of Snake and Salmon) there is a very considerable rapid nearly as great from the information of Scgt. Ordway as the great falls of the Columbia the river 200 Yds. wide." This information, comparing Cougar rapids with the Celilo Falls of the Columbia, sets it apart.

Ordway's reference to "the great falls of the Columbia" could only be Celilo Falls, near present day The Dalles, Oregon. The Celilo Falls were inundated in 1957 by the rising waters behind The Dalles Dam, but prior to that were one of the great salmon fisheries of the world. There remain hundreds of historical descriptions and thousands of photographs of Celilo, and both authors retain vivid memories of it before its 1957 inundation. Only Cochrane Rapids and Big Cougar Rapids on this portion of the Snake compare with Celilo.

Although Celilo was more than twice the size, in both drop and volume, than any of the middle or lower Snake rapids, there are some aspects of the Cougar Bar, Cochrane Rapids site that are worthy of comparison, albeit on a smaller scale. For example, at Celilo the river appeared to drop sideways, falling from the northern (Washington) shore of the Columbia towards the southern (Oregon) shore generally; that is to say, the falls were not formed by a ledge of rock going in a straight line from shore to shore, but by a series of ragged ledges forming a series of islands and drops that ran parallel to the northern and southern shore. This is the situation, too, at Cochrane Islands. Some are large fields of river rock thrown into islands in the river center, and there also are large basalt formations thrusting upwards, and the current flows past, between, and sometimes over these rock ledges.

No other rapid on the Snake looks remotely like Celilo. In Ordway's time the rapids may have been even more abrupt, since in both the late nineteenth century and early twentieth the rapids were blasted with explosives to improve the channel for steamboat navigation.[9]

It's possible that Ordway's being reminded of Celilo was based on something he saw other than the river conditions, which triggered a comparison. Ordway did not write it, but both Clark and Lewis described the lodge (where Ordway, Frazier and Weiser were required to wait outside) as having a flat roof. Flat roofs were typical of many of the dwellings on the Columbia's shores at Celilo.

Or perhaps it was the trade Ordway witnessed going on around him? Again, this would not be on a scale with Celilo, where massive exchanges of goods transpired between the products of both the Plains and the Pacific, but the Cochrane Rapids, Cougar Bar area, and even downstream to Cache Creek and McDuff Rapids was rather an area where the Wallowa Nez Perces and those of the Clearwater and lower Salmon region connected. Traveling, socializing and trading were high on the agenda, too, of their Umatilla, Cayuse, and Walla Walla relatives (Sahaptian speakers, although the Cayuse also had their own primary language) coming to this area of the Snake through the Wallowa country from the Blue Mountains and Grande Ronde River country, and beyond.

Access makes a trading center possible, and the See-wy-yaa village produced a prime commodity: early salmon. In that rugged canyon, nature allows trails in few places. And many a ridge that at first looks like a promising route ends in cliffs or steep rockslides. Other trails parallel streams, but likewise disappear in bluffs and waterfalls. While some trails allow people and horses to reach the canyon from the east and others from the west, there are few places where trails from both east and west converge simultaneously on the Snake's banks. Cougar Bar and downstream environs for several miles constitute one such location. The relatively gentle riverside terrain and the convergence of east and west trails at a prime fishing spot make the Cougar Bar and See-wy-yaa village the likely Wallowa-Clearwater-Salmon hook up.

The presence of Ordway, Frazier, and Weiser may have posed a temporary imposition upon the village hospitality. Late May was the early stage of the salmon season, and Ordway wrote that the Indians "have but fiew Salmon." Ordway does not say how many salmon he was able to trade for, nor what items he used to strike his deal but, in his journal entry of May 31, the day he and his men left Snake River, he made the comment that some of the young Indians "stole some of our fish."

No one has ever questioned Ordway's statement, the only documentary record of the incident, yet a critical examination of it seems merited on several grounds. Theft in Nez Perce society was rare. This is reflected in the journals of all expedition members. But throughout the expedition, incidents of theft were treated seriously. Why did Ordway not earnestly pursue this case as other episodes of theft were addressed at other times during the expedition? Why were the "thieves" not directly confronted nor redress sought through the offices of Twisted Hair making the expedition's case to the Fishing Leader? And if fish were taken, why were only "some" of the fish stolen and not "all"? Answers to such questions may provide insight into the "stolen" fish.

Imagine Ordway and his men awakening on the morning of May 31. Did they look about and discover the fish were missing, or did they actually witness the "theft"? There are few trees on Cougar Bar and none of any height, only the Hackberry and Thornbrush Tree (Columbian Hawthorn). Where did they hang the salmon? Maybe they hung them on drying scaffolding constructed of driftwood. It is easy to imagine hanging heavy salmon too low for protection from coyotes, wolves, or camp dogs. And again, if there was a real theft committed by young Indians, why were only "some" stolen and not all? Maybe the 17 salmon that the expedition packed out of Snake River Canyon were the salmon hanging highest in the brush, and every other fish, the salmon hanging within reach, was taken by camp dogs.

Every Nimíipuu fishing village had a Fishing Leader, known as *lewtek'enew'éet*.[10] His responsibilities were manifold and including foremost, the equitable distribution of available fish. At the end of May 1806, the large Chinook salmon were not in sufficient numbers in the Clearwater River for the villages located there to harvest adequate fish to feed their people. This is why many people migrated to downriver locations to make early interceptions of the upriver migrating salmon. The fish migrated into Snake River before the Clearwater, and that is one reason why Twisted Hair and others traveled to the Snake River: more salmon, sooner.

By custom or law, visitors to any of the fishing villages had to defer to the "Fishing Headman," or Fishing Leader. This is why Ordway wrote on the 30th that "a number of [Indians?] left eairly with nearly all the Salmon which was caught so we had to wait here to day expecting to git some salmon" and why he observed the following day that "our old chief [Twisted Hair] and his man stayed as they had got no fish yet."

Why did Ordway receive salmon ahead of Twisted Hair? Did the village *lewtek'enew'éet* (Fishing Leader) follow a courtesy of dealing first with guests who had the furthest to travel? Perhaps, but maybe, too, there were simply no more trading goods to be bargained for, and the three white men, who were never invited, posed a temporary imposition upon meager village resources. Still, the whites received the usual hospitality, and then it was time for Ordway and company to move on.

Another possible explanation was that the white men had traded for salmon with persons not authorized by custom to strike a deal. In a time of abundant salmon, this violation might have passed unnoticed, but since there were as yet few salmon, maybe another trading group arrived at See-wy-ya whose presence also demanded village hospitality—meaning, they needed to be fed. If salmon acquired in an "unauthorized trade" were hanging nearby, they were likely subject to an "adjustment" by the Fishing Leader.

There are other scenarios of cultural misunderstanding. Trade amongst the Nimíipuu was never exclusively an economic activity—it involved diplomacy and ritual that represented several levels ranging from friendship to quasi-kinship. A relationship had to be established before trade could begin. What if Ordway, Weiser, or Frazier made eye contact with a Nez Perce woman, she looked back at him, and he continued to exhibit an obvious interested stare?

In the tribal view, that behavior showed desire for a romantic liaison, one of the best levels of a trade relationship. It is possible, even likely, that the young men did not realize even a temporary "marriage" implied a legitimate expectation that the woman's relatives could claim property belonging to her "husband." This was not something bad, wrong, or immoral; on the contrary, it was practical and a positive and good behavior. Many of these temporary trading patterns became life-long and even extended between families through generations.

The relatives of any of the women involved with Ordway or either of his men could walk into their camp and legitimately claim whatever they chose. For example, if a woman's brother took any item from her lover, it was said that the lover had been "brother-in-lawed." Maybe Ordway got "brother-in-lawed," and maybe he was lucky to get out of camp with his horse and saddle.

This custom has been practiced well into the twentieth century. While there is no documentary evidence that sexual relations occurred at the Snake River village, the possibility cannot be ignored. It cannot be argued that the good sergeant was above such behavior; he had already been involved in a scrape over a woman during the Mandan winter.[11]

Is it possible that the sergeant and his men traded some of their precious goods for sexual favors instead of the salmon requested by the captains, and then explained their lack of a larger catch on "thieving" young Indian males? The captains might be predisposed to believe them and would not be trotting off 70 miles to check out their story.

The morning after the salmon were supposedly stolen, Ordway wrote, "got up our horses eairly and Set out on our return." Twisted Hair remained behind waiting for his own salmon, so Ordway, his men and horses traveled back over the "same road" to "the village we left the day before yesterday." They recrossed Wapshelli Ridge to the Salmon River, then rode along the north bank a few miles to Deer Creek and ascended to the village where they had traded for the two Spanish mill dollars the night of Wednesday, May 28th. They made this leg of the journey without a Nez Perce guide, the only portion traveled so far without one. However, they had ridden this trail just a couple of days earlier with Twisted Hair showing the way, and it was an area of distinctive geographical features—a difficult route, but easy to follow.

Once at the village, they were likely ready to spend the night, but the local *miyóoxat,* "directed us another way whi[ch] he said was nearer & a better road and Sent 2 boys to show us the way to a village on the road. They took us over a verry bad hill down on the Thommonama river [Salmon river] again then left the river ascended a high long hill near the top of which is a large village we Camped near Sd. village as night came on." This was a new trail but, again, they had guides, "2 [Nimíipuu] boys."

The "verry bad hill" crossed by Ordway was likely Hoover Point ridge, and it was in this area which Chief Whitebird, Chief Joseph, and others led the non-treaty Nez Perces away from General Oliver Otis Howard following the Battle of Whitebird Canyon, the first fight in the 1877 war. After crossing this "verry bad hill," the entourage was back on the Salmon River only a few miles upstream from where they had been a few hours earlier. They were near the mouth of Maloney Creek, and then began to once again ascend out of Salmon River canyon on a series of high benches which separate Maloney Creek from Divide Creek.

In the foreground lies a pile of rocks where tribal youth have been sent to face the sunrise in a vigil seeking their Weé yekin or Guardian Spirit. At the bottom of the canyon the Salmon River is seen at what is now called Horseshoe Bend. It was near here that Frazier, Weiser and Ordway, led by two Nimiipuu youths, began making their final ascent out of Salmon River Canyon (May 31, 1806). They followed a trail on ridges that brought them near the top just to the left of Cottonwood Butte, seen here on the skyline. Photograph by Richard Storch, 2002.

Somewhere near the top, perhaps near modern day Keuterville, Idaho (Idaho County), they spent the night in "a large village." The next morning, Sunday, June 1, they were set on the road again by a young man who got them headed in the right direction down a creek "flowing east," probably down the headwaters of Cottonwood Creek and likely through the modern hamlet of Cottonwood, Idaho (Idaho County).[12] About noon, they came to a lodge "where the trail left the creek," which places them at a traditional camping location known in the early Settlement period as "Chapman's Crossing," located where the 1863 reservation line crosses Cottonwood Creek.[13]

That afternoon, they paralled Cottonwood Creek on the south side "thro the high plain a good road" and, by evening, they were at another village, located on a portion of the flat bottom near the mouth of Cottonwood Creek and the South Fork of the Clearwater River. Ironically, this was the same village site which was attacked by General Howard on July 6, 1877, and which resulted in driving the non-treaties on a run for Montana and, ultimately, for those who refused to surrender, to Canada.

But the ancestors of some of those welcomed Ordway and men to their village and, as Ordway wrote, "they appeared verry friendly to us and gave us a large cake of uppah."

The last day of this adventure (Monday, June 2), they rode down the South Fork of the Clearwater to where it emptied into the Clearwater proper. Ordway mentions passing two more villages and, then about noon, they arrived opposite Camp Chopunnish and crossed over in an "Indian canoe," having been deprived of passage in the expedition's craft because of its being wrecked. They swam the horses across safely, and they were back with some spoiled and some excellent salmon. All in all, it had been a remarkable adventure.

They had traveled with a lot of tribal guidance, from Camp Choppunnish on the Clearwater River, to the lower Salmon River, and on to what would become known as Hells Canyon. This 7,913-foot gorge forms a portion of the modern boundary between the states of Oregon and Idaho. Sergeant John Ordway, the trip leader, accepted help from more than a half dozen different Nimíipuu for various portions of the trip.

Where the people are gathered in this photograph is the likely camping place of Ordway, Frazer and Weiser for the nights of May 29-30, 1806. They were led here by Chief Twisted Hair to secure salmon and they were successful in getting back to Kamiah valley with seventeen. This view is towards the west at what is now the Oregon side of lower Hells Canyon. There was no good "road" in 1806, and this condition has not changed; access today is by floating, jet-boat, horseback or hiking. Photo courtesy John W. Fisher.

Lewis and Clark and Sergeant Patrick Gass wrote down accounts of the one-week journey based upon what they were told by the participants but, in most modern accounts, the trip is given scant attention. Yet Ordway, Frazier, and Weiser were the first United States citizens to gaze into Hell's Canyon and the first to actually descend into it, although at the "shallow" northern end. They were also the first to see where the surging Salmon River joined the powerful Snake, and the first to view Oregon's Wallowa Mountains and Idaho's Seven Devils Mountains.

But they were not on a sightseeing mission; instead, they were on a quest for salmon for the Corps of Discovery to consume immediately and perhaps to preserve for the march over the Bitterroot Mountains. In this, they were only partially successful, yet their travel alone was an accomplishment. Their ride of Saturday, May 31, where they climbed out of Hells Canyon, descended into the lower Salmon gorge, climbed out of it nearly to the top, crossed over Hoover Point Ridge, and descended to the Salmon once again, only to then ascend out of the canyon one last time, deserves to go in the annals of great horseback rides of the West, and Nez Perce guides had been instrumental in nearly every leg of the journey.[14]

ENDNOTES

1   James P. Ronda, "Frazer's Razor: The Ethnohistory of a Common Object," *We Proceeded On* v7 no. 3, pp. 12–13.

2   *JLCE*, 9:316.

3   John J. Peebles, "The Return of Lewis and Clark " *Idaho Yesterdays* (Summer, 1966), part 3, p. 21. Hereafter cited as Peebles, "The Return of Lewis and Clark."

4   Merle Wells, "Lewis and Clark in Idaho," *Idaho Yesterdays* (1990).

5   Field proofing by Steve Evans, spouse Connie, Allen V. Pinkham, and Northwest historian and author Carole Simon Smolinski began in 1998, and continued with visits by these and others, including Nez Perces Rodney Carter, his Yakima wife Cindy, and others each year from 1998 to 2005.

6   Alice Fletcher, "Notes…." Authors notified Idaho state archaeologist Ken Reid and officials of Hells Canyon National Recreation Area, who administer the canyon's public lands. In addition, John A.K. Barker, river guide and professor (emeritus, Lewis-Clark State College, Lewiston, Idaho), acting with LC scholar Steve Russell and Idaho Fish and Wildlife Sam McNeil (retired), after considerable investigation, came to the same conclusion, confirmed by Idaho state archaeologist Kenneth C. Reid using a ground penetrating sonar device, that Cougar Bar was the site of the first white penetration of Snake River's Hells Canyon. See John A.K. Barker and Steve F. Russell, Ph., D. "Sgt. Ordway's Salmon River Fishing Expedition." Brochure published through Bonneville Power Administration, Idaho Governor's Lewis and Clark Trail Committee, and the Idaho State Historical Society, printer unknown, 2004. Hereafter cited as Barker and Russell, "Sgt. Ordway's Salmon River Fishing Expedition."

7   Good description of fishing techniques in Dan Landeen and Allen V. Pinkham, *Salmon and His People: Fish & Fishing in Nez Perce Culture* (Lewiston, ID: Confluence Press, 1999).

8   *JLCE*, 9:317.

9   Carole Simon-Smolinski, adjunct professor, Lewis-Clark State College, Lewiston, Idaho (retired). Author of *Hells Canyon on the Middle Snake River: A Story of the Land and Its People* (Lewiston, ID: Confluence Press, 2008).

10   Aoki, *Nez Perce Dictionary*, p. 1157.

11   Ronda, *Lewis and Clark Among the Indians*. Has to do with Ordway's problems at Mandan village over a married woman, p. 106.

12   Barker and Russell, "Sgt. Ordway's Salmon River Fishing Expedition."

13   This Cottonwood Creek begins on Cottonwood Butte and flows generally east and empties into the South Fork of the Clearwater River. Explained due to proliferation of "Cottonwood Creeks" in the region.

14   Contents of this chapter with accompanying slideshow used previously by authors (etc).

Chapter 13

Last Days at the Long Camp

While Sergeant Ordway and Privates Weiser and Frazier were off on their junket, the interaction between local villagers and the expeditioners on the Clearwater continued at a relaxed pace. York, La Page, and Charbonneau returned from upriver with roots, and Collins, Shannon, and Colter came in with eight deer, a new high in venison production. Perhaps equally as exciting was the news that they were able to hunt on the north side of Collins (Lolo) Creek when they found a ford where they could cross with their horses. This was the first indication that the party would be able to reach the Oyáyp (Weippe) Prairie, the launching spot for the Bitterroot crossing.

In what seemed like a miracle, the chief, who had been immobile for so long, on this day showed definite improvement and was able to use his hands and arms, and seemed "much pleased with the prospect of recovering, he says he feels much better than he has for a great number of months." The captains consented for him to remain with them and repeat the sweat treatments. This was a great boon to the reputation of the white captains, first of all because they achieved results and, secondly, because they did so through the highly regarded sweat ceremony of the Nimíipuu themselves. After a few more sweats, Clark reported that he entertained "Strong hope of his [the chief's] recovering by these Sweats."[1] Even little "Pomp" was better this day and showed no fever.[2]

On Thursday the 29th, the Americans decided to build a corral big enough to hold at least a portion of their scores of horses. To catch a horse running at large with 60-plus other horses was indeed a chore. The Indians would catch whatever they wanted by using the lasso from the back of another horse. Clark observed that they were "extreemly dextrous in throwing a Rope and takeing them with a noose about the neck."[3]

The Nez Perce and Shoshones had learned this skill from the Spanish, and soon the Americans would be learning these same techniques, but they had not yet learned them in 1806. It was a source of amusement to the young Nez Perces that the whites had difficulty catching their own horses. With the corral, at least a portion of the horses would be rotated in and kept handy or, as Clark wrote, they could be taken "at pleasure." This made the Americans less dependent upon the young Nez Perces, who were not always available to catch the horses owned by the white men. Whether or not the Nez Perces used the corral prior to 1806 is unknown; however, they soon began constructing their own corrals.

Initially, the men of the Corps also depended upon the Nez Perces for crossing the Clearwater, but the young soldiers finished their own canoe, a large dugout, on the afternoon of May 26th. The canoe was capable of hauling a dozen persons at one time, so it must have been of great length and weight.

They had already been using it for three days when the accident occurred. Shannon and Collins were crossing to the south bank to trade with the villagers on the opposite shore (and upstream) when the canoe was driven broad side, with the full force of a very strong current, against some standing cottonwood trees. This information alone, from Lewis's entry for the 30th, indicates the river was at an extremely high level, up into the cottonwoods on the far side, far beyond its normal banks. The canoe was "instantly filled with water and sunk."

Potts, an "indifferent swimmer," who was also in the canoe, made it to shore "with much difficulty."[4] Three blankets, a coat, and some other merchandise were lost, but fortunately no one drowned or was seriously injured. The following day (May 31), Chief Tun-na-che-moo-toolt (the Broken Arm) and a large party of Nez Perces gathered on the shore opposite Camp Choppunish and attempted to raise the canoe. The journalists do not describe how they tried to raise it, only that they were "unable to effect it—."[5]

Upstream that same day (May 31), Charbonneau and La Page were coming down a trail on the north side of the Clearwater when their pack horse tumbled off a cliff and into the water. Some Nez Perce on the south bank witnessed this alarming event and, when the pack horse swam to their side, they chased it back into the river, where it eventually re-embanked, undoubtedly downstream from the bluffs it originally fell from.

Unfortunately, the water destroyed some paint and a portion of the horse's load was lost—a dressed elkskin and several small articles. The remaining goods from the horse pack were laid out to dry, and Charbonneau and La Page camped on the spot. The Nez Perces recognized the trading opportunity and camped across from Charbonneau and La Page with their own supply of roots to trade. Early the next morning (June 1), the Indians, using a raft, started across, struck a rock "upset and lost thir cargo." Thus everyone returned to their respective camps, "the river having fallen heir to both merchandize and roots."[6]

A Tale of Two Tomahawks

In a second incident on June 1st, Drouillard and Red Grizzly Bear left for a village to the south where, the captains were informed, resided an Indian who had two tomahawks belonging to the expedition. The first tomahawk, which belonged to the late Sergeant Floyd, was supposedly stolen at Canoe Camp in the fall. The other was left carelessly in the camp on Mosquito Creek (Big Canyon Creek, May 7) by either Clark or Lewis.[7] Drouillard and Red Grizzly Bear, who were sent to retrieve the tomahawks, met Chief Cut Nose en route to the prairie, where the three found the tomahawks in one village.

The journals do not tell how the tomahawk left behind at Mosquito Creek was reclaimed, but they got it back. The other, belonging to the late Sergeant Floyd, had been taken at Canoe Camp, but sold to another. Sadly, the man who bought it was in the act of dying when Cut Nose, Red Grizzly Bear, and Droulliard came upon his village. Further, the family of the dying man was determined to bury the tomahawk with him as a token of respect, just as they regularly buried other personal property with the dead and sacrificed horses upon the gravesites.

Cut Nose understood their grief. His own wife had recently died, and he and her relatives sacrificed many horses on her burial spot. But Lewis and Clark had hoped to return Sergeant Floyd's tomahawk to his family. Once Chief Cut nose understood the importance of the tomahawk by way of Droulliard's signs, the chief was able to convey the information to the family of the dying man. A handkerchief, two strands of beads to the family, and two horses, given by the chiefs and to be killed according to custom, influenced the success of the transaction.

June 2nd, Cut Nose, Red Grizzly Bear, and Drouillard returned to Camp Chopunnish with both tomahawks. This peaceful conclusion was a feat that would have been impossible without intervention by the Nez Perce leaders, and Droulliard especially credited the offices of Chief Cut Nose.[8] In an interesting postscript, Sergeant John Ordway wrote that the tomahawk which both captains reported as stolen at Canoe Camp was not stolen, but lost by Captain Clark, and "which the chief kept for us."[9] Another story with no small amount of mystery to it.

The success of the above mission was balanced by the bad news that Captain Lewis's horse, the one he rode over the Bitterroots in September and hoped to ride back across in a matter of weeks, was beyond recovery from its castration wound, and he had to order it shot. With his favorite horse dead, he was now of the conclusion that the Indian method of gelding was superior to their own technique, as all the Indian-gelded horses were fully recovered.[10] It was about noon on June 2, also, that

Sergeant John Ordway and Privates Frazier and Weiser returned from the Snake and Salmon rivers.

On the third of June, Chief Tun-na-che-moo-toolt (the Broken Arm) came into the whites' camp with three warriors and spent the night. He brought the information that they had sent a man over the mountains to discover news of the east side of the Bitterroots, especially to find out what had happened to the Salish over the winter. The news that interested the captains the most was simply the fact that the Indians were able to send someone across.

Then why couldn't the exploring party of Lewis and Clark cross over, also? This question the Nez Perces answered with the advice that it would be best to continue to wait upon the snow melt, as the horse feed on the trail was buried under the snow and thus unable to sustain the riding and pack stock for the duration of the travel. Besides, creeks that must be crossed were too deep and fast for horses. Although not mentioned in the journals of Clark or Lewis, Ordway wrote in his entry for the 5th of June that the Nez Perce courier "went over one mountain and in attempting to cross a creek which was high and rapid his horse fell and hurt him So he turned back to wait untill the water falls."[11]

The captains were disappointed that they had to wait and, in their journals they expressed discouragement regarding the return of the salmon. They had hoped to use the returning salmon as a major source of protein for the journey over the Bitterroot Mountains. The salmon, however, would come in their own time and, as the fish run escalated, the salmon would become available to the bank fishermen. The old-time Indians said that, when the full migration was at hand, you could hear them coming. The white leaders were impatient about the salmon's schedule.

They knew, through the Nez Perces and the report of Sergeant Ordway, that chinook were available in the Snake, but it was too far away, and they did not have "merchendize with which to purchase the salmon,"[12] even if they did arrive in the Clearwater in time for an ample harvest. Lack of salmon power gave them no confidence in securing salmon for themselves.

In lieu of those fish, the captains leaned towards traveling up the Clearwater breaks on their north, to the "Quawmash Grounds beyond Colins Creek" (Oyáyp Prairie), and to secure game and dry meat for the crossing of the Bitterroots. This they would do around the 10th, with a view of beginning their cross mountain journey about the middle of June, the time the Nez Perces had been telling them all along that would allow travel with horses over the Lolo.

The morning of June 4, the captains repeated their promises to Chief Tun-na-che-moo-toolt (the Broken Arm), Cut Nose and Red Grizzly Bear regarding peace and trade. Once again, the captains invited them or their representatives to travel with them as far as the falls of the Missouri. At the Falls, they would participate in a peace-making with the "Minitarres of Fort dePrarie," and the "Blakfoot Indians."

This was a repetition of the same theme emphasized by Lewis and Clark at the Grand Council of May 12th and really amounted to a reiteration and confirmation with the Americans' imminent departure. Clark also emphasized that travelers could not only accompany Lewis to the north (to the Blackfeet), but also others could go into the Three Forks area with him and come to an understanding with the Shoshones. If a peace was not forthcoming with the tribes on the Marias, Lewis pointed out, the young men of the Nez Perce could inform their fellows so as to remain on guard "untill the Whites had it more in their Power to give them more effectual relief."[13] This sounded good, but the Nez Perces correctly had their doubts about the possibilities of peace with the Blackfeet. Their reply was that they would think about it, but probably would go onto the plains in force later in the year and remain on the east side through the following winter.[14]

Traveling over the pass later in the summer and hunting in conjunction with the Salish and their friends and relatives would be in keeping with their usual pattern. They were periodically at peace anyway with certain bands of the Shoshone and were willing to make and entertain overtures but, with regard to the Blackfeet, it was wiser to hunt and travel in force, united with allies. This was their reality, and they did not need reminding from the Americans to be "on guard."

In the afternoon, the chiefs and warriors returned to their villages, but not before Chief Tun-na-che-moo-toolt (the Broken Arm) invited the captains to his village to have one more talk and to give them some roots for the journey over the mountains. The captains promised they would visit him as requested, on "the day after the tomorow," the 6th of June.

"The Indian Chief" who was being treated with the sweats was given another on the 5th and appeared to continue to improve. Sacajawea's son also had improved to where the poultice was discontinued and a new ointment made of pine resin, beeswax, and bear's oil mixed. The swelling was still hard, but the inflammation was gone, and he was recovering fast.[15]

Robert Fazier, who may have kept a journal and was reputed as making progress in learning the Nez Perce language,[16] received permission to visit Twisted Hair's lodge on June 5th. He informed the captains that the lodge was only about 10 or 12 miles away and that he had left roots there while on the fishing junket with Ordway and Weiser. He wished to pick up these roots. When he did not return this same day (June 5), there appeared no alarm in Camp Chopunnish, and he appeared the next day with Chief Twisted Hair as his companion. His extended absence would have been a source of anxiety at another phrase of the journey, but the friendship between the Nimíipuu and the Corps was now so strong that the captains had come to relax about security measures.

On May 9, when the Americans were traveling from Mosquito Creek (Big Canyon Creek) to Commearp Creek (Lawyer's Creek), they camped near the lodge of Twisted Hair and at that time, it was about the distance from Camp Chopunnish as indicated by Frazier. However, when Ordway, Weiser, and he were traveling to the Salmon River on their fishing junket, they found Twisted Hair encamped on Lawyer's Creek a few miles southwest of the present hamlet of Craigmont, Idaho, at least twice the mileage indicated by Frazier, and this is the camp where the roots had been left.

Had Twisted Hair moved back to the village location of May 9 and brought Frazier's roots with him? Did Frazier want to go to the upper Lawyer's Creek village, and only told the captains the distance was short to encourage them to allow him passage? If his motive were simply to retrieve roots left the night of May 27, why did he not return from Salmon River through the village where they spent the night of May 27? These are questions which will probably never be answered, but circumstances surrounding Frazier's activity invite suspicion and speculation. What was going on between Robert Frazier and the Nez Perces?

Chief Twisted Hair returned to Camp Chopunnish with Frazier, but Lewis could not talk with him because interpreter Drouillard and Clark were off visiting Chief Tun-na-che-moo-toolt, as the captains had promised on June 4. Twisted Hair, unable to converse with Lewis, recrossed the river, and Frazier went with him.

In the meanwhile, Clark's visit with Chief Tun-na-che-moo-toolt enabled the Americans to hear, once more, that the Nimíipuu were not going to cross over the mountains until later in the summer, weeks after the Corps planned to cross. This knowledge led Lewis and Clark to believe that they would receive no help from the Nez Perces in crossing, although Chief Tun-na-che-moo-toolt gave Clark dried *qém'es* for the journey and, in addition, the men with Clark were able to trade for even more roots. Upon examination, they now found that the entire party had enough roots saved up for crossing the Bitterroots.[17]

Chief Tun-na-che-moo-toolt informed Clark that some young men might yet travel with the Corps in crossing the mountains, but that they would have to be selected in council of several bands that would meet near the headwaters of Commearp Creek (Lawyer's Creek) on the prairie.[18]

If the young men to accompany the Corps were selected after the Corps had already left, Chief Tun-na-che-moo-toolt informed Clark they would hurry and catch the party enroute. Clark seemed skeptical of this and confided to his journal that they would not receive "any assistance from them as guides," but would seek guides from the Salish in the neighborhood of Traveler's Rest, the mouth of Lolo Creek and the Bitterroot River.

Chief Tun-na-che-moo-toolt explained to Clark that many "of the Small chiefs of the different Bands of his nation had not heard our word from our own mouths;" some were present in his camp and were glad to see Clark. This was Clark's cue to relate some of the American program to these chiefs as he had done at the Grand Council of May 12.

This was no doubt an assurance to the chiefs who had heard already, from others, the American proposal for peace and alliance. It would have been embarrassing for Chief Tun-na-che-moo-toolt if Clark had not reiterated what he had said earlier.

Chief Tun-na-che-moo-toolt told Clark also that Shoshones had contacted the "Ye-E-al-po" Nation[19] in an effort to create the kind of peace they had heard about from Lewis and Clark the previous year "of the of the East fork of Lewis's river," and that they "were resolved to pursue our Councils."[20]

To dramatically punctuate his own interest and commitment to Clark, Chief Tun-na-che-moo-toolt produced two pipes. One was a present to Clark and the other, he announced, came from the Shoshones, and Clark was to return it to them. This pipe was stone and "curiously inlaid with Silver"[21] to which Clark decorated the stem with blue ribbon and white *wampum* that he informed Chief Tun-na-che-moo-toolt, "was the emblem of peace with us."[22]

The Clark party returned in the afternoon, accompanied by Red Grizzly Bear, the two young chiefs and several others. They met Frazier and Twisted Hair coming from camp Chopunnish, and Twisted Hair told Clark that he could not accompany the Americans across the mountains because "his brother was Sick &c.--."[23]

On June 7, an overcast morning with a few drops of rain, the two young Chiefs left Camp Choppunnish for their village on nearby Lawyer's Creek and took Gass, McNeal, Whitehouse, Goodrich, and Charbonneau with them to trade. These members of the expedition were supposed to get rope for the horse packs and bags for their roots. Gass, Charbonneau, and Goodrich came back in the afternoon having obtained only a little string. McNeal and Whitehouse remained with the villagers on Lawyer's Creek for the night. They probably needed more negotiations with the young ladies for root bags.

Red Grizzly Bear crossed over to the Americans' camp during the day and brought Robert Frazier a new horse, a nice gift in response to some Canadian pacs Frazier had earlier given to Red Grizzly Bear. These Canadian pacs were a high-topped, fur-lined, doubled-soled moccasin. Obviously Virginian Private Robert Frazier, who tried to learn *Nimipuutímt,* the Nez Perce language, was popular with at least some, if not all, the local tribespeople.

On Sunday, June 8th, 1806, the Americans were getting ever closer to leaving the Kamiah Valley. The timing seemed about right; "The sick

Cheif is fast on the recovery," Lewis wrote, and the child of Sacajawea was nearly well and "Bratton has so far recovered that we cannot well consider him an invalid any longer."[24] This was an amazing cure or an uncanny miracle. Clark used all his knowledge for months on Bratton, yet in the end it was the Nimíipuu sweat which seems to have effected a cure.

Sunday, June 8, was marked, too, by a visit of a dozen warriors led by Cut Nose, and the captains got to see some Cayuse tribesmen for the first time, perhaps the same ones who reported on the Shoshone overture relayed to the captains on June 6.[25] They did a little horse trading, and the men played games and held races. The Indians, they found, were "active" and one proved as fast as the fastest American runners, Reubin Field and the Shawnee half-blood, Drouillard. Also on this day, some Nimíipuu men and some members of the Corps, working together, finally dislodged the canoe that had been pinned underwater against some cottonwoods by the strong spring current on May 20.

The morning of June 9 brought the Americans one day closer to the end of the expedition's time at their historic camp, later called the Long Camp, or Camp Chopunnish. That morning the horses were brought in to be made ready for beginning the trek up the long slopes leading to the dividing bench between Collins Creek (Lolo Creek) and the Kamiah Valley and to the Oyáyp (Weippe) Prairie beyond. Several mares and colts were traded to the Nez Perces for horses better able to bear the strenuous trails ahead. The captains managed to exchange one "indifferent" horse for a "very good horse" by throwing a leather shirt into the bargain. Xáx̣aac ʻilpʼílpʼ (Red Grizzly Bear) and several others took leave and set out for the prairie towards the Salmon and Snake rivers, so did the Chief Tun-na-che-moo-toolt (the Broken Arm).

Chief Cut Nose, Lewis wrote, "borrowed a horse and rode down the Kooskooske River a few miles this morning in quest of some young eagles which he intends raising for the benifit of their feathers; he returned soon after with a pair of young Eagles of the grey kind; they were nearly grown and prety well feathered."[26] John Ordway added to this startling information when he reported that Chief Cut Nose captured the birds by using a rope and climbing to the nest in a tree and "[with] the feathers of these eagles the Indians make head dresses war like & paint them & is a great thing among them." Charles Willson Peale was a friend of President Jefferson's who created one of the first museums. Many of the artifacts of the expedition eventually found their way to Philadelphia to Peale's museum. He made a memorandum of some, perhaps all, of the items he received from the president. According to "Peale's Memorandum of Specimens and Artifacts," one item consisted of:

Feathers which were at various times presented to Captn. Lewis and Clarke by the principal Chiefs of the nations inhabiting the Plains of Columbia, whose custom it is to express the sincerity of their friendship by cutting feathers from the crowns of the War Caps and bestowing them on each as they esteem.[27]

This statement clearly reveals that the famed "war bonnet," often referred to as the "plains bonnet," was firmly entrenched with the Nez Perces. The origin of the styled, eagle-feathered headdress, called, *tu'ynu∩suus* [28] amongst the Nimíipuu, is mythological.

The First Nimíipuu *Tu'ynu∩suus* (Eagle-Feather Bonnet)

as told by Elmer "Whiskey" Paul

Waqipaníx, a long time ago, two brothers lived at Píite Village, on the south fork of the Clearwater River. One brother was married to a beautiful young maiden, and they were deeply in love, but she was secretly loved and coveted by the other brother.

He made up a plan and one day approached his married brother and proposed an adventure. He said that they should take a long rope and go upstream to some granite cliffs, Sept-a-qul-watia-kin wespu, today known as Huddleston Bluffs, and hunt eagles. It was agreed they would obtain feathers and trade them to other Indians. They traveled far upstream and then climbed higher and higher until the south fork [Clearwater] was a tiny thread below them.

The married brother allowed himself to be lowered from the top of the cliff a long ways to a rock ledge where there was an eagle's nest. Then his brother put his plan to action. He pulled up the rope and left his brother on the ledge. Now his brother was trapped, there was no way to climb from this difficult spot and so he knew his brother was doomed and would never be seen again.

He returned to the village and reported the sad news that his brother had fallen, he was dead and it was impossible to retrieve his body. The village grieved for the young man and the family grieved, too. And the beautiful young widow grieved. But the brother consoled her and promised to help her, to become the one responsible to protect her and provide fish and wild game and become her husband in every way. This is what he wanted all along, to fulfill the obligations of *pinúukin* [this was a custom that a brother must accept the responsibility of a deceased brother's wife and family. Even if a brother already had a wife, he had to accept his wife's sister as a wife, too, if she lost her husband].

Back on the ledge, the deserted brother was, at first, in shock and did not understand what had happened, but gradually he understood his brother's deceitful plan. He knew why, too late, why he had been abandoned to die.

However, he crept around the rock ledge and came to an eagle's nest where there were four baby eagles. He climbed into their nest and waited, then when a parent flew to the ledge with a rabbit it was torn apart and he was offered a portion. The parent eagle seemed to accept him, and both parents brought food. Sometimes fish were brought to the nest, other times meat from other creatures killed and delivered by the father and mother eagle.

The weeks went by and the parent birds continued to feed the eaglets and the Indian brother. The eaglets accepted him also as a nestmate, a relative. The young eagles exercised their wings daily and, after many months, they were ready to leave their rocky perch and fly. This went on for more months, until they were large and strong, and their soaring skills were keen and their confidence was at its peak. Finally, they took pity upon their Indian brother whom they had come to love, but who could not soar as they could.

This was his chance, his only hope, at last an opportunity to return to his village. The young eagles allowed their legs to be wrapped with rawhide, which the young man then looped around his wrists. It was now or never, he thought once more of his beautiful wife, he raised his arms and, as the eagles flapped their wings, he slid from the ledge into the canyon air.

They all landed in a tangle of birds and brush at the canyon floor. They had dropped hundreds of feet, but not so fast that they were injured. The Indian brother untied the legs of the eagles and unlooped the rawhide from his wrists. Then each mighty *tipiyeléhne,* each eagle, gave several black and white tail feathers to their friend and brother, and instructed him on constructing a special headress to be worn on special occasions to symbolize that they are of the same family, different but related. The eagle would always be the messengers the connection between the man and the spirits above. The feathers would represent bravery, honor, and brotherhood. The human brother now had to return to his people who lived in the canyon and tell about his experiences and what he had learned. The people could take feathers one time from eagles, and then they must be released.

The young woman was getting water at the spring when

she saw him approaching. Was it a dream? The young man walking towards her was thin, but otherwise he looked as her late husband. He had waited where he could watch the spring, waited until he saw his wife coming for water. Then he stepped forth and approached her. First she was in shock and disbelief, then she was crying and ecstatic, her husband was not dead, but alive.

You might think that he would seek vengeance against his brother, but he did not. He was beyond vengeance, and he thought his brother was pitiful. His mission was to deliver the instruction and messages from his eagle family and to rejoin his wife, that was all. It was for the village council to decide his brother's fate, and their ruling was banishment for life.

The returned brother instructed the people with his learning from the eagle family, as he was supposed to do. He taught all the meanings symbolized by their feathers, and the proper respect that must be paid the eagle and the construction of the bonnet and its use. And this is the way it remains today. *wáaqo' kaló'*. That is all.[29]

Elmer Paul of Lapwai, Idaho shows the buffalo hide drum he made and had Nimiipuu artist Nakia Williamson paint a portrait of Chief Looking Glass, the younger, son of Chief Ram's Horn (Looking Glass, Sr.) who aided the expedition. Photograph by Steve Evans.

Alex Pinkham, Sr., veteran of WWI with his granddaughter Lynn Pinkham (Menninick), great granddaughter of Antonia Matthews (mother of Annette Pinkham Blackeagle and grandmother of co-author Pinkham).

That evening, "one of the young Chiefs who had given both Capt Lewis and my Self a horse came to our camp accompanied by 10 of his people and continued with us all night."[30] There was amusement and games in camp, too, that night, "pitching quates, Prisoners bast running races &c—," according to Clark. Nothing is said of sentiment regarding leaving the Nez Perces—the Americans seemed focused on advancing toward the Oyáyp Prairie and the trail leading towards their home. Most of the Nez Perces had moved off in pursuit of their annual rounds. The young chief and his small retinue remained with the Corps of Discovery for their last night at the "Long Camp."

ENDNOTES

1   *JLCE*, 7:310.

2   Ibid., 7:297.

3   Ibid., 7:307.

4   Ibid., 7:308.

5   Ibid., 7:315.

6   Ibid., 7:322.

7   Clark says Lewis left it, Lewis says Clark did it. *JLCE*, 7:322–4.

8   *JLCE*, 7:326.

9   Ibid., 9:319.

10 Ibid., 7:328.

11 Ibid., 9:319–20. Also see Gass, *Journals,* p. 192.

12 *JLCE*, 7:332.

13 Ibid., 7:334.

14 Ibid., 7:333.

15 Ibid., 7:336.

16 Gass, *Journals,* p. 193.

17 *JLCE*, 7:339.

18 This may have been at the village where Ordway, Frazier and Weiser spent the
    night of May 7, and where Frazier had recently gone to retrieve his roots and re-
    turned to Kamiah Valley with Twisted Hair. Or it may have been another village

location nearby. The headwaters of Lawyer's Creek is located in the foothills of Craig's Mountains and is close to the breaks of the lower Salmon River.

19   Waiilatpus, or Cayuse, allies and relatives of the Nez Perces.

20   *JLCE*, 7:341.

21   Ibid., 7:340.

22   Ibid., 7:341.

23   Ibid., 7:342.

24   Ibid., 7:346.

25   Ibid., 7:341.

26   Ibid., 7:348.

27   Jackson, *Letters*, p. 477, quoting Charles Wilson Peale's "Memorandum of Specimens and Artifacts."

28   Aoki, *Nez Perce Dictionary*, plate 3, following p. 1280.

29   In 1926, historian Lucullus Virgil McWhorter acquired a myth of the origination of the Nez Perce Warbonnet. The theme is the same as Elmer Paul's, but the bluff described is "Whe-alp" on the Columbia River northwest of Spokane Washington. In Peo-Peo'lah-Likt's (Bird Alighting) version, the returning brother finds his wife in her lover's arms, and he kills them both. In Gordon Fisher's version, the couple is found in their bed at their home village on the south fork of the Clearwater, and he shoots both with arrows.

30   Jackson, *Letters*, p. 349.

Chapter 14

The First Attempt to Cross

It was still too early to leave for the Bitterroot crossing, still too much snow and high water and not enough horse feed. But the Americans were determined and, in their hurried state of mind, it was better to let them go. The level of the Clearwater was down, but this only marked the beginning of when one could reasonably consider going, not that it would yet be possible. It would be much easier later, when the mountain grass was high and rich. That is when many Nez Perces would cross over to their friends and relatives among the Salish and the buffalo country. The morning of June 10th, the Americans were up early, wrangling the horses, getting them ready to move to Oyáyp (Weippe) Prairie, the jumping-off point to the Lolo Trail, the Bitterroot Mountain crossing.

The distance from Camp Chopunnish to the Quawmash Flats was not far, perhaps 12 miles, but it was 3 miles up to get out of the Kamiah Valley then back down into the depths of Lolo Creek, Lewis and Clark's Collins Creek, and a difficult ford, then another climb to Oyáyp Prairie, the Quawmash Flats. They crossed Lolo Creek safely, but some of their packs got wet. Eight Nez Perces had joined the Lewis and Clark group even before they reached the rim of the Kamiah Valley, and informed the whites that they, too, were going to hunt the area of the Quawmash Flats, but the captains believed the Nez Perces were along "in expectation of being fed."

If this was true, and there is no evidence that it was, the Indians were disappointed, because the hunters of the expedition shot mostly squirrels and none of the meat was shared. The captains stopped sharing on the premise that "we Should use all frugallaty as well as employ every exertion to provide meat for our journey."[1] The Americans were not in their more leisurely Long Camp mode any longer. They were back to familiar old traveling discipline, and their old habits of seeing Indians as pilferers and exploiters returned, as well. Just a few weeks earlier, sharing seemed a good idea. That was when the Americans were hungry and the Indians shared their food with them.

The next morning, June 11, the hunters turned out at dawn and, about noon, most returned. Labiche came back with a black bear and Gibson, a large buck.[2] Tribal hunters turned out, also, but did not fare well, and the expeditioners, again, did not share. One of the Nez Perces traded horses with one of the Americans, then all Nez Perces returned to their own camp, about three in the afternoon.[3]

On June 12, a lone Nez Perce came to their camp on the eastern border of the Oyáyp Prairie, and he remained for the night. On the 13th, he traded his good horse for another, one "which had not perfectly recovered from the operation of castration,"[4] but, in addition, the Nez Perce received an axe and a knife and rode away satisfied with his prizes. It would be June 21, a full week later, before any other Nez Perce would be seen by the Lewis and Clark party.

Without any Nimíipuu guides, the traveling party struggled. The journals of the captains reveal both were apprehensive about the crossing. Lewis confessed in his journal that "the snow and the want of food for our horses will prove a serious imbarrassment." And Clark, echoing his friend, "even now I Shudder with the expectation with great dificuelties in passing those Mountains."[5]

Their concerns were well founded. They left Oyáyp prairie on June 15, traveling generally southeast to where they recrossed upper Lolo Creek (crossed a dozen miles downstream on their way to Oyáyp Prairie on June 10), but incessant rains made the day uncomfortable and the trail dangerous. They were in a thickly timbered region, too, and crisscrossed blow-downs combined with the mud and six foot and higher brush to impair their travel. Still, they rode on, "with much dificuelty."[6] Finally, the rain let up.

The next day, June 16, they were on Hungry Creek, small but deep and "a perfect torrent." They saw increasing amounts of snow in pockets and so little horse feed that, when they found an inadequate amount, they still deemed it wise to camp and use that which was available. The last part of the day, they were riding over packed snow that was eight feet deep in some places and obscured the trail.

They traveled down Hungry Creek about seven miles and were forced to cross it several times. It was ice cold. A few times they avoided crossing the creek by riding up steep brushy side hills and around rocky outcrops as an alternative. There was just no easy or safe way to go. Then they left the creek bottom, ascending a long steep ridge, higher and higher towards the main divide between the Kooskooske (Clearwater) and the Chopunnish (North Fork Clearwater), the ridge which would lead them to Lolo Pass, down Lolo Creek to Traveler's Rest in the Bitterroot Valley.

As they gained altitude, they encountered ever-deepening snow until it became 15 feet in places. Deep snow was not all bad; for a time they were able to go over downed timber, steep rock slides, and even brushy areas which were buried. Where the snow was packed hard, riding went smoothly but, when the horses broke through the surface layer, conditions were impossible. Where was grass for horse feed?

The explorers considered their fate with starved out horses, and the fate of their journals and collections if they should lose the trail in the deep snow and the maze of ridges that lay ahead. The opinions of the men were sought and, when their best woodsmen could give them little assurance of success, the leadership concluded, "Under these circumstances we conceived it madnes...to proceed without a guide."[7] Patrick Gass's version of this event was simple and straightforward. When there were no prospects for horse feed and the road was impossible to find, a halt was called "to determine what was best to be done."

Considering the facts, "it appeared not only imprudent but highly dangerous to proceed without a guide of any kind."[8] In an extraordinary moment, both Clark and Lewis realized and admitted that they were dependent for their lives upon the Nez Perce. In both their journals, they recorded their determination to keep their horses healthy at Oyáyp until they could procure "an indian to conduct us."[9]

In short, they had to turn around and backtrack, the only time in the entire expedition where this proved necessary. They constructed makeshift scaffolding on which to store much of their baggage so that it would not be damaged by the melting snow or molested by animals. This was a somewhat risky thing to do, given the importance of their equipage, but it made little sense to haul it all back down the slopes, and Lewis and Clark were by this point taking risks they would not have considered the previous year, perhaps even the previous month. With a deep sense of disappointment, they turned back, downhill, to Hungry Creek. As they did so, the weather began to "Set in to hailling & raining at this time verry cold and disagreeable."[10] Once back on Hungry Creek, they turned their horses upstream and rode up it about two miles, then camped for the night.

June 18 was cloudy, and it showered cold rain several times during the day. The horses had scattered in the night searching for grass, and it took some time to collect them and get them saddled. Shields and LaPage were left behind to try and bring up two horses that could not be located.

Drouillard and young Shannon were directed by Lewis to travel ahead of the main group, to ride quickly back to the Oyáyp Prairie and then to the "Chopunnish Indians in the plains beyond the Kooskooske (Clearwater) in order to hasten the arrival of the indians who had promised to accompany us or to procure a gude at all events and rejoin us as soon as possible." Ordway says they were to go "to the villages of the *pel-oll-pellow* nation," which in this instance was an obvious reference to the Nez Perce living on the Clearwater.[11]

While Drouillard and Shannon sought guides as instructed, the main group rode on the backtrail at a slower pace towards the Oyáyp Prairie. They were attempting to preserve the condition and strength of their horses. Even at low speed, the going was tedious and even came to a complete stop when John Potts, one of four men clearing brush with a large knife, gave himself a nasty gash in the leg. Lewis stitched and bound Potts's leg.

But then in a ford of the icy, torrent Hungry Creek, Colter's horse was swept from his feet, and both "were driven down the creek a considerable distance rolling over each other among the rocks."[12] Welcome to the land that would be called Idaho. Many tales that began as his do not end as happily. In this instance neither he nor his horse was seriously injured. Colter even saved his rifle, but lost his blanket.

By nightfall, the main party was back on modern Eldorado Creek, a branch of Collin's Creek (Lolo), and were able to find horse feed. The mosquitoes were bad even though they were but a short distance from winter snows. The captains hoped that, with enough game and fish, they might be able to save several days' rugged travel by holing up where they were and awaiting the arrival of the sought-after Nez Perce guides. They spent three nights at this camp, June 18-20, but the guides did not arrive. The hunters were none too successful and fishermen armed with Indian style gigs could not consistently land fish. Hunters even tried, unsuccessfully, to shoot steelhead seen in Eldorado Creek.

Cruzatte brought in several morel mushrooms for Captain Lewis, but he did not have grease to cook them in, and he had left all their salt in their cache of the 17th, so Lewis pronounced even the delicate morel "truly an insippid taistless food."[13] He just was not the happy camper.

By June 20, it was becoming obvious that the main party would have to retreat even further to the Oyáyp Prairie. That morning, hunters had turned out in all directions, and only one bear, a black bear in poor condition, was brought in. The fishermen made serious war on the steelhead trout using "2 guigs a Bayonet fixed on a pole, a Scooping nett and a Snar made of horse[hair]," yet killed only six, not enough to feed all the troops. That evening Labiche and Cruzatte came in with a deer, but the decision had been made already: it was time to pack up once again.

The morning of June 21 was fair, a good day for travel, yet all felt "some mortification in being thus compelled to retrace our steps through this tedious and difficult part of our rout, obstructed with brush and innumerable logs of fallen timber which renders the traveling distressing and even dangerous to our horses."[14] In fact, that day Cruzatte's horse took a broken limb from a fallen log into his groin, which made him useless.[15] When the party reached Collin's Creek, they met two Nez Perces who were heading over the Bitterroots. These were not the guides sought by Drouillard and Shannon, but they had seen them. This left the captains wondering what had happened to their emissaries. There was good news, however: the Nez Perces had with them three horses and a mule which had escaped and headed back to the good grass at Oyáyp. The Indians correctly figured that the Americans must be short four head and returned the stock to Lewis and Clark.

The two Nez Perces themselves brought four supernumery horses with them, but gladly turned around and rode about a half mile down Collins Creek to a good spot where all horses could graze and the combined party could dine and talk. The Indians agreed to hold up their own travel to accompany the Americans if they were ready to try again in two days' time. They rode back as far as Crane Prairie to wait there. Patrick Gass and several other Americans were left behind to hunt, and everyone else made it back to the old Oyáyp Prairie camp of June 10–14 at around 7 p.m. that night. In one week of tremendous effort against difficult conditions, they had traveled exactly nowhere. The Nez Perce said *mimíc'itpas* (they don't listen).

ENDNOTES

1   *JLCE*, 8:11.

2   Ordway wrote that Gibson killed a buck, and Labiche shot a bear, a buck and a crane, *JLCE*, 9:321. Gass also confirms that two bucks were killed, not one. Gass, *Journals,* p. 193.

3   *JLCE*, 8:17.

4   Ibid., 8:23.

5   Ibid., 8:24.

6   Ibid., 8:25.

7   Ibid., 8:31.

8   Gass, *Journals,* p. 195.

9   *JLCE*, 8:32, 33.

10 Ibid., 9:324.

11 There have been a variety of speculations as to the meaning of the references to the pel-oll-pellow nation, as spelled by Ordway (*JLCE*, 9:324) on June 18, 11806, and various other spellings, such as Whitehouse's polot pello or Flathead Nation (*JLCE*, 11:325). Alvin Josephy and Gary Moulton speculate about who these names refer to more precisely. Obviously, Whitehouse's equation of the polot pello as Flathead is incorrect. Whitehouse consistently referred to the Nez

Perces as Flatheads. Josephy's ideas can be examined in Josephy, *Nez Perce Indians and the Opening of the Northwest,* pp. 649–51. Moulton's speculations can be found in *JLCE,* 7:348 n. 1. We believe that the reference is to the residents of a Nez Perce village in the Kamiah Valley, which was sometimes used as a general appelation to all Indians in the region on the west side of the Continental Divide. Robert Frazier used the name "Pallotapollars" on a map, published in Charles G. Clarke's *The Men of the Lewis and Clark Expedition: A Biographical Roster of the Fifty-One Members and a Composite Diary of Their Activities from All the Known Sources* (A.H. Clark Co., 1970), pp. 204–5.

The late Zoa Swayne of Orofino, Idaho, used the term "Tee-e-lap-a-lo" as a village site in Kamiah Valley, located on lower Lawyer's Creek, meaning "place of the crawfish," and so identified by Nez Perce tribal leader, now deceased, the respected Harry Wheeler in Swayne, *Do Them No Harm!,* pp. 5, 7, 145, 326, Chapter 11, n. 1).

The late Lynus Walker, father-in-law of author Evans, and Marcus Oatman, tribal elder and World War II combat veteran, both identified the village location and title based upon the village location by a spring named for a small variety of crawfish, called the *ti'ila,* peculiar to Lawyer's Creek. The location is near Kamiah Second Presbyterian (Indian). In Aoki, *Nez Perce Dictionary,* p. 779, *ti laapaloopa* is listed as the locative form. This village was across the Clearwater from the Long Camp and about a mile upstream. It was the closest village to the Long Camp, and most certainly the Nez Perces with whom the Americans had been, in Lewis's words, "most conversant," the Nimíipuu that they had been camped "next door" to for 30 days and nights.

12 *JLCE,* 8:35.

13 Ibid., 8:37.

14 Ibid., 8:43.

15 Ibid.

Chapter 15

The Second Attempt

Even though the Americans had gone nowhere in one week, they now had a better understanding of the true trail conditions, and they had better prospects for success. Even if the regular Nez Perce guides did not materialize, they had two others waiting at Crane Meadows who were willing to show the way and were confident of the trail.[1]

On June 22, Clark found some beads in his waistcoat pocket and gave them to Joseph Whitehouse with instructions to ride back into the Clearwater Valley and trade for the salmon, which they now knew were plentiful. In the meantime, the hunters of the main party had phenomenal good luck, with a deer and three bear falling to their bullets. Back at the Collins Creek (Lolo) camp, the Field brothers killed a small "pheasant,"[2] actually one of several grouse species.

The morning of Monday, June 23, came, and still there was no sign of Shannon, Drouillard, or Whitehouse. The captains were concerned that something had happened to those sent to the river, and guides would not be forthcoming. To compensate for the possibility of no guides coming from the Kamiah region, Robert Frazier and Peter Weiser (of the uncelebrated Salmon River and Hells Canyon expedition) were sent west to Crane Meadows and beyond to the Collins Creek camp with instructions for Gass, Reubin and Joseph Field, and Weiser to try to catch up with the two Nez Perces crossing the Bitterroots. Gass immediately took his three men and Frazier, left Weiser, and quickly followed up his instruction to follow the Nez Perces and "blaze the trees well as they proceeded."

Later on the 23rd, Drouillard, Shannon, and Whitehouse returned from the Clearwater accompanied by the brother of Cut Nose and the two young chiefs (unnamed, also)[3] who had presented Lewis and Clark "each with a horse on a former occasion at the Lodge of the broken arm [Chief Tun-na-che-moo-toolt]." This reference was presumably to the ceremony at the Grand Council on Lawyer's Creek (Commearp Creek) on May 12. The captains both wrote of these three, "Those are all young men of good Charrector and much respected by their nation."

As if confirming the terms of the American Alliance, they also assured the captains "that thir nation as well as the Wallar-Wallars [Walla Wallas] have made peace with the Shoshones agreeable to our late advice to them."[4] The horses were brought in close to camp to be ready for an early start on June 24.

The main party got an early start and, by lunch, had met up with Frazier, waiting alone on Collins Creek. Peter Weiser, Patrick Gass and the Field brothers had pushed ahead to catch the two Nez Perce who were camped ahead on the trail. The plan was to closely follow the Nez Perce guides while blazing trees along the correct route to clearly mark the trail for the mail party The captains and the remainder of the expedition were not far behind. After they "nooned it as usual" they continued to their old camp of the 18th-20th (on Eldorado Creek, Idaho County, Idaho). They were getting to know this portion of the trail better than they wanted. But it was here that they joined up with Sergeant Gass, Peter Weiser, the Field brothers, and the two young Nez Perces. Gass had persuaded to wait with them for Lewis and Clark by offering them each a pair of moccasins. Therefore, on the evening of June 24, on today's Eldorado Creek, the party was completely reunited, and had a total of five Nez Perces accompanying them. Incidently, each young man was related to tribal spokesmen, either Cut Nose, Red Grizzly Bear, and Twisted Hair.

That same evening, the young Indian men entertained the Americans by setting fire to spruce trees, which created "a very suddon and immence blaze from bottom to top." These trees were described as "tall trees," and, many in the area grew to excess of a 100 feet. "[T]hey are a beatifull object in this situation at night," wrote Lewis, and it reminded the expedition members of a display of fireworks.[5] The purpose of the fires, the Nez Perces told Lewis and Clark, "was to bring fair weather" for the trip over the mountains.[6]

But the weather on the 25th was wet, and only one Nez Perce left camp with the expedition. The others said they would catch up later, but the captains feared that they were preparing to abandon them, writing that one of the guides complained of illness "which I did not much like as such complaints with an indian is generally the prelude to his abandoning any enterprize with which he is not well pleased."[7] But the captains were wrong, and the four who remained behind caught up with the main party by the time of their lunch stop on a branch of Hungry Creek. They proceeded down the branch to Hungry Creek and camped "about one and a half below the campment of the 16th inst."[8]

The next day, the 26th, the party climbed out of the canyon of Hungry Creek and finally reached their cache of the 17th, their old turnaround point from their first attempt to reach the east side of the Bitterroots. It took several hours to rearrange packs to accommodate the extra equipment, and they cooked a meal and measured the depth of the snow. Based upon marks left on the 17th, they judged that the snow had melted about four feet, yet about seven feet remained.

The Indians, as recorded in the journal entries of both captains, hastened all to ride on, because it was a long distance to the next place where horse feed might be found, and there was none at the scaffold "cache." Despite some heavy rainfall on top of the existing snowdrifts, the entire party followed the Nez Perce's directions up and down the rugged and steep dividing ridge between the North Fork of the Clearwater to the north and the Lochsa drainage to the south.

In the evening, they arrived at the side of a steep mountain, not a good camping spot except that the snow on one side of the mountain had melted off, revealing excellent feed for the expedition's horses. Without careful maintenance of their livestock's strength, made possible by their Nez Perce guides, the expedition's fate may be fairly judged.

The intimate knowledge of the mountain conditions at this time, including the location of horse feed and spring water, was critical.[9] The captains' decision not to persist in their ill-judged plan to make the Bitterroots transit alone, but to turn back to Oyáyp (Weippe) Prairie and obtain Nez Perce guides before making a second attempt, was one of the most intelligent choices they ever made. Another Nez Perce man joined them at this camp with the intention of accompanying them the full distance over the mountains—Lewis said all the way to the Great Falls.[10] This made a total of six Nez Perce guides, and each had two or three horses, which means the cavalcade included over 80 head of riding and pack stock.

Although the Nez Perces urged the entire troupe forward on the 26th, the next day the Nimíipuu guides asked them to hesitate at a prominence along the route they called the Smoking Place. It was on this elevated point "the nativs have raised a conic mound of Stons of 6 or 8 feet high and erected a pine pole of 15 feet long. from hence they informed us that when passing over with their families some of the men were usually Sent on foot by the fishery at the entrance of Colt Creek in order to take fish and again meet the party at the quawmash glade on the head of Kooskoske river. from this place we had an extencive view of these Stupendeous Mountains principally Covered with Snow like that on which we Stood."

This remark was telling of the Nez Perce prowess at mountain travel. To send men off the ridge on foot was to have them drop over 3,000 feet in the roughest timber-strewn and rocky country imaginable. Once on the river, the modern Lochsa, they were to catch fish, dry them, and continue upstream to the headwaters, where they would rendezvous at Packer Meadows with their families traversing the mountains on horseback.

Of course, in taking this 40-plus mile detour, the young men walking had to carry whatever fish and game they secured back up the 3,000-plus feet they lost when they left the ridge and still not be so late as to unduly delay the horseback throng following their main trail. It was a very physical side trip.

The midsummer travel conditions the Indians experienced with their families were leisurely compared to the push of this deep-snow crossing by the Americans in a hurry. Lewis and Clark appreciated their difficult situation. This is indicated clearly in a few telling lines from their journals.

Clark wrote: "we were entirely Serounded by those mountains from which to one unacquainted with them it would have Seemed impossible ever to have escaped, in short without the assistance of our guides, I doubt much whether we who had once passed them could find our way to Travellers rest in their present Situation for the marked trees on which we had placed Considerable reliance are much fewer and more difficuelt to find than we had apprehended. those indians are most admireable pilots."

Lewis's version of the last line reads, "these fellows are most admireable pilots." It is interesting to note the many later historians who credit the individual heroics of the American captains in the survival of the exploring party, when it is clear from their own hand to whom they attribute their success on this occasion.

The pause at the Smoking Place was not long, but it indicates the respect Lewis and Clark had come to feel for their most hospitable hosts, the Nimíipuu. Lewis wrote, "After haveing Smoked the pipe and Contemplating this Scene Sufficient to have dampened the Spirits of any except Such hardy travelers as we have become, we continued our march."[11] Thus, according to the journals of the captains, the stop at the smoking place was spectacular and a dramatic setting, but brief.

The expedition, following the traditional trail, left the main dividing ridge between the North Fork Clearwater and the Lochsa and dropped off into a basin on the North Fork side of the ridge, then reascended the main ridge and after a few miles made camp for the night of Friday, the 27th, a camp similarly situated to the night of the 26th "tho' the ridge was somewhat higher and snow had not been so long desolved of course there was but little grass."[12]

Under the guidance of the Nez Perces, the exploring party had made good distance under extraordinary circumstances. Patrick Gass said that it was over "some of the steepest mountains I ever passed. The snow is so deep that we cannot wind along the sides of these steps, but must slide straight down."

The next day was a shorter and easier day because the Nez Perces recommended a noon stop. Early camp was dictated by the conditions. The lack of adequate horse feed on the 27th caused the horses to scatter in the night, and when they were gathered up the next morning, they appeared gaunt.

The Indians knew there would be no grass found beyond their noon location on the 28th and, thus, they suggested that the Corps travel no farther that day, but rest and allow the horses to graze. Gass described their location, "On the south side of this ridge there is summer with grass and other herbage in abundance; and on the north side, winter with snow six or eight feet deep."[13]

The morning of the 29th, everyone packed up to proceed on the trail leading east but, after a few miles, the ridge ended, and the travelers were required to ride down to the Crooked Creek Fork, which empties into the Lochsa below, cross that branch, then climb back up a steep timbered ridge where they connected with their old trail of September 1805. Riding through timber for a few miles brought them to a small meadow, today called Packer Meadow, where they rested and grazed their horses. This was the divide between the Clearwater running west and the Lolo Creek running north and east into Clark's Fork.[14] They rode down Lolo Creek for about seven miles, where they reached the Lolo Hot Springs.[15]

The journal entries confirm what is already known about the Indians and the hot springs: they thoroughly enjoyed them. The whites did, also, and soaking in the hot water had to be a relief after the difficult riding they had all been through. The captains both noted, "the Men and the indians amused themselves with the use of the bath this evening. I observe after the indians remaining in the hot bath as long as they could bear it run and plunge themselves into the Creek the water of which is now as Cold as ice Can make it; after remaining here a fiew minits they return again to the worm bath repeating this transision Several times but always ending with the worm bath."[16] This was no different than their traditional hot and cold baths, except that they did not have to do the preparation of the rocks to create the hot water—nature had done it for them.

The Nez Perces were concerned about the tracks of two bare-footed Indians found near the hot springs, as they supposed them to be from distressed Salish, perhaps some of their friends or relatives who might have been attacked by Minnetares. Lewis mentions the tracks in his journal entry of the 29th, and the following day mentions that the Nez Perces "express much concern for them and apprehend that the Minnetares of fort de Prarie have distroyed them in the course of the last winter and spring, and mention the tracks of the bearfoot Indians which we saw yesterday as an evidence of their being much distressed."[17]

Traveler's Rest

The camp of June 30 was on the south side of Lolo Creek, just above its entrance into Clark's River, the same camp location used by the explorers on September 9–10 to prepare for their westward trek over the Bitterroots. It was called "Travellers Rest", and it proved to be a good base in late June of 1806, as a resting spot for men and horses, and as a spot to prepare for the division of the group.

The captains wanted to explore both the Yellowstone River and the Marias, which they had merely glimpsed on the westward trip. Thus, they planned that a portion of the party accompany Clark to the headwaters of the Jefferson River where the canoes had been cached, then further subdivide, some to proceed down the Missouri, while Clark and others crossed to the Yellowstone. In the meanwhile, Lewis would ride horseback to the Falls of the Missouri and explore the Marias, then meet with that portion of the Clark party which brought the canoes downstream from the Jefferson.

The plan was for all to rendezvous at the juncture of the Yellowstone and the Missouri. By this time, they had been out of the snow and back in the Missouri River watershed for several days, but now the mosquitoes were again troublesome.[18]

The exploring party spent all day of the 30th descending the lovely valley of Lolo Creek, although some of the travel was forced by brush and fallen timber to the steep, but open, north sidehills. On one such trail, Lewis's horse placed both hind legs too close to the edge and tumbled downhill with Lewis about 40 feet. Both horse and rider were lucky to avoid injury.

The first day at Traveler's Rest, all the hunters turned out with excellent results; a dozen deer were killed. The meat was welcomed, but the absence of the Salish was of great concern to the Nez Perces, who still feared that tragedy had befallen them. According to the plan of the officers, the Nez Perces were going to continue on with Lewis for a while, but the Indians were anxious for their Salish friends and relatives.

This anxiety may be what prompted the "talk" that Ordway mentions the officers had with the guides on July 1. The possible demise of their Salish relatives illustrated the tragedy of continuous warfare to the Nimíipuu. Thus, they "told our officers that they wished to live in peace and bury their war Stripes in the ground."[19] It was understood that the Americans wanted peace—that is what they said—thus, the Nez Perces said, again, they wanted peace also.

However, if peace was not at hand, they did desire to keep the friendship of the Americans and get the guns vital to protecting themselves from attacks by their gun-bearing enemies. To emphasize the friendship with the Americans, the warrior who overtook the party on the 26th in the Bitterroots gave Captain Lewis an excellent horse, "which he said he gave for the good council we had given himself and nation and also to assure us of his attattchment to the white men and his desire to be at peace with the Minnetares of Fort de Prairie."[20]

Clark wrote that the man who gave Lewis the horse had his ears opened regarding peace and hoped that Lewis would see the Gros Ventres (Hidatsa), make a good peace with them, and show them the horse "as a token of their wishes & c."[21]

On July 1st, Lewis had Shields cut off the barrel of private Richard Windsor's weapon, after he had "birst his gun near the muzzle" a few days earlier. Lewis then exchanged the short-barreled model with "the Cheif" for the one he had given him earlier for guiding them over the mountain. He was presumably referring to the son of Red Grizzly Bear, perhaps one of several sons who carried the name Black Eagle in his lifetime. Chief Tun-na-che-moo-toolt (the Broken Arm), who was also the son of Red Grizzly Bear, also carried the name Black Eagle.

It was his sister, too, who was rumored to be the mother of Clark's child. If true, in the Nez Perce sense of things, this young man who traded rifles with Lewis was the brother-in-law of William Clark. Lewis witnessed the young man shooting his new short-barreled rifle and reported, "he was much pleased with the exchange and shot his gun several times; he shoots very well for an inexperienced person." Lewis was the first army officer to comment on Nez Perce marksmanship, but he would not be the last.[22]

Clark described a valuable bit of intelligence on July 1, which was provided by one of the Nez Perces, though he does not say which one. The news was from the far side of the Bitterroot River, which the Indian swam. He explored the vicinity on the far bank, and returned to tell that the Salish (called Tushepaws here by Clark) had been camping 64 lodges strong, but had moved downstream. This was good news to the Nez Perces. It was now obvious their friends had not been rubbed out by enemies. Nevertheless, the guides were ready to return home and told the captains as much.

Instead of the guides leaving immediately, Lewis wanted them to continue for a few days with him to ensure he got on the correct trail to the great falls of the Missouri. The captains issued "a medal of the Small Size to the young man Son to the late Great Chief of the Chopunnish Nation who had been remarkably kind to us in every instance, to all the others we tied a bunch of blue ribon about the hair, which pleased them very much."[23]

This "Son to the late Great Chief of the Chopunnish Nation" was one of the young men (unnamed) who had presented Clark and Lewis "each with a horse" on May 12th, at the Grand Council.[24] Neither of these young men was identified by name at the time of the Grand Council. After Lewis had given him "a medal of the small size," the young guide "insisted on exchanging names with me according to their custom which was accordingly done and I was call Yo-me-kol-lick which interpreted is 'the white bearskin foalded'."[25]

Thanks to Yo-me-kol-lick's insistence upon the name exchange ceremony, and Lewis's rendition of it in his journal, we know the name of the compelling young Nez Perce who guided the Lewis and Clark expedition on their return through the Bitterroot Mountains. The journal entries of all laud the skill and tenacity of all the guides, and the time of the crossing was cut from 10 days in the Fall of 1805 to 1 week in the Spring of 1806, and under much more difficult traveling conditions.[26]

The evening of July 2nd, the day of the name exchange ceremony, a little celebration was held in which the Indians and some of the whites ran their horses and "several foot races betwen the natives and our party" were held. These races ended, Lewis wrote, "with various success." He added, "these are a race of hardy strong athletic active men," indicating his recognition of their qualities and his respect.[27]

On July 3, the exploring party split, and Lewis wrote, "I took leave of my worthy friend and companion Capt. Clark and the party that accompanyed him. I could not avoid feeling much concern on this occasion although I hoped this seperation was only momentary."[28] A little mystery is introduced by Lewis when he mentions that he "proceeded down Clark's river (Bitterroot) seven miles with my party of nine men and five indians."

Where was Nez Perce number six? Here's how we account for them. Two were on the eastbound trail and picked up as the party proceeded east, three were recruited and were brought up by Drouillard, and one caught up as everyone was traveling along on Thursday, June 26, the evening they camped after picking up their caches on Willow Ridge along the Lolo Trail. Perhaps in the original journal, Lewis wrote a six that looked like a five, but by our reading of the Moulton edition, there is a Nez Perce missing.

True to their promise, the Nez Perces showed Lewis the way to the great falls on the 3rd of July. After leaving Clark's party, they rode down the Bitterroot River five miles, passing the entrance of the "East branch of Clark's River," today's Clark Fork River, on the opposite bank and continuing on for two more miles. Here the Nez Perces recommended · the crossing be made. The mid-day was spent making rafts and, by 3 p.m., all was in readiness, and the three small rafts constructed were used to ferry men and equipment across. Each time the rafts crossed, a little riverbank was lost due to the swift current, until only Lewis and a couple of poor swimmers were left. The Indians had already swum across with their horses and their baggage towed in little basin-boats constructed of deerskins.[29] The horses used by Lewis were swum across, also, but when Lewis and the last of his men attempted their crossing, they were swept into faster water and only made shore with some difficulty. Lewis wrote they were swept "a mile and a half before, we made shore," and the raft they were on sunk as they did so.[30] Everyone rode (back upstream) about another three miles and camped.

At camp, the Nez Perces informed Lewis through signs to Drouillard that the explorers could not now miss the road to the great falls of the Missouri. They informed Lewis of the river now known as the Blackfoot River, and told him to go up that stream, ascend it until they crossed into the drainage of the Medicine River (Sun River), and follow it down to the Missouri and the great falls. This road they called "Cokahlarishkit or the river of the road to buffaloe."[31]

The Nez Perces were not interested in going any farther in east along the buffalo trail with Lewis. They were concerned about "their enimies the Minnetares," and instead of riding any farther with Lewis, would descend the Clark's Fork and attempt to locate their friends and relations, the "Shalees" (Salish).[32]

It is worthy to note that the judgment of the Nez Perces was sound, especially in light of Lewis's later encounter on the Marias River. While still in Kamiah Valley, on June 4th, he and Clark had suggested that several young Nez Perces accompany them east and camp at the mouth of the Marias to await Lewis who, according to Clark, thought it was probable he "Should meet with Some of the bands of the Blakfoot Indians and Minitarres of Fort de Prarie, that in Such Case Capt L. would indeavor to bring about a good understanding between those indians and themselves, which when effected they would be informed of it through the young men thus Sent with him. and that on the contrary Should he not be fortunate enough to meet with those people, nor to provaile on them to be at peace they would equally be informed through those young men, and they might Still remain on their guard with respect to them, untill the Whites had it more in their Power to give them more effectual relief."[33] Good thing the young men took the guidance of their chiefs, good they went to their friends, the Salish, and good they did not hold their breath waiting for the whites "to give them more effectual relief."

Another young Nez Perce showed up at their camp the morning of July 4. "[H]e proved to be the same young man who had first attempted to pass the rocky mountains early in June last when we lay on the Kooskooske and was, "obliged to relinquish the enterprize in consequence of the debth and softness of the snow."[34] This man made another try, after the Lewis and Clark expedition was already on the Lolo Trail, then finally caught up to Lewis's portion of the Corps at 6 a.m. on the 4th, the same day the other Nez Perces were preparing to leave Lewis and go back to Clark's Fork to search for their Salish relatives.

On July 4, 1806, Lewis's camp was located in what might now be called East Missoula. It was here, on America's 30th birthday, that the Nez Perces had their final contact with the American expedition.

Lewis gave them "a shirt a handkercheif and a small quantity of ammunition."[35] He had also given them some meat brought in by his hunters, which the Nez Perces had cut thin to dry for their return journey. Shortly after 11 a.m., Lewis ordered his party to saddle up in preparation to ascend the Blackfoot River on the trail the Nez Perces called *qoq'áalx̣ 'iskit* (literally "buffalo road," meaning here "the road to buffalo").[36] But before the Americans and Nez Perces separated, Lewis brought out a pipe to smoke "with these friendly people." Lewis wrote that "these affectionate people our guides betrayed every emmotion of unfeigned regret at separating from us; they said that they were confident that the Pahkees (the appellation they give the Minnetares), would cut us off."[37] These were the last written words in their journals concerning the Nez Perces by any members of the Corps of Discovery.

The young Nez Perces left their Montana camp of July 4th and rode out of Lewis's journal and off the historical records of the Lewis and Clark expedition. From Lewis's journal, we only know they intended to travel north looking for their Salish relatives, but whether they found them or not is unwritten and forgotten. For these young guides and the Nez Perce Nation, the time spent with the Corps of Discovery was over. The exploration team would be disbanded that fall (1806), but the association and alliance with the Americans was just beginning.

ENDNOTES

1   Gass, *Journals,* p. 197. He says the Indians intended to go over with the American party.

2   Ibid. Really a grouse, as pheasants were not indigenous.

3   Ralph Space, forest supervisor for the Clearwater National Forest and local historian, claimed that his Indian informants stated their belief that one of the young chiefs was a son of Red Grizzly Bear, and the other, a son of Chief Twisted Hair. If this information is accurate, it means that this son of Red Grizzly Bear was the brother (or half-brother) of Chief Tun-na-che-moo-toolt (the Broken Arm) and brother (or half-brother) of Clark's Nez Perces's wife. The other young chief, a son of Twisted Hair, would have been the older brother of later, Chief Lawyer, or perhaps an older half-brother since Twisted Hair had two wives. See Space, *The Lolo Trail,* p. 34. Additional information from Mylie Lawyer.

4   *JLCE,* 8:47.

5   Ibid., 8:50.

6   Ibid., 8:51.

7   Ibid.

8   John Peebles, 1966, map has this camp marked on a map which he figures is within a few hundred feet of its true and original location. See Peebles, "The Return of Lewis and Clark."

9   Gass mentioned the showers of the afternoon of the 26th, which Lewis and Clark do not. See Gass, *Journals,* p. 198. They were camped upon Bald Mountain in the Clearwater National Forest, there is a primitive road around the mountain.

10   *JLCE,* 8:53.

11   Ibid., 8:57.

12   Ibid., 8:58. Incidentally, three mule deer were sighted near this camp, and the Indians told Lewis and Clark that there were many "sheep" in the mountains. However, the Indians called them "white Buffalow," Clark's translation, really mountain goats. They were probably referred to as "buffalo" due to the shoulder hump giving a similar appearance to the buffalo.

13   . Gass, *Journals,* p. 199.

14   Missoula County, Montana. There are two Lolo Creeks. The first, called Collins Creek by Lewis and Clark, is now Lolo Creek, Idaho. The second runs from Lolo pass east into Montana.

15   Packer Meadows is at the head of Pack Creek (Idaho County, Idaho), and runs into Brush Creek, the Crooked Fork Creek, which in turn drains into the Lochsa River, a branch of the Clearwater River.

16   *JLCE,* 8:64.

17   Ibid., 8:66. The Salish are called Ootslashshoots by Lewis; Clark spells their name Oatlashshots in his entry for the same day, Monday, June 30, 1806.

18   Ibid., 9:329.

19   Ibid.

20   Ibid., 8:75.

21   Ibid., 8:78.

22   Ibid., 8:75. In the 1877 war and its aftermath, many remarks were made by participants in the conflict of the accuracy of Nez Perce rifle fire. Many of these are recorded in standard works of the war of 1877, such as Beal, Josephy, Greene, or see Bruce Hampton, *Children of Grace: The Nez Perce War of 1877* (New York: H. Holt, 1994), p. 111. Hereafter cited as Hampton, *Children of Grace.*

23   *JLCE,* 8:77–78.

24   Ibid., 7:247.

25   This name may have been the name, too, of his father killed the year before by

the Gros Ventres (Hidatsas). The "Yo-me" in the name is Lewis's rendition of the Niimiipuu word *hiyuum*, meaning grizzly, and *capaalkoliiksa,* to fold something up. See Aoki, *Nez Perce Dictionary*, pp. 171, 1159.

26   The original crossing, from Traveler's Rest to Oyáyp (Weippe), took from September 11 until September 20 (Clark) and 22nd (Lewis). The trip of June, 1806, began with guides, on the 24th and arrived at Travelers' Rest on June 30.

27   *JLCE*, 8:79.

28   Ibid., 8:83.

29   Moulton suggests that the small craft were made from inflated deerskins, however the phrase, "little basons of deer skins," seems more descriptive of a small bull-boat type of craft with hide stretched over a willow frame, just large enough to float their bedding and supplies.

30   *JLCE*, 8:83–4.

31   Moulton describes this route in *JLCE*, 8:87 n. 9, and identifies Lewis's word as the Niimiipptimpt, or Nez Perce language word for buffalo (*qoq'áalx*) and trail (*'ískit*).

32   *JLCE*, 8:85.

33   Ibid., 7:334–5.

34   Ibid., 8:88.

35   Ibid.

36   Spelled Cokahlarishkit by Lewis, *JLCE*, 8:85.

37   *JLCE*, 8:88.

Chapter 16

The Nez Perces
and Lewis and Clark After 1806

Lewis and Clark and their men made a good impression on the
Nimíipuu. One quality the Indians valued was healing power. Clark
possessed this, and it was considered the sign of a leader who was
connected to the spirit world. The second virtue that the tribesmen
held in highest esteem was martial abilities, as revealed often in
weaponry and exhibitions of marksmanship by the captains and their
men. The third value was salmon power: the understanding of, or
acceptance of, the mystery of the salmon, its sharing of itself with
humans and all that its sacrifice meant. Part of "salmon power" was
patience, a virtue important to harvesting the Creator's gift. The
old people declared the white men *q'uyíiy* (full of odor), and said
hipeqyíyimne (they were in a hurry).

When the Americans came back to the Clearwater country in the
spring of 1806, they were still in a hurry, despite the advice from all
headmen that the conditions in the high Bitterroot country were not
yet conducive to travel. Before Lewis and Clark left for the mountains,
they wanted salmon, too, but again they showed little patience. This
was while the Americans were traveling and first camped in Kamiah
Valley. Finally, they accepted that they must wait for the snow to melt
and wait for the salmon before leaving. This is when they made their
best impression. Then the Americans were generous, likeable and fun,
and the counsels of their leaders were wise.

Yet the Americans still left too early. After a few weeks, they
became anxious to leave and could not wait for the salmon's arrival.
Their impatience revealed an unwillingness to embrace the power or
validity of salmon's mystery, and their disregard of knowledgeable
tribal leaders regarding deep snow and lack of horsefeed forced the
Corps to retreat. They might have listened and made it easier on
themselves and their horses.

Still, Jefferson's choice of leadership was excellent. Both captains respected the importance of ceremonial pipe smoking and, whenever possible, they tried to follow other tribal traditions and protocols. The Nimíipuu took notice and were appreciative; in fact, Lewis and Clark's conduct and the general behavior of the Americans stood out by way of contrast with the many whites who came after them.[1]

In the early years after Lewis and Clark, the United States and the Nez Perces needed one another. The May 1806 alliance held throughout the fur trade era, as well as the early missionary period that overlapped the heyday of the beaver hunters. The most severe tests of the alliance between the Nimíipuu and the United States came with the wars between the United States and traditional Nez Perce allies: their relatives, the Cayuse, Palouse, Yakima, and their sometime allies, the Coeur d'Alene and Spokánes. Nez Perces were torn in their loyalties between their old friends, relatives, and allies on the one hand and the United States on the other.

Lewis and Clark promised the Nez Perces that more Americans would be coming to the mountains with additional trade goods. However, it was the Canadian David Thompson, representing the North West Company of Montreal, who arrived next with items of trade. He established Kootanae House, a long ride north for the Nimíipuu (on the Columbia's upper reaches in modern British Columbia), but they purchased goods there as early as 1809.

Thompson's goods were not American, but guns, powder, and lead were available, as well as steel arrow points and war axes, all of which helped the Nez Perces to defend themselves in their core territory and on buffalo hunts to the plains. And the domestic material goods, such as needles, cotton thread, scissors, metal cookware, and textiles, undoubtedly made life a little easier. Bells, ribbons, and colorful imported beads helped the people achieve a more colorful and enriching existence.[2]

None of the men of the Corps of Discovery ever returned to the Nez Perce country, but some did return to the Rockies as mountain men trappers. A short list of these intrepid men would include John Colter, George Drouillard, John Potts, and Peter Weiser. John Thompson, Joseph Field, and Pierre Cruzatte may have also become mountain men. They may have met Nez Perces in the regions east of the Bitterroots but, if they did, it was in an unofficial capacity; they no longer represented the government of the United States.

There were other mountain men, new arrivals, who did enter Nez Perce territory to winter with some of the bands and marry some of their belles. Many names might be mentioned here, but suffice it to say that three of the most prominent mountain men in the history of the

Northwest, Robert "Doc" Newell, William Craig, and Joe Meek, each married one (or more) Nez Perce wives. Other trapper-traders, perhaps slightly less notable in the annals of the Rockies, included James Conner, George Ebberts, and Louis Raboin.

One of the direct benefits of the Nez Perce and American mountain men association was mutual security. When trading with the Americans, the Nez Perces often received rifles superior to the trade guns their enemies got from the British.[3] In their many scrapes with tribal opponents, the Americans found the Nez Perces among their most reliable allies, and the trappers were always active in fights against Nez Perce enemies, especially the Blackfeet.

Even with British, Canadian, and American trade goods and American fighting men on their side, the Nez Perce situation was not simple or ideal. The Americans were not the only white presence in the Pacific Northwest. Alexander Mackenzie had crossed the continent north of the 49th parallel just a few years ahead of Lewis and Clark, which, along with David Thompson, enhanced the British claim.

The Spanish and Russians also made claims, although confined mostly to the Pacific shore. The Spanish and Russian claims were eliminated by diplomacy in 1819 and 1821, respectively. The British, Canadians, and Americans were a presence in the interior. The Canadian North West Company with headquarters in Montreal, the Hudson's Bay Company of London, and a variety of American fur companies and independent trappers all vied for domination of the profitable fur trade.

Competition was treacherous and sometimes violent, and the complicated politics nearly always caused great confusion amongst the Nimíipuu and other tribes. One American, John Clarke, an employee of John Jacob Astor's Pacific Fur Company, in a fit of anger, hanged a Nez Perce whom he suspected of pilfering a drinking goblet. This episode occurred in 1813, at a Snake River village near the mouth of the Palouse River.[4]

There were other incidents of violence and subsequent narrow brushes with reciprocal violence between some Americans and Nez Perces. These may be regarded as isolated cases in the overall picture and, generally speaking, the Nez Perces and American trader-trappers maintained peace and amity. But, with the increase in white presence in Nimíipuu territory, tensions inevitably began to rise to dangerous levels.

The viability of the American-Nez Perce alliance was never more evident than in a fight that broke out at the end of the 1832 rendezvous. The Battle of Pierre's Hole was fought on July 18, 1832, in what is now southeast Idaho. Seven Nez Perce and Salish were killed and several wounded that day, including Chief Lawyer, one of the sons of Twisted

Hair. A band of Gros Ventres (Hidatsa) were the enemy on this occasion, and they suffered nine deaths and an unknown number of wounded. When the Americans and their Salish and Nez Perce allies tried to renew fighting the next day, they found their enemy had withdrawn under cover of night.[5]

While Lewis and Clark had attempted to diplomatically stress the benefits of intertribal peace, the fur trade, which followed on the heels of Lewis and Clark, combined with new technologies, increased rather than decreased intertribal warfare. More fighting and new diseases sweeping through scattered villages must have weighed heavily upon tribal leaders. The Nez Perces often felt they were on the brink of a great national trauma. Minimally, they must have felt a great anxiety.

Ancient Nez Perce religious beliefs inextricably bound spiritual power of the individual with worldly success or failure;[6] therefore, it was natural that they saw potential solutions to their problems emerging from a spiritual realm. Emerging prophets and prophecies were the norm in plateau culture, and the Nez Perces were used to visionaries proselytizing in their villages. It was, in fact, a part of their religious tradition.[7] Many changes had come to the Nimíipuu, but their traditional religious life remained strong.

In 1829, just three years prior to the Nez Perce fight at Pierre's Hole, a Spokane Indian named Spokan Garry created a sensation when he began preaching the Christian gospel to all who would listen. The Salish-speaking Spokanes were a tribe to the north of the Nez Perces, with whom the Nez Perces were familiar. In the years immediately following the departure of Lewis and Clark, the Spokanes were the Nez Perces' primary source of guns and ammunition, which they received from the Canadian North West Company trading post in their country.[8] After the Hudson's Bay Company's 1818 construction of Fort Nez Perces at the mouth of the Walla Walla River, the Nez Perces had an easier access to essential goods. Spokane House was abandoned in 1826.

The Spokanes had sent Spokan Garry, a chief's son, and the nearby Kutenai tribe, also Salish speakers, sent a young man dubbed Kutenai Pelly to the Red River School, run by the Church of England Missionary Society in present-day Manitoba. The religious fervor created by Garry's preaching likely stirred the Nez Perces, who had already asked George Simpson of the Hudson's Bay Company to send teachers and religious leaders to the Nez Perce. It was undoubtedly the hope and belief of the Nimíipuu that whatever learning they might acquire would only enhance their existing access to spiritual power. In other words, they were less interested in converting to Christianity than in adding more spiritual dimensions to their already rich spiritual lives.

In 1830, two Nez Perce youths, Ellice and Pitt, were sent, via Fort Colvile and a Hudson's Bay Company brigade, to the Red River School.[9] Spokan Garry, Kutenai Pelly and three other youths also traveled back to the school. Ellice was connected to the Lewis and Clark Expedition through his grandfather Xáxaac 'ilpilp (Red Grizzly Bear) on his mother's side, and his father was none other than Twisted Hair.[10] Perhaps the youth named "Pitt" was a relative of a chief too, but there is no record available. While Ellice and Pitt were off to the Red River School, Chief Red Grizzly Bear and a council of Nez Perce headmen determined to send another delegation to Lewis and Clark in St. Louis.[11]

The 1831 Journey to St. Louis

A council of headmen decided that four men would attach themselves to Lucien Fontenelle and Andrew Drips of the American Fur Company. Two of the travelers were older—Black or Speaking Eagle and Man of Dawn—and two younger—No Horns on His Head and Rabbit Skin Leggings.[12] They began their sojourn riding up the dusty trail out of Kamiah Valley towards the Oyáyp (Weippe) qém'es grounds, the same route ridden by Lewis and Clark as they left Nimíipuu country 25 years before.

This was the jumping-off point for the Lolo Trail, one of the primary routes used from ancient times by the Nimíipuu to reach the east side of the Rockies and the plentiful buffalo. This was the same narrow tread that Chief Looking Glass the younger, son of Chief Looking Glass (We-ark-koompt, Flint Necklace), who had helped Lewis and Clark; Joseph the younger; and the other chiefs and their people would ride to escape General Oliver Otis Howard's federal army just 46 years hence. When the four pilgrims reached the Bitterroot River, they crossed and followed the Clark's Fork upstream to the Deer Lodge (Montana) Country.

By June 19, 1831, they were enjoined with fur traders Fontenelle and Drips and camped with them just north of Monida Pass on the present-day Idaho-Montana border.[13] Their next destination was Cache Valley, Utah, where the entire group would combine with the Rocky Mountain Fur Company brigade before continuing east. Early that fall, the four Nez Perces finally reached St. Louis, where they were sad to learn that Meriwether Lewis was dead.[14] The four were directed to or led to William Clark, then serving as Superintendent of Indian Affairs. They communicated through the universal sign language with Clark. Was there an interpreter? Clark kept no record of their meeting; he only alluded to them in a later report to Secretary of War Lewis Cass.[15]

Soon after the initial meeting, one of the older delegates, one called Tipyahlanah, Black or Speaking Eagle, died of disease (October 31, 1831). Tribal tradition says he died in Clark's home.[16]

Chief Tun-na-che-moo-toolt, the "Broken Arm" also carried the name Tipyahlanah, "Black or Speaking Eagle." He is one and the same man identified by Lewis and Clark as one of the leading men at the Grand Council in May 1806 and the chief who directed them to their "long camp" location.[17]

Informant Jonathan "Billy" Williams claimed that Black Eagle, Speaking Eagle, and Tun-na-che-moo-toolt were the same person, and he would have known; he rode with the four famous ones for a distance as they left Kamiah.[18] Black Eagle (Chief Tun-na-che-moo-toolt, the Broken Arm) was also the recipient of a small Jeffersonian peace medal and an American flag, and he was a son of Chief Red Grizzly Bear. He was also a close relative, a "brother," meaning first cousin in Nimíipuu relations, to Chief Lawyer.[19] In December 1831, Man of Dawn also died of disease. Both he and Black Eagle (Chief Tun-na-che-moo-toolt, the Broken Arm) remain buried in St. Louis.[20]

More Than Trusted Friends

Clark's legacy among the Nez Perce tradition recalls that he took a lover while in Kamiah. She is reputed to be either Red Grizzly Bear's younger sister or his daughter. At any rate, she was left pregnant, and the story goes that she gave birth to a son who became known by the name "Daytime Smoker" (Haláx túuqit), after his father, and also called simply "Clark."[21] By the time of the 1855 treaty, he was also known as "Capon Rouge."[22]

The portrait by Gustavus Sohon, compared with the Charles Wilson Peale portrait of Clark, strongly corroborates that the story is true, in which case Clark would have been either "uncle" or "brother-in-law" to Chief Black Eagle (Tun-na-che-moo-toolt, the Broken Arm). Tribal historian Chief Many Wounds, Sam Lott, wrote that Clark recognized Black Eagle (Tun-na-che-moo-toolt, the Broken Arm)[23] and that would help explain the reason the four Nez Perces received Clark's personal hospitality. This relationship might also help explain the puzzle of why Clark, usually a meticulous record keeper, failed "to register even the briefest mention of their presence in the city."[24] Lewis, too, had gone through the shirt-trading ceremony and was also "a relative." Lewis was dead, of course, but the Nez Perces did not know that fact when they left Kamiah.

This portrait of William Clark by Charles Wilson Peale reveals the close physical likeness to the Nez Perce Indian, Daytime Smoker, drawn by artist Gustavus Sohon at the 1855 Treaty in the Walla Walla Valley. The Nez Perce often referred to Clark as "Daytime Smoker" because of his tobacco habit (at left). Daytime Smoker, also known as Capon Rogue often called himself "Clark." Drawing by Gustavus Sohon, Washington State Historical Society, 1918.114.9.42 (at right).

Kate McBeth, missionary to the Nez Perces, writing from Kamiah just a century after Lewis and Clark's departure, was not far from the truth when she wrote that "it seems quite natural that when the Nez Perces were perplexed about how and what to worship, their eyes and hearts should try to follow the trail of their trusted friends, believing if their troubles were laid out before 'the crowned ones,' they would know the truth."[25]

The point is simply that, while the motive or motives for the journey have been widely debated, except for missionary McBeth, the relationship between these Nez Perces and Lewis and Clark has been overlooked or ignored. And yet she did not know, or refused to recognize, that the Nez Perces were more than mere trusted friends: Clark and Lewis were Nez Perce relatives, wealthy, powerful "family" who could help in their time of need.

Beginning in 1829, the Nimíipuu likely felt a need for help. Northwest natives, especially on the lower Columbia, were experiencing another pandemic. No one knows exactly what the disease was—it may have been measles, malaria or smallpox—but it wiped out entire villages. The effects of this pandemic would have been known and felt upstream on the plateau.

The Nimíipuu's traditionl answer to sickness was through spiritual power, which was not seen as a separate category from medicine or a thing apart from everyday life.[26] But their old knowledge did not work on the white man's diseases. They needed to add knowledge of the white man's spirit power to protect them from new diseases.[27] In White accounts of the 1831 journey, the questions revolve around whether or not the Nez Perces were looking for "the book." The answer is not so simple.

When the anthropologist Alice Fletcher asked the Presbyterian Jonathan "Billy" Williams if they (the four) were searching for "the Bible," he replied: "no, they went to find Lewis and Clark and learn about the better way to worship God. The people were poor and miserable and often hungry and they knew not where to look for help in their trouble and they were sure that Lewis and Clark could tell them."[28]

This is what Jane Gay wrote that Billy Williams told her companion, allotting agent Alice Fletcher. One can hardly help but wonder what information Billy Williams withheld from Fletcher, or what Fletcher or Gay censored from their interview with Williams. For example, was there any mention of Clark's son? Did the four bring news to Clark of his son, or any other expedition members' progeny?

It seems there was no single purpose in the visit of the four Nez Perces to St. Louis, but many purposes. In one sense, the pursuit of religious wisdom, and all that entailed, was an obvious response to the religious task of the Lewis and Clark expedition. President Jefferson's Attorney General, Levi Lincoln, recommended a religious purpose in the expedition's final instructions. This was a political move to hold conservative Federalist opposition to the expedition at bay.[29] While the journals of the expeditioners do not record religious discussions with the Nez Perces, tribal memory does recall that they occurred.

For example, Chief Timothy, who was a child at the time of the Lewis and Clark visit and who later became one of missionary Reverend Henry H. Spalding's first converts and a Nez Perce minister, used this memory in sermons he delivered. He used to say, "[Lewis] look at sky he point up high over clouds where sun stands and moons—he look up one eye open—he point up he show some paper with marks writing on it—then Sacajawea told people what the white man's book meant, about white God Spirit."[30]

It is not surprising that the Nez Perces should link their interest in religion to "little marks on paper." The Nimíipuu saw Lewis, Clark, Ordway, Frazier, and Whitehouse made marks on paper. The white men could write things down, and they could look at the marks and read their meaning. They also had books, collections of little pieces of paper with marks on them, and could read their words. What was the magic of the little marks on paper?

The curiosity about writing and the desire for learning made the Nimíipuu want the power that came with it. The Bible was purported to be proper religious instruction, the little marks would teach it, but they must be able to understand the marks. They wanted to know the mystery of writing, about literacy and, in that sense, they were truly touched by the American enlightenment. Were they capable of learning the system? Of this they had no doubt—white men had learned it and so had Spokane Garry.

Sam Lott, Chief Many Wounds, wrote that the delegates in St. Louis received an answer to their requests of Clark: "Clark make sign back, mean, yes, we send man."[31] With this answer the two youngest delegates, No Horns and Rabbit Skin Leggings, the only two left alive, bided their time in any way they might waiting for spring and a return to their home country.

On March 26, 1832, the two younger men of the Nez Perce delegation accompanied trader Lucien Fontenelle onboard the steamboat Yellowstone, and began the long journey back to their people. The famous artist George Catlin was on the same journey up the Missouri, and when he became acquainted with them, he painted their portraits. Sadly, No Horns grew sick and died before they reached their journey's end, and he was buried somewhere in the vicinity of the mouth of the Yellowstone River.

This left only Rabbit Skin Leggings of the original four, but he too was destined to ill-fate. He never got back to the Kamiah country, but continued with Fontenelle's pack string as far as the Rockies, then joined up with a group of buffalo-hunting Nez Perces. He spent almost a year with them, and no doubt he related everything that had befallen him and his comrades. Rabbit Skin Leggings died in mid-March 1833 while fighting against the Blackfeet.[32]

Missionaries Come

The journey of the Nez Perces to St. Louis received wide publicity amongst both Protestants and Catholics in the United States. The Protestants, in the form of the American Board of Commissioners for Foreign Missions, were the first to respond and had the greatest immediate impact upon the Nez Perces. Jason Lee, the Methodist, came west in 1834. He did not stay with the Nez Perces to preach, but continued west into the Willamette Valley.

Dr. Marcus Whitman and Reverend Samuel Parker came to the fur rendezvous of 1835, and met many Nez Perces in attendance. Whitman returned east from the rendezvous to marry and garner more support for a mission to be established the next year, and Parker traveled into the Nez Perce homeland with those tribesmen via the Southern Nez Perce Trail.[33] Parker did not remain, but continued on to Fort Vancouver and returned to the east coast by sailing ship. The next year, however, Whitman was back, accompanied by his young wife Narcissa, and Henry Harmon and his wife Eliza Spalding. Both families established missions: Whitman near Walla Walla and Spalding at the mouth of Lapwai Creek on the Clearwater, 120 miles from Whitman and centrally located in the Nimíipuu country. In the next few years, a smattering of other missionaries, joined by refugees from the collapsing fur trade, trickled into and near the lands of the Nez Perces and neighboring tribes.

The missionaries were followed by masses of emigrants flooding the Oregon Trail in the middle 1840s. Diseases came to the people once again, this time born by the wagon trains of emigrants, and again the old cures failed. In the meantime, the flood of white American settlers helped to convince Great Britain to agree, by treaty, to abandon all of their claims below the 49th parallel. Now all sovereignty issues would be settled between the tribes and the United States. A series of crises and misunderstandings led the Cayuse to kill the missionaries Marcus and Narcissa Whitman in November 1847. A Nez Perce element wanted to kill the Spaldings, too. If that had been carried out, the resulting chaos might easily have escalated into a general outbreak of interior Northwest tribes. However, the threat to the Spaldings was quelled by a strong Nez Perce element that favored peace and adherence to the American-Nez Perce alliance dating back to the councils with Lewis and Clark.

A group of settlers formed the Oregon Volunteers and attempted to punish those Cayuse who were directly responsible for the demise of the Whitmans in what has been called the Cayuse War of 1847. The Whitman killing was provoked in no small measure by white intrusion into the Pacific Northwest—American intrusion that was encouraged by the Whitmans, the Spaldings, and a sprinkling of other Anglo-American missionaries. The Cayuse were historic allies of the Nez Perce, and they, too, had welcomed Lewis and Clark. In short, the Nimíipuu were allied to both the Cayuse and the Americans in 1847, and the Whitman tragedy forced them into a difficult choice. Ultimately, the peace faction won out, and Nez Perce warriors assisted the Oregon Volunteers in trying to capture the warring Cayuse faction.

Finally, a handful of Cayuse surrendered and, in 1850, five were hanged in Oregon City. Later, in 1854, the Nez Perces also helped fight some Shoshones who were considered responsible for killing some American emigrants.[34] This was an easier choice, as the Shoshones were often enemies of the Nez Perce.

The Treaty of 1855

This treaty was and remains a sacred document among the Nez Perces. It is sometimes referred to as the Stevens Treaty after one of its primary promoters, Washington's Territorial Governor Isaac Ingalls Stevens, who also served simultaneously as Superintendent of Indian Affairs and as the leader of the most northerly of four Pacific Railroad Survey groups.[35] In the treaty he initiated with the Nez Perces, the United States recognized tribal dominion over more than six million acres of Nez Perce heartland. Before Lewis and Clark, and up until June of 1855, the time of the negotiation of the treaty, the Nez Perces exercised great influence, if not outright sovereignty, over more than twice the territory recognized in the treaty.

Yet in many ways, mainly in the expressed recognition of sovereign rights, the Treaty of 1855 was the formal recognition of an existing relationship between the Nez Perce tribe and the United States. This relationship had begun with the May 1806 agreements made at the Grand Council near Kamiah. In a sense, that treaty, made official with varied ceremonies, was now—49 years later—officially signed on paper.

The Treaty of 1855 was closely tied to Lewis and Clark's diplomacy through several important persons involved in the treaty-making. The man recognized as "Head Chief" by the whites, and the first to sign the 1855 agreement, was Lawyer, son of Twisted Hair. Lawyer was one of the young boys who first saw Clark's arrival at Oyáyp Prairie and had been found hiding in the tall grass by Clark, who had given him some ribbons. Lawyer was probably one of the youngsters who kept an eye on the American horse herd in the winter of 1805–6, and was likely present at the Grand Council on Qemyep Creek, later named Lawyer's Creek in his honor. He had been active in the fur-trading and buffalo hunting in his day, and was seriously wounded fighting alongside American trappers during the Battle of Pierre's Hole in 1832. Another headman who signed the 1855 treaty was Ta-Moots-Tsoo the Younger, or Timothy. He was baptized and given the new name of Timothy by missionary Spalding. He had been at Oyáyp with his father, Ta-Moots-Tsoo the elder in 1805, and had rushed with him back to their village along the Snake River to prepare for Lewis and Clark's arrival. Like Lawyer, Timothy was perhaps 10 years old at the time.[36]Another young man who helped care for the Expedition's horses and grew up to become a leader of his people and the tenth signer of the 1855 Treaty was Tah-moh-moh-kin.

Chief Lawyer by Gustavus Sohon,
Washington State Historical Society,
1918.114.9.53 Collection # 1918.114.9.53

Descendants of Twisted Hair. Lawyer family, left to right, son Archie, father Corbett, daughter Mylie, mother Lillian, June 1930. Photo courtesy Pensrose Library, Whitman College, Native American Collection, Box II, Nez Perce folder.

The second man to sign the 1855 Treaty was not at Walla Walla when the treaty proceedings began, but arrived late from the buffalo country, agitated that perhaps his country had been signed away.[37] Known to his people as Apush Wa hykt, or Flint Necklace, he had been referred to as the Bighorn Chief by Lewis and Clark. It will be remembered that it was through a misunderstanding that he received the name Looking Glass from Lewis.[38] There may have been other 1855 Treaty signers who were adults at the time of Lewis and Clark, but the only one the authors could confirm is Chief Looking Glass, Sr. How many other signers of the 1855 Treaty were directly influenced by their experience with Lewis and Clark is lost. In 1855 their party was still remembered favorably, so perhaps many others were influenced by the tribal memory and signed.

Gustavus Sohon was a 30-year-old German-born artist who was at Walla Walla during the treaty proceedings in 1855, and he drew many of the important leaders.[39] One Indian was pushed forward by others to have his picture drawn though he was not a "chief." It was explained to Sohon that the light-complexioned Nez Perce was known as "Pi-nahua-ut-at," or Capon Rouge, Red Head, and it was said he was the son of William Clark.[40]

This man was about 50 years old and also went by the name "Clark," but the pronunciation of the name was not exactly like Clark as a white American might speak it, for there was no "r" in the Nimipuutímt, the Nez Perce language. The name probably sounded more like "Claak." The man also carried the name Halax tuuqit, or Daytime Smoker, a name given to Clark by the Nez Perces because of his tobacco habit. There is an unmistakable similarity between the man's face and that of Captain Clark. Halax tuuqit showed up at Mormon Fort Limhi on the East Fork of the Salmon River in the summer of 1855 and was known as "Clark" to the Mormon pioneers there.[41]

The Nez Perces were at the zenith of their political and military unity and influence at the 1855 treaty proceedings, and this is reflected by the outcome in the 1855 document. But many other tribes dealing with Isaac Stevens did not fare so well, and war broke out with other tribal groups soon after the 1855 proceedings. These new outbreaks, such as the Yakama War, which involved elements of Spokanes, Coeur d'Alenes, and others, again forced the Nez Perces to make difficult choices. It was similar to the hard decisions made by the Nez Perce as the Americans warred upon their Cayuse friends and relatives after the Whitman tragedy.

Leading headmen of the Nez Perce were the sons of headmen who treated with Lewis and Clark and had pledged their friendship. The natural assumption in 1806 was that there would be no falling out between the Americans and any of the tribal relatives and friends of the Nimíipuu, because it was believed that they, too, enjoyed an alliance status.

In 1858, when Col. Edward J. Steptoe attempted to cross Palouse, Spokane, and Coeur d'Alene territory, the native warriors thoroughly routed Steptoe with considerable cost in material and in dead and wounded. Yet the Nez Perces helped Steptoe and the bulk of his forces escape from the Rosalia, WA region to south of the Snake River and Walla Walla. Later, Colonel George Wright led an expedition that punished those Indians, and he was accompanied by Nez Perces who were issued uniforms and served as both regulars and scouts. Just as in the case of the Cayuse troubles of the 1840s, although the Nez Perces acted with unity, they were of a divided opinion. But, in the course of events, they chose peace with the Americans and to honor their written contract, the Treaty of 1855, the embodiment of the old Nez Perce-Lewis and Clark Grand Council of 1806.

But many harbored doubts about the Americans when they were forced to choose conflict over friendship with ancient allies. The Nez Perces were witnesses to the poor treatment of the Cayuse, Palouse, and Yakamas, like them all former friends to Lewis and Clark. Americans, such as Governor Stevens, who coveted potential gold-bearing grounds and potential railroad routes, seemed friendly only as long as convenient to American purposes. Some Nimíipuu now felt that Lewis and Clark had misled them.

This was the beginning of a serious lesson for the Nez Perces, because the deceitful side of American policy, the policy introduced by Thomas Jefferson through Lewis and Clark, was coming to fruition. On the one hand, peace and friendship were offered and maintained as long as practical and convenient for the Americans. The Nez Perces suspected they might be making wrong choices by siding with the Americans against ancient allies.

This was the other side of the prophecies that both good and bad would come from the white people. This was the negative aspect of a cultural clash, a conflict that was represented politically by the reverse side of the seemingly benevolent Jeffersonian Indian policy. American policy, like the Jefferson peace medal, had two sides.[42]

The Treaty of 1863: The "Steal Treaty"

For half a century, the Nez Perces were able to reap the benefits of the American alliance, but when gold was discovered on Nez Perce lands in 1860, the duplicity of American Indian policy came to the forefront in the form of the Treaty of 1863. The six and a half million acre reservation homeland recognized by the government in 1855 was suddenly cut by ninety percent. And when headmen who represented bands who lived outside of the government's new miniscule boundary refused to sign away their homes, the government agents, represented by Calvin Hale, Superintendent for Indian Affairs in Washington Territory, simply ignored them and found others to sign.

This treaty is still called "the steal treaty" to this day by the Nez Perces.[43] Chief Lawyer and some of the other headmen, such as Utsinmalikan, fought bitterly for weeks against Hale's authority, then against the small size of the new reservation. But Hale was backed by six companies of American troops brought to Fort Lapwai, recently created just a few miles from the treaty grounds.

The Nez Perces were told that the troops were there to protect the Indians, but when some Yakamas and Palouse showed up in Big Thunder's camp just a mile from the proceedings, Hale had soldiers escort them away. Mylie Lawyer, great granddaughter of Chief Lawyer, maintains that the chief was told privately, "in no uncertain terms," that he had better sign "for the good of the people."[44] And it is a historical fact that the troops who were supposedly present to protect the Indians were used to coerce them.[45]

For a few years, the Salmon River chiefs, the headmen of the Wallowa country of northeastern Oregon and the leaders from Asotin country and the Blue Mountain area of southeastern Washington Territory went about their business, but they were pressed on all sides by miners and squatters. Many problems arose, and even bloodshed, but it was always the Indian whose blood was spilled and whose women were violated. Still the bands continued their seasonal rounds, gathering berries and roots and fishing for salmon, but now tending cattle more than traveling to the buffalo country. Finally, after many murders and rapes by Americans that went unpunished by the civil authorities,[46] and repeated government demands for the Indians to move onto the reservation, a few desperate warriors lashed back in two raids along the Salmon River. This gave the United States government an excuse to attack the Nez Perce bands who recognized only the 1855 Treaty. These bands were sometimes referred to as non-treaties because they had not signed the 1863 "Steal Treaty."

The 1877 War

The Nez Perces did not want to go to war against the United States and, as Captain David Perry and his men from Fort Lapwai approached a combined village at Whitebird Canyon in the early light of June 17, 1877, three rode towards Perry with a white flag in an attempt to parley. A volunteer fired his rifle in their direction, and Nez Perce sharpshooters returned fire. The 1877 War had begun.

The War of 1877 is one of the best known stories in the annals of war between the United States and Indians. It is popularly known by non-Indians as "Chief Joseph's War" and "the Nez Perce War," but it was not a war wanted by the Nez Perce or promoted by Chief Joseph, the headman of only one of about half a dozen bands that ended up fighting. The United States army suffered defeat in this first battle, suffering a staggering 66 percent casualty rate. Soon the victorious bands were joined by two small groups of Palouse who threw in their fate with the Nimíipuu.

The war is often seen as a romantic expression of a freedom-loving people fighting against overwhelming odds. Through 11 engagements, 5of them pitched battles, the fighting bands either won or held their own in a 1,500 mile running gunfight against thousands of American soldiers. The war finally ended on the wind- and snow-swept plains of north-central Montana. Most "histories" of the 1877 war end with Joseph's famous surrender speech. Whites love the story of the war and emphasize the role of the noble Chief Joseph and the resourceful Nez Perce.

The war was a tragedy and, in some ways, its constant retelling at the expense of other tribal history is more tragic still. It was a war between David and Goliath, only this time Goliath prevailed. The deeper story of the Nimíipuu embraces 10,000 years, all of it available through archeology and associated sciences, as well as a published mythology and oral history. Two hundred years of Nez Perce existence is available through the study of written accounts in the English language, yet most writers have chosen to focus on just one year: 1877. This emphasis upon this single event, with only cursory attention to the years before and after the June to October "war," tells us more about the Anglo-American than it explains about the Nez Perces. Soon after the Nimíipuu surrender, a *NY Times* reporter wrote the war "was in its origin and motive nothing short of a gigantic blundered crime."[47]

Typically overlooked or de-emphasized is that "the war" only involved a portion of the tribe—mostly, but not exclusively, the non-Christian Nez Perces, those who had their aboriginal lands stolen outright by the United States government. And the "surrender" which ended the major military operations was really a "conditional surrender," in which only a portion of the people "quit fighting" with the understanding that they were to retain what property they still possessed, including their horses and equipment, and that they would be returned to their homes in the spring. Especially downplayed by the officers who participated, who created the core of primary sources on the conflict, was the fact that a large segment of the combatants and their associated families escaped into Canada (where some of their descendents remain).

General Oliver Otis Howard and Colonel Nelson Miles wrote their versions of events and helped create the myth that Chief Joseph was a military genius, a "Red Napoleon."[48] For many years the mythological, romanticized version of events dominated white America's view but, in the last half-century or so, a more accurate synthesized picture has emerged. Within the framework of Nimíipuu history, and especially within the context of the Nimíipuu-Lewis and Clark experience, the entire affair should be seen as a tragedy and a debacle, as well as the blunder and crime.

This was the conflict that never should have happened, the fight that wise leaders, such as Twisted Hair, Red Grizzly Bear, Tun-na-che-moo-toolt (the Broken Arm), and others, believed they were guarding against by endorsing the agreements of May 1806 at the lower Commearp Creek (Lawyer's Creek) Grand Council. There, the Americans traded rifles and ammunition to the Nez Perce men, taught them marksmanship, and shared the sacred pipes.

Maybe if Lewis or Clark were around, their counsels might have prevailed, and there would have been no army attacks on Nez Perce villages. Maybe Clark's own son, "Claak," the *haláx túuqit*, Daytime Smoker, would not have been caught up in the war with the United States and driven into exile to die.[49]

But Lewis and Clark were long gone, and it is a fact that they led the military "reconnaissance in force" that first spied out the land for the United States government. And, later, when he served as Superintendent of Indian Affairs, Clark's humanitarian views were sometimes ignored, as when Indians were seen as a threat to American progress or American peace.[50] The Nimíipuu understood the 1806 agreement to mean intermarriage and perpetual trade and military co-operation. The war of 1877 was not how the story was supposed to end.

Exile, 1877–1885

The policies initiated by Lewis and Clark revealed only the smiling benevolence and paternalistic side of American policy. After them came the aggressive acquisitiveness of the Americans, which brought cultural destruction and death. The Nez Perces had held fast to their promises to Lewis and Clark and the Americans through great turmoil and, if the paternalistic and benevolent side of American Indian policy would have held sway, the 1877 War might have been avoided. Americans' commitment to justice and fair play might have overcome American lies and greed.

But American benevolence and largess did not hold sway, even with the loyal Nez Perces. The 1877 War was the Nez Perces' turn to be on the receiving end of the duplicitous American policy, the policy for which Lewis and Clark served as the cutting edge. It was a racist and land-hungry policy, but the policy's 1805-06 face was gentlemanly, the face of the Virginian on the peace medal, and the faces of Lewis and Clark.

As long as the tribes were useful in the international struggle for empire, as long as the fur trade was uppermost to a regional economy, peace and alliance held sway. When tribal alliances were no longer desirable or needed, the United States cast them aside. Thoughtful New Englanders and Virginians alike understood that fact and knew what would happen next.

The historical precedent had already been set, for Jefferson's policy was the child of the policies of the Federalists, and theirs was the step-child of the British colonial policies which preceded them. In turn, Jeffersonian policy, it must be remembered, was the genesis of the near-genocidal Jacksonian Indian policy, an American policy so vicious that Adolf Hitler later claimed it as an inspiration to his own concept of concentration camps.[51]

The fighting ended on October 5, 1877, but then the prisoners were taken to Ft. Keogh in eastern Montana, where the conditions of the conditional surrender, the promises, were shattered one at a time. The prisoners were disarmed and could no longer hunt, and their horses, blankets, saddles, and bridles were taken from them, "stolen" in anyone's language. Then, instead of being settled for the winter in preparation for their return to the Idaho reservation as per Nelson Miles' promise, they were shipped to Fort Leavenworth for the winter of 1877–78, and many were buried there.

The following summer, they were removed from their shabby camp, where many were dying of old wounds and disease at Malaria Flats just outside Fort Leavenworth, and hauled by railroad to Indian Territory, where they fought in every way left at their disposal just to survive.

Finally, at 1:15 pm on Friday, May 22, 1885, 268 men, women, and children, the remnants of the Nez Perce and Palouses who had resisted the United States in 1877, pulled out of the Arkansas City train depot headed for the Northwest.

They had lost more lives while incarcerated by the United States than they lost in combat.[52] And once they arrived back in the Pacific Northwest, they were again divided. Some were sent to the Colville agency in north central Washington Territory, and the remainder were allowed to settle in Idaho on the Lapwai agency. Yellow Wolf reported that at Wallula (Washington Territory), the interpreter asked "Where you want to go? Lapwai and be a Christian, or Colville and just be yourself."[53]

There were people who died during the war and some during exile who were old enough to have remembered Lewis and Clark. And many others who were involved in the 1877 conflict who were second generation and, in one way or another, connected to Lewis and Clark. There was, of course, Daytime Smoker, already mentioned, who went through the war and died in the Territory, and his daughter Iltolkt, probably Clark's own granddaughter, and her baby who were P.O.W.s.[54]

Chief Joseph himself had a *qaláca'c* (paternal Grandfather), who had helped welcome Lewis and Clark's people at a Snake River village.[55] Chief Looking Glass, killed at the last Battle, was son of Old Looking Glass (the Ram's Horn, Weah-Koo-Nut).[56]

Young Chief Looking Glass made a tremendous effort to keep himself and his band out of the 1877 conflict, but when their Clear Creek village was attacked, they were forced to join the hostile faction or be killed. The bands of Toohoolhootzote, Chief Joseph, Chief Whitebird, and Palouse headmen Hatolikin and Huis Huis Kute likewise had little or no choice.

One warrior, Red Spy, was killed just after the last battle; he was the son of mountain man William Craig and a Nez Perce mother—part of the Indian-white progeny, like Daytime Smoker, a direct result of the alliance between the United States introduced by the Grand Council of May 11, 1806.

There were likely many more undocumented and forgotten who were closely tied to Lewis and Clark. All the bitterness and lost treasure and death created by the 1877 conflict and subsequent exile was avoidable and unnecessary.

The Allotment

When the 1877 war began, the warriors of the bands that had reluctantly adhered to the treaty of 1863 abstained from fighting against the United States and, in some cases, actually scouted for or fought on behalf of the army against their own relatives. Making that choice was not easy but, like the choices forced upon the Nimíipuu previously, they did what they felt they had to do in order to survive.

However, they were mistaken in the belief that their loyalty would insure their own property and freedom, for their land, supposedly protected inside the boundaries of the 1863 Treaty, had not escaped the covetous eyes of the Americans. The Dawes Severalty Act, or Allotment Act of 1887, was a government plan that was supposedly written to help American Indians, but really crafted to steal more tribal lands. The Dawes Act would apply to nearly every Indian reservation. Each reservation would be carved up into small square acreages, and each Indian "awarded" a parcel. All the lands not "allotted" in that fashion would then be opened for white settlement. Even before the Allotment Act, it will be remembered that the Nez Perces had already lost most of their magnificent homeland. Once sprawling over 13 million acres in parts of three states, it had been reduced to a small core after the ratification of the 1863 Treaty in 1869.

Beginning in 1889, and continuing through 1892, the government surveyed fewer than 2,000 80-acre and 160-acre parcels for individual Nez Perces. When government allotting agent Alice Fletcher left the Nez Perce reservation in the fall of 1892, the solid block of Nez Perce property was shattered, and a map of the reservation showed only a weak checkerboard pattern of tribal lands.

In 1895, when the "open" lands were offered to homesteaders and town builders, the Nez Perces were a sudden minority in their own homeland, or the miniscule portion that was left. It was only 90 years since Lewis had written, "this country would form an extensive settlement."[57]

This was the final blow to Nez Perce freedom and a comeuppance for those Nez Perces who had remained loyal to the United States even in the face of the 1877 War. The tribal land base was in shambles. Fletcher's assistant, Jane Gay, wrote many letters and took dozens of photographs during the four years of the allotment.[58] Her records, corroborated by agency records, show that the Nez Perces who were forced to bow to the allotment process were often educated and successful farmers and livestock raisers. They were an element who, in many cases, wore "civilized dress," had cut their hair like the white man, and were devoted members of the Presbyterian, Methodist, or Catholic faiths.

No matter. They were Indians and not citizens of the United States, and the prophecy was fulfilled: The big nation shoved the small nation around and drew lines upon the earth. Is it a wonder that the memory of Lewis and Clark deteriorated to a thread by the close of the war, the exile, and the allotment? Many Nez Perces felt, and many still feel as the Montana Salish Chief Charlo, friend of the Nez Perces, that support of Lewis and Clark had been a mistake.[59]

In less than a century, disease and the empire-building Manifest Destiny of the United States hammered the proud Nimíipuu nearly into oblivion. From the 7000-10,000 Nimíipuu of 1805–6, the tribe had dwindled. At the time of allotment, the Idaho population was under 2,000; by the end of the century, there were less than 1,400. Worse, their culture had been deliberately and systematically weakened. Many of the cultural carriers, those who knew the ways of the people, had not survived the crushing power of the United States army, or the stifling death of the post-war exile.

Where the Nimíipuu had once reigned sovereign, they were forced to seek an agent's approval for any kind of major activity and could not even leave the reservation's boundaries without permission. At the time of Lewis and Clark, Nimíipuu law was supreme; 100 years later, the people were nearly gone and their means of subsistence was taken from them or destroyed. They were surrounded by alien government, forced to answer to state, county, and even municipal officials. In the words of Archie Phinney, a Columbia University Ph.D., and himself the grandson of a Nez Perce woman and an American mountain man, the people were "pitiable," and the tribe was "rendered helpless."[60]

How the Story Ends

Chief Joseph, whose grandfather welcomed Lewis and Clark in October of 1805, died in exile at Nespelem, Washington, on September 21, 1904. This was just a year before the opening of Portland, Oregon's, World's Fair and Exposition, and the Lewis and Clark Centennial Exposition. Joseph's death caused a vacuum of leadership at Nespelem and in Idaho where his influence was still felt. The Nez Perces were invited to join in the celebration at Portland, but they were not in the mood. Their search for new leadership occupied some of their activities and custom called for little or no participation in celebratory activities until one year had passed after Joseph's death.

The Lewis and Clark Exposition began June 1, more than three months short of the one year wait.[61] The tribesmen were experiencing too many internal difficulties to reach out,[62] and it is not surprising that they showed little interest in the Exposition.

There was an exception to the general lack of interest, however, and that was manifested in an abiding concern surrounding Sacajawea. The suffragists regarded her life as an exemplary and appropriated her as an icon representing the women's suffrage movement.[63] Perhaps the idea of the vote attracted the interest of the Nez Perces who were as yet unenfranchised.[64]

After the 1877 War, the exile, and allotment, it is understandable that the Nez Perces might feel bitterness toward the United States government, the U.S. Army, and Lewis and Clark, but the memory of Sacajawea was still revered, and when the railroad offered some seats on the train to Portland, a few tribal folks went with a plan to see the unveiling of the Sacajawea statue. At the "Idaho Building," they likely saw a grain display showing "Twisted Hair and Sacajawea being portrayed on the wall in multicolored wheat and seeds."[65]

The Nimíipuu interest in Sacajawea was also due to the relationship between her and the Alpowa band of Nez Perces led by Chief Ta-Moots-Tsoo. His son, not more than ten years old in 1805, was called Ta-Moots-Tsoo the Younger, later called simply Chief Timothy (1796–1891). He was much impressed by the teenaged Shoshone bride of Charbonneau, maybe even "taken" by her as only a young boy might be. There are echoes remaining suggesting that Sacajawea favored the Alpowa band and young Ta-Moots-Tsoo and that, years after the Lewis and Clark expedition, she returned to visit them (in modern southeast Washington state).

So, despite much tribal disenchantment with the white explorers due to the bitter feelings stirred by the 1863 "steal treaty," the 1877 War, and the Allotment theft, interest in Sacajawea remained, and at least some of the tribal visitors to the World's Fair and Lewis and Clark Exposition of Portland, Oregon were relatives of Chief Timothy—he had been dead for only 14 years.

Captain William Clark nicknamed Toussaint Charbonneau's wife "Janey." Chief Timothy's daughter, Jane, born in 1842, may have been Sacajawea's namesake. With this mantle, she led Captain E. O. Pierce to Idaho's first gold strike and, like Sacajawea, she married a white man, a Harvard graduate working for the government named John Silcott. Jane was independent and, around 1880, she rode her horse and led a pack horse loaded with her camp outfit and gifts from her father's people to Sacajawea in the Wind River country of present-day Wyoming. The source of this story, or legend, comes from Chief Peo-Peo-Tah-Likt (Bird Alighting), relative of Jane and Chief Timothy and train passenger to Portland for the unveiling of the Sacajawea statue.[66]

Peo-Peo-Tah-Likt was a veteran of the 1877 War and friend to Yakima rancher and chronicler of Nimíipuu history Lucullus Virgil McWhorter. Chief Peo-Peo-Tah-Likt followed McWhorter's example of recording tribal history on paper. His cousin, Sam Lott, had been to school and was a sympathetic listener. McWhorter had been interviewing tribal folk, beginning in 1907 and continued until his death in 1944. He interviewed both Lott and Peo-Peo-Tah-Likt in the 1920s, and Lott began interviewing Peo-Peo-Tah-Likt himself in the 1930s. Of course Peo-Peo-Tah-Likt had been passing his stories along his entire adult life, but writing them on paper was a breakthrough.

The importance of this effort was encouraged by the educated, mixed-blood cousin of Peo-Peo-Tah-Likt named Joe Evans (no relation to the co-author of this book), who owned a small museum in Spalding, Idaho, near where the Lewis and Clark expedition stopped for lunch on October 10, 1805, on their way downstream to the Pacific. Evans and his wife had a dozen typed-up, hand-bound books made of Peo-Peo-Tah-Likt and Sam Lott's work, *Historical Sketches of the Nez Perces.*

Chief Peo-Peo-Tah-Likt's father remembered Lewis and Clark. Peo-Peo was a young warrior in the 1877 War and later lived with Sitting Bull in Canada. He returned to Idaho for the allotment in the late 1880's and began working to establish tribal government. With his Cousin, Sam Lott (Many Wounds) the great-grandson of Chief Red Grizzly Bear, they wrote their own history, Historical Sketches of the Nez Perces *(1935). Photographs courtesy Washington State University MASC Cage 55, by L.V. McWhorter (on left); Nez Perce National Historical Park, NEPE-HI-0528 (on right).*

The Jane Silcott-Sacajawea connection, gleaned from this short book (only 27 pages long), claims that Jane found Sacajawea on Wind River and remained with her about one month. She left many gifts and brought many back home, including a buckskin dress, allegedly the very one worn by Sacajawea on her trip to the Pacific and back. She decorated it with beads from both Lewis and Clark, and had further decorated it over the years to be her funeral dress. Instead, she exchanged dresses with Jane just before Jane's return to Lewiston, Idaho Territory.

In the foreword to their small book, a testimony regarding both Sam Lott (Many Wounds) and Peo-Peo-Tah-Likt is offered. It states: "They represent the finest type of American Indian, they are strong of character, honest, and their integrity unquestioned. They possess good judgment, kindly forbearance for erring whites, and outstanding qualities of leadership." This was written in 1935.[67]

Missionary Marcus Whitman was assisted in some of his endeavors by his young nephew, Perrin Whitman, who escaped the so-called "Whitman Massacre" of 1847. Perrin often worked as an interpreter to the Nez Perce and, living with them, raised a daughter, Francis. This young woman became a close friend of Chief Timothy's daughter Jane, and later married Charles Monteith, Nez Perce Indian Agent (1882–86). Jane's friend Francis wrote in 1937 (long after Jane's tragic death in a house fire in 1895) that "I...verify the story by Sam Lott (Many Wounds) regarding Jane Timothys visit to Wyoming to visit Sacajawea. I actually saw the articles she brought vack [sic] with her from Sacajawea. Some of them are now in posession of Mr. And Mrs. Joe Evans."[68]

There are two versions, similar but slightly different, and only a dozen or so copies of Peo-Peo-Tah-Likt and Sam Lott's *Historical Sketches of the Nez Perces* and the information therein is subsequently little-known in scholarly circles. The unique perspective of these trail chroniclers will not settle the long-standing historical questions revolving around Sacajawea's death, but may help keep the bright fires of controversy burning.

Less controversial in the Clearwater country, several Nez Perce men made major contributions to the future study of Lewis and Clark (and the Nez Perces) on the Lolo Trail. James Stuart was an educated Nez Perce who had been assistant to and interpreter for Allotment Agent Alice Fletcher. It was Stuart who was present as interpreter for the ethnographic work that Fletcher did with tribal historian Jonathan "Billy" Williams.[69] And it was Stuart who acted as guide and informant to *The Trail of Lewis and Clark 1804-1904* author Olin D. Wheeler.

Much of the Lolo Trail is located in what is now called the Clearwater National Forest, carved out of the older Bitterroot Forest Reserve. One time supervisor of the Clearwater was forester Ralph Space. He traveled the Lolo Trail 50 years beginning in 1924. Informed by tribal members Harry Wheeler, Corbett Lawyer, and William Parsons, he published a small book, *The Lolo Trail* in 1970. He based its contents on his own research and experience and his Nez Perce informants.[70]

In 1905, the beginning of the Lewis and Clark Centennial in Idaho, and the year of the creation of the Clearwater National Forest, money became available for trail maintenance. Charlie Adams, son of a white man by the same name and a Nez Perce woman, was reputed to be a grandson of Twisted Hair (from his mother's side). Adams was well versed in the lore of the Lolo Trail and was hired by the Clearwater National Forest to trace and cut out the Trail. He was ably assisted in this work by Walt Sewell, a white man who passed on his knowledge, gleaned from Adams, to Orofino historian Zoa Swayne,[71] who acknowledged Adam's contribution along with four dozen more Nimíipuu who enriched her work, *"Do Them No Harm!" An Interpretation of the Lewis and Clark Expedition Among the Nez Perce Indians.*

Charlie and Sophia Adams. This man was the son of a white miner named Charlie Adams and a Nez Perce mother from Ahsahka, at the juncture of the North Fork Clearwater River and the main Clearwater. A reputed descendent of Chief Twisted Hair, Adams worked for the early Forest Service on trail maintenance and impacted the work of author Olin D. Wheeler and many others with his willingness to share his knowledge of tribal history and the lore of the Lolo Trail. Nez Perce National Historic Park, NEPE-HI-2432.

Early in the Twentieth Century, however, Nez Perces were not merely struggling to maintain their identities and history, but really fighting for survival. Anthropologist Herbert Spinden, in his landmark study of the Nez Perces originally published in 1908, concluded, after a talk with agency doctor J.N. Alley, that unless something be done regarding disease among the Nez Perces, they would "soon be only a name."[72] The concept of the "vanishing American" was no myth in the early decades of the Twentieth Century, and the Nez Perces suffered losses similar to other tribes. They numbered less than 1,500 at the time of the Lewis and Clark Centennial, and it seemed they might disappear altogether.

As in the rest of the United States, sickness and death stalked their homes during the influenza outbreak of 1917. By 1922, the year of the government's survey of reservations, called the Merriam Report, the Nez Perces on the Idaho reservation "were only about 1,300 scattered over a large area among approximately 20,000 whites."[73]

In response to this situation, the Nez Perces formed the Nez Perce Indian Home and Farm Association. The Association consisted of all adult members of the tribe and was headed up by a council. The president was James Stuart, who had been interpreter to Alice Fletcher and aide to historian Olin D. Wheeler on the Lolo Trail. The vice-president was Jesse Paul, descendent of Man-of-Dawn, who traveled to St. Louis in 1831, and Chief Utesinmalicum, who died in Washington, D.C., in 1868. Secretary of the new organization was Corbett Lawyer, grandson (through Archie Lawyer) of Chief Lawyer and great grandson of Twisted Hair.

At least two of the remaining six members of the council were also linked to Lewis and Clark; Ellis Khip-khip-pel-kehken traced his lineage back to Twisted Hair through that chief's second wife, Tah-se-wy-ma or Heyumeotwy. Peo-Peo-Tah-Likt was also a councilman; his father witnessed Lewis and Clark's arrival, and he himself had always been loyal to the Americans. But living peacefully in Chief Looking Glass's camp on Clear Creek in 1877, he had been shot by a soldier and wounded and, thereafter, he joined the war. He never surrendered at the Bear Paws, but escaped into Canada where he lived with Sitting Bull for a while.

Eventually Peo-Peo-Tah-Likt drifted back into the United States and to the Nez Perce reservation. He traveled to Washington, D.C,. with Joseph in a attempt to regain the Wallowa or a portion of the Wallowa country, and he tried and failed to be elected Chief of the Nez Perce after the death of Joseph in Nespelem in 1904. Always free and independent, he was a strong participant in the early pow-wow and rodeo circuit, and he volunteered to help his war brother Yellow Wolf and Yakima rancher-historian Lucullus V. McWhorter to rewrite tribal history.

Slowly, through the thirties of the Great Depression and World War Two, the Nez Perce population climbed, and interest in sovereignty and self-governance ascended simultaneously.

The Nez Perce Farm and Home Association was the real beginning of modern tribal government, and many of those who promoted it were tied to Lewis and Clark. Thus the tribe, or at least the Idaho portion of it, were well on their way to recovery before the advent of the New Deal and the Indian policies of the Franklin Roosevelt administration. In fact, the Nez Perces rejected the Indian Reorganization Act of 1934, claiming they did not need the authorization of the 1934 Act—they operated under the inherent right to self-governance.[74]

Nez Perces served in World War One, like Alex Pinkham, father of one of this work's authors. Well over a hundred served in the various branches of the United States armed forces during World War Two, and many were killed in action. An examination of the cemetery in Nespelem, Washington, shows the many sacrifices made by Wallowa Band descendents who remained in exile. In other words, the Nez Perces, like other Native Americans all over the country, have put their lives on the line in numbers often out of proportion to their small population bases. It is the same all over Indian Country, and Indian communities truly honor their veterans. Nez Perces served in the Korean War, the Vietnam War, the First Gulf War, the Second Gulf War, and in Afghanistan. As this book is being written, several dozen Nez Perces are on active duty, and a half dozen are in Afghanistan and Iraq.

Despite the consistency of tribal service to the United States, governmental entities often ignore the treaties, the agreements the government itself insisted upon. While the United States, through its emissaries Lewis and Clark, recognized Nez Perce sovereignty over the big game animals in their tribal region, and the treaties of both 1855 and 1863 recognize that right, state and local governments are widely divergent in their recognition of those rights.

Idaho has often opposed Nez Perce hunting, fishing, and gathering rights on the one hand, and occasionally supported treaty rights on the other. And there is the bizarre situation where the state of Montana invites Nez Perces to participate in a buffalo hunt of excess Yellowstone animals (2007–8) and, in Oregon, a Nez Perce Indian, Irvin Watters, a World War II U.S. Navy combat veteran (and informant for this work), was arrested on charges of hunting out of season and found guilty.[75] Tribal gaming and tribal tax policies are two other areas that demand vigorous tribal defenses, yet these are just a few among many others.

Recently, the State of Idaho has negotiated a landmark water rights settlement with the Nez Perce Tribe called the "Snake River Basin Adjudication Settlement." Dennis Colson, University of Idaho legal historian and law professor, believes that, in the years to come, it will rank in importance with the Treaties of 1855 and 1863.

And on the story flows. Like the Salmon and Clearwater rivers that dominated the Nimíipuu homeland, the story of the places and the people persist. Now the homeland is shared with the non-Indians, the descendents of the Americans who first showed up in the personages of the men of the Lewis and Clark Expedition. The salmon that were the protein mainstay of the people then have all but disappeared; some, in fact, are extinct.

But the Clearwater River, although blasted in places for steamboat navigation, and crowded by highway and railroad embankments, remains one of the most beautiful rivers in America. The Salmon River, the longest river in the United States that flows its entire length within one state (Idaho), is not inside the 1863 Reservation boundary. Its wild untamed waters remain an inspiration to all Americans and are still dear to the Nimíipuu who visit the Salmon's interior mountains to harvest fish, big game, berries, roots, and tipi poles.

The lower Clearwater, passed in canoes by Twisted Hair, his brother Al-We-Yas, and the Lewis and Clark Expedition in 1805, is now the scene of U.S. Highway 12 and the Clearwater Casino, where bingo and slot machines have replaced the old tribal "badger gamble," but the stick game songs and gamble are still seasonally practiced with fun and tribal profit foremost in mind. Downstream just a few miles, Lewis and Clark might be suprised to see the mighty smokestacks of Potlatch Industries on the south riverbank, the city of Lewiston's leading industry.

While the west wind still blows furiously where the Clearwater enters the Snake, the boatman no longer need fear the currents. They have been quelled by the water backed up by the Lower Granite Dam. And downstream on the Snake, three more dams stop the Snake's once turbulent and magnificent waters. Advocates of the dams are proud of the electricity, the navigation, and jobs now possible, but the chinook and sockeye salmon have paid with their lives, and land lost under rising waters has cost thousands of northwest people their livelihoods.

Lewis and Clark did not seem to have an intuitive understanding of the sea-run fish, and neither do the dominant whites who control the region today. The politicians seem willing, if not always eager, to sacrifice nature for the profit of the few. The loss of the nutritious salmon, delivered to the river homes of Indian and non-Indian alike over thousands of miles at no cost, is certainly one of the great tragedies of the last 200 years.

The Fisheries Department of the Nez Perce tribal government is one of the tribe's largest organizations and still works and dreams of fish recovery. Yet many have lost all hope of recovering the way of life tied to the salmon as long as the dams kill the smolts, the salmon young. Sweat house smoke and the sound of drumbeats rise on the Nez Perce Reservation at traditional gatherings and, likewise at Native Christian churches, people pray for a miracle, that politicians will come to understand the enormity of the stake and authorize removal of at least a few of the dams. Perhaps the expeditioners, witness to the change of the last two centuries, would now understand the complexity of their arrival in Nimíipuu country. This is the dual legacy of the Lewis and Clark Expedition to the Nez Perces: the promise of friendship, cooperation, and security, on the one hand, and the final destruction of their culture and way of life on the other. Where will it end?

The Nez Perce nation has remained loyal to the United States. Today, as in previous generations, the Nez Perces are tied to non-Indian America by treaty and by the oldest bond of all, the bond of blood. Tribal men and women have worn the uniform of the U.S. armed services in major wars and police actions, and many have died. The tribe is alive and, despite many problems, many of the people thrive.

But the United States is a nation of hundreds of millions of people, and the Nimíipuu still number fewer than their few thousand who were alive in the years of the Lewis and Clark Expedition. And so we do not know how the story ends, for the story of Lewis and Clark and the Nez Perce Indians is the story of the relations between a small nation and a colossus one. And the flourishing of the small nation depends considerably upon whether or not the United States will find the understanding and generosity of spirit to fulfill its highest ideals and honor its own promises, and respect the Nez Perces. For the Nez Perces once played a critical role in the Nation's western development. The existence and fate of the Nimíipuu are part of the mix that makes the United States unique in the world. Thus the story is not ended, for new pages are written daily.

ENDNOTES

1   Alice Fletcher in *Nez Perce Country*, quoting Jonathan "Billy" Williams. Sappington, "Alice Cunninghamn Fletcher," p. 1. Robert Lee Sappington, Caroline D. Carley, Kenneth C. Reid, and James D. Gallison, "Alice Cunninghamn Fletcher's 'Ethnographic Study in the Columbia Plateau," *Northwest Anthropological Research Notes* vol. 23 no. 2 (Spring, 1995), pp. 177–220. Hereafter cited as Sappington, "Alice Cunninghamn Fletcher," vol. 23.

2   For a detailed accounting of the Nez Perces and fur trade embroilments, see chapter 2 in Josephy, *Nez Perce Indians and the Opening of the Northwest.*

3   Arima, *Blackfeet and Palefaces,* p. 109. The Author describes an early nineteenth century raid against a Nez Perce village in the buffalo country, and Apauk, a young Blackfoot warrior, took the rifle of a young Nez Perce adversary while he was reloading. He noted "the captured gun was different from those of the Saskatchewan River traders, having a long eight sided barrel and a slim polished stock with a side compartment for ball patches." Ed Steerman, of Lewiston, Idaho, friend of the authors and black powder firearms expert explains that this episode shows a contrast between the smooth-bore fusil, with a large trigger guard, with a 24-gauge or .58 caliber of the Saskatchewan River traders, and the American Fur Company trade rifle used by the Nez Perce, which was more accurate due to the grooved or "rifled" barrel which cast a flatter trajectory.

4   The Palouse River is in modern-day southeastern Washington State. For a more detailed accounting of the John Clarke episode, see Josephy, *The Nez Perce Indians and the Opening of the Northwest*, pp. 49–50, also Trafzer, *Renegade Tribe,* pp. 15–16.

5   William C. Hayden, "The Battle of Pierre's Hole," *Idaho Yesterdays*, Vol. 16 no. 2 (Summer, 1972), pp. 2–11.

6   Walker, *Conflict and Schism in the Nez Perce Acculturation,* p. 30.

7   See Leslie Spier, The *Prophet Dance of the Northwest and its Derivatives:
     The Source of the Ghost Dance* (Menasha, WI: George Banta Publishing Co.
     1935), pp. 8, 12, 19. Another helpful source is Clifford E. Trafzer and Margery
     A. Beach, "Smohalla, the Washani, and Religion as a Factor in Northwestern
     Indian History," in Clifford E. Trafzer, guest ed., "American Indian Prophets
     and Revitalization Movements," *American Indian Quarterly* (1985) pp. 309–24.
     Also, Walker, *Conflict and Schism in the Nez Perce Acculturation,* pp. 18-30.

8   Josephy, *Nez Perce Indians and the Opening of the Northwest,* p. 54 n. 20.

9   Josephy, *Nez Perce Indians and the Opening of the Northwest,* pp. 88–9.

10   Ellis's real name was Elli-Wii-Ass; he was named after Twisted Hair's brother,
     Elli-Wii-Ass, who maintained the easternmost camp at Oyáyp (Weippe) Prairie
     during the *qém'es* (camas) season. Whites named the younger Elli-Wii-Ass
     "Ellis" when he attended the Red River School. His mother was Tah-See-Uy-Ma,
     or He-yume-otwy, Twisted Hair (aka Tsap-tso-kalpskin)'s second wife. Twisted
     Hair's first wife, Wits-kees-poo or Tsa-kap, was mother to Alieya, one of the
     young boys sighted by Clark at Oyáyp (Weippe) Prairie on September 20, 1805.
     Alieya was also known by the name Ha-Hul-Ho-Tsote, and grew up to become
     Chief Lawyer. Information from Mylie Lawyer.

11   The journey to St. Louis came as a result of a council who selected the delegate.
     See Peo-Peo-Tah-Likt, *Historical Sketches of the Nez Perces,* Cage #1218, p. 17.

12   McBeth, *Nez Perces Since Lewis and Clark,* p. 30. See also Aoki, *Nez Perce
     Dictionary,* pp. 72, 754. The word *Tipiyelehne* is used in myths, legends, and
     personal names, and *ciixne* (spoke), or *cixneweet* (speaker or talker). This also
     from elder Horace Axtell.

13   Josephy, *Nez Perce Indians and the Opening of the Northwest,* p. 94.

14   Peo-Peo-Tah-Likt, *Historical Sketches of the Nez Perces,* Cage #1218, p. 17. Peo-
     Peo-Tah-Likt, *Historical Sketches of the Nez Perces,* Unpublished manuscript,
     Cage #4681, p. 14.

15   William E. Foley, *Wilderness Journey: the Life of William Clark* (Columbia, MO:
     University of Missouri Press, 2004), pp. 253–4. Hereafter cited as Foley, *Wilderness
     Journey.* Clark also alluded to the Indians in his "1830 Report on the Fur Trade,"
     reprinted in *Oregon Historical Quarterly,* vol. XLVIII (March 1947), pp. 25–33.

16   Peo-Peo-Tah-Likt, *Historical Sketches of the Nez Perces,* Cage #1218, p. 17; Peo-
     Peo-Tah-Likt, *Historical Sketches of the Nez Perces,* Unpublished manuscript,
     Cage #4681, p. 14.

17   McBeth, *Nez Perces Since Lewis and Clark,* p. 30. *JLCE,* 7:249.

18   McBeth, *Nez Perces Since Lewis and Clark,* p. 30. Jonathan "Billy" Williams told
     this story to Kate McBeth many times, the last in 1894, the year before he died.

19   Interview, Mylie Lawyer, May 14, 2003.

20   "A Memorial to the Historic Journey of four Nez Perce Warriors in 1831," a pamphlet from the from the Nez Perce St. Louis Warriors Project, 2003, p. 13. The two Older Nez Perces are buried in Calvary Cemetery, St. Louis, Missouri.

21   Josephy, *Nez Perce Indians and the Opening of the Northwest,* p. 313.

22   David L. Nicandri, *Northwest Chiefs: Gustav Sohon's Views of the 1855 Stevens Treaty Councils* (Tacoma, WA: Washington State Historical Society, 1986) p. 67. Hereafter cited as Nicandri, *Northwest Chiefs.* Also note David L. Bigler, *Fort Limhi: The Mormon Adventure in Oregon Territory, 1855–1858,* (A.H. Clark Co., 1970), pp. 79–80. Hereafter cited as Biger, *Fort Limhi.*

23   Peo-Peo-Tah-Likt, *Historical Sketches of the Nez Perces,* Unpublished manuscript, Cage #4681, p. 13.

24   Foley, *Wilderness Journey,* p. 254.

25   McBeth, *The Nez Perces Since Lewis and Clark,* p. 31.

26   Walker, *Conflict and Schism,* p. 30.

27   Larry Cebula, *Plateau Indians and the Quest for Spiritual Power, 1700–1850* (Lincoln, NB: University of Nebraska Press, 2003), p. 39.

28   Gay, *With the Nez Perces,* p. 50.

29   Sammye J. Meadows and Jana S. Prewitt, *Lewis and Clark for Dummies* (Hoboken, NJ: Willey Publishing Co., 2003), p. 97.

30   Peo-Peo-Tah-Likt, *Historical Sketches of the Nez Perces,* Cage #1218, p. 17. Alice Fletcher's investigations as to the purpose of the St. Louis trip found Nez Perce elder Billy Williams explaining that Speaking Eagle found contradictions between religious pronouncements of the King George men and Lewis and Clark. He wanted to settle some of these questions. See Sappington, "Alice Cunninghamn Fletcher," vol. 23.

31   Peo-Peo-Tah-Likt, *Historical Sketches of the Nez Perces,* Cage #1218, p. 17.

32   Josephy, *Nez Perce and the Opening of the Northwest,* p. 293.

33   Josephy, *Nez Perce and the Opening of the Northwest,* p. 134–38. Also see Ernst Peterson and H. E. Anderson, "Rev. Samuel Parker and the Southern Nez Perce Trail," *Montana The Magazine of Western History,* Vol. XVI, No. 4 (October, 1966), pp. 12–27.

34   Josephy, *Nez Perce and the Opening of the Northwest,* p. 313.

35   Josephy, *Nez Perce and the Opening of the Northwest,* p. 292–3.

36   Chief Timothy biographer, Rowena L. Alcorn, holds that Timothy was born in 1800, see Alcorn, *Timothy, A Nez Perce Chief.* Peo-Peo-Tah-Likt estimated Timothy was eleven years old in 1805, placing his birth in 1794. See Hereafter cited as Peo-Peo-Tah-Likt, *Historical Sketches of the Nez Perces,* Cage #1218, p. 11.

37   Most of the Nez Perces arrived May 24, Looking Glass rode into council the afternoon of June 8, as everyone was about to sign. When he learned that

evening that Nez Perce lands were protected in the treaty, he agreed to sign the next day, June 9. Josephy, p. 328.

38 Lewis gave We-ark-koompt (Flint Necklace, Bighorn Chief, Ram's Horn) a small round mirror with a metal frame and an eyelet for hanging around the neck and repeated the words "looking glass" three times, which the Nez Perces took to be a naming ceremony. The Looking Glass name dates back to this event. "Indian" file, Asotin County Historical Society, Asotin, WA. File contents likely author Judge Elgin V. Kykendall.

39 Nicandri, *Northwest Chiefs,* pp. 65–95.

40 Nicandri, *Northwest Chiefs,* p. 67. Clark may have also fathered a son by a Salish woman. Their son was later baptized as Peter Clark. See Foley, *Wilderness Journey,* pp. 119–20, and Salish-Pend d'Oreille, *The Salish People,* p. 107. See also photo of Tzi-kal-tza on page 114. This is the same man the Nez Perce identify as Daytime Smoker, the name they also used for William Clark.

41 Bigler, *Fort Limhi,* p. 80.

42 For a thorough narrative analysis of Jeffersonian Indian policy, see Wallace, *Jefferson and the Indians.*

43 That the 1863 treaty was and remains "the Steal Treaty" is common knowledge in Nez Perce country. Good accountings may be found in McWhorter, *Hear Me, My Chiefs!* Also see Josephy, *Nez Perce Indians and the Opening of the Northwest.* See also Slickpoo and Walker, *Noon Nee-Mee-Poo.* See more recently, *Treaties Nez Perce Perspectives,* contributors, Horace Axtell, Kristie Baptiste, David Cummings, Rick Eichstaedt, Carla HighEagle, Dave Johnson, Julie Kane, Diane Mallickan, Allen Pinkham, Julie Simpson, Antonio Smith, Patrick Sobotta, Angelan Sondenaa, William Swagerty, Rev. Henry Sugden, Rebecca Miles Williams (Lewiston, ID: The United States Department of Energy and Confluence Press, 2003). From the perspective of attorney John K. Flanagan, "The Invalidity of the Nez Perce Treaty of 1863 and the Taking of the Wallowa Valley," *American Indian Law Review,* vol. 24, no. 1 (1999), pp. 75-98.

44 Interview with Mylie Lawyer, July 23, 2002.

45 That the treaty was coerced becomes obvious in the historical works of Lucullus McWhorter or Alvin Josephy in Josephy, *Nez Perce Indians and the Opening of the Northwest*, pp. 425–30. Also see source documents provided in Dennis W. Baird, Diane Mallickan, and William R. Swagerty, *The Nez Perce Nations Divided: Firsthand Accounts of Events leading to the 1863 Treaty* (Moscow, ID: University of Idaho Press, 2002).

46 McWhorter, *Hear Me, My Chiefs!,* Chapter 8, "The Crimson Trail - a Story of White Atrocities," pp. 116–31, gives the reader a fair idea of the type of crimes committed against the Nez Perces that went unanswered by government.

47 Hampton, *Children of Grace*, quoting *NY Times*, p. 312.

48   Steven Ross Evans, "Chief Joseph and the Red Napoleon Myth," Washington State University MA thesis, 1969, and Mark H. Brown, "The Joseph Myth," *Montana The Magazine of Western History* (January, 1972).

49   Daytime Smoker, son of William Clark, was buried at the Nez Perce Cemetery in Kay County, Oklahoma. At some point in time, the graves were plowed up and the headstones shoved into a nearby ravine. Later, a small portion of the former cemetery was fenced off and a single monument erected.

50   Foley, *Wilderness Journey*, p. 256. The concept of the Lewis and Clark expedition as a reconnaissance-in-force was emphasized to the authors by Clifford Allen, a Nez Perce elder and himself a veteran of the Army's 82nd Airborne Brigade.

51   Jon Toland, *Adolph Hitler*, 2 vols. (Doubleday, 1976), 2:802.

52   410 were taken prisoner, 268 were delivered home. See Clifford E. Trafzer, *Northwestern Tribes in Exile: Modoc, Nez Perce, and Palouse Removal to the Indian Territory* (Sacramento, CA: Sierra Oaks Publishing Co., 1987). Also see J. Diane Pearson, *The Nez Perces in the Indian Territory: Nimíipuu Survival* (Norman, OK: university of Oklahoma Press), pp. 209, 286.

53   Lucullus V. McWhorter, *Yellow Wolf: His Own Story* (Caldwell, ID: Caxton Printers, 1940). p. 290.

54   McWhorter, *Hear Me, My Chiefs!*, pp. 498–9.

55   This maintained by Joseph in an interview by Charles N. Crewdson of the Washington, D.C. *Evening Star*, December 12, 1903.

56   Allalimya Takanin, or Chief Looking Glass, the younger, was the son of Weah-koo-Nut, the Ram's Horn, Apash Wyakaikt (Flint Necklace), Looking Glass, Sr. Looking Glass the younger was shot, killed, and buried during the Bear Paw Battle, September 30 to October 5. Accounts differ as to which day he died. McWhorter, *Hear Me, My Chiefs!*, p. 495, says he was shot in the forehead on the last day of the fighting.

57   Friday, May 9, 1806. *JLCE*, 7:234.

58   Gay, *With the Nez Perces.*

59   James Hunter, *Scottish Highlanders, Indian Peoples: Thirty Generations of a Montana Family* (Helena, Montana: Motnana Historical Society Press, 1996), pp. 155–6.

60   Archie M. Phinney, "Nimíipuu Among the White Settlers," *Wicazo Sa Review* (Fall 2002), Vol. 17, No. 2, pp. 21–42.

61   Chief Joseph died September 21, 1904. The Lewis-Clark Exposition opened June 1, 1904, well short of the desired one-year memorial wait to participate in public affairs.

62   Dennis and Lynn Baird, *In Nez Perce Country: Accounts of the Bitterroots and the Clearwater After Lewis and Clark* (Moscow: ID, University of Idaho Library), 215–6. Hereafter cited as Baird and Baird, *In Nez Perce Country.*

63 Ronald W. Taber, "Sacagawea and the Suffragettes: An Interpretation of a Myth," *Pacific Northwest Quarterly*, LVIII (January, 1967), pp. 7–13.

64 Although many Nez Perces were eligible for citizenship 20 years after the allotment, Nez Perces were not allotted until 1889–1892, thus not qualified for citizenship until 1909–1912.

65 Baird and Baird, *In Nez Perce Country*, p. 214.

66 See William L. Lang and Carol Abbott, *Two Centuries of Lewis and Clark: Reflections on the Voyage of Discovery* (Portland, OR: Historical Society Press, 2004), pp. 71–88.

67 And may be found at Spalding, Idaho's Nez Perce National Historical Park Archives. NEPE 623, p. 3.

68 Letter from Francis Whitman Monteith "to whom it may concern," p.6 Washington State Historical Society, MS 55 Folder 7, Tacoma, Washington.

69 Baird and Baird, *In Nez Perce Country*, pp. 228–9.

70 Space, *The Lolo Trail*.

71 Baird and Baird, *In Nez Perce Country*, pp. 231.

72 Spinden, "The Nez Perce Indians."

73 Slickpoo and Walker, *Noon Nee-Me-Poo*, p. 227.

74 This information from Dr. Bill Willard, author of unpublixhed manuscript on Dr. Archie Phinney. Dr. Phinney was an educated Nez Perce (Columbia University) and served as Director of the Northern Idaho Indian Agency. Archie's brother George Phinney lived in Lapwai valley and served on the Nez Perce Farm and Home Association.

75 He supposedly shot an elk out of season; however, his treaty right precedes and predates the game laws of the State of Oregon. Watters filed to appeal the case, but sadly passed away before the appeal was heard.

All interviewees are members of the Nez Perce Tribe

CLIFFORD ALLEN
(1934–Present) Tribal elder, a U.S. Army veteran, 82nd Airborne, served on Nez Perce Tribal Executive Committee (NPTEC), the governing body of the Nez Perce Tribe of Idaho, owned his own construction outfit, historical researcher.

HORACE AXTELL
(1924–Present) Tribal elder, has done an autobiography with help from Margo Aargon, called *A Little Bit of Wisdom.* An Army veteran of WWII, Pacific Theater, career Potlatch Mills worker, pow-wow dancer, story teller, college language teacher (Lewis-Clark State College, Lewiston, Idaho) and renown leader in Seven Drum Religion.

CECIL CARTER
(1922–2011) Tribal elder, a U.S. Army veteran of WWII, European Theater, career Potlatch Mills worker and supervisor, story teller and college language teacher (Lewis-Clark State College, Lewiston, Idaho).

as told by Cecil Carter: Chapter 1, Page 16

GORDON FISHER (Yosyos Tulikeciin)
(1936–2011) U.S. Army veteran, Vietnam 1966. Career in industry, language teacher with Nez Perce tribal language program and story teller.

as told by Gordon Fisher: Chapter 1, Page 17

MYLIE LAWYER
(1912–2006) Tribal elder, career in the Indian
Service, collector and oral historian.

REV. DAVID J. MILES, SR.
(1904–1994) Tribal elder, U.S. Marines, Panama,
U.S. Army WWII veteran, European Theater,
school teacher, basketball coach, ordained
Presbyterian minister, language teacher
Lewis-Clark State College.

BEATRICE MILES
(1916–2007) Tribal elder, wife of Rev. David Miles,
story teller, oral historian.

IRVIN C. WATTERS, SR.
(1927–2006) Tribal elder, veteran of U. S. Navy,
gunner's mate on destroyer, Pacific Theater, WWII,
rancher, logger, rodeo cowboy, musician, served on
NPTEC, activist and artist.

as told by Irvin Watters: Chapter 2, Page 37

JAMES WALKER

(1969–Present) Salmon and Snake river whitewater guide, sawmill worker, tribal fisheries employee, assistant in tribal horse program, tipi-maker, grandson of tribal elder Lynus Walker, son of co-author Evans.

LYNUS WALKER

(1913–2000) Tribal elder, early rancher and career with Clearwater National Forest, mill worker and supervisor, served NPTEC, president of the Presbyterian Camp Association, story-teller.

WILLIE BRONCHEAU

(1945–Present) Tribal elder, lifelong resident of the Clearwater River, and famous Chinook fisherman and cultural informant.

WALLACE WHEELER

(1918–Present) Tribal elder, veteran of U.S. Army, Ranger WWII, Pacific Theater, thirty-eight plus years with the Bureau of Indian Affairs, story teller.

NANCY JOHNS LOOKINGGLASS
(1927–2010) Tribal elder, Kamiah valley resident and direct descendent of Old Chief Lookingglass, career with Indian Health Service, lifetime affiliate of Second Presbyterian Church (Indian) and Lookingglass pow-wow.

EDITH LOOKINGGLASS STROMBECK
(1932–2004) Tribal elder, Kamiah valley resident and direct descendent of Old Chief Lookingglass, career housewife, lifetime affiliate of Second Presbyterian Church (Indian) and Lookingglass pow-wow.

DELORES LOOKINGGLASS WHEELER
(1926–2013) Tribal elder, Kamiah valley resident and direct descendent of Old Chief Lookingglass, career with Kamiah schools hot lunch program, lifetime affiliate of Second Presbyterian Church (Indian) and Lookingglass pow-wow.

JEANETTE EDWARDS SCOTT
(1932–2009) Tribal elder, U.S. Air Force veteran, career Air Force civilian employee, cultural informant.

ROBERTA EZEKIAL
(1932–2010) Story teller, master of traditional craft, cultural and root knowledge.

MARCUS OATMAN
(1926–2012) Veteran of U.S. Army, Pacific Theater, career sawmill worker, fisherman, story teller.

ALEX M. PINKHAM, SR.
(1895–1975) Veteran of U.S. Army WWI in France, U. S. Marshall, served on NPTEC, oral historian.

as told by Alex Pinkham: Chapter 13, Page 205

EUGENE WILSON
(1917–2005) WWII veteran of U.S. Army Air Force, 60 plus missions as navigator and bombardier in a B-26 over North Africa, and Europe, career Indian Health Service, cultural informant.

ELMER PAUL
(1920–1994) WWII veteran of U.S. Army, story
teller, career ranch hand, cultural consultant to both
Anthropology Departments at University of Idaho
and Washington State University.

as told by Elmer Paul: Chapter 13, Page 205

OLIVER FRANK
(1906–1992) Worked for many years in public
service in greater Los Angeles area, Indian adviser
to Los Angeles Mayor, Sam Yorty, worked with
Hollywood Indians to help organize Native American
aid organizations for re-located tribal people in
Los Angeles area, Boy Scout adviser, lecturer and
consultant to various colleges and universities. 1967
Los Angeles Indian Fair, Man of the Year.

as told by Oliver Frank: Chapter 1, Page 9

HARRY WHEELER
(1884–1963) Son War of 1877 veteran,
Weeahweoktpoo, later known as Presbyterian minister
Rev. William Wheeler, and father of authors' informant
Wally Wheeler, Harry Wheeler was an oral historian
who helped Clearwater County, Idaho, historians Ralph
Space and Zoa Swayne with their works.

as told by Harry Wheeler: Chapter 1, Page 19

Acknowledgements

Our journey to explore the events shared by the Nez Perce Indians and the Corps of Discovery during parts of the years 1805 and 1806 began for us in 1998. We found that there was much more to the story than we initially anticipated and thus our journey has lasted fifteen years.

Nez Perce National Historical Park (NPNHP) of the National Park Service (NPS) are to be commended and thanked for their contribution to our telling of the Lewis and Clark-Nez Perce experience. Our gratitude is extended to former Park Superintendent, Frank Walker and current Superintendent, Terri De Grosse and longtime Archivist Robert Applegate, CA, and new Archivist, Dr. Tabitha "Beth" Erdey. We recognize Kevin Peters (NPNHP Park Ranger) Nez Perce, for his cultural knowledge and his insightful artwork. Also we thank Nakia Williamson-Cloud (Nez Perce) for his skill and authenticity in depicting the Nez Perce at the time of first contact in the giant mural and a half-dozen smaller historical based paintings at Park headquarters in Spalding, ID. Thanks go out also to former NPNHP Interpreter Otis Halfmoon, Nez Perce, (now of NPS). We have heard him speak about Lewis and Clark and we took notes. Thanks also to Diane Mallikan, Nez Perce, a scholar in her own right, who, along with her co-author Dennis Baird, shared vital secondary sources and personal knowledge. Park Curator, Bob Chenowith, an expert on the dugout canoe of the Pacific Northwest aided us materially in our rendition of the Lewis and Clark voyage on the Clearwater River, Snake River and Columbia portion of their journey.

We thank Lynette Miller and Joy Werlink of the Washington State Historical Society Archives in Tacoma, for documents and timely service. Thanks, too for aid from Bernice Pullen of the Clearwater Historical Museum in Orofino, ID. John Capwell of the Garfield County Historical Society in Pomeroy, WA, opened for us on a museum "closed" day, and we remain grateful. Chet Orloff of the Oregon Historical Society sent us research materials concerning the Portland Centennial Celebration.

Expertise in Lewis and Clark era weaponry was shared with us by Edgar Wayne Steerman of Lewiston, ID. Ed is a benefactor to the Museum of the Fur Trade, Chadron, NE, and a long-time friend to us who has been historical adviser and cheerleader on the Lewis and Clark and the Nez Perce and other projects. Chuck Knowles of Moscow, ID and John Fisher of Potlatch Creek, ID have also advised us on period weapons. John has doubled as an expert on the medical aspects of the expedition and acted as photographic technician while simultaneously acting as unofficial

liaison between ourselves and the Dakota Institute Press. The authors
have Lewiston, ID historian and photographer, Garry Bush to thank for
our book jacket portraits. Mr. Chuck Raddon, retired from the US Forest
Service, and Lewis and Clark enthusiast has encouraged us before, during
and since the local Bicentennial Commemoration.

Dr. Loran Olsen, retired Washington State University Musicologist, has
been a friend and mentor. Another friend currently living in Port Angeles,
like Dr. Olsen, is Richard Storch. He has shared his expertise in his study
of historic Plateau photographs. For making their specialized knowledge
available, the authors will be forever indebted.

Carole Smolinski, historian, now retired from Lewis-Clark State
College, first suggested to the authors a first-hand field investigation
of the Sergeant John Ordway journey from Kamiah Valley to lower
Hells Canyon and the return. Pioneering research had been done on this
subject by John Peebles and Merle Wells but there were new discoveries
to make. Carole, Allen, Steve and his spouse Connie hiked portions
of the Ordway route. The authors independently discovered what they
believed to be the Ordway camp of May 29-30, 1806. In other excursions
which involved boating, hiking and horseback riding, others participated
in our field research as well. This included Diane Mallikan (NPNHP),
photographer Richard Storch, Rod and Cindy Carter (Nez Perce, Yakama,
respectively), Macoy Oatman, former Chairman of the Nez Perce Tribal
Executive Committee, and Lester Lowe, formerly of Discovery Outfitters
(Riggins, ID). Lapwai Creek neighbor Dick Jain, who cowboyed in the
Wapshilla Ridge area between the Salmon and Snake rivers and wintered
twice on Cougar Bar in lower Hells Canyon of the Snake rendered
invaluable intimate knowledge of the village location and local trails.
Simultaneously trail expert Steve Russel, teamed with former Idaho
Fish and Game Regional Director Sam McNeil, and outfitter John A.K.
Barker of Barker River Trips were making some similar investigations.
Though the investigations were technically independent of one another,
co-author Evans and John Barker were friends, neighbors and colleagues
at Lewis-Clark State where John also served the Speech and Drama
Department for 32 years. Through friendship and a lot of coffee both field
investigations benefitted from the other and information was shared with
and confirmed by Idaho State Archeologist Ken Reid.

We appreciate the cordiality and assistance of staff including Julie
Baehr at the Fremont County Library for materials related to Sacajawea
historical issues. Fremont County Library Archives contain boxes of "pro"
and "con" evidence for her 1884 death at Wind River. Thanks to several

former students (Lewis-Clark State, Lewiston, ID) Brenda Hahn and Angie Miles (Hermann) who both wrote "Sacajawea" research papers, and University of Idaho (Moscow, ID) graduate student and Lewiston businessman Jock Pring who investigated Nez Perce tribal interest in the Portland, OR, Lewis and Clark Centennial Exposition (1905). Pring found their primary interest was only in the Sacajawea statue dedication. We want to recognize English Professor, Benjamin Kent Evans (son of co-author Evans), of Central Wyoming College, Riverton, WY. He made two major revisions of the first three chapters of our manuscript.

We want to thank Midori C. Raymore, Coordinator for the Lewis-Clark National Historic Trail Foundation Challenge Cost Share Program (2002). She guided us through the application process and when our proposal was accepted, we were able to record sixteen interviews with tribal members. Those interviewed were Clifford Allen, Horace Axtell, Willy Broncheau, Cecil Carter (1922-2011), Roberta Ezekial, Gordon Fisher (1936-2011), Nancy Lookingglass Johns (1928-2010), Mylie Lawyer (1912-2006), Marcus Oatman (1926-2012), Allen Pinkham (interviewed by co-author Evans), Jeanette Scott (1930-2009), Mary Jane "Tootsie" Souther, James A. Walker, Irvin C. Watters (1927-2006), Delores Lookingglass Wheeler (1926-2013), and Wally Wheeler. DVD's have been placed in the Lewis-Clark State College Library and the Nez Perce National Historical Park Library Archives. Administration of our grant and technical expertise were all provided by the Educational-Technical office at Lewis-Clark State College, ably administered by Dave Taylor and his Assistant Doris Miles with technical support from Jason Goldammer and cameraman Dan "Tukes" Kane whose tribal membership and cultural knowledge and familiarity with many of our interviewees greatly enhanced whatever we may have accomplished.

Our investigations soon made us acutely aware of our indebtedness to many Chopunnish, Nimiipuu or Nez Perce from the generations since Lewis and Clark. In one way or another and to varying degrees some Nez Perce refused to forget or let go of some aspect of the stories associated with the first encounters with these strangers from the East.

We will never know all their names but we acknowledge and salute the efforts of both the unknown and the known. Auyeen (Mylie Lawyer's spelling) or Bullet-Through-the-Dress, earned her name when a lead ball from a Gros Ventre rifle cut a hole through the hide of her dress as she brought up a fresh horse to her husband, Chief Lawyer, during the famed Battle of Pierre's Hole in 1832. Known to the whites as Tillie Lawyer, she drilled her young grandson in Nimiipuu history as he lay in his blankets near the fire of his grandmother's tipi in Kamiah Valley, near the Long Camp of Lewis and Clark in 1806. The grandson, named Corbett Lawyer, as an old man, lay by the fireplace in his daughter's home in Lapwai, ID, and retaught the stories Tillie Lawyer had taught him. His daughter's name was Mylie Lawyer and the authors had the great privilege to sit by her fireplace as she told us Tillie Lawyer's stories. We wrote them down and thus pass them to you, the reader. Her younger brother, Archie Lawyer was also a help to us.

Reading the two volumes of Olin D. Wheeler's *The Trail of Lewis and Clark, 1804-1904*, brought forth the names of Charlie Adams (Nez Perce) and James Stuart (Nez Perce) who served as assistant to Special Indian Agent Alice C. Fletcher, Allotting Agent, and Harry Wheeler, 1884-1963 (Nez Perce and Carlisle football center), the son of Weeahweoktpoo (later Presbyterian minister Reverend William Wheeler, ordained 1888) renowned warrior of the 1877 Conflict. The authenticity of Olin D. Wheeler's work on the Nez Perce portion of the trail was to a considerable extent due to these three educated and historically conscious Nez Perce.

These names we mention are only a part of the historical parade of heroines and heroes who have struggled to establish and maintain a tribal memory. Sam Lott or Many Wounds (1860-1935) the grandson of Black Eagle, aka Broken Arm, who died in St. Louis, wrote, in his best English, tribal sagas as told him by his cousin Nez Perce patriot, Chief Peo Peo Tah-Likt or Bird Alighting (1856-1935). Sam Lott's daughter Rena Katherine Ramsey (1918-1999) was a strong cultural carrier and friend to the authors. Kamiah elder, Kewkewluya (Jonathan "Billy" Williams (1822-1895) acted as tribal historian to Presbyterian missionaries and anthropologist Alice C. Fletcher to insure a tribal voice. While Chief Joseph's nephew James Reuben used his own writing and speaking skills to fight for and maintain Nez Perce power and influence over Nez Perce stories. The early twentieth century found educated Nez Perce such as Star Maxwell successful banker and advocate and Nez Perce anthropologist Archie Phinney both making notable published collections of tribal history and mythology.

We want to remember Nez Perce elders Elmer Paul (1920-1994), grand-nephew of Chief Yellow Wolf (1856-1935) for his many contributions, and gratefully remember also Reverend David J. Miles (1904-1994) and his wife Beatrice (1916-2007). Mrs. Miles told the Watkuweis story many times and often added the portion regarding the wolf spirit power of Watkuweis. Eugene Wilson, Nez Perce (1917-2005) of Tempe, AZ, and his older brother Angus Wilson of Kamiah contributed materially to our understanding of the Lewis and Clark among the Nez Perce story and tribal history and culture generally. Co-author Evans" father-in-law Lynus Walker, Nez Perce (1913-2000) of Kamiah and Oliver W. Frank (1908-1992) of Kamiah pointed out camp and trail locations as well as other cultural and historical information.

Co-author Allen V. Pinkham received much of his historical and cultural education from his late father Alex Pinkham (1895-1975), who learned much from his father, 1877 war veteran, John Pinkham and from three old men that were oft quoted to Allen. One of these was a relative, likely a great grandson of Chief Cut Nose of the Lewis and Clark journals, named John Cut Nose. Co-author Pinkham wrote of these memories of the three old men in a chapter for Alvin M. Josephy, Jr.'s book, *Lewis and Clark Through Indian Eyes* (Alfred A. Knopf, 2006). Co-author Pinkham also credits his siblings, all older, for his knowledge of tribal history and culture. They are from the oldest to the youngest, Albert, Audrey, Priscilla, Alex Jr., Alfred, Loretta and Alvin, and Bernadine.

We recognize the work of linguist Dr. Haruo Aoki as vital to our effort and his monumental *Nez Perce Dictionary*, and the monumental accomplishment of Dr. Gary E. Moulton in editing The Journals of the Lewis and Clark Expedition. Our task would have been impossible without their achievements. We were dependent too upon the academic direction and help of James Rhonda, William L. Lang, and Carl Abbott, and tribal academics, Phillip Cash Cash, and Ronald Pond as well as the pioneering book by Nimiipuu writer Allen P. Slickpoo, Sr. and his co-author, anthropologist Deward E. Walker, Jr.

Marianne Keddington-Lang, Oregon Historical Society gave us a great deal of constructive criticism and encouragement following the completion of our first manuscript in 2007. Currently retired college faculty also helped with ideas and information, Alan G. Marshall, Lewis-Clark State College anthropologist and William Johnson retired English professor were both helpful, as was Lillian A. Ackerman of Washington State University who always answered our calls with answers to our questions and gave us many kind references. And we give special thanks also to David H. Stratton of the Washington State University History Department, retired, for his encouragement.

We recognize Sandi Broncheau-McFarland, Nez Perce, for her work as Administrator for the Nez Perce Nimiipuu National Historic Trail for the Forest Service in preservation of the Nez Perce and Lolo Trail through Idaho and Montana. We also thank Barbara and the late Harlan Opdahl,

Triple O Outfitters, for their horsepack trips on the Lolo portion of the Lewis and Clark and the Nimiipuu Trail; their hospitality and skill will always be appreciated. Likewise we want to recognize Weippe residents Eugene and Molly Eastman for the academic and field work of the Nez Perce and Lolo Trails. They are in the tradition of Olin D. Wheeler and Ralph Space. They know the history and ground perhaps equal to or better than any other living persons and are actively engaged in preserving the same. Their spirit of cooperation and sharing are greatly appreciated.

Thank you too, Silas Whitman, current Chairman of the Nez Perce Tribal Executive Committee (2013) and his staff and tribal departments which assisted us in our endeavor. We appreciate the Cultural Resources Department Director, Mrs. Vera Sonneck, Nez Perce, Josiah Pinkham (son of co-author Allen Pinkham) and Nakia Williamson-Cloud for their sharing of resources and comments. The Land Service Department of the Nez Perce Tribe headed by Mr. Kim Cannon placed his office and staff at our disposal for development of historical maps. Thanks to all employees, Edith "Wook" Powaukee, Nez Perce, Jane McAtty, Nez Perce, and Elaine Ellenwood, Nez Perce, and Laurie Ames who gave us a great deal when we were most in need.

The Tribal Language Department has been helpful on our entire journey, Angel Sobotta (a Chief Red Grizzly Bear descendent) along with linguist Harold Crook and the Nez Perce Circle of Elders. Stites, ID, elder Rachel Zumwalt's views are appreciated, along with Sweetwater elder Francis Paisano and other elders Bessie Scott, Bernice Moffett, Florene Davis, Florene Rickman and language teacher James McCormack.

Finally we thank our immediate families not only for their support but the many sacrifices they were forced to make due to the length of our commitment to this volume. Co-author Evans' children, Ben Evans, James Walker and Lisa Burks shared the burden along with co-author Pinkham's children, Lynette, Allen Jr., Levi, Timothy, Josiah, and Tisa. Connie Evans provided a great deal of moral support and material aid for the fifteen-year duration and was our technical aid at our office in Lapwai, ID. Connie and Christiane Pinkham-Stuk (Allen Pinkham's granddaughter) were responsible for assembling and checking the glossary along with tribal language program's Thomas 'Tutlo' Gregory. Our initial manuscript was typed by Shirley Guzman (co-author Evans's sister-in-law), and all subsequent versions were completed by our secretary of the last four years, our technical assistant and, sometime editor and critic (who should receive some kind of medal), we salute Alycia Shedd of Lewiston, ID.

Our thanks go out to Lapwai resident Heath Wilson for donating the rights to his painting used on the book cover and to the artist John Seven Wilson (Nez Perce), who knows the country. And the book would never have been published without the assistance and support of the good people at The Dakota Institute Press, David Borlaug and the editorial efforts of Clay Jenkinson and the patience and skill of Sarah Trandahl the editorial assistant who brought all of the book parts together and co-ordinated all the work with the authors in Idaho through the telephone and email, a long tedious process. And lastly we appreciate Clay S. Jenkinson for writing our Preface and Fred E. Hoxie for writing the Foreword to this book and his many other contributions to Native America, including his services with co-author Pinkham on the Board of Trustees of the National Museum of the American Indian.

Books

Ackerman, Lillian A. *A Necessary Balance: Gender and Power Among the Indians of the Columbia River.* Norman: University of Oklahoma Press, 2003.

Alcorn, Rowena L. and Gordon D. Alcorn. *Timothy: A Nez Perce Chief, 1800-1891.* Fairfield, WA: Ye Galleon Press, 1985.

Allen, A.J. *Ten years in Oregon: Travels and adventures of Doctor E. White and lady, west of the Rocky mountains, with incidents of two sea voyages via Sandwich Islands around Cape Horn, containing, also, a brief history of the missions and settlement of the country ... description of the soil, production and climate.* Ithaca, NY: Andrus, Gauntlett, & Co., 1850.

Anastasio, Angelo. *The Southern Plateau: an Ecological Analysis of Intergroup Relations.* Moscow, ID: University of Idaho, Laboratory of Anthropology, 1975.

Aoki, Haruo. *Nez Perce Dictionary.* Berkeley, CA: University of California Press, 1994.

Arima, Eugene Y. *Blackfeet and Palefaces: The Pikani and Rocky Mountain House: a Commemorative History from the Upper Saskatchewan and Missouri Fur Trade.* Ottawa: Golden Dog Press, 1995.

Baird, Lynn, and Dennis W. Baird. *In Nez Perce Country: Accounts of the Bitterroots and the Clearwater After Lewis and Clark.* Moscow, ID: University of Idaho Library, 2003.

Baird, Dennis W, Diane Mallickan, and William R. Swagerty. *The Nez Perce Nation Divided: Firsthand Accounts of Events Leading to the 1863 Treaty.* Moscow, ID: University of Idaho Press, 2002.

Betts, Robert B. *In Search of York: The Slave Who Went to the Pacific with Lewis and Clark.* Boulder, CO: Colorado Associated University Press. 1985.

Bigler, David L. *Fort Limhi: The Mormon Adventure in Oregon Territory, 1855-1858.* Spokane, WA: Arthur H. Clark Co, 2003.

Boyd, Robert. *People of The Dalles: The Indians of Wascopam Mission.* U of Neb. Lincoln and London, 1996.

Cebula, Larry. *Plateau Indians and the Quest for Spiritual Power, 1700-1850*. Lincoln, NB: University of Nebraska Press, 2003.

Clarke, Charles G. *The Men of the Lewis and Clark Expedition: A Biographical Roster of the Fifty-One Members and a Composite Diary of Their Activities from All the Known Sources*. Glendale, CA: A.H. Clark Co, 1970.

Cox, Lloyd M. *In the Days When the Rivers Ran Backwards*. Lewiston, ID: L.M.Cox, 1994, 1995.

Eastman, Gene, and Eastman, Mollie. *Bitterroot Crossing: Lewis and Clark Across the Lolo Trail*. Second edition. Northwest Historical Manuscript Series, University of Idaho Library, Moscow, Idaho, 2005.

Evans, Steven Ross. *Voice of the Old Wolf: Lucullus Virgil McWhorter and the Nez Perce Indians*. Washington State University Press, Pullman, WA, 1996.

Fazio, James R., and Mike Venso, *Across the Snowy Ranges: The Lewis and Clark Expedition in Idaho and Western Montana*. Moscow, ID: Woodland Press, 2001.

Fisher, John W. *Medical Appendices of the Lewis and Clark Expedition*. 8th edition. Self-published, 2006.

Foley, William E. *Wilderness Journey: The Life of William Clark*. Columbia, MO: University of Missouri Press, 2004.

Garry, Jim, *Weapons of the Lewis and Clark Expedition*. University of Oklahoma, 2012.

Gass, Patrick, and Carol L. MacGregor. *The Journals of Patrick Gass: Member of the Lewis and Clark Expedition*. Missoula, MT: Mountain Press Publishing Co., 1997.

Gay, E.J., Frederick E. Hoxie, and Joan T. Mark. *With the Nez Perces: Alice Fletcher in the Field, 1889-92*. Lincoln, NB: University of Nebraska Press, 1981.

Gilman, Carolyn. *Lewis and Clark: Across the Divide*. Washington, D.C.: Smithsonian Books, 2003.

Goble, Dale, and Paul W. Hirt. *Northwest Lands, Northwest Peoples: Readings in Environmental History*. Seattle, WA: University of Washington Press, 1999.

Halsey, Cheryll, and Robert R. Beale. *Lewis and Clark and the Shahaptian Speaking Americans*. Fairfield, WA: Ye Galleon Press, 1983.

Hamill, Chad S. *Songs of Power and Prayer in the Columbia Plateau.*. Corvallis, OR: Oregon State University Press, 2012.

Hampton, Bruce. *Children of Grace: The Nez Perce War of 1877*. New York: H. Holt, 1994.

Hunter, James. *Scottish Highlanders, Indian Peoples: Thirty Generations of a Montana Family*. Helena, MT: Montana Historical Society Press, 1996.

Huser, Verne. *On the River with Lewis and Clark*. College Station: Texas A & M University Press, 2004.

Jackson, Donald. *Letters of the Lewis and Clark Expedition with Related Documents, 1783-1854*. Urbana: University of Illinois Press, 1962.

Josephy, Alvin M. *The Nez Perce Indians and the Opening of the Northwest*. New Haven, CT: Yale University Press, 1965.

____. and Marc Jaffe. *Lewis and Clark Through Indian Eyes*. New York: Knopf, 2006.

Landeen, Dan, and Allen Pinkham. *Salmon and His People: Fish & Fishing in Nez Perce Culture*. Lewiston, Idaho: Confluence Press, 1999.

Lang, William L., Carl Abbott, Roberta Conner, and Christopher Zinn. *Two Centuries of Lewis and Clark: Reflections on the Voyage of Discovery*. Portland, OR: Oregon Historical Society Press, 2004.

Marshall, Alan G. "Unusual Gardens: The Nez Perce and Wild Horticulture on the Eastern Columbia Plateau," Chapter 9 in Dale D. Goble and Paul W. Hirt, eds., *Northwest People: Readings in Environmental History*. Seattle and London: University of Washington Press, 1999.

McBeth, Kate C. *The Nez Perces Since Lewis and Clark*. New York: F.H. Revell Co, 1908.

McWhorter, Lucullus V. *Yellow Wolf: His Own Story.* Caldwell, ID, Caxton Printers, 1940.

____. and Ruth B. A. Bordin. *Hear Me, My Chiefs!: Nez Perce History and Legend.* Caldwell, Idaho: Caxton Printers, 1952.

Meadows, Sammye J., and Jana S. Prewitt. *Lewis & Clark for Dummies.* Hoboken, NJ: Wiley Publishing Co., 2003.

Moulton, Gary E., ed. *The Journals of the Lewis and Clark Expedition.* Vols 1-13. Lincoln: University of Nebraska Press, 1983–2002.

Neumann, George C., Frank J. Kravic, and George C. Woodbridge. *Collector's Illustrated Encyclopedia of the American Revolution.* Harrisburg, Pa: Stackpole Books, 1975.

Nez Perce Tribe of Idaho, *Treaties: Nez Perce Perspectives.* Lewiston, ID: Confluence Press, 2003.

Nicandri, David L. *Northwest Chiefs: Gustav Sohon's Views of the 1855 Stevens Treaty Councils.* Tacoma, Wash: Washington State Historical Society, 1986.

____. *River of Promise: Lewis and Clark on the Columbia.* Washburn, ND: The Dakota Institute Press, 2009.

Northwest Anthropological Research Notes. Moscow, ID: University of Idaho, 1967.

Pambrun, Sam. *The Corps on 84: A Travel Guide.* Pendleton, OR: Umatilla County Bicentennial Sterring Committee.

Parker, Samuel. *Journal of an Exploring Tour Beyond the Rocky Mountains.* Auburn, N.Y.: J.C. Derby & Co, 1846.

Pearson, J. D. *The Nez Perces in the Indian Territory: Nimiipuu Survival.* Norman: University of Oklahoma Press, 2008.

Plamondon, Martin, II. *Lewis and Clark Trail Maps: A Cartographic Reconstruction:* Volume I. Pullman, WA: Washington State University Press, 2000.

Relander, Click. *Drummers and Dreamers: The Story of Smowhala the Prophet and His Nephew Puck Hyah Toot, the Last Prophet of the Nearly Extinct River People, the Last Wanapums.* Caldwell, Idaho: Caxton Printers, 1956.

Rice, Harvey S. *Native American Dwellings and Attendant Structures of the Southern Plateau.* Cheney, Wash: Archaeological and Historical Services, 1985.

Ronda, James P. *Lewis and Clark Among the Indians.* Lincoln: University of Nebraska Press, 1984.

Salish-Pend d'Oreille Culture Committee and Elders Cultural Advisory Council, Confederated Salish and Kootenai Tribes. *The Salish People and the Lewis and Clark Expedition.* Lincoln: University of Nebraska Press, 2005.

Shawley, Steve. *Nez Perce Names and Notes,* Appendix I. Moscow, Idaho: University of Idaho, 1977.

Simon-Smolinski, Carole. *Hells Canyon and the Middle Snake River: A Story of the Land and Its People.* Lewiston, Idaho: Confluence Press, 2008.

Slickpoo, Allen P. Sr., and Deward E. Walker, Jr. *Noon Nee-Mee-Poo (We, the Nez Perces): Culture and History of the Nez Perces.* Lapwai, Idaho: Nez Perce Tribe of Idaho, 1973.

Space, Ralph S. *The Lolo Trail: A History of Events Connected with the Lolo Trail Since Lewis and Clark.* Lewiston, Idaho: Printcraft Printing Inc., 1970.

Spier, Leslie. *The Prophet Dance of the Northwest and Its Derivatives: The Source of the Ghost Dance.* Menasha, Wisconsin: George Banta Publishing Co., 1935.

Spinden, Herbert J. *The Nez Perce Indians.* Lancaster, PA: New era Print. Co., 1908.(Reprinted: Kraus Reprint, New York and Millwood, 1964, 1974), pp. 237–8.

Swayne, Zoa, and Carol A. G. Bates, ed. *Do Them No Harm!: Lewis and Clark Among the Nez Perce.* Caldwell, ID: Caxton Press, 2003.

Thompson, Scott M. *I Will Tell of My War Story: A Pictorial Account of the Nez Perce War.* Seattle, Wash: University of Washington Press, in association with the Idaho State Historical Society, Boise, 2000.

Thwaites, Reuben G., George W. Ogden, W. Bullock, and Josiah Gregg. *Early Western Travels.* Cleveland, OH: Arthur H. Clark Co, 1905.

Tonkovich, Nicole. *The Allotment Plot.* Lincoln, NE: University of Nebraska Press, 2013.

Townsend, John K. "Narrative of a Journey across the Rocky Mountains," reprinted in Reuben Thwaites, *Early Western Travels*, Cleveland, 1905.

Toland, John. *Adolf Hitler.* Volume 2. Garden City, NY: Doubleday, 1976.

Trafzer, Clifford E. *Grandfather, and Old Wolf: Tamánwit Ku Súkat and Traditional Native American Narratives from the Columbia Plateau.* East Lansing, Mich: Michigan State University Press, 1998.

____. *Northwestern Tribes in Exile: Modoc, Nez Perce, and Palouse Removal to the Indian Territory.* Sacramento, CA: Sierra Oaks Publishing Co., 1987.

____. and Richard D. Scheuerman. *Renegade Tribe: The Palouse Indians and the Invasion of the Inland Pacific Northwest.* Pullman, Wash: Washington State University Press, 1986.

Walker, Deward E., Jr. *Conflict and Schism in Nez Perce Acculturation: A Study of Religion and Politics.* Pullman, WA: Washington State University Press, 1968.

Wallace, Anthony F. C. *Jefferson and the Indians: The Tragic Fate of the First Americans.* Cambridge, MA: The Belknap Press of Harvard University Press, 1999.

Wana Chinook Tymoo. Portland, OR: Columbia River Inter-Tribal Fish Commission, 1991.

Wheeler, Olin D. *The Trail of Lewis and Clark, 1804–1904: A Story of the Great Exploration Across the Continent in 1804-6; with a Description of the Old Trail, Based Upon Actual Travel Over It, and of the Changes Found a Century Later.* New York: G.P. Putnam's Sons, 1904.

Journals

Ackerman, Lillian A. "Marital Instability and Juvenile Delinquency Among the Nez Perces," *American Anthropologist,* 73:3 (June, 1971).

Anderson, William M, and Albert J. Partoll. "Anderson's Narrative of a Ride to the Rocky Mountains in 1834," *Frontier and Midlands* (Autumn, 1938).

Brown, Mark H. "The Joseph Myth," *Montana, the Magazine of Western History* (January, 1972).

Chenowith, Bob. "Wali̇imliyas: The Nez Perce National Historical Park Dugout Canoe Collection and Dugout Canoe Use Among the Nez Perce Indians." *Journal of Northwest Anthropology,* 42:2 (Fall, 2008) pp. 167-204.

Clark, William. "1830 Report on the Fur Trade," reprinted in Oregon *Historical Quarterly*, vol. XLVIII (March, 1947), pp. 25–33.

Flanagan, John K. "The Invalidity of the Nez Perce Treaty of 1863 and the Taking of the Wallowa Valley." *American Indian Law Review*, 24.1 (1999), pp. 75-98.

Hayden, William C. "The Battle of Pierre's Hole," Boise, ID: *Idaho Historical Society,* vol. XVI (Summer, 1972).

Modie, Jonathan. "Celilo Legacy." *Wana Chinook Tymoo (*Winter, 2008), p. 4.

Murdock, George Peter. "Notes on the Tenino, Molala, and Paiute of Oregon," *American Anthropologist.* n. s., 40 (July-September 1938), pp. 395-402.

Osborne, Douglas. "Nez Perce Horse Castration—a Problem in Diffusion," reprinted in *Northwest Anthropological Research Notes*, 2:(1/2) (1955), pp. 113-122.

Peebles, John J. "The Return of Lewis and Clark," *Idaho Yesterdays,* vol. 10 (Summer, 1966), pp. 16-27.

Peterson, Ernst, and H. E. Anderson. "Rev. Samuel Parker and the Southern Nez Perce Trail," *Montana Magazine of Western History,* vol. XVI, no. 4 (October, 1966).

Phinney, Archie M. "Nimi̇ipuu Among the White Settlers," *Wicazo Sa Review*, 17.2 (2002), pp. 21-42.

Pinkham, Allen V. "Childhood Memories of Fishing at Celilo Falls." *Oregon Historical Quarterly.* 108.4 (2007), pp. 586-595.

Ray, Verne F., and Nancy Oestreich Lurie. "The Contributions of Lewis and Clark to Ethnography," *Journal of the Washington Academy of Sciences.* 44 (November, 1954), pp. 358-70.

Ronda, James P. "Frazer's Razor: The Ethnohistory of a Common Object," *We Proceeded On,* vol. 7 no. 3 (August, 1981), pp. 12–13.

Sappington, Robert Lee and Caroline D. Carley. "Alice Cunninghamn Fletcher's 'Ethnographic Gleanings Among the Nez Perces,'" from *Northwest Anthropological Research Notes,* vol. 9 no. 1 (Spring, 1995), p. 20.

Sappington, Robert Lee, Caroline D. Carley, Kenneth C. Reid, and James D. Gallison. "Alice Cunningham Fletcher's 'The Nez Perce Country,'" *Northwest Anthropological Research Notes,* vol. 29 no. 2 (1995).

Sappington, Robert Lee. "The Lewis and Clark Expedition Among the Nez Perce Indians: The First Ethnographic Study in the Columbia Plateau." *Northwest Anthropological Research Notes,* vol. 23 no. 1 (Spring, 1989).

Seton, Alfred. "Mackenzie's Post of the Clearwater River, 1812-1813," *Idaho Yesterdays,* vol. 18, no. 3 (Fall, 1974), pp. 24-32.

Taber, Ronald W. "Sacagawea and the Suffragettes: An Interpretation of a Myth." *Pacific Northwest Quarterly,* LVIII (January, 1967), pp. 7-13.

Trafzer, Clifford E., and Margery A. Beach. "Smohalla, the Washani, and Religion As a Factor in Northwestern Indian History." *American Indian Quarterly,* 9.3 (1985), pp. 309-24.

Warren, D.E. "Spotted Horse No Recent Arrival," *Lewiston Morning Tribune,* Lewiston, ID (January 6, 1963).

Walker, Deward E., Jr., *The Nez Perce Sweat Bath Complex: An Acculturational Analysis,* vol. 22 (Summer, 1966), pp. 133-71.

Wells, Merle. "Lewis and Clark in Idaho," *Idaho Yesterdays* (1990).

Other

Evans, Steven Ross. "Chief Joseph and the Red Napoleon Myth," Washington State University MA thesis, 1969.

Frank, Oliver. unpublished manuscript.

Lott, Sam, and Tholekt, Peopeo, with Mary Evans. *Historical Sketches of the Nez Perces: Personal Incidents in the Lives of the Famous Chiefs of the Nez Perce.* Typescript. Nez Perce National Historical Park Archives, Spalding, ID, 1935.

Marshall, Alan. "Nez Perce Social Groups: An Ecological Interpretation." Ph.D. dissertation, Washington State University, 1977.

Peo-Peo-Tah-Likt, Chief, and Chief Many Wounds (Sam Lott). *Historical Sketches of the Nez Perces*, typed unpublished draft from Cage #1218, Manuscripts, Archives and Special Collections, Washington State University, Pullman, Washington, 1935.

Peo-Peo-Tah-Likt, Chief, and Chief Many Wounds (Sam Lott). *Historical Sketches of the Nez Perces*, typed unpublished draft from the Evans Collection, Cage #4681, Manuscripts, Archives and Special Collections, Washington State University, Pullman, Washington, 1935. This version is several pages longer than the #1218 manuscript and while both contain much of the same material, each has some events not covered by the other or includes different details of similar or same events.

Peo-Peo-Tah-Likt, Chief, and Chief Many Wounds (Sam Lott). Account 2.1. *Historical Sketches of the Nez Perces*, Excerpts from with editing by Dennis Baird, University of Idaho, Moscow, Idaho. Source from Evans Collection, Cage #4681, Manuscripts, Archives and Special Collections, Washington State University, Pullman, Washington.

Russell, Steve F., Ph., D. "Sgt. Ordway's Salmon River Fishing Expedition, brochure published through Bonneville Power Administration, Idaho Governor's Lewis and Clark Trail Committee, and the Idaho State Historical Society, printer unknown, 2004. Further information from Idaho Department of Fish and Game, Clearwater Region, 1540 Warner Avenue, Lewiston, ID 83501, (208) 799-5010, or contact Steve F. Russell. Historic Trails Research, 26393 520th Ave., Ames, IA 50014, www.historic-trails.com.

Spalding Sweathouse, Jesse Redheart.

Taber, Ronald W. "Sacagawea and the Suffragettes: An Interpretation of a Myth." *Pacific Northwest Quarterly* LVIII (Jan 1967) 7-13

VanArsdol, Ted. "History of the Alpowai." Unpublished manuscript in posession of the authors, 1972.

Glossary

The following is a list of Nimíipuu terms used in this book. For further reference, see Haruo Alki's *Nez Perce Dictionary,* University of California Press, 1994.

A few of the terms are transcribed into English in slightly different ways by different informants who are quoted in this book. In such cases, the initials of the informant are added in parentheses.

Alex M. Pinkham (AMP) Alice Fletcher (AF)
Alvin Josephy (AJ) Elmer Paul (EP)
Eugene Wilson (EW) Harry Wheeler (HW)
Lynus Walker (LW) Mylie Lawyer (ML)
Oliver Frank (OF) Ralph Space (RS)
Sam Lott (SL) Zoa Swayne (ZW)
Gustavas Sohon's 1855 Stevens Treaty Councils (GS)
Lewis and Clark in their journals (LC)

Terms

A
'ápa – loaf of ground qáaws (see below) (Aoki)
'apa'áal – May or June, season of 'apa' (see above) (Aoki)

C
ciq'áamqal – dog (Aoki)
Cokahlarishkit (LC) – Buffalo Trail (see qoq'áalx 'ískit below)
coqóycoqoy – tipi (Aoki)

E
eaus – a pole/paddle combination, 10 feet or more long, usually made from red fir wood

H
háama – man (Aoki)
hamoolcix – implies cuteness and treated like children; this word is a 2nd person plural present tense verb "we are like children" (Aoki)
hímiin – wolf (Aoki)
hin-olt-sin – they dawdle as if we were children (AF)

hipeqyíyimne – they were in a hurry (Aoki)
hipt – food (Aoki)
hoopop – pine tree moss (Aoki)

I
'iceyéeye – coyote (Aoki)
'ilcweew'cix kaa 'iceyéeye – monster and coyote (Aoki)
'isx̣íipit – act of becoming a Shaman (Aoki)
'iweepne – wife (Aoki)
'iyehneno's – canoe pole (Aoki)

K
kaak sun ma – sturdy brush (OF)
kayxkáyx – clean, clear (Aoki)
kopluts – war clubs
kuhet'iniit – long house (Aoki)
kuus – water (Aoki)

L
lewtek'enew'éet – Fish headman, distributor of fish, especially in reference to salmon during the season (Aoki)

M

maamin – an appaloosa horse

mexsem'e pi'squ – mountain tea, mountain Labrador (*ledum glandulosum*) tea

mimic'itpas – people who don't listen / are disobedient (Aoki)

mim'yooxat – chiefs (Aoki), elders also often say mimíyooxat

miyóoxat – singular of above

N

naaqc – one (Aoki)

naaqc heenek'e – once again

naco'ox – salmon, note: this form is only to show the extra vowel included when suffixes are added,should be nacó'x when spoken (Aoki)

nee saa wai loo – mythological reference to coyote (OF)

Nimíipuu – Nez Perce people

Nimipuutímt – Nez Perce Language (Aoki)

P

papc'ícqiy or papcícqi – fir tree pitch (Aoki)

pilpil'uus – entrails (Aoki)

pinuukin – husband's brother (Aoki)

piskis – door (Aoki)

Q

qaaws – root vegetable

qacano – competent, versatile, fearless

qalaca'c – paternal grandfather, qaláca –(vocative) paternal grandchild (Aoki)

qawsqaaws – a variety of common cow parsnip that grows in swamps in the mountains (Aoki)

qém'es – camas, onion shaped root (Aoki)

qeqi'it – wild potato (Aoki)

qi'iwn – old man (Aoki)

qo'opas – tripe, stomach (Aoki)

qoq'aalx – buffalo

qoq'aalx 'iskit – Buffalo Trail (Aoki), more commonly referred to as k'usey'ne'iskit

qu'nes – condor (Aoki)

quuynu – Beaver musk, castor; used to make love potion (Aoki)

q'uyi'iy – full of odor (Aoki)

S

Sahaptins – linguistic group

sap-soo-wayikt – a method of crossing horses over a river (EW, LW, AP)

see-wy-yah – a sudden turn or bend of the river around a promontory

sexni'm' – fall season (Aoki)

si'k'em – horse

sooyáapoo – white man (Aoki)

T

ta'c – good (Aoki)

tamacilpt – circle of tipis (EP)

    temee – place (Aoki)

    cilíilp – circle (Aoki)

tew'yelenew'eet – camp crier (Aoki)

tili'pe' – fox (Aoki)

tipiyele'hne – eagle (Aoki)

tiweet – medicine man (Aoki)

tiwata'aat – medicine woman (Aoki)

tiwelke – enemy to be fought (AMP)

tiwe'lqe – enemy to be fought, specifically Bannocks and Shoshone (Aoki)

tok'ó'niit – tule house, mat lodge, long house (Aoki)

tuuk'es – digging stick (Aoki)

tu'ynu'suus – tail feather crown, Sioux-type war bonnet made with tail feathers, eagle feather bonnet (EP)

W

wáaqo' kaló' (now yóq'o kaló') – that is all (Aoki)

    wako kalo – that is all (OF)

wali'im'niit – old time housing (Aoki)

waqipanix – a very long time ago (Aoki)

weye 'uuyit (possibly could use 'anoqónmapa, 'anoqonpa, 'anóqitpa) – first coming, (Aoki) we-dhuh, we-tuh, wit-uh − building rafts from driftwood

wéetes − earth (Aoki)

wéeyekin − guardian spirit (Aoki)

wéeyekweecet or wéeyekweyeecet − medicine dance; guardian spirit dance (Aoki)

wewéex̣p − spring season (Aoki)

wew'íimn − wild celery (Aoki)

weya úuyit − first coming (Aoki)

wistamalwiyáat − camp chief (Aoki), one who is the chosen decision maker while traveling

wistitám'o − sweathouse (Aoki)

Y

yáaka' − black bear (Aoki)

yee ya weets a koo saa − it is a pitiful thing you are doing (OF)

yú'c − pitiable, poor (Aoki)

Names of Individuals

Aleiya − Child's name, son of Twisted Hair (ML)

Al-We-Yas − Twisted Hairs Brother (ML)

Cuts-Sah-nim − Principal Chief

Ellis Khip-khip-pel-kehken − man's name (ML)

Halax̣ túuqit − name, thought to be Clark's son

halax̣ − daytime

túuqit − smoker

aka Pi-nahua-ut-at, Capon Rouge, Red Head

Hatolikin or Natolikin − man's name, also means buck antelope

Hiyóom'asanm wehéyqt − Grizzly Bear Claw Necklace, (Aoki)

Hiyúum páax̣at tim'íne − Chief's name, Five Big Hearts

hiyúum − mythical grizzly bear (Aoki)

páax̣at − five (Aoki)

tim'íne − heart (Aoki)

Huis Huis Kute − Palouse leader

Ipnáatkian − elderly woman, relative of Oliver Frank

Ke-Pow-Han − Palouse leader

Kew-Kew-Kew'-lu-yah − Jonathan "Billy" Williams

Neesh-ne-park-ke-ook − Cut Nose (LC)

Nusnu −ee-pah-kee-oo-keen − Cut Nose (ZS, HW)

Peo-Peo-Tah-Likt − Bird Alighting (SL)

Tah moh moh kin or Yah moh moh kin − herded horses for the Lewis and Clark Expedition, possibly the 10th 1855 Treaty signer

Ta-Moots-Tsoo − Chief Timothy, a little boy when Clark arrives at Weippe

Ta-Moots-Tsin (ZS)

Tah-se-wy-ma or Heyumeotwy − Chief Twisted Hair's second wife (ML)

Te-toh-kan Ahs-kahp − looks like brothers (ZS, HW)

Tetoharsky (LC)

Tsuts Pilkin − a man who was an excellent horse man (HW)

Tunnachemootoolt − Broken Arm, aka, Black Tailed Eagle, Blackeagle, Speaking Eagle (AJ)

Tin-nach-e-moo-toolt (ZS, HW)

Utsinmalikan − Nez Perce leader

Watai-Watai-How-Lis − Son of Ke-Pow-Han

Watkuweis − woman's name meaning returned from afar

We-ah-koomt − Rams Horn, aka Looking Glass, Sr., Flint Necklace (ZS)

We-ark-koomt (LC)

Apash wyakaikt (AJ)

Weah-koo-nut (RS)

'apáswahayqt (Aoki)

Xáxaac 'ilpilp – Chief Red Grizzly Bear (Aoki), White Bird Band leader

from White Bird area

Hohastillpelp (LC)

Yel-lep-pit, Chief – Walla Walla Chief

Place Names

Alpowai – creek that runs into Snake River, few miles downstream from Clarkston, WA

'Asáha – Seven Mile Creek, creek that runs into Tucannon River (L-C visited 1806)

Ciwí ikite – Coyote Gulch, near Lewiston, ID

Epa tok maaux – Chimney Peak in the Selway Crags (OF)

Pí ite – Village South Fork of the Clearwater River (Aoki)

Pik'uunen – Snake River (Aoki)

Qosispah – Palouse village

Siláyloo – Celilo, OR, possibly a non-Nez Perce word (Aoki) (Weck'upupe is one of the Nez Perce words for Celilo Falls. It means "something sticking on the sides" and is likely a reference to the lamprey that were caught there. I would recommend some analysis on the word with elders etc. to ensure proper spelling. It came from the Garth notes and although his orthography is better than most, it still has some challenges. *J.Pinkham*)

Sept-a-qul-watia-kin wespu – Granite cliffs, Huddleston Bluffs (EP)

Siseeqiymexs – Seven Devils Mountains (Aoki)

Tamáanma – village site located at the mouth of the Salmon River with the Snake River (Aoki)

Wal'wáamaxs – Wallowa Mountains (Aoki)

Weippe – current spelling of Weippe, ID

'Oyáyp (Aoki)

Wyam – Celilo Falls area

X̱uyéeɫp – Columbia River (Aoki)

Index

ERRATA SHEET for *Lewis and Clark Among the Nez Perce*,
by Allen V. Pinkham and Steven R. Evans

Page 43, note 1, for "Harkola" read "Hakola"

Page 44, note 9, for "described as being covered" read "described tipis on Weippe Prairie as being covered"; for "1813-2002" read "1913–2002"

Page 44, note 11, for "Cunninghamn" read "Cunningham"

Page 50, image caption, for "Nakia Willismson" read "Nakia Williamson-Cloud"

Page 73, note 30, for "Coulter's River" read "Colter's River"

Page 75, line 6, for "Celio" read "Celilo"

Page 75, line 12, for "Chief Ta-Moots-Tsoo" read "Chief Ta-Moots-Tsoo (Timothy)"

Page 82, note 11, for "Scheurman" read "Scheuerman"

Page 82, note 12, for "Droulliard" read "Drouillard"

Page 98, note 5, for "Chick" read "Click"

Page 99, note 41, for "no.1" read "north"

Page 138, note 27, for "9/Unusual" read "Unusual"

Page 155, note 7, for "James R. and mike Venso's" read "James R. Fazio and Mike Venso's"

Page 156, note 23, for "Allen P." read "Allen Pinkham"; for "Red Grizzly Bear, Worrolen, aged 106, in 1926" read "Red Grizzly Bear, Worrolen, aged 106, In 1926"

Page 157, note 40, source is *Early Western Travels* Volume 21

Page 185, line 1, read name as "Kew-Kew'-lu-yah (Jonathan "Billy" Williams)"

Page 213, note 11, for "11806" read "1806"

Page 218, line 11, for "mail party" read "main party"; for "Gass had persuaded to wait with them for Lewis and Clark" read "Gass had persuaded them to wait for Lewis and Clark"

Page 255, line 12, read name as "Ellis Khip-khip-pel-lehken"

Page 262, note 61, for "1904" read "1905"

Page 265, Mylie Lawyer, add "Great-great-granddaughter of Chief Twisted Hair"

Page 281, add "Pond, Ronald James. *The Jefferson Peace Medal: A Cultural Phenomenon Passed Down from Chief to Chief in Walla Walla Culture, circa 1805–1986.* Pullman, WA: WSU Plateau Center for American Indian Studies, Plateau Studies Series: Monographs and Edited Volumes, Monograph 1, 2008."

Page 290, for "Ellis Khip-khip-pel-kehken" read "Ellis Khip-khip-pel-lehken"; for "Kew-Kew-Kew'-lu-yah" read "Kew-Kew'-lu-yah"

Page 295, read index entries as "Kew-Kew'-lu-yah (Jonathan "Billy" Williams)" and "Khip-khip-pel-lehken, Ellis"